"Like *Letters from the Earth,* Twain continues to live long after his death. Now we have Laura Trombley's fascinating narrative of his last days. . . . The pieces fall into place: The funniest man on earth is revealed to be a much more complicated soul."　　　　　—Ken Burns, filmmaker

"A remarkable investigative effort. . . . Gripping."　　　—*The Oregonian*

"Researched to a 'T,' *Mark Twain's Other Woman: The Hidden Story of His Final Years* tells a story of dysfunction, deceit and duplicity the likes of which we associate not with Mark Twain—but with the pages of Henry James."　　　　—Brenda Wineapple, author of *White Heat* and *Hawthorne* and a winner of the Pushcart Prize

"In this often revealing work, Trombley punctures the myth that Twain was affable and easygoing in his dotage."　　　—*The Boston Globe*

"While presenting the case for Lyon, Trombley has some interesting things to say about the difficulties of being a 'new woman' in America one hundred years ago."　　　　—*St. Louis Post-Dispatch*

"Trombley has proved to be adept at peeling back Samuel L. Clemens's carefully constructed persona and forcing scholars to reconsider some basic assumptions."　　　—Bruce Michelson, president of the Mark Twain Circle of America

"The points of friction in the story of Twain and Lyon mirror a Victorian drama."　　　—*Los Angeles Times*

"A remarkable book about an even more remarkable relationship. This friendship, which went sour, makes for engaging reading and is historical reporting at its very best. Laura Skandera Trombley brings both Twain and this very determined woman into sharp focus."
　　　　　　　　　　　　　　　　　　　　—*Tucson Citizen*

## LAURA SKANDERA TROMBLEY

# Mark Twain's Other Woman

Laura Skandera Trombley was raised in Southern California and attended Pepperdine University, where she earned her BA and MA summa cum laude, and the University of Southern California, where she earned a PhD in English and was a Lester and Irene Finkelstein Fellow. She is the president of Pitzer College in Claremont, California, and the author of three books about Mark Twain and dozens of articles. She lives in the Pitzer president's home with her son, Sparkey.

www.lauratrombley.com

# Mark Twain's Other Woman
## The Hidden Story of His Final Years

## LAURA SKANDERA TROMBLEY

VINTAGE BOOKS
A DIVISION OF RANDOM HOUSE, INC.
NEW YORK

FOR SPARKEY

*My Son*

*My Gift*

FIRST VINTAGE BOOKS EDITION, MARCH 2011

*Copyright © 2010 by Laura Skandera Trombley*

All rights reserved. Published in the United States by Vintage Books, a division of
Random House, Inc., New York, and in Canada by Random House of Canada Limited,
Toronto. Originally published in hardcover in the United States by Alfred A. Knopf,
a division of Random House, Inc., New York, in 2010.

Vintage and colophon are registered trademarks of Random House, Inc.

The Library of Congress has cataloged the Knopf edition as follows:
Trombley, Laura Skandera.
Mark Twain's other woman : the hidden story of his final years /
Laura Skandera Trombley.—1st ed.
p.   cm.
Includes bibliographical references and index.
1. Twain, Mark, 1835–1910—Last years. 2. Twain, Mark, 1835–1910—
Relations with private secretaries. 3. Twain, Mark, 1835–1910—Relations with women.
4. Authors, American—19th century—Biography. 5. Authors, American—
20th century—Biography. 6. Lyon, Isabel, 1863–1958. 7. Private secretaries—
United States—Biography. I. Title.
PS1332.S53 2010
818'.409—dc22 [B] 2009048367

Vintage ISBN: 978-0-307-47494-0

*Author photograph © Erinn Hartman*
*Book design by Iris Weinstein*

www.vintagebooks.com

Printed in the United States of America
10  9  8  7  6  5  4  3  2  1

# Contents

# Illustrations

# Preface

Sitting alone in a little room in an old house in Montreal, I am
thrown back through the years—by a single packet of written
matter, which proves to be the "forms" dictated by Mr. Clemens to
me as his private secy. For answer to letters, invitations, the gifts
of books—His private secretary—so private that the very mention
of me is with held from the world by the turn of fate—Private—

—ISABEL VAN KLEEK LYON

An enduring mystery in Mark Twain's life concerns the events of
his last decade, 1900 to 1910. Despite a multitude of published biographies, no one has ever determined exactly what
took place during those final years and how his experiences affected
him, both personally and professionally. Writers have speculated on
whether his final years were ruled by a growing misanthropy, or
whether he retained his keen sense of humor as he made his incisive
social commentary. The public version for nearly a century has been
that Twain went to his death a beloved, wisecracking iconoclastic
American, undeterred by life's sorrows and challenges. "I am not *an*

American," Twain defiantly wrote, "I am *the* American." However, lives
are complicated, Twain's extraordinarily so, and as one long intrigued
by the vagaries of Twain's life, I sensed that there had to be more to
the story than the carefully cultivated, homogenized version that had
been intact for so long. While writing my cultural biography *Mark
Twain in the Company of Women* in the early 1990s, I became interested
in exploring the relationships he enjoyed with women throughout his
life—sexual, emotional, intellectual, and professional. Contrary to
what I found in previously published biographies, my conclusion then
was that Twain was heavily dependent upon women, and that from the
outset of his writing career he had routinely sought feedback from
women he had befriended and respected. Twain, naturally, expressed it
best, saying that he had not had "much of a literary friendship with
men." He did so with women, among them his mother, Jane Clemens;
his friend and mentor Mary Fairbanks; his spouse, Olivia, and daughters Susy, Clara, and Jean; and more than a hundred women writers
from five countries.

While researching the personal connections Twain cultivated with
women, I found that contrary to contemporary perceptions of his work
(that he wrote principally about boys and men), females had always
been a mainstay of his writing. He covered their activities as a reporter;
highlighted them in the short stories "Hellfire Hotchkiss" and "Wapping Alice," among many others; included them in his most celebrated
works, *Tom Sawyer* and *Adventures of Huckleberry Finn;* featured them in
two later novels, *Personal Recollections of Joan of Arc* and *Pudd'nhead Wilson;* wrote hundreds of letters to prepubescent "Angelfish"; and spent
the last year of his life writing "The Death of Jean" and the "Ashcroft-
Lyon Manuscript."

After publishing my book, I was haunted by a lingering feeling that
there was much about his final years that remained to be discovered. I
decided to further investigate the individual I suspected had played the
largest role in his life during that period and who possibly held the
answers to my questions about Twain's life and writings. Why had his
mood turned so bitter toward the end of his life? What was the reason
for his estrangement from his daughters? Why did he compose the
bizarre "Ashcroft-Lyon Manuscript"?

The key that turned the lock and helped reveal the answers to these
questions and many more was Isabel Van Kleek Lyon. For a hundred

years, Isabel Van Kleek Lyon has been the mystery woman in Mark Twain's life. After the death of his wife in 1904, Twain spent the last six years of his life largely in Isabel's company. To free himself from having to deal with professional and business matters, he willingly delegated the management of his schedule and finances to her. She was slavishly devoted to Twain: running the household staff, nursing him during his various illnesses, arranging amusements to keep boredom at bay, managing his increasingly unmanageable daughters, listening attentively as he read aloud what he'd written that day, acting as the gatekeeper to an enthralled public, and overseeing the construction of his final residence, Stormfield.

And then something happened that led to a dramatic breakup.

This book is an exploration of their relationship. In his final months, Twain resorted to giving vituperative press conferences and ranting in personal letters about how Isabel had injured him. He was obsessed with her and wrote about her for hours every day, all the while suffering from angina pains and attacks of gout. His feelings were so strong that he needed almost a ream of paper to express them. Yet, despite the inordinate attention Twain gave her before his death, Isabel has remained a friendless ghost haunting the margins of Mark Twain's scholarship. For decades, biographers deliberately omitted her from the official Twain story. Her potentially destructive power was so great that Albert Bigelow Paine, Twain's handpicked hagiographer, allowed only one timorous reference to her in his massive three-volume work, *Mark Twain, a Biography* (1912).

My curiosity was further piqued when I visited the Mark Twain Papers & Project at the University of California, Berkeley, in the early 1990s and examined its Isabel Lyon materials. Robert Hirst, the general editor of the project, patiently carried out stacks of dusty boxes and folders. No formal cataloging of the collection had ever been done. In a cardboard box, I discovered Isabel's original daily reminders, diary, notebooks, date book, and letter book. She had exhaustively recorded the events of each day she had spent in Twain's presence. In a manila folder, I found letters written by Twain scholars decades earlier, and without exception they agreed that Isabel was "a slovenly writer and not a perceptive observer." This was a forgotten woman.

What had been her attachment to Twain? I wondered. How had her writings come to be part of the Mark Twain Papers & Project? I was intrigued by the voluminous and eloquent personal record she had kept of her years with him and the small regard she was held in by the scholarly establishment. Isabel's is the only such detailed record of Twain's last years that exists. Why had her papers been dismissed? Could it be that as a member of the working class, a secretary, she had been considered unimportant by members of the scholarly community? Perhaps there was something more to all of this, a deeper reason that no one had discovered. I decided that I would read through all of her writings.

I soon realized that there were some unusual aspects to Isabel's ephemera, beyond the fact that it was scattered all over the country, from California to Texas, Wisconsin, and New York. There was the sheer size of the collection; Isabel wrote constantly during her years with Twain. Also, her daily reminders and diary are heavily edited, and in some cases hunks of pages have been ripped out. There is no mention of when this editing took place or why, or whether she was the one who removed the pages. In addition, Isabel made an undated, edited, handwritten copy of her 1906 daily reminder. It appears that she made this separate second version with the intention of either misleading anyone who would read the reminder or as a backup in case the original was stolen. Finally, as I discussed this project with various scholars, archive directors, and memorabilia collectors, I heard repeated rumors of a 1909 diary that had mysteriously vanished.

It took years to transcribe the personal writings that Isabel left behind, my eyes straining to decipher the handwriting she had scratched out. Thoughts obscured, in order to protect her inner life from voyeurs like myself. For Isabel was a possessor of secrets about the Clemens family so enormous that Twain and his daughter Clara were determined that she be forever silenced. There is irony in the fact that one of America's greatest writers devoted the end of his life to ensuring that one woman would never be able to tell her stories. After Isabel had been summarily fired by Twain, he lived one year longer, full of malice and terribly lonely. Mentally and emotionally he could never let her go. Twain finally delivered his coup de grâce in a letter sent to his daughter Clara, branding his former companion "a liar, a forger, a thief, a hypocrite, a drunkard, a sneak, a humbug, a traitor, a conspirator, a filthy-minded & salacious slut pining for seduction."

Twain had spent decades ruminating over how to control future depictions of his life. He had chosen Albert Bigelow Paine as his official biographer in part because of his tractability, and went so far as to direct that parts of the autobiography he dictated remain unpublished until one hundred years after his death—a wish that has been granted by the Mark Twain Papers & Project. With no one left to contest him and with his authorized biography and autobiography representing his final say on the subject, Twain's monolithic version of his life would stand forever. Paine ever so delicately noted in the preface to his biography that "certain happenings" included within would "differ materially from the same incidents and episodes as set down in the writings of Mr. Clemens himself," volunteering that in his autobiography Twain "made no real pretense to accuracy of time, place, or circumstance—seeking . . . 'only to tell a good story.' " Paine was quick to reassure the reader that his biography was unfailingly accurate, as it was "supported by a unity of circumstance and conditions, and not from hearsay or vagrant printed items." Isabel, with her intimate knowledge of the family's secrets, had become an infuriating annoyance—the only obstacle standing in the way of Paine's account and Twain's "good story."

Against this background, in 2001 I had a conversation with Isabel's grandnephew, David Moore, then in his early seventies, in which he reminisced about his beloved relative: about how loving Isabel had been toward him, always giving him a fifty-cent piece on his birthday ("A lot of money in those days"); how she frequently visited him when he was a boy and how he looked forward to seeing her; how when she moved to New York City she lied about her age because she was afraid prospective employers would think she was too old; how she loved Christopher, her Siamese cat; and how after she died, David traveled from Connecticut to New York with his parents and older sister to clear out her small apartment ("crammed with stuff"). David told me that his sister had known her best, but that she had died. He asked if I knew what Mark Twain had said about his great-aunt: "So you know about him calling her a slut?" I told him I did. It was at that moment that I realized that biography is a genre that bleeds.

The purpose of this book is to lift the layers of what has come to be accepted as truth about Mark Twain's life and to explore what actually existed in the beginning and what finally remained at the end. Indeed, this account directly contradicts the well-established, genteel, and genial image of one of America's literary icons. This is a story that Mark Twain was determined no one would ever tell.

# ONE

# "TOO PERFECT FOR LIFE"

## THE LATE 1880S–FALL 1905

Today has been very full of the joy of living—I wrote letters and read some in the morning. Looked out of my window just in Time to see Dear Mother look up at me on her way home from Church and in the afternoon she came over. Later I played cards with my chief. Some day the penalty for having such perfect living will come.

—ISABEL VAN KLEEK LYON

*Clemens family at their Hartford home. Left to right: Clara, Olivia, Jean, Mark Twain, Susy*

B y all rights no one should have ever heard of Samuel Langhorne Clemens. He should have lived and died a cipher of rural nineteenth-century America. Certainly his modest beginnings presaged a difficult, abbreviated existence. Yet life takes unexpected turns, and the course that his journey took as Mark Twain would have strained the credulity of the most dedicated fiction reader.

Born two months prematurely, red-haired Samuel Langhorne Clemens arrived to his parents, thirty-two-year-old Jane Lampton Clemens and thirty-seven-year-old John Marshall Clemens, on November 30, 1835. His birthplace was a tiny two-bedroom rented cabin with an outdoor lean-to kitchen in the village of Florida in Monroe County, Missouri, located at a fork of the Salt River. He joined four young siblings: ten-year-old Orion, eight-year-old Pamela, five-year-old Margaret, and three-year-old Benjamin. Another brother, Pleasant, had died in infancy six years earlier. For a time it looked as though he would suffer Pleasant's fate. No one in his family much expected him to survive. His mother later wrote, "he was a poor looking object to raise." Of Florida, Twain joked that the dusty little settlement "contained a hundred people and I increased the population by 1 per cent. It is more than many of the best men in history could have done for a town. It may not be modest in me to refer to this, but it is true. There is no record of a person doing as much—not even Shakespeare. But I did it for Florida, and it shows that I could have done it for any place—even London, I suppose." Yet in the midst of these decidedly inauspicious surroundings, there was an augury that hinted that this child just might be special. For weeks prior to his birth, the bright trail of Halley's Comet crossed the nighttime sky.

After a departing shower of sparks and the passage of years, interest in the comet's appearance receded. But not so for Jane Clemens, who told and retold the story of the mysterious visitation and how it foretold great things, and most important, not for Twain, who by the end of his life embraced the notion that Halley's Comet had heralded his coming. He possessed a strong affinity for the celestial body, expressing his hope that he would make his exit when it returned during its seventy-five-year cycle: "I came in with Halley's Comet in 1835. It is coming again next year (1910), and I expect to go out with it. It will be the greatest disappointment of my life if I don't go out with Halley's Comet."

Maybe Twain felt that a passing comet provided the best explanation for his remarkable life. That this son of Missouri would grow up to be the most famous author in the world and the first global celebrity was so implausible that even Twain had difficulty making sense of his rise: "The Almighty has said, no doubt: 'Now here are these two unaccountable freaks; they came in together, they must go out together.' " The accomplishments of this "freak" were so many and his fame so enormous that by the end of his life he had come to be considered by those who knew him well as otherworldly. According to a close friend, "He always seemed to me like some great being from another planet—never quite of this race or kind."

The family failed to prosper in Florida, and so in 1839 they moved twenty-eight miles northeast, to the bustling riverside town of Hannibal, Missouri, in Marion County. The little boy quickly adapted to his new surroundings and acquired a closely knit group of friends. His boyhood adventures exploring the environs of Hannibal with Tom Blankenship and Laura Hawkins would later be immortalized in his most beloved works, *Tom Sawyer* and *Adventures of Huckleberry Finn.*

With the untimely death of his father when he was just eleven years old, his formal schooling ended and his mother apprenticed him to a Hannibal printer named Joseph Ament to learn the trade. Trained as a boy to move individual letters, he would grow up to become a compulsive writer of words. In 1851, he went to work with his brother Orion, who owned a small newspaper, the *Hannibal Western Union.* It was while working at the *Union* that he began writing humorous sketches that were occasionally published. Two years later, he traveled north working as an itinerant typesetter in Saint Louis, Philadelphia, and New York City. After a few years spent wandering, he decided he would travel to South America to sail the Amazon and make his fortune in "COCA, a vegetable product of miraculous powers," which he had read, in a book about the Amazon, "was so nourishing and so strength-giving that the native of the mountains of the Madeira region would tramp up hill and down all day on a pinch of the powdered coca and require no other sustenance." His plan was to travel by river from Cincinnati to New Orleans and then set sail for Pará (a port city in northern Brazil), where he would establish himself in the lucrative cocaine trade.

While on board ship he met Horace Bixby, a legendary riverboat pilot. By the time he disembarked in New Orleans, plans for South America had been abandoned in favor of working for Bixby. Bixby had agreed to mentor the young man and they worked together on the Mississippi River from 1857 to 1861. On April 9, 1859, Twain received his steamboat pilot's license. Working as a pilot brought him not just increased income, but an enhanced social status. To the end of his life, he would regard earning his pilot's license as one of his proudest accomplishments. He reluctantly decided to leave the river and the ship he was piloting, the *Alonzo Child,* only when the American Civil War broke out, in 1861, and commercial traffic on the Mississippi was curtailed.

At loose ends, he accompanied his brother Orion to Nevada, where he had been appointed secretary of the new territory. After trying his hand at silver prospecting, Twain worked as a reporter for the *Territorial Enterprise* in Virginia City, Nevada. It was in 1863, while he was with the *Enterprise,* that he began signing articles with the pseudonym "Mark Twain"—meaning two fathoms deep, indicating safe passage, a fond allusion to his time spent working on the river. His first big success as an author came in 1865, when he was living in San Francisco and his short story "Jim Smiley and His Jumping Frog" was published in the *Saturday Press* on November 18. The story was a sensation, and Twain became known as a western humorist. Newspapers and magazines across the country reprinted this tall tale of an inveterate gambler and his shot-filled frog, Dan'l Webster.

While in San Francisco, Twain worked as a newspaper correspondent, and in 1867 he registered as a passenger on the *Quaker City*'s maiden voyage to the Mediterranean, with a trip to the Holy Land as part of the tour. He persuaded the San Francisco *Alta California* to pay his traveling costs in return for the letters he would send them. These letters ultimately served as the material for *The Innocents Abroad. Innocents* became a best seller, with more than seventy thousand copies sold in its first year, and remained the best selling of all of Twain's books during his lifetime.

While on board the *Quaker City,* Twain befriended young Charles Langdon of Elmira, New York. After the trip's conclusion, Charles invited him to attend a reading by Charles Dickens in New York City. There he met Langdon's father, Jervis Langdon; his mother, Olivia Lewis Langdon; and his sister, Olivia Louise Langdon. Twain was immediately attracted to the well-educated, wealthy, pretty young woman, and after a year-and-a-half-long courtship, the two were married, on February 2, 1870, in the parlor of the Langdon mansion in Elmira.

A decade younger than her husband, Olivia proved to be Twain's ideal companion. Erudite, genteel, and possessed of a keen sense of humor, Olivia encouraged her spouse's literary pursuits. The couple moved to Buffalo, New York, where Twain had become a co-owner of the *Buffalo Express* newspaper. Their first child, a son, Langdon, was born nearly nine months to the day after their wedding. Buffalo did not suit them and their son Langdon was a sickly child who passed away after just nineteen months. The couple relocated in 1871 from Buffalo to Hartford, Connecticut, where they had three more children and resided for the next twenty years. This period constituted the happiest time of Twain's life. The Clemenses spent their winters in Hartford and summered in Elmira, at Susan Crane's home, Quarry Farm. Susan was Olivia's older sister, and it was there that Twain did most of his writing.

To those around him, Twain possessed a seemingly endless amount of energy. His intense intellectual curiosity compelled him to crisscross the globe (he sailed the Atlantic Ocean twenty-nine times) and to amass an enormous personal library with thousands of volumes. He was an individual who craved conversation, and he flourished as the center of attention. For Twain, dialogue was everything, and it is estimated that he wrote fifty thousand letters over the course of his lifetime in addition to more than three thousand newspaper and magazine articles and more than thirty books. His creative capacity appeared limitless, and when he was not writing he talked. The only impossibility, it seemed, was for Twain not to express himself. He was so confident of his imaginative powers that he claimed he never needed to worry about inspiration: "I made the great discovery that when the tank runs dry you've only to leave it alone and it will fill up again in time, while you are asleep—also while you are at work at other things and are quite unaware that this unconscious and profitable cerebration is going on."

In addition to his correspondence, newspaper articles, and book-length manuscripts, he was a dramatist and wrote scores of short stories. By age fifty-four he had written many of what would come to be considered classics of American literature. His books *The Innocents Abroad* (1869), *Roughing It* (1872), *The Gilded Age* (1873), *The Adventures of Tom Sawyer* (1876), *A Tramp Abroad* (1880), *The Prince and the Pauper* (1881), *Life on the Mississippi* (1883), *Adventures of Huckleberry Finn* (1884), and *A Connecticut Yankee in King Arthur's Court* (1889) had catapulted him into the highest ranks of American writers, and he was read and beloved by the general public as well as by the literary elite. Writing to his close friend William Dean Howells, Twain bragged about his proletarian popularity: "High and fine literature is wine, and mine is only water; but everybody likes water." A beloved public intellectual in his later years, he frequently wrote opinion and critical essays that were widely published. Over the course of his career Twain managed to move from being regarded as a satirical humorist to a serious author, a feat no other American writer could claim. During his lifetime, Twain was declared to be the "one living writer of indisputable genius" in the United States. And while Twain is remembered for his writing legacy, perhaps his greatest talent, which unfortunately no one today will ever see or hear, was his ability to command the platform as one of the greatest stand-up comedians who ever lived.

## 2

By early 1890, Mark Twain had every reason to be well satisfied with his life. Living in his spectacular mansion in Hartford, Twain adored his close-knit family circle, and at age fifty-five he relished fatherhood. Pictures from that period show a beaming Twain with his dignified, attractive forty-five-year-old wife, Olivia, and their three lovely daughters. Susy, eighteen years old, wanted to become an author and at age thirteen had written a biography of her father; Clara, age sixteen, studied piano and voice and dreamed of a concert career; and Jean, just ten years old, loved animals and making mischief. The local newspaper, the

*Hartford Courant,* proudly claimed that Twain "has taken a leading place in literature, in society, and in business in America." The entire family enjoyed socializing and frequently opened their home to friends and visitors for lavish evenings of fine dining and entertainment.

His literary reputation well established, Twain was also recognized for his financial acumen, and highly regarded for his humanitarian inclinations. When his publishing firm, Charles L. Webster and Company, published Ulysses S. Grant's memoirs in 1886, he was regarded as Grant's savior, rescuing the dying general's family from certain poverty. *Personal Memoirs of Ulysses S. Grant* became a best seller, and Grant's family received an astonishing $400,000 (75 percent of the royalties, according to their contract with Webster and Company), giving them a Gilded Age tax-free fortune.

While Twain was never deficient in ego, even he appeared to be a bit overwhelmed by his good fortune: "I am frightened at the proportions of my prosperity. It seems to me that whatever I touch turns to gold." For this little-schooled country boy from Missouri, all that success meant Twain had conquered the impossible. *Harper's Weekly* hailed him for lifting "himself high in the ranks of American authorship. He is not only a humorist, but he is a writer of rare and peculiar power. . . . While other men are living on what they have done, Mr. Clemens is continually progressing. He is a growing man, and each year he accomplishes some new feat in literature." In a profound sense, Twain had come to symbolize America's promise and hopes for continued prosperity.

3

Into this heady atmosphere of congratulation, wealth, and celebrity walked twenty-six-year-old Isabel Van Kleek Lyon. One afternoon in the late 1880s, Mrs. Harriet Whitmore asked Isabel to deliver a package of books to her good friend Olivia Clemens. Isabel was glad to do this task for her mistress, as it provided a welcome break from her duties as governess to the Whitmores' six children.

Isabel was let into Clemens's Hartford home by George Griffin, the family's African American butler, and led across a marble floor into the ground-floor library where Olivia was waiting. While Isabel was no stranger to wealth (as a child she had enjoyed the privileges of

*Hartford house exterior (above) and library (below)*

the upper class due to her parents' affluence and social status), she had never before witnessed such opulence as this. The "Steamboat Gothic"–style mansion had cost approximately $120,000 to build in 1874. Designed by Edward Tuckerman Potter, the house had the effect of awing and overwhelming its visitors. The exterior featured a curved front porch, soaring turrets, fancy red brickwork, and colored roof tiles. With nearly twenty rooms, the house boasted a staff of seven and Hartford's first telephone in a private residence. Guests were received in an extravagant entrance hall with wood-paneled walls and ornamental detail carved by Leon Marcotte of New York and Paris. Candace Wheeler, America's first female decorator, had designed the hall and stenciled the room's original paneling in silver, with the walls and ceiling painted red with patterns of dark blue. The library was an ornate space designed by Louis Comfort Tiffany's firm. A massive carved wooden fireplace mantel, originally from Ayton Castle in Scotland, dominated the room.

After delivering Harriet Whitmore's books into the hands of Mrs. Clemens and politely chatting with her, Isabel made her exit. She did not see Twain that day. Her opportunity came a short time later when their paths crossed at the home of the Whitmores. Franklin Gray Whitmore, Twain's business advisor and close friend, belonged to the Friday Evening Club, a regular gathering of Hartford men who drank whiskey, smoked cigars, and played billiards with Twain in his study throughout the 1880s. The Whitmores were also old friends of Isabel's parents. Twain was invited for an evening of cards, and he arrived sans Olivia ready to play competitive whist. Isabel was recruited to be his partner and quickly managed to trump his ace—a rather unsubtle way of entering the game. Years later, Isabel gleefully recalled to her close friend Doris Webster, "A kind of war broke out around the table but I said nothing and continued to play, taking all the remaining tricks. Trumping his ace was my only way of getting in."

Petite and attractive, with liquid brown eyes, long chestnut-colored hair, and porcelain skin, Isabel was twenty-eight years younger than Mark Twain, whose red hair was now going gray. She was representative of a new working class remembered today as the "new woman." These turn-of-the-century white women were employed as secretaries, governesses, stenographers, or clerks; they were formally educated, they lived away from home, and they enjoyed greater freedoms than their

*Georgiana Van Kleek Lyon and Isabel Van Kleek Lyon*

mothers ever had. Most of the "new women" lived independently for a few years prior to marriage while earning a living wage, typically $10 a week.

Twain realized that he had found a good whist partner in Isabel. When he was invited for a return engagement, he agreed to come only "if I can play with the little governess." Clever gamesmanship would come to define their relationship.

At the time of their convivial meeting, Isabel was still emotionally raw from a series of tragic personal losses. Born on December 15,

1863, in Tarrytown, New York, Isabel was the oldest of the three Lyon children. Her parents, Charles and Georgiana, were considered members of the town's gentry. Georgiana Van Kleek was Charles's second wife and was twenty-four years younger than her husband. Her family was Dutch and her father had owned a good portion of Hartford's prestigious Hudson Street. Education ran in the Lyon family. Charles Lyon likely first met Franklin Whitmore when the two were studying at Columbia University in the early 1860s. Charles was a published writer and orator, an author of Greek and Latin textbooks as well as assorted learned essays. The Lyons resided at their country estate, Spring-Side, located near where the Bear Mountain Bridge stands today, overlooking the Hudson River. Spring-Side was adjacent to Irving Park, a one-hundred-acre property owned by Charles. In 1859, four years before Isabel was born, Charles had decided to subdivide Irving Park and advertised it in a lavish illustrated monograph. Individual lots were available for purchase with financing information included.

But Charles Lyon died suddenly, on May 12, 1883, with his ambitions of becoming a real estate magnate unrealized, and the comfortable life Isabel assumed was always to be her birthright disappeared. She had just turned nineteen. Charles left no appreciable estate other than the family home. Making matters worse, Isabel's uncle, William T. Lyon, died just fifteen months after his brother, on August 13, 1884. The remaining family members moved to Farmington, Connecticut, where they rented an elegant home, Oldgate, still standing today, and the women took in sewing to support themselves. The house was located near the well-known Miss Sarah Porter's school, and the family established a social connection with the faculty. With her father and uncle deceased and no inheritance forthcoming, Isabel was forced to enter a life of service, and she embarked upon a series of nanny positions. Her first known job was with the Claghorne family in West Hartford, and from there she joined the Whitmores in Hartford.

Shortly after Isabel's card-playing evening with Twain, she left the Whitmores on excellent terms, and in December 1890 she moved to Philadelphia to begin employment with the Danas: "Surrounded by French speech, manners, thoughts & servants. It is an entirely new experience & one wholly unlooked for. If I had planned for weeks the position could not have been more to my fancy." Charles Edmund Dana was a well-known art critic and professor at the University of Pennsylvania. Isabel was pleased to join a family who shared a university affiliation, like her own, and she enjoyed caring for Millicent Dana, age ten. Yet early in her tenure with the Danas, Isabel wrote an anguished letter to her confidante Harriet Whitmore, revealing that she appeared to be haunted by more than her family's past difficulties:

> I cannot tell you how very happy your letter made me. My life has started all over & I could not tell what might have been said or done in these strange weeks. People become so sadly and easily prejudiced. But, my past is quite past—So very much has occurred—that my brain has not yet ceased whirling.

Isabel declined to clarify just what had prejudiced people against her. A possible explanation for her distress might have been her brother, Charles, who was leading a dissolute life with an Englishwoman by the name of Poppy, whom Isabel suspected was his mistress. Charles's family disapproved of their relationship, and the couple had gone to live with Poppy's sister. Poppy had a little girl whom she initially claimed had been adopted, although Isabel believed that she was really Charles's daughter. Isabel and Charles had a falling-out over his circumstances. Isabel confessed to Harriet Whitmore that she "had so much trouble that my mind was & has since been at a very low ebb. There is nothing in life like mental trouble to under-mine one's health." Between begging Harriet to "read between the lines" and assuring her that her happiness would return when she could "forget a little," Isabel was pleased to note that her wages had increased to "$500 a year and that seems a great deal when I am not expected to teach either music or French."

### 4

Twelve years would pass before Twain's and Isabel's paths crossed again. During this time, Mark Twain endured the deaths of beloved family members as well as a series of deepening financial crises. Still in mourning over the death of his mother, Jane Lampton Clemens, in October 1890, and that of his mother-in-law, Olivia Lewis Langdon, in November, the winter of 1890–91 saw Twain battling crippling financial reverses. By late spring the entire family, Twain, Olivia, Susy, Clara, and Jean, were exiled by economic circumstances to live as expatriates in Europe. They reluctantly closed their beloved Hartford home and set sail for France. House expenses had averaged $30,000 a year in Hartford, while in Europe the family was able to rent housing and avoid the sizable expenditure of social entertaining.

At the same time, Twain's Webster publishing firm failed, and on April 18, 1894, at age fifty-nine, Twain entered into voluntary bankruptcy. His debt—approximately $100,000—had been caused by a combination of exorbitant personal living expenses and disastrous speculation. Once heralded in the press for his business expertise (perhaps he believed his generous clippings too much), Twain had made multiple bad investments. The most expensive and unfortunate of these ventures was the Paige typesetter, into which he had poured over a quarter of a million dollars. The entire investment was a loss.

After exploring all possible financial avenues, Twain reluctantly accepted that the only path back to fiscal solvency was through lecturing. He had no taste for the stand-up circuit anymore and was loath to have to consider treading the boards once again—"heart-torturing," he called it. But he had no alternative. In April he signed a contract, and on May 11, 1895, the Clemenses sailed from Southampton, England, to New York to begin an around-the-world tour intended to rescue the family from its monetary woes. Twenty-three-year-old Susy and fifteen-year-old Jean were left with friends and family in Elmira. Twain appealed to his trusted friend Henry Huttleston Rogers, the Standard Oil baron, as he set off from New York, to "Pray for me."

On July 14, Twain commenced his speaking tour in Cleveland, accompanied by Olivia and twenty-one-year-old Clara. In less than thirty days, he performed in twenty-two cities, including a stop in Vancouver, before sailing west. The family's journey lasted a brain- and body-numbing twelve months and took the three ultimately to the southern tip of Africa. In total, Twain headlined almost 150 shows on five continents, and the halls where he appeared were filled to overflow capacity. The trip turned out to be a tour de force; everywhere, a worshipful press and crowds of devoted fans hailed him. Twain capitalized on his lecturing success by writing a popular travelogue, *Following the Equator,* published in 1897.

While the tour was a triumph and allowed Twain to follow the good advice Olivia and Henry Huttleston Rogers had given him—namely, to repay his creditors dollar for dollar—it dealt him a devastating personal blow. The three Clemenses sailed from Capetown, South Africa, arriving in Southampton, England, on July 31, 1896. After landing, they impatiently waited for Susy and Jean to set sail from New York so that the family could be reunited. A letter arrived explaining that Susy was ill, followed a few days later by a reassuring cable informing them that she would be all right, although her recuperation would be lengthy. Olivia and Clara immediately set sail for New York to assist with her recovery.

Twain was alone when a second cable arrived, on August 18, informing him that Susy, his favorite daughter and the child most similar to him in many respects, had died an agonizing death from meningitis at the family's home in Hartford while her mother and sister were still en route. For two weeks, Susy's fever spiraled and she grew delirious, sometimes wandering through the empty house. She watched the traffic passing on Farmington Avenue and called out, "Up go the trolley cars for Mark Twain's daughter. Down go the trolley cars for Mark Twain's daughter." As the infection spread, she went blind. She found a gown belonging to Olivia hanging in a closet and spent her last hours stroking and kissing the dress, believing in her delirium that her mother was dead. She clutched the dress and wept with grief. Near the end, she lapsed into a coma. When she died, Susy was just twenty-four years old. In an entry for his autobiography Twain declared, "It is one of the mysteries of nature that a man, all unprepared, can receive a thunder-stroke like that and live." For the rest of his life, Twain mourned his lost daughter. Olivia, Clara, and Jean returned to England after Susy's burial in Elmira and they remained in Europe in deep mourning for four years.

The homesick family finally returned to the United States in 1900. When the sixty-four-year-old Twain disembarked from the S.S. *Minnehaha* on October 15, he was greeted by hordes of reporters who hailed him as a "genius," a man of "unsullied honor," and "the bravest author in all literature." The New York *World* exclaimed the next day, "There was the familiar bushy hair, the twinkling, semi-mysterious eyes, the peculiar drawling voice, half Yankee, half Southern, the very low turn-down collar of the West and the immaculate shiny silk hat and long frock of the effete East. He looked as young as he did twenty years ago, and younger than he did when he shook American dust off his feet in 1891." *The New York Times* declared that Twain "never looked better, was in splendid humor." Reporters noted that at dockside he was as spontaneously funny as ever, and quoted what became a famous aphorism: "I never told the truth in my life that someone didn't say I was lying, [and] I never told a lie that somebody didn't take it as a fact." America lay before him, rushing to adore and deify him.

His family could not emotionally bear to return to Hartford and settled instead in a rented town house in Manhattan at 14 West Tenth Street. Twain's days of writing books that were to become literary classics were behind him, and he embraced the life of a celebrity while associating with the millionaire industrialists Henry Rogers and Andrew Carnegie and such political and cultural luminaries as President Roosevelt, Woodrow Wilson, Jane Addams, and Helen Keller. He basked in the extravagant flattery given him and happily chose from dozens of social invitations and lucrative lecturing opportunities.

For the next seven years, Twain would be interviewed and quoted by the press more often than anyone else. He became America's best-known pundit, leaving his daughter Clara to wonder out loud how her father "could manage to have an opinion on every incident, accident, invention, or disease in the world." He encouraged the press to ask him about all contemporaneous topics and even invited them to come photograph him smoking in bed. Twain reveled in his popularity and

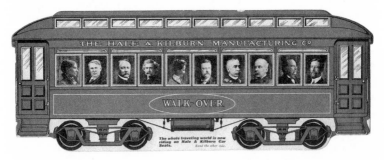

*An advertisement for the Hale & Kilburn Manufacturing Co. Faces in the trolley window, left to right: Clara Barton, Thomas Edison, unknown, Mark Twain, Madame Curie, President Teddy Roosevelt, General Nelson Miles, Admiral George Dewey, President Grover Cleveland, unknown*

*Mark Twain cigar box. The selling phrase on
the box: "Known to Everyone—Liked by All"*

understood that in large measure the public's continuing interest in
him was related to his obliging the press.

In record time, Twain had come back from being a failed business-
man and was seen once more as an icon of integrity and accomplish-
ment. Recognized and read worldwide, he exulted in his astonishing
achievement. Such was his iconic status, as one critic has observed,
Twain "was almost a living statue." A cigar-box label, circa 1910,
succinctly conveys the goodwill he enjoyed: "Mark Twain: Known to
Everyone—Liked by All."

Isabel's life in the interim was a troubled mixture of familial insta-
bility and loss. On April 25, 1893, thanks to her long-term employment with the Danas, she had saved enough money to purchase some
land from her sister, Louise, and brother-in-law, Jesse Moore, for $200.
A small house, Choisy, was constructed for her mother just south of
Louise's home, financed with the remainder of the proceeds of the sale
of their house in Tarrytown. (The house stands today at 143 Main Street
in Farmington.) On December 5, 1893, tragedy struck the family again
when Isabel's brother, Charles, died at age twenty-four. In a manuscript
detailing the Lyon family's history in Tarrytown, his death is recorded
as a heart attack.

Years later, Isabel confided to Jean Clemens that her brother's death
was a suicide. Brother and sister had reconciled by that time, yet

Charles's relationship with Poppy was unraveling due to his drinking and gambling. Isabel worried that he had fallen in with a "bad set of very fast young men." Charles wrote Isabel a confessional letter about his misery and, immediately afterward, she received a cable informing her that her brother had died. Upon returning home Isabel visited the physician who had performed her brother's postmortem examination and said, " 'Charlie committed suicide.' He was so amazed that he blurted out: 'How did you know that?' which finally proved it." Charlie had deliberately overdosed on morphine. A horror-struck Isabel could not bear to tell her mother, and the public record was falsified.

Losing her brother was a tragedy compounded by the manner in which he died. The specter of suicide in the nineteenth century was so terrifying that families went to great lengths to hide the truth. Society regarded suicide as a disgrace, and all surviving relatives were left stigmatized by association. The children of a suicide bore the risk of being socially ostracized, and their chances of marriage were substantially reduced, as it was strongly believed that they and any of their offspring would have a propensity for insanity and violence as well as suicide. This was an era of "strong family ties," and it was imperative that families do nothing to risk their social standing. Isabel must have felt a particular kinship with Jean to reveal her family's great secret. Perhaps she thought there was the possibility of common ground in view of the fact that Jean suffered from an illness that also carried a social stigma— epilepsy, a cruel disease that was little understood and greatly feared. In April 1894, four months after her brother's death, a grieving Isabel accompanied the Danas on a tour of Germany and Italy, her second trip with them to Europe.

5

While Twain had regained his financial equilibrium, a shadow was cast over his heady mixture of affluence and notability, and it came in the form of Olivia's declining health. She had spent a lifetime fighting serious maladies. In her youth she had made a miraculous recovery from spinal tuberculosis that the members of her family and closest friends had expected would finish her. She had endured four pregnancies and survived the heart-wrenching deaths of her son, Langdon, and her daughter Susy.

While Olivia was understandably both proud and relieved at her husband's phoenix-like professional and financial rebirth, their restored affluence also meant an enormous increase in their social activity. Olivia's delicate health and Twain's fame would result in an invitation to his former whist partner, Isabel Lyon, to come work for the family. Keeping up with all of the correspondence directed toward Mark Twain had become an enormous task that Olivia and her daughters could no longer perform, and so the family looked for assistance. They consulted their old friend Harriet Whitmore, who enthusiastically recommended Isabel. On June 30, 1902, Olivia effusively thanked Harriet:

My dear Friend:

Indeed I was most glad to get your letter (as I always am) and especially glad of the news that it contained regarding Miss Lyon. Yes, I am going to want just such a person in the Autumn. I have been wishing ever since you spoke to me of her that I could see her.

Now if I can possibly manage it I will plan to have her come up here for a few days and see me. We have a guest room, until Clara gets here then we shall have none. This week there is coming a young lady to spend July with Jean. If I can get in a few days between her going & Clara's coming I will ask Miss Lyon to be my guest for a few days, making her my guest from the time she leaves the Hartford (or Farmington) station.

I [would] like better if possible to arrange to have Miss Lyon have a boarding place outside. With one exception I have always done this & have found it more satisfactory. I think also Miss Lyon would find it so. We can of course talk that all over.

I am deeply grateful to you for letting me know of her & I should have been greatly distressed if she had slipped away from me after what you said about her & I could not help hoping she would break her present engagement.

The visit was a success, and Isabel was hired. She was thirty-eight years old when she arrived early in October 1902 at Riverdale-on-Hudson. Mark Twain was a month shy of his sixty-seventh birthday. The family had taken a three-year lease on a lavish twenty-eight-acre estate named Wave Hill overlooking the Hudson River and the Palisades.

Isabel was thrilled with her new situation. She later told Doris Webster that she had been honest with Twain about her lack of training as a social secretary: "But I said I can't possibly use a typewriter and I don't know shorthand. M.T. said 'Well I wouldn't have one of those goddam machines in the house and I couldn't read it if you did write shorthand.' " (Twain undoubtedly realized the incongruity of his remark, since he had purchased a typewriter for $125 in 1874 and had later boasted about being the first author to type a manuscript, namely *A Connecticut Yankee in King Arthur's Court.*)

Isabel's professional limitations notwithstanding, the Clemenses were delighted with her. In keeping with the customs of the other "new women" as well as with Olivia's wishes, Isabel did not live in. She was quite pleased with her salary, as Twain paid her more than average, $50.00 a month, an increase of $8.40 a month over what she had been paid by Charles Dana.

From the outset, Isabel's effectiveness was gauged more by her talent at dispelling the anxiety the family was feeling about Olivia's deteriorating condition than by her secretarial expertise. She worked for the Clemens family eight months before ever interacting with Olivia. Two months after her arrival, a grateful Clara expressed her appreciation to Harriet Whitmore:

> I want to tell you how thankful we are that you told us about Miss Lyon for she is really a treasure and enormous comfort;
>
> She not only is sweet and attractive, entirely lacking any disagreeable qualities but she is also a pleasure for she has a cheerful manner and way which are particularly welcome in a house at time of illness & consequent depression.
>
> I am so glad we have her & I know my Mother will be when she knows her.
>
> I see her very little & still have quite an affection for her.

Isabel immediately understood the special advantages her position held and began keeping a written record of her time with America's most famous author and celebrity in the form of letters she sent to her mother, Georgiana. Months afterward, she was distressed to discover that her mother had purposely destroyed her correspondence. Georgiana excused herself, claiming that the letters were "so personal" she felt they should not be saved. To preserve her observations, beginning in 1903 Isabel began keeping a series of daily reminders and a diary.

While Clara may have delighted in her "cheerful manner," Isabel was a woman burdened by painful secrets. On New Year's Day 1903 she wrote, "Alone I watched the New Year in, and the old one gently die, before I went to bed & to sleep—Two days ago a blackmail letter came and I did not like it—It froze my very heart." Perhaps the sender was someone who knew about her dissolute brother and threatened to expose his unprincipled lifestyle and sudden death. She never says.

Isabel was immediately awestruck by Twain. She was impressed by the famous individuals who wrote and visited him as well as by his lavish surroundings. Yet she possessed enough insight and intelligence to look beyond glamour and wealth. Early on she noted that there was a profound difference between the man Samuel Langhorne Clemens and his public persona, Mark Twain, and wondered how he was able to manage the weight of his public identity: "His private humor was one of his most darling possessions—Subtle—often profound & often Soaring with a swift birdlike flight into the upper reaches of men's Mental skies. Never the obviousness of Mark Twain, Timed & Tuned for a mixed audience."

By June 1903, Isabel, in her notations, had developed a nickname for Twain: Marse Clemens (with variations "Marse C" and "Marse"). The name was a likely pun on Thomas Nelson Page's Marse Chan, the main character in a short story by the same name from his collection entitled *In Ole Virginia* (1887). Page was a significant southern author, and there would have been an edge to Isabel's pun, as Marse Chan was a slaveholder in the antebellum south. While Isabel dutifully acted out her proletarian life of service, she never lost her ambivalence toward it. Later she largely dropped the "Marse" slaveholder reference, substituting a new term of submission, calling Twain simply the King in her private notes.

## 6

Isabel found Twain's daughters fascinating and treated them with great deference. On the surface theirs was a life of incredible privilege, free of worries about money and social status. There must have been many long nights when Isabel could not help but think about what might have been had her father been more successful in business before his death or if her uncle and brother had not passed away. She regarded the strikingly beautiful Clara with a mixture of wide-eyed admiration and increasing

*Young Clara Clemens*

envy. Clara possessed a mon-eyed kind of glamour and had only recently returned from Europe, where she had been studying voice. Her intention was to embark upon a career as a professional contralto.

In January 1903, Isabel wrote that she had lunched with Clara and found her "enchanting": "A Sweet Sweet morsel of a woman"; and "Alluring beyond words." Clara was petite with a heart-shaped face, russet curls, and an hourglass figure. A lover of clothes and jewelry, she was always smartly coiffed and stylishly dressed in photographs. Her expression belied the kind of self-assurance possessed by the pretty who have been told all their lives just how attractive they are. There was a certain childlike quality to Clara with her plump cheeks and primped appearance. She grew quickly fond of Isabel, enjoying the older woman's admiration of her as well as her usefulness to the household. But just a few months after Isabel began her employment, she and Clara were involved in their first awkward scene concerning Twain:

This morning as I sat writing in the drawing room, the closed door cautiously opened and in visited S.L.C.'s [Samuel Langhorne Clemens's] head, followed by himself in nightshirt, blanket gown, bare legs and black felt slippers. We settled some business drawing checks etc. and then C.C. [Clara Clemens] appeared (charming C.C.) telling him to go up stairs and get into his clothes. He refused. She was firm. He was for dictating letters. She was firm. So off he trotted, not to get into his clothes, but to go to bed again. Appearing at the landing a few minutes later he called. "Is Clara gone?" I said "no"—and he said "Then I'll go back to bed." We chuckled much. He is delightful.

In that moment, Isabel had aligned herself with Twain against Clara.

Isabel's relationship with Jean was more consistent. While Clara more closely resembled her mother, Jean was every bit her father's daughter in appearance. Taller than Clara, Jean had a long, angular face that bore the unmistakable Clemens nose. Brunette, dark-eyed, and slender, she possessed a formal attractiveness and grace. In photographs she is always standing ramrod straight, with her hair pulled away from her face into a bun, and she is less fashionably attired than her trendily

*Jean Clemens as a young woman*

corseted sister. Judging from her rather stiff expression, Jean was much more comfortable behind the lens, "kodaking," than standing before it. Ill at ease and socially awkward around people her own age, Jean preferred romping with children and caring for animals. More intellectual than her pleasure-seeking sister, Jean was fluent in several languages, an avid reader of history, philosophy, and literature, and an advocate of animal rights. Isabel's first mention of Jean came in relation to her health. Early in January 1903, she noted that when she saw Jean that morning, "she looked badly. Showing how ill she has really been." At the time, Jean was suffering from pneumonia with a high fever. Later in the week, Isabel wrote that Clara and Twain "have been having a sad time trying to keep Jean's illness from Mrs. Clemens."

Jean's bout with pneumonia, while serious, proved a relatively minor event when compared to her chronic malady—as early as 1896, when Jean was fifteen, she had begun to experience blackouts that eventually were diagnosed as epileptic seizures. Twain tried to explain his daughter's condition to Henry Rogers in a letter written when Jean was in her twenties: "Jean's head got a bad knock when she was 8 or 9, by a fall. Seven years ago she showed capricious changes of disposition which we could not account for; and four years ago the New York experts pronounced her case epilepsy. This we learned when we got back from around the world. We put her into the hands of the world's head expert in Vienna, who said that in some cases this disease had been outgrown, but that he knew of no authentic instance of its cure by physicians." Twain's attribution of the cause of Jean's ailment was in agreement with the prevailing medical wisdom at the time. A late-nineteenth-century medical textbook, *Diseases of the Nervous System: Or, Pathology of the Nerves and Nervous Maladies,* which Jean's doctors likely used as a reference, provides an exhaustive list of causes for epilepsy including "fright, anxiety, grief, over mental exertion, dentition, indigestion . . . blows on the head, falls, sunstroke."

Based on descriptions in family letters and Isabel's writings, it appears that Jean suffered from idiopathic epilepsy, a form of epilepsy that typically occurs in children and teenagers. Treatment included giving the patient "bromides of potassium, lithium, and sodium, and the oxide of zinc." At times she took thrice-daily doses of sodium bromide, a sedative. Bromides were dangerous business and reserved as a last resort for patients with severe epilepsy. Doctors would prescribe them in order to completely suppress attacks, but often they were so strong that patients would be reduced to a "constant hebetude" (a dullness of mind and mental lethargy).

In conjunction with their prescriptions, patients were advised to avoid alcohol, eat more "vegetable than animal food," and to regard sexual intercourse as presenting "great danger." Medical textbooks gravely warned that masturbation would cause "in general the greatest number of fits," and "intellectual employment requiring deep thought is injurious." The recommended lifestyle was clean, asexual, healthy country living with plenty of exercise, including such pursuits as "gardening, horse exercise, the gymnasium, swimming." Jean and her family had spent years seeking cures at various European and American sanitariums, and they believed with a hope born of desperation that frequent osteopathic sessions would have a beneficial effect. Yet, despite the family's heroic efforts, Jean continued to suffer from both petit mal and grand mal seizures. Current research asserts that if epileptic patients do not achieve seizure control through drug treatment within two years of their initial diagnosis, only a handful of these unresponsive patients will "ever achieve control." Jean, without benefit of modern drug therapy, was not among those fortunate few, and she would spend the rest of her life searching for a cure.

Epilepsy was little understood at the time, and those who suffered from the disease were regularly stigmatized and shunned by society, shunted off to mental asylums, poorhouses, and jails. The Clemenses did their best to protect their daughter from the social effects of the disease, and her condition was never publicly mentioned. Barred from ever entering the social whirl that young women of her wealth and status would typically embrace, in accordance with medical opinion at the time Jean spent a great deal of her time outdoors. A budding amateur naturalist, she loved hiking and being in the woods. Isabel frequently wrote about the days they spent together watching black and white creeping warblers, hummingbirds, and field sparrows through their opera glasses.

While Isabel had daily contact with Clara and Jean, her interactions with Olivia were decidedly more remote. After Olivia had spent months incommunicado, Isabel's first work done directly at her request came in April 1903, when Isabel wrote to Frank Whitmore on Olivia's behalf regarding the dismantling of the Hartford home. The family had painfully concluded that they could never live there again because of their memories of Susy, and so in the spring the mansion was sold for a paltry $28,000, less than a quarter of its original cost. Acting upon Olivia's orders, Isabel asked Frank "if the little cherubs over the door between the dining room and library have been taken down. If not will you kindly have them removed at once, before anyone has a chance to see them and believe that they are a part of the house; for they go with the mantelpiece."

Selling their home was traumatic for all the members of the family, but it proved particularly upsetting for Olivia. This was the home she had helped design, whose construction she had overseen, and the strain of sorting out the family's effects took a heavy toll on her physical health and mental state. Isabel carefully recorded her rare sightings of Olivia: "I saw Mrs. Clemens twice in 1903. Riverdale; frail & very lovely in her flowing black silk garments, & soft white lace shawls, or scarfs. She didn't try to be a picture out of the lovely Italian School. She was that picture in the quaint frocks made of rare stuffs; & with her glorious dark eyes that said every thing to you, or said nothing."

Isabel was "summoned" by Olivia in June, and by her careful record was allowed to spend exactly six and a half minutes in her presence. Olivia was reclining on a couch and Isabel observed, "Such a tall woman with thinnest of hands. She wore a black silk wrapper—and when she smiles she is very lovely. C.C. [Clara Clemens] sat over at one side & watched us." Isabel politely wrote that she found Olivia "charming"—"I do not wonder that Marse worships her." On that same day, Isabel painstakingly wrote above the date in her daily reminder that Twain had given his first gift to her, a signed photograph of himself. Abjuring a more prosaic gift like a book or an essay, Twain instead gave Isabel an image of himself to gaze upon. One could hardly imagine a comparable luminary, such as William Dean Howells, doing such a thing. With Olivia unable to give him much notice because of her ill health, Twain seemed to be inviting Isabel to fulfill his thirst for attention. The next day Isabel noticed Olivia momentarily taking air on the balcony: "Oh she is sweet beyond words. Instantly putting one at ease—as the greatest Souls Ever do. By their Simplicity."

While Isabel was filled with admiration for the Clemenses, she was simultaneously trying to escape her working-class life by attempting to establish a romantic relationship with another famous humorist. John Kendrick Bangs was one year older than Isabel, and, like her, he had been born in New York State. He had graduated with his doctorate from Isabel's father's alma mater, Columbia, and had spent an additional year studying law there. A journalist, dramatist, and author, Bangs was called "the Humorist of the Nineties." He was the editor, at various times, of *Literature, Harper's Weekly, New Metropolitan,* and *Puck.* Bangs and Twain knew and liked each other, and they published each other's work. Just prior to Twain's return to the United States in the fall of 1900, likely as a ploy to drum up the newspapers' interest in his return, Twain announced to the press that he had decided to make a presidential run against McKinley on the Plutocratic Ticket and nominated Bangs as his running mate. The American public loved the joke.

Twain and Bangs belonged to the same social set, and Isabel met Bangs courtesy of Twain. A month after she began working for the Clemenses, Twain's sixty-seventh birthday dinner was held at New York City's Metropolitan Club. Bangs attended, along with such literary and business luminaries as William Dean Howells, Hamlin Garland, George W. Cable, Booth Tarkington, and Henry Rogers. Four months later, on April 5, 1903, Bangs's wife, Agnes, died, and he was

*John Kendrick Bangs*

left a highly eligible widower with three young sons. Isabel wrote in her daily reminder: "How I kept on a strange sympathy with that man when he lost his wife . . . but it didn't find a footing. He didn't need the Sympathetic wave for he married his Type writer ever so soon." Despite Isabel's best efforts, just a little over a year later, on April 27, 1904, Bangs married Mary Blakeney Gray, formerly his secretary. On Ascension Sunday 1905, while riding a Fifth Avenue bus with her mother, Isabel caught a glimpse of her former crush driving in a fancy Victoria carriage with his new wife. Instead of being bitter about her lost opportunity, she comforted herself with the thought of new possibilities:

> But That's no harm—I've known of several men who have married several Times—They Couldn't live without the Companionship & Sympathy of a woman. And I like the thought of it—There's a comfort in sitting beside a man sometimes—for instance this morning in church. I sat beside a quiet man. He scarcely moved.

Evidently, Isabel had a soft spot for wealthy humorists, a strong yearning for the good life, and a large dose of ambition—and she would have another chance.

## 7

The Clemens family had begun planning another move to Europe in the hope that a change in climate might improve Olivia's condition. Early in June 1903, Twain asked Isabel to accompany them to Florence. She excitedly agreed and was disappointed when plans for renting a suitable villa failed. Twain, thinking that Italy was impossible, for a brief period gave serious consideration to relocating the family to California, but finally a villa in Florence was secured.

After an exhausting summer spent packing and caring for the increasingly incapacitated Olivia, the Clemenses sailed in October, along with Katy Leary, the family's longtime housekeeper and Olivia's personal nurse. Isabel and her mother were originally supposed to travel with the party, although due to an injury to Isabel's eye, the women were delayed two weeks. (Isabel would seek treatment for her wounded eye for years without finding relief.) On November 7, 1903, Isabel and Georgiana set sail from New York Harbor on the S.S. *Lohn* under the command of Captain Bolte. Isabel delighted in the adventure of it all:

> This begins my third trip to Europe. As the days of life increase in value, the wit to write of them decreases—Their significance is too profound—But now we are away out in midocean. . . . The big pier, and the scores of emigrants and all the spirit of sea life made Mother look sad, and our hearts nearly burst. I realized what we were leaving and also what it meant to Mother.

During a brief landing at Gibraltar, Isabel was elated to learn that the "very young man" who was acting as her guide had traveled with Twain and his daughters two weeks prior. She briefly deliberated whether to tell him about her attachment to the Clemenses and decided against it. In Gibraltar she and her mother had an exciting hiking and carriage tour, and she was pleased to make the acquaintance of a handsome soldier. When the ship docked in Naples, Isabel was disappointed to see the "quality" passengers disembark. Isabel and her mother left the ship in Genoa and spent the night at the Eden Palace Hotel. The next day the two caught their train to Florence.

On Friday, November 20, they finally arrived and were met at the station by Jean Clemens, wearing an incongruous lorgnette. The next morning Isabel and her mother started for the Villa di Quarto,

where Mr. & Mrs. Clemens are established for the Winter & which place was to be the Seat of my work. We drove for a long way through the city which was not interesting. drove through fog & a damp penetrating air. to finally pass the barriere & to wind along a narrow walled-in road, to a height above the fog where the villa is situated about 3 1/2 or 4 miles from Florence. I don't know why my heart kept sinking. but it did— and I kept looking at Mother to see how she took it. but she was pretty much stunned by this time. However. I don't think I'll write how disappointed, discouraged, & despairing we were when we discovered that the Quarto villa was so far from Florence that we could not be established in a pension. It is enough that we found right here on the villa property a nice little furnished villino. It is rented by one Mori-Ubaldini, a flourishing clock maker on the Piazza del Duomo, who uses it for 2 or 3 of the hot Summer months, when to stay in the city is an impossibility,—or a discomfort. It is neatly furnished. is built all of stone of course. And we pay the modest sum of 250 lire or fifty dollars for . . . six months.

*Villa di Quarto*

Isabel's dark mood lightened when she saw her charming "villino," and she was heartened by the friendliness of her Italian neighbors. While "boarding out" was typical at the time and Isabel was agreeable to the expense, Twain's expectation that Isabel should pay for her own living expenses would come back later to torment both of them.

On January 17, 1904, writing from the "Villino di Quarto," Isabel reflected on what had happened to her over the previous two months, including sailing to Italy and assisting Twain in his initial dictations for his autobiography. In her journal she worried that due to all of her recent activity she had been unable to keep her entries current. She decided that she would go back and try to remember and write about the prior two months before they vanished forever, "for someday I shall want to read it. No one else will ever care, but I shall."

Isabel thought that the Villa di Quarto, the Clemenses' leased mansion, was hideous. On January 17, she wrote that the villa could have been "a very Splendid Barracks":

> It was built for Cosimo I. & has been lived in by royalties of one kind & another from time to time but at present is owned by the wife of the Count Raybaudi-Massiglia. I say the wife. for Count Massiglia is far away serving his country as Consul, in Persia or Siam. and he is likely to stay there too; and it seems to me that for the sake of peace, or freedom, he has left this villa in the hands of the Countess.

Isabel's opinion of the Countess was colored by the fact that she had known her in Philadelphia (when Isabel was working for the Danas) and strongly disliked her then. In Philadelphia, the Countess was rumored by polite society to be an adulteress. Now, Isabel describes her as "vicious," with "painted hair," a "coarse voice," "slit-like . . . eyes," "dirty clothes," and "terrible manners."

WHEN THE TWO WOMEN MET at the villa, the Countess denied ever having previously met Isabel, although Isabel "made it quite plain to her that she had." To the consternation of Florentine society and consistent with Isabel's impression of her, the Countess had built an apartment over the stables and lived there with "the big Roman steward of the place." Isabel cattily recorded a comment made by a Florentine acquaintance about the Countess's behavior: "Mr. Cecchi at the

Bank asked me if the woman thought herself in the wilds of Africa. that she could outrage every law of Social life, & still be accepted as a member of it. Here she remains. a menace to the peace of the Clemens household."

During her stay in Italy, Isabel experienced newly found freedoms and became intoxicated with the beauty of the Tuscan countryside. She exclaimed over the sights of Florence, and she was also taken with the beauty of the olive orchards, especially as they appeared at night: "At first the high stone walls on either side of the high road were very disappointing. Now they are less so, because one can remember the mysterious loveliness of a moon-light drive along that same high road, when the Soft olive trees bending over the walls, suggest untold lovelinesses within & one's imagination can run to glorious riot."

The country isolation proved beneficial for Twain's ability to concentrate, and he managed to produce a number of short pieces: "A Dog's Tale," "You've Been a Dam Fool, Mary. You Always Was," "Italian Without a Master," "Italian with Grammar," and "Sold to Satan." But it was "The $30,000 Bequest" that was the most substantive of the lot. For decades Twain had explored themes of transvestitism and exchanged genders in his short stories and novels. He had always been irresistibly drawn to the contexts and implications of gender, and in these tales he was identifying and satirizing social constructions of gender roles and power distribution within the restrictions of his society. Two of his prior gender-switch tales, "John Brown and Mary Taylor" and "Hellfire Hotchkiss," practically serve as drafts for "The $30,000 Bequest." The story features two main characters—Saladin Foster, nicknamed Sally, and Electra Foster, nicknamed Aleck. Sally is a devoted husband and father who daydreams about spending a $30,000 bequest to be left to him by a distant male relative on the occasion of his death. Aleck is a loving wife and mother as well as a talented money manager and investor. The story consists of the two fantasizing about investing and spending their future bequest until Aleck has managed to parlay the initial $30,000 into an imaginary $300 million. All is lost, though, in an imaginary Wall Street crash. After their fantasy bankruptcy, the two discover that the relative left no estate. They are shattered. The story, which ends with their deaths, can almost serve as Twain's cautionary tale about the perceived rewards and disappointments incurred in the pursuit of wealth.

With Olivia ever in seclusion, Twain and Isabel spent the long winter days together. During this period Isabel's position in the household was transformed into something more than that of an employee—she became Twain's confidante. She was delighted by how their relationship was evolving and was clearly infatuated with her employer. On January 8, in a letter to Harriet Whitmore, she had rhapsodized about her recent interactions with Twain and his growing dependence upon her:

> Perhaps you may be interested to know how very entirely Mr. Clemens absorbs all my time—every minute of it—even my evenings. I attend to an infinite number of Things for him, and when he is lonely and restless we play cards—play cards? Why I play with him all day Sunday even. He is delicious; this morning he had a run of very bad luck and biting his cigar hard he said "Christ couldn't Take Tricks with the kind of cards you give me." Oh darling Mrs. Whitmore you have given me all this joy, and Truly I am the wealthiest woman ever. There is a side of the life here that is most exquisite and hallowed; and Mr. Clemens lives much in the past—There are days when he restlessly paces the "lonely house." and he has not yet begun any real work—beyond a short article on "Copyright" that appeared in *N. American Review* for January.

*Olivia Langdon Clemens, 1895*

I have very little to do with Jean—never go out with her any more; you see Mr. Clemens wants his secretary on deck—and when he can have her services when he needs them.

Obviously, Isabel was not bored with keeping Twain company during the Italian country winter, and she was ecstatic about his growing need for her. As she attended to his thirst for constant attention, he was also fulfilling her longing for a lost birthright. Perhaps the time they shared represented a welcome return for Isabel to her father and childhood: Tarrytown and Florence merged; images of Charles Lyon and Twain combined; the Lyons' country home Spring-Side morphed into the Villa di Quarto; and the Hudson and Arno Rivers converged. Isabel had an early and traumatic introduction to life's hardships due to her father's death and she looked to Twain as a compassionate benefactor. Here in Italy, Isabel had one of the most famous men in the world all to herself, to love, to admire, and to desire—and was happy to serve him.

But Twain and Isabel's cozy times were interrupted when he developed acute bronchitis and gout so severe that his feet became inflamed and swollen. After recovering from his illness, he effected a transition of seismic proportions. Twain's wife, Olivia, had been his primary literary audience throughout their thirty-four years of marriage, during which she had listened to him read his prose and had provided feedback. With Olivia bedridden and the daughters apparently little involved with him, Twain turned to Isabel. "About January 14, Mr. Clemens began to dictate to me. His idea of writing an autobiography had never proved successful, for to his mind autobiography is like narrative & should be spoken. . . . In fact he loves the work." With the worshipful Isabel as his eager audience, Twain was finally able to maintain his focus and the autobiography dictations began in earnest. He rejoiced to his old friend William Dean Howells two days later: "I've struck it! And I will give it away—to you. You will never know how much enjoyment you have lost until you get to dictating your autobiography. . . . Miss Lyons does the scribing, & is an inspiration, because she takes so much interest in it."

Isabel was equally pleased: "Last week we began an entrancing occupation; that of having Marse C. dictate—not letters, but words for a book. He is making his journal of describing this villa and the work is the most interesting Ever. In these days we have written about 3000 words. Working for an hour or a little more, Each morning."

Their partnership thus established, Twain shared material with Isabel that he found too risqué for his family. One day, he called her into his bedroom and asked her to type for him (notwithstanding their earlier conversation about her lack of skills, apparently Isabel had some proficiency with the typewriter): "Somewhere in the Bible there is a story about the woman whose soul was being damaged by Some jewels she owned & so she gave them to her sister. This illustrated the fact that Mr. Clemens has been writing Something that is so strong, that he cannot give it to Jean to type, because he does not know how nearly her soul is lost; he is not willing to 'shove her in among the goats,' but I only can get the machine & do the typing."

Twain's confidence in Isabel was double-edged: apparently she had already fallen among "the goats" and did not have to be protected as the afflicted Jean did. There is also a note of sexual triumph in Isabel's entry, her subtext proclaiming that she has replaced Olivia and regards herself as more intimate with Twain than his daughter was.

Twain and Isabel's dictation sessions ended abruptly on February 2. The Countess Massiglia owned an apparently homicidal donkey that managed to break out of his stall and threaten the unsuspecting Isabel as she walked nearby. By Isabel's account, the donkey was a public menace that had previously mauled and killed two people.

> I dropped out of sight behind some bushes. & though I did not feel afraid, a strange terror took possession of me for I knew that if he could get at me he would kill me. He snorted around outside the bushes— until he was sent along on his way, by the two contadini from whom he had escaped, and who were hastening along after him, trying to Catch him. Like one in a nightmare I fled up the long winding hill. but before I reached the top my heart began to fail me—or in its efforts to do its work well, it Seemed to be bursting beyond its limits—For 5 days I lay like one in a dream, but soon I pulled myself together enough to go unsatisfactorily about my work.

Clara Clemens confirmed Isabel's peculiar account in a letter she wrote to a friend several days after the incident: "Miss Lyon was pursued by that donkey that killed two men & injured a third, & although she escaped him the shock was so great on her nerves that she has been lying ever since half unconscious with a pulse so weak that part of the time it can't be felt. So you know the nurse said today she was afraid Miss Lyon might die & if she didn't die that she would be ill for several months with nervous prostration." Twain wrote to his publisher, Frederick A. Duneka, general manager of Harper and Brothers, blaming the donkey attack for the "sudden standstill" in his writing, and reporting that Isabel's "life was about frightened out of her—since which time she has lain half-conscious in her bed at home, and the doctors cannot foretell what the outcome will be." The dictations would not resume until the end of March.

February proved to be a difficult month not just for Isabel, but for Twain, Olivia, and Clara as well. Twenty-nine-year-old Clara had long chafed under the strict restrictions her parents had set for her, and after Susy's death their grip had tightened. Twain insisted that his daughter be chaperoned, and begrudged any potential suitors paying attention to her. While Europe normally held great appeal for her, she had only reluctantly accompanied her parents and sister to Italy. She resented being treated like a child and was desperate to strike out on her own and lead an independent life. The depth of her resentment and animosity was revealed in a letter she wrote to her close friend Dorothea Gilder (daughter of Richard Watson Gilder, a prominent poet, editor in chief of the *Century Illustrated Monthly Magazine,* and founder of the Authors' Club). Sure that her friend, who was younger by eight years, would keep her confidence, Clara confessed her guilt to Dorothea about an awful incident involving a screaming confrontation with her father— a rant, in fact, that the entire household had witnessed.

I have reached the very lowest stage a human being can drop. I have had an attack of what everyone in the house calls hysteria the one thing of all others I have always despised most.

I should not believe it had happened if I were not so lame & sore all over, today and seem curiously weak.

For Heaven's sake I hope you never will be seized as I was yesterday for the shame on me today is indescribable, when one of the servants came in to my room this A.M. & said that all the servants wished to express their sympathy I felt as if I should never stop flushing.

I don't know why I was so suddenly seized but at any rate I was seized by something & began to scream & curse & knocked down the furniture Etc. Etc. 'till everyone of course came running & in my father's presence

I said I hated him hated my mother hoped they would all die & if they didn't succeed soon I would kill them, well on & on for more than an hour, I don't know all I said but mother hearing the noise & being told that I was overwrought got a heart attack and as you can imagine today I can hardly meet anyone's eyes. Of course I am as hoarse as a crow & am terribly bruised from knocking myself against things. Doesn't it sound like the commonest vulgarest actress? It all comes of controlling controlling controlling one's self 'till one just bursts at last in despair. The whole winter has been & still is ghastly, my mother has been growing steadily worse, the doctor's tone is always discouraging, there is constant war with that Countess & my father is trying to sue her (with right of course) we expect to leave to move out of the house any minute & there it is, my mother couldn't be moved if the house were burning. . . .

I should think everyone would consider it dangerous to come near our family. . . .

I never had such a strange feeling before in my life as I have today, I keep blushing at intervals & then feeling resentful—do tell me have you ever acted so that people were frightened away from you & admitted to you afterwards they thought you were insane? If you haven't I pray you never will. I am in bed half the time nowadays anyway but this minute it seems to me I should like never leave it.

This is not exactly a letter it's sort of a "please do tell me that you have or that you know some one that had a similar attack," it seems to me I don't belong in good society anymore. very affectionately yrs. C.C.

Clara later pleaded with Dorothea to destroy the letter, yet her friend ignored her wishes. Clara's ferocious outburst proved more than Olivia could bear, and the stress only added to her nearly constant pain.

Isabel Lyon had no physical contact with the "other" lady of the house during this period; within her writings, there survives only one document that links her and Olivia at this time. During the month of March, Isabel sent Olivia a brief note on behalf of Twain asking if she remembered an expected visitor, Katherine Bates. Olivia wrote back at the bottom of the note that she did and that if she was well enough when Miss Bates visited Florence she would be happy to see her. Although the two women were part of the same household, they occupied separate compartments of Twain's life. Now, both were seriously ailing simultaneously, and Clara made her own bid for attention and retreated to her bed as well. One can only imagine Twain's sense of being under siege. As someone who was accustomed to having his needs met immediately and everyone's attention focused on him, this change in the balance of the household must have proven to be enormously unsettling.

Isabel knew about Clara's breakdown and the ugly threats she had made against her mother and father, although she was far too circumspect to comment directly in her journal about what had happened. A week after the incident, Isabel discreetly jotted down a note on a loose piece of paper that she had visited Clara, "to have a word with her." Isabel now was privy to powerful, intimate knowledge about the family and had gained frightening insight into Clara's emotional state of mind. At the same time, Clara realized that Isabel possessed information about this highly embarrassing personal episode in her life and that realization must have caused her considerable discomfort. Shortly afterward, Isabel gave Clara a new nickname in her writings: Santissima. In Italian, *Santissima* means the most saintly, the most revered, the most holy. A church in Florence dedicated to the Virgin Mother is named Santissima Annunziata. With this latest display of her fearsome temper Clara bore little resemblance to any saint, and Isabel's seeming endearment may actually have functioned as a pointed parody of Clara's troubled disposition. The two women would never again share an entirely comfortable relationship.

Writing to Harriet Whitmore less than a month after the incident, Isabel omitted any mention of Clara's attack in her determinedly upbeat letter:

> Mrs. Clemens has not had the good winter that the first weeks after her arrival promised—She has not left her room for a long long time, but she seems to be improving now—and all are hoping that the lovely Spring days will bring Strength with them.
>
> Mr. Clemens is just up after two weeks in bed with hard bronchitis—he is still coughing a good deal.
>
> Clara and Jean are quite well. Both are studying hard—and Clara is doing beautiful things with her voice. I am present at all her lessons, and the development is marvelous. Someone after hearing her sing, was heard to say "What a wonderful black Contralto from such a little creature!"

Italy is very beautiful these days—and the Villa di Quarto overlooks one of the loveliest views about Florence—Mr. Clemens sends many messages to you and to Mr. Whitmore.

On April 8, Olivia had another heart attack—this time with Clara in the room to witness her agony. Later that same month Twain confided to Henry Rogers, "The past week has been awful—she has had bad nights, and been obliged to sit up in bed for hours, in order to get her breath. . . . Three nights ago her pulse went up to 192, and nothing but a subcutaneous injection of brandy brought her back to life."

The Clemens family's troubles aside, at the end of February Isabel had made a friend outside of her immediate circle. Don Raffaello Stiattisi was a local priest from whom she began to take Italian lessons. Over the next few months, she grew very fond of the handsome priest and the two frequently spent time together. Her attraction to Don Raffaello, while genuine, certainly had a bit of the character of forbidden fruit to it in view of his priestly vocation. Nevertheless, the two had a number of outings together, sometimes accompanied by Clara or by Isabel's mother, Georgiana. Isabel dreamily recounted a beautiful evening they had spent together:

*Clara Clemens and Don Raffaello Stiattisi,*
*Florence, Italy, 1904*

We sat out of doors, heard lovely music and watched the city lights come out. The hills of Fiesole were a wonderful dark blue, a glorious sunset was making it all too beautiful, and the Arno stretched along like a pearl necklace, with its curving line of lights. Best of all, always and forever was Don Raffaello with his beautiful face, his lovely buoyancy of manner, and his great sweetness of soul. We stayed to watch the view, and to watch some intelligent young soldiers experimenting with a newly invented method of telegraphing, by means of flashes of light. We could see the answering flashed from a hill between Fiesole and Quarto and it was all too lovely. Then we took the train home, and walked from the Piazza del Duomo down to the hotel.

With the arrival of the Italian spring Isabel's spirits soared, and on April 14 she exclaimed, "And we came over here to live—It is Too perfect for life. There are no flaws." This joyous declaration strikes an odd note considering the events of February and Olivia's heart attacks.

And indeed, less than six weeks later, on a warm, clear, Sabbath evening in June 1904, Olivia finally surrendered to her last illness, progressive heart disease, and quietly slipped away. She was fifty-eight years old. Although the family obviously knew that Olivia was gravely ill, in a time when severe and prolonged illnesses commonly forecast the worst, it is equally true that they were utterly unprepared for her death. Katy Leary held Olivia in her arms as she died, and bore witness to the terrible moment when Twain saw his deceased wife:

> Mr. Clemens ran right up to the bed and took her in his arms like he always did and held her for the longest time, and then he laid her back and he said, "How beautiful she is—how young and sweet—and look, she's smiling!" It was a pitiful thing to see her there dead, and him looking at her. Oh, he cried all that time, and Clara and Jean, they put their arms around their father's neck and they cried, the three of them as though their hearts would break.

Olivia's corpse was lifted into a coffin and moved to the parlor. Clara collapsed beneath her mother's casket and sobbed uncontrollably, then stood up and went to her mother's bedroom and threw herself into her mother's bed. She finally went to her own room, lay down in her bed and remained motionless and silent for four days. Twain spent a night kneeling and pacing next to Olivia's coffin.

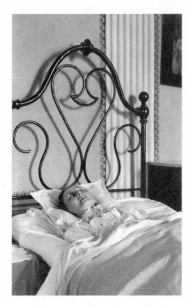

*Olivia Langdon Clemens, dead at age fifty-eight, Florence, Italy*

Isabel captured the enormity of Olivia's death and the family's intense reaction to it in three cryptic lines:

June 5—Mrs. Clemens died at nine
    in the evening.
    Clara is prostrate—
    Life is Too desolated—

A year later Isabel recalled, "Today is the anniversary of the great Tragedy of this family . . . after a sweet chat with Santissima, Mrs. Clemens's light went out— Now I can see Mr. Clemens's face when I flew to his room & told him to go to Mrs. Clemens's room—'Is it an alarm?' he said—but I didn't know—they only told me to run & get him."

The passing of Olivia had a less histrionic but much more devastating effect on Jean. Amazingly, she had the fortitude to take a number of photographs of her dead mother as personal keepsakes. In Jean's photographs, Olivia looks creased and worn, with her mouth slightly open. She is dressed entirely in white, still wearing her bedclothes. When her mother died, Jean suffered a seizure, the first in over a year, and for the rest of her life she would never be free from such attacks for so long a time. Jean, her mother's beloved baby, was now dependent upon her grief-stricken father and sister to help manage her illness.

While the shocked family members prepared to return to the United States, Isabel steeled herself for a difficult good-bye to the priest, Don Raffaello. On June 16 she wistfully recorded, "The trunks are pulled out. life in Italy is almost finished—Don Raffaello comes every evening for a little or a long while—He grows more beautiful Each day as priest and man."

On June 28, three weeks after Olivia's death, the remaining Clemenses bade farewell to Italy and boarded the *Prince Oscar* along with Isabel, Georgiana, Teresa Cherubini (the Clemenses' Italian maid), and Olivia's coffined corpse. When the ship docked, on July 12, at 7:00 p.m. in New York, the family was greeted with a directive signed by President Roosevelt and his cabinet that allowed them to bypass customs. Twain, Clara, and Jean immediately left the ship to spend the night at the stately Wolcott Hotel, while Isabel, her mother, and Teresa went to the more modest St. Denis. The next day the Clemenses departed for Elmira, where Olivia would be buried, and the task of passing the nineteen pieces of luggage through customs fell to Isabel. She later noted with satisfaction in her journal that she had managed "to get the 16 Trunks booked to Lee [Massachusetts] without paying extra for overweight of 2500 lbs." Twain had decided to rent a home on Four Brooks Farm, Richard Watson Gilder's property in Lee, as an appropriate summer and fall retreat. Isabel arrived first with the mountain of luggage.

At the end of June, a worried Twain had written to Charles Langdon, his brother-in-law, that unless Clara found some relief soon from her "strain," "she will go down with a crash and her present two-thirds nervous breakdown will take on an additional third and be complete." Clara's confused mental state was magnified at her mother's funeral. The private service took place on July 14 at the Langdon's home in Elmira. The ceremony was held in the parlor where Twain had married Olivia thirty-four years earlier. Olivia's final resting place was next to her deceased son and daughter in the Langdon plot on a grassy hill less than a mile from her family's home. At the cemetery an inconsolable Clara tried to jump into her mother's grave as the coffin was lowered, and she had to be physically restrained by her bereaved father. Two days after the funeral, Clara arrived at Four Brooks Farm in Lee, "pale weak exhausted," followed by Twain, Jean, and Katy Leary. By all appearances, Clara's feelings of guilt and loss must have been unbearable.

There is a single surviving letter in which Twain expresses the full extent of his grief over losing Olivia. In the letter, written less than two weeks after her funeral, Twain revealed his most emotionally vulnerable side to Susan Crane, Olivia's older sister.

Dear Susy—
     Yes, she did love me; & nothing that I did, no hurt that I inflicted upon her, no tears that I caused those dear eyes to shed, could break it

down, or even chill it. It always rose again, it always burned again, as warm & bright as ever. Nothing could wreck it, nothing could extinguish it. Never a day passed that she did not say, with emphasis & enthusiasm, "I love you so. I just worship you." They were always undeserved, they were always a rebuke, but she stopped my mouth whenever I said it, though she knew I said it honestly.

I know something, & I get some poor small comfort out of it: that what little good was in me I gave to her to the utmost—full measure, the last grain & the last ounce—& poor as it was, it was my very best, & far beyond anything I could have given to any other person that ever lived. It was poverty, but it was all I had; & so it stood for wealth, & she so accounted it.

I try not to think of the hurts I gave her, but oh, there were so many, so many!

With Twain's beloved wife dead, Isabel would now become a key part of the family dynamic. Isabel was the willing "Typewriter" who would give Twain the "Sympathetic wave."

## 8

At the time of Olivia's death, Isabel was forty years old and feeling the burdens of her age. She had a permanently injured eye, frequent headaches, and suffered from bouts of depression. A glowing beauty in her youth, Isabel had now become what she never could have imagined growing up—a spinster. Years of work and worry had etched themselves into her face, and her rich brown hair had become streaked with gray. Photographs exposed rawness in her expression, a nakedness born of past disappointments. Although men had found her attractive, none of her relationships had lasted. Isabel was now at a crossroads, and she was keenly aware that her opportunities had dwindled. Olivia's demise created a vacuum that Isabel would do her utmost to fill on a permanent basis. She had always been a crafty cardplayer, and she could not afford to waste her few remaining good hands.

At Lee the careful housing arrangement that Olivia had insisted upon—that Isabel would live outside the family's residence—was abandoned. Isabel and Twain began living in the same house, and during their future travels they usually lodged at the same hotel. Twain had made a career of questioning and challenging propriety, and this change in living arrangements was a substantive departure from his earlier expressed views. While he prided himself on his iconoclasm, where sexual propriety was concerned he was extremely sensitive to public opinion. Two years after he and Isabel started living in the same house, Twain told an indignant Jane Addams that the reason he withdrew his support for Maxim Gorky was because Gorky was rumored to be staying in a hotel with his mistress. "[Gorky] could not offend against one of the strongest of our customs." Twain was well aware that his immediate family felt such an arrangement with Isabel was inappropriate, although he brushed off Clara's objections to Isabel's live-in status by joking, "No, I want her here. She's like an old pair of slippers to me." Isabel was happy to comply, her earlier criticism of Countess Massiglia's behavior with her servant and public perception of such an arrangement apparently forgotten. For Isabel, Twain's immediate emotional needs took precedence over what anyone would say—damn propriety.

Isabel was privately challenging decorum with her continued attraction to Don Raffaello. After her return to America, she often expressed her longing for the priest: "I wonder if I am glad or sorry that I miss him so much." On July 28, she wrote and then crossed out, "Oh stretching straining heart that reaches out to Florence." Isabel's Florentine romance became a diversion for her during the long summer nights in Lee, and in August, she inked over another entry, in which she had exulted, "Today I have an uplift. Perhaps it comes surging out of my soul by the Continuous and beautiful Thought of Italy. Last night I dreamed of Don Raffaello, and it was sweet dreaming. I like to wander alone into the fields here and Talk across seas to Italy. It makes sweet living." Isabel and Don Raffaello corresponded for months and often sent each other small gifts. Although Don Raffaello had promised to visit her in America (and Twain was persuaded by Isabel to write a letter of introduction for him), he fell into ill health, "lost money," and never did.

Approximately one month after Clara's arrival at Lee, she left for New York. Isabel described Clara's condition in a record she later crossed out:

> Santa Clara went away with Katy [Leary] today. Last night we talked the night away, for I did not go to my room until dawn was breaking. The Strain of living here has been too great—She Cannot stand the

Sounds in the Tiny house. Two days ago with a strange effort of her will she got up. Saying it was only a question of will—And simply because her mind would not be normal that did not mean that the body was ill—The body must be ignored. She went alone last Evening down to the little river—fearing to face the new life she has taken up—(for she is making herself the housekeeper) and feeling that She must be guided. And so after the sad reaching out by the little river, She felt She must go—and it is best—though what it will be for me—With Santa Clara away—I don't like to think.

An emotionally shattered Clara entered Dr. Angenette Parry's sanitarium at 117 West Sixty-ninth Street in New York City. Clara became further distraught when she learned that just a week and a half later, Jean, an avid equestrienne, was struck by a streetcar in Lee while riding in the moonlight with Rodman Gilder, Richard Gilder's son. Jean was knocked unconscious and her horse, Rhea, was killed. Twain traveled to New York to tell Clara about her sister's accident, and unfortunately, with his tendency toward exaggeration, he further upset his daughter. Horrified by her father's alarming words, Clara immediately traveled back to Lee to see Jean. Jean's injuries proved to be relatively minor: "a broken tendon in her left ankle. And her face and back were bruised and disfigured and she suffered much. But was very plucky." Twain's only comment to Isabel was that "the Whole affair was simply another stroke of a relentless God." After spending three days with her sister, a "hysterical" Clara returned to Dr. Parry's care. In September, Clara checked herself into a second sanitarium, in Norfolk, Connecticut, to continue her recuperation. At the end of September, she returned to New York and Dr. Parry, where she remained under doctor's orders to have virtually no contact with her family until spring. Grief-stricken and depressed, Clara was restricted to her bed and not allowed to read her mail for several months.

With remarkable speed, Twain, Isabel, and Jean established a routine life of relative normalcy. The three spent their evenings together playing euchre and reading excerpts from Thomas Bailey Aldrich's *Ponkapog Papers* and Rudyard Kipling's *Five Seas*. Richard Gilder, along with his oldest child, Dorothea, and oldest son, Rodman, were frequent guests, and on July 26, the popular author "[Alice] Hegan Rice, who wrote 'Mrs. Wiggs of the Cabbage Patch' " paid a social call. Isabel was

*Andrew Carnegie*

fers." Twain's illnesses drove Isabel frantic with worry, and she became his personal nurse: "He seems quite helpless from the gout & nearly fell in reaching his arm chair—I caught him as his ankles gave way—and it alarmed me." For treating his various ailments, Twain favored alcohol. When he felt a cold coming on he would automatically reach for whiskey. Sick or well, Twain smoked constantly. His daily intake was approximately forty heart-clenching "smokes" every day. Isabel suspected his dependence actually might have hidden health benefits: "Sometimes I think he must draw nourishment from his smoking, for he smokes so much. & he doesn't seem to get any thing but good out of it—for himself & for others of us too." Isabel was fascinated by the essential attachment that Twain had to tobacco and the palliative effect that tobacco apparently had on him:

I doubt if any smoker has ever been better loved & revered by the spirit of his tobacco than Mr. Clemens is—I've never seen any Smoke issue so confidingly, never seen any that is so loathe to leave the smoker. This lingers—lingers, curls around him with the grace of a spirit, and then melts unwillingly worshippingly away—it always has a message for him. Perhaps he hears it. Or perhaps he doesn't.

disappointed with Rice because she thought she appeared "very unliterary and inconsequent. Mr. Clemens says that Mrs. Wiggs is not literature so there is less need than might be for a literary flavor to Mrs. Rice." But the slow, quiet country pace of Lee proved boring for Isabel: "It has been a long waiting up in those hills," and she was restless to depart for the social whirl of New York City with Twain and Jean at the end of November.

Twain had leased a house in New York at 21 Fifth Avenue for a period of three years. Isabel was thrilled to leave her country surroundings and loved the new home: "This house is . . . nicely oldish—with gothic adornments over the doorways & windows on the main floor. When it shall be finished—weeks hence—it will be harmonious." Twain and Isabel's abode, with its fashionable address, was located next to the venerable Brevoort Hotel. James Renwick, Jr., the architect of Saint Patrick's Cathedral and Grace Church on lower Broadway, had designed the building approximately sixty-five years earlier. Isabel thought the surroundings provided a suitable frame for her King:

the real picture of Mr. Clemens standing as I have seen him, near the arch of the Gothic window in the middle with the fading light of the

*Mark Twain House on left, with gothic windows; Brevoort Hotel on right. New York City, 1935*

afternoon softening our blemishes & enhancing his great charm as he [crossed out: stands smoking with] stops in his walk with his cigar between his fingers the smoke & like incense curling affectionately about him as he waits to hear the remark of some person present, or waits to catch a thought of his own to . . . give to his listeners.

With Clara under medical care and away from her family, Isabel assumed the household duties, capably managing the servants and organizing Twain's meals: "Tonight at dinner the Soup was not very good and Mr. Clemens said 'The cook didn't put her heart into that Soup—it was probably her foot.'" As for keeping the staff happy, Twain's tongue-in-cheek recommendation to Isabel was to "be good to Them—put a hunk of pie under Their pillows every night." Unamused by his advice, Isabel huffed from her newly elevated status: "The attitude that one has to assume toward servants in this city."

At 21 Fifth Avenue, the card playing continued in full force with Hearts and 500 as favorite choices: "This evening after dinner we played 500—a very good game. & after Jean left us—which she did at an early hour for she has [a] cold—Mr. Clemens and I continued—Rodman Gilder came in for an instant to pay his respects—but he wouldn't stay to take a hand in the game. And after he left Mr. Clemens and I continued until eleven. I won most of the games." A bad strategy with Mark Twain. Isabel amusedly observed that when Twain played cards with her and Jean, he did not rein in his language:

When Jean is in Mr. Clemens's room and we play cards—or don't—he gives a freer vent to . . . his words and is therefore a dear delight. Tonight he had nothing but little "spot" Cards. & he called them a "perfect puke of spot Cards." Ah his babbling is of a Strength—Jean remonstrated—and In a chuckle of joy he Told about a man—a good man—who many years ago was stranded somewhere in Mexico . . . without a cent. He hunted every where for work, and finally they offered him a chance to personate Christ in . . . one of the religious processions . . . depicting Christ on his way to Calvary. The street was lined with godless folk who pelted him with rotten eggs—bad bananas, and hideous other things. The man stood it with great dignity until the Storm was too hot then putting down his cross he said "If I wasn't personating God Almighty, Id show yer a Thing or Two." I think it was apropos of the fact that a "perfect puke of spot cards" was nothing to what . . . Mr.

Clemens could say if he were not upholding his dignity as Jean's father. That's what I think.

Between the around-the-clock card games, Twain gave Isabel her first lesson on the Orchestrelle, which she called "a truly wonderful instrument." Built by the Aeolian company, the Orchestrelle could be played by hand like a piano or powered by foot. Twain's Orchestrelle was the largest model built and cost $2,600. He reportedly visited the factory while it was under construction to listen to its tone. His desire was that it should sound as much like a pipe organ as possible. The Aeolian was delivered along with five dozen sheets of music. The enormous Orchestrelle towered over the diminutive Isabel. Over the next few years she would spend countless hours playing it at Twain's request; he demanded to hear his favorite songs again and again.

Listening to music from the Orchestrelle was therapeutic for the aging literary giant, and he rarely missed his daily session. Isabel understood that the "Aeolian satisfies . . . him [crossed out: as nothing else can]." Whenever Twain moved to Dublin, New Hampshire, or Tuxedo, New York, to spend the summer, the Orchestrelle was carefully dismantled, transported via train, and painstakingly reassembled. On particularly tedious evenings, when Isabel's attempts to find visitors proved fruitless and cards failed to distract, a morose Twain entreated her to play two special selections that reminded him of his lost daughter, Susy, and his wife:

I have been playing to Mr. Clemens, playing his favorites—and after I had played many things that he loves, I took up the Largo—He sat in the big green Tufted chair quite near me, with his back Toward me, and when I had finished it he said—"If you're not tired play the Susie one." That is the Intermezzo. I played it & he said "I can fit the words to both those pieces, as the coffins of Susie & her mother are borne through the dining room & the hall & the drawing room of the Hartford house, Susie calls to me in the Intermezzo & her mother in the Largo—& they are lamenting that they shall see that place no more—" Oh, his soul is so lonely—Days are when it is so Terrible—

Painful gout and bronchitis kept Twain in bed for five and a half weeks during December 1904 and January 1905, greatly adding to his gloom: "He is weak & depressed—It is heart sickening—for he suf-

*William Dean Howells*

In spite of his drinking and smoking, Twain finally regained his health, and he eagerly plunged into the New York social whirl, visiting with Henry Rogers, Thomas Bailey Aldrich, and William Dean Howells. Andrew Carnegie came to chat and gave Twain some of his personal Scottish whiskey, a blend so treasured that Carnegie shared it with only three other people—presidents Cleveland, Harrison, and Roosevelt. Robert J. Collier sent Twain two boxes of expensive cigars: "Fuel," Twain gleefully called them, "for the New Year."

Between his puffing and comings and goings, Twain indulged in his supreme talent—he talked and talked and talked to Isabel:

> Today Mr. Clemens hasn't worked at all—[Twain had just completed "Eve's Diary."] He came down stairs & talked with me for a long time about the wonders of Darwin. & he strikes so into the heart of Things— [crossed out: how he makes the heart of you sob while he is talking & you waken in the dead of night with the sob still in you.] . . . It has been a memorable day because he has talked so much. & he makes you to see visions—Oh Such visions when the silver flow of his speech starts. Oh but he lives a Strong inner life.

With Isabel as his constant companion, Twain regaled her with humorous tales about his life. Isabel described Twain's conversation as "Like a dream edifice, for you don't know what is coming next, & his talks build on into exquisite towers & pinnacles & when he sits down the wonderful structure he has built, fades away & you have only & imperishable memory of a hauntingly beautiful thing that you can never remember & never forget."

One afternoon, Twain's memory was jogged when Jean's dog Prosper le Gai (an enormous St. Bernard) came sniffing around while he was having tea with Isabel, Jean, and a Mrs. Dwight. Twain entertained the group with a story about how he had nearly been prevented from visiting Augustin Daly (a famous playwright who adapted *Roughing It* and *Ah Sin*) in his New York office during the mid 1880s.

Prosper appeared just then—& that threw the talk into the lovely story of Mr. Clemens's trip to New York to keep an appointment with Mr. Daly. And how Mr. Daly's big Irishman wouldn't admit Mr. Clemens,—he hadn't admitted anyone to that Sanctum for 25 years without instructions from Mr. Daly to do so—This day there hadn't been any instructions. . . . Mr. Clemens had been told how to find the Sanctum—Go into a court—from a street & go to the first door that you see—There was the door but behind it was the big Irishman—No—Mr. Clemens couldn't see Mr. Daly—And no one was allowed to smoke there either. So Mr. Clemens put his cigar down—But . . . that morning the New Haven news dealer who boarded the train had . . . only New Haven papers . . . they were better than nothing—So Mr. Clemens bought one & read it all—advertisements even—one whole page was given up to a Bench Show [an animal show], & the only illustration was that of a big prize $10 000 St. Bernard—Mr. Clemens read it all—Read the dimensions & weight & name of that dog—got the name of the head man of the Bench Show too—As he stood trying to convince the big Irish-man that Mr Daly wanted to see him—that the business was of interest to . . . Mr Daly . . . and the Irishman . . . blandly said "Yes they all say that—" a big St Bernard . . . entered the little room—The Irish-man's face changed as the Splendid creature walked in—& he had just asked Mr. Clemens the nature of that business—& Mr. Clemens told us that he couldn't say he was a lecturer, he wouldn't stand any show with the Irishman—but he did say he was the bench show man from New

Haven. The Irishman flew around, pulled off his vest—hadn't any coat on—& dusted the only Chair for Mr. Clemens—& Mr. Clemens did it all for us—he dusted the chair—he was the happy worshipful Irishman to a dot—& he told us how he guessed the length & height & weight of that dog so captivating the Irishman that he showed Mr. Clemens the way up to Mr. Daly's sanctum to the utter amazement of Mr. Daly.

This was not the first time Twain had spun his Daly yarn, but Isabel had never heard it before, and she loved his impression of the bench-show man. Not surprisingly, Twain told Isabel stories that reflected well on him. In his telling, he was worry free as well as the focus of her attention. Another anecdote related how Twain's nephew Samuel Moffett had made his way in journalism.

[Samuel] had been left a sum of money by his father's death, & he put it in a fruit farm; "but the worms came along & they ate up the fruit then the trees, & then they started for the house, but Sam left about that time." He tried all sorts of ways to find work out there in California & finally wrote to Mr. Clemens asking for a letter of introduction that might bring him work on a newspaper. Mr. Clemens said he'd do it if his nephew would abide by the rules that he would give him. And the rules were these: Ask for his work—but for work without any pay—do anything he was asked to do—Sweeping out the office if need be—and never mention the pay—let his employer do that. Moffett did it. And he climbed steadily until now the Editor of the *World* is trying to induce him to decline a very good offer from *Collier's* weekly—for they want him to take charge of an Historical Department—a most congenial work for Mr. Moffett. While at a very good salary—and the *World* people want him to assume a responsible and well paying assistant-editorship on their own paper. They would pay a higher salary than *Collier* will—but . . . the latter position is worth more than just mere money.

This tale is a curious one, and highly suspect as to its historical accuracy. Twain predictably cast himself in a favorable light as the wise, thrifty uncle whose sage advice launched young Samuel's career. Yet when Samuel Moffett's father died, he was only five years old—a bit young to be investing in fruit farms. Also, William Moffett, Samuel's father, was a Saint Louis merchant whose business was ruined by the Civil War, and there was no money for such a bequest to his young son. After William's death, the surviving family members (his mother, Twain's sister, Pamela, and siblings Annie and Samuel), managed on his modest life insurance. Samuel Moffett eventually did enter the newspaper business, at age twenty-two, working for a paper in Oakland, California, while a student at the University of California at Berkeley. Indeed, Twain's embroidered recollection resembles the "model boys" stories (the best known of which was Horatio Alger, Jr.,'s novel *Ragged Dick*), where the lead characters were moralistic role models ordained to do good. Earlier in his life Twain had mocked these stories, and had published a satire, "The Story of the Bad Little Boy," in 1865, when Samuel Moffett celebrated his fifth birthday.

Why Twain shared such an elaboration with Isabel is worthy of consideration. Twain was wracked by a lifelong insecurity, and his story serves to portray him as benevolent and caring. This was a time when his relationship with his daughters was becoming increasingly distant, and his paterfamilias account could be interpreted as a means of reassuring himself against possible accusations of neglect. In retrospect, it is significant that Twain chose to tell Isabel, a working woman who had lost her father, about the success of a fatherless young man, approximately her age, who was fortunate enough to have had such an important benefactor. Unlike the industrious Samuel, no matter how hard Isabel worked or how thrifty and virtuous she was, there was no encouragement offered by anyone that ultimately she could become an assistant editor and entertain competing employment offers. For Isabel's generation there was no female analogue to Ragged Dick. In telling Isabel the story, Twain may have been revealing his willingness to act as her patron, albeit more in a traditional patriarchal sense than a professional one.

During their first year together after Olivia's death, Isabel and Twain's bond intensified. Although they had been born on opposite sides of the Mason-Dixon Line (he in Missouri and she in New York), had dissimilar upbringings, and were separated by a yawning generation gap, they were members of the same intimate club of pain and memory. The roots of their special affinity had been created decades earlier when they experienced the death of their fathers at a vulnerable age: Twain, a sensitive child, was only eleven years old and Isabel was just nineteen. While it is impossible to know the full extent to which they were emotionally affected by losing a parent, in reading through their personal papers and remembrances one sees telling signs.

Twain's reminiscences to Isabel about his father, John Marshall Clemens, were apparently not numerous, but the ones Isabel recounted were quite sentimental and at odds with Twain's own ambivalent portrayal of him in his autobiography. Isabel recorded two occasions when Twain spoke to her about John Clemens. On Saturday morning, March 24, 1906, a teary-eyed Twain blurted to Isabel, " 'This is the day my father died, fifty nine years ago' . . . as he looked at the date on the morning newspaper—*The Times*—He remembers it all distinctly for he was just at the age when events stamp themselves indelibly—He drew the sparkle in his eye back into its sheath . . . after he saw & received the copy of *Simplicissimus* [a satirical German weekly magazine] that I brought in to him."

Twain told Isabel he would share with her the only joke his father had ever made in his presence: "He went with his father when a very little boy, into a room where there were many loaves of bread—200 or more, & the bread was very moldy & covered with blue cobwebs. It surprised the boy, & he asked his father where it came from, & he answered. 'From Noah's Ark.' " A simple joke, but so unexpected from a usually taciturn man that this rare moment of camaraderie would be remembered by Twain for the rest of his life. In 1950 Isabel told Doris Webster that while Twain shied away from mentioning his father, he spoke quite frequently about his mother.

Isabel's writing about her own father is remarkable for its silence—he makes scarcely a ripple in the hundreds of pages she generated during her six and a half years with Twain. On July 28, 1904, she spent the evening playing euchre with Twain and Jean when Richard Gilder stopped by to visit. Richard and Twain began reminiscing about Horace Greeley (the founding editor of the *New York Tribune*), prompting Isabel to recall when she had met him:

> I was a little bit of a girl & got into a Broadway stage with father & mother. I sat or stood between my mother & a man upon whose knee I rested my little hand and I remember that Father whispered something to Mother that made her look very proud for her little daughter's hand was on Horace Greeley's knee & he didn't brush it off.

In Isabel's retelling of her childhood memory, the status reference is clear—beaming parents watching their child hold a famous man's knee. This is the only mention Isabel is known to have made of her father, and he is a sidebar in a story about Horace Greeley. While she makes constant, often daily, references to her mother, Charles Lyon is a ghost to whom his daughter almost never gives voice. For Twain and Isabel, fathers were a convenience, their deaths inconvenient. As adults, Isabel clung to her mother and Twain talked about his. Mothers were the central figures for the two.

John Marshall Clemens and Charles Harrison Lyon may have exacted an emotional toll on their families, but in both cases financial catastrophe followed. In the years prior to John Clemens's death, his family had endured a steady downward economic spiral and faced bankruptcy. When he died, of pneumonia at age forty-eight, his unexpected passing left his wife and four children in dire straits from which they escaped only years later, after Twain became a successful lecturer and writer. As a double cruelty, Twain endured the humiliation of insolvency twice in his life—the first time at his father's hands, the second at his own. Isabel, too, knew how it felt to be reliant upon the charity of extended family and neighbors. When Charles Lyon died, Isabel entered the petit bourgeois life, a circumstance she resented. Her halcyon country days abruptly ended, and she was forced to depend upon the kindness of family friends for employment. She had been raised to understand the importance of social position, and she understood that her family had lost theirs along with their wealth.

Their mutually troubled pasts left Isabel and Twain particularly vulnerable when death repeatedly visited their family members. Although early and sudden death was a frequent visitor in all social classes in these times, the loss of loved ones was never routine. In addition to surviving his wife, two children, and his parents, Twain had lost his sisters Margaret and Pamela, and brothers Benjamin and Orion, as well as his younger brother, Henry. The emotional balance Twain had been able to establish as a family man was ruptured by the death of Susy and utterly broken with Olivia's passing. Jean's horrible illness was more than Twain could bear to deal with by himself, and Clara was becoming ever more isolated from her family.

Isabel also struggled with incapacitating emotional stress. With her father, uncle, and brother gone, Isabel remained close to her sister,

Louise Moore, and formed a particularly reverential relationship with her mother, calling her "Saint Mother." Isabel constantly worried about Georgiana's health and well-being, and found her physical presence so comforting that she rented a room for her at 19 East Ninth Street, near Twain's residence. When her mother was away, Isabel complained about how "very lonely" she was, while wondering how she dared to "be lonely in the presence of a loneliness like Mr. Clemens's." Isabel's fretting frequently resulted in tension headaches that sometimes lasted for days; she

*Louise and Charles Lyon*

described them as "strange, nervous," and "Terrible." She complained that they "shut me away from physical & mental activitie." Surely the stress of her living situation exacerbated Isabel's condition, yet that was likely just one of the causes. Isabel's "emotional strain" or depression may have been due to the mysterious blackmail threat, to her unresolved grief over her family's devastation, her fear that she might suddenly lose her mother, and her frustration over not establishing a more permanent relationship with Twain.

For years Twain and Isabel were witnesses to the disintegration of their family circles. It was only natural that the two of them, with their twin histories of grief and displacement, would find each other compatible.

9

The winter, spring, and summer of 1905 were an especially happy time. Isabel raved about Twain: "Never never on Sea or shore of spiritual or terrestrial being Could there be a man to equal Mr. Clemens. The subtlety of his magic and he doesn't know it. He cant half enjoy himself and Oh the pity of it—for he would so appreciate himself—It is Cruel. After dinner Jean & finally I gave him music until a late hour. I am stupefied." Living with Twain and associating with his friends, Isabel was becoming who she felt she always should have been. She was a lady reinvested with social status, who had time to read and think and write. She had been reborn.

Twain was increasingly relying upon Isabel to deal with matters that he chose not to entrust to his daughters. She was given carte blanche to control the household accounts, deal with merchants, and write checks. She also read all of Twain's personal mail and was charged with keeping the curious and adoring public at bay. When someone tried to contact Twain through Isabel, he jokingly called it "tampering with the sentinel." Isabel was well aware of the privileges associated with her position, and visitors frequently reminded her of her good fortune. A Mrs. Judd, who had called on Twain, fussed over Isabel after her visit with him: "She showered very sweet speech upon me & kissed my forehead in homage for the man, who stands as my Complete master. She said that I will not need a heaven when I die for I have it here. She doesn't half suspect the truth of her words. She wondered how I 'managed it' to become his secretary. Those things aren't managed They just Come to one—& you mustn't try to 'manage' them into existence."

Such modest demurring aside, ensuring her future was exactly what Isabel had in mind, and part of her management included a revised opinion about adultery. When the handsome American journalist and author Poultney Bigelow came to visit Twain a year after their return from Italy, Isabel expressed her sympathy for his rather tangled personal relationships in a diary entry she later crossed out: "His love for another woman than his wife, you don't see that behind the mask of him. Why don't I condemn the man or woman who loves outside of his or her marriage bond? Most married women of my age do condemn, and roundly—but I don't." Isabel's sexual wishes are right on the surface, and she clearly identifies with the other woman and the philandering man.

When Twain was ill and incapacitated, Isabel was sometimes asked to speak for him. In early January 1905, a reporter invited Isabel to make up a statement from Twain that he was willing to publish, a comment about the recent report that he was suffering from illness. Isabel declined the reporter's journalistic largess. And it was Isabel to whom

Twain turned to a month earlier when he desired that the books in his personal library be organized: "For 3 days I have been very busy classifying the hundreds of books of Mr. Clemens's library—and Coming across many interesting volumes. It is exhausting work." Isabel spent weeks "trying to find places for the books that are scattered—piled—on the library floor"; her task was significantly delayed when, in February, she discovered Katy Leary, who had always been entrusted with such tasks in the past, "vigorously declassifying those books. & arranging them according to color & bindings—So there is a hodge podge of science & poetry—history & fiction now. But it was funny enough to be enjoyable." Isabel was amused, but not deterred. She held her ground, and her system of classifying Twain's books replaced Katy's.

Isabel was granted access to all of Twain's private papers, and she immediately realized that his manuscripts were very valuable. In January, she observed: "Quite an interesting man—Mr. Hellman" had come inquiring if "Mr. Clemens has any manuscript to sell. He has bought nearly all of Mr. John Fiske's mss. And others too of value Some of Howells & N. Hawthorne." Twain was not interested in peddling his manuscripts. On one occasion, Isabel found "among Mr. C's papers" the obviously precious "note book that he used on *The Quaker City* [the ship on which he traveled while writing what became *Innocents Abroad*] in 1867." She was hunting for manuscripts in the study one day, when Twain entered and recounted an observation William Dean Howells had made:

> he Said that a few days ago Mr. Howells made the remark That Mr. Clemens possessed a great advantage over him, because he never had to put any love scenes in his book. Mr. Clemens said that he couldn't do it anyway—if he ever put a girl in a book he Soon found that he had to make an excuse to drop her overboard. While poor Mr. Howells has to have love scenes & the task of having them to Suit him is a terrible one.

This was the second time Twain had mentioned to Isabel his reluctance to include romantic passages in his work. The first occasion occurred when a dramatist interested in adapting *Personal Recollections of Joan of Arc* visited him. After the individual had departed, Twain told Isabel that if the adaptation were done, one of his "striking" conditions was "that there could be 'no love passage in it.' " Twain later explained to Isabel that his insistence was due to his inability to write a "successful play" containing a "love element, which he said he could not handle—He never knew what to do with the woman."

By early 1905, Twain was preoccupied with securing his literary legacy, and he made Isabel an offer that was, for him, unusually generous. He asked her to edit his letters. This was an extraordinary request considering her dearth of editorial experience, and one that was guaranteed to inflame his daughters' jealousy. Twain's invitation indicated that he trusted Isabel to portray him in the most sympathetic manner imaginable. Isabel was politically savvy enough to approach his offer with extreme caution:

> Today Mr Clemens talked with me on the editing of his Letters. He wished me to do it—Gently I protested & told him that Clara was the logical one for that. And though he said "Ben [his nickname for Clara] would never be interested in that." I believe he knew that I . . . am right—for the authority must rest with some one heavy and deep in the knowledge of how Mrs Clemens could wish the publication.

At the same time, Twain was considering who would be the appropriate person to write his authorized biography. In June, he told Isabel that he was ready to "appoint his biographer," namely his old friend William Dean Howells. Isabel naturally concurred with Twain's choice and declared that Howells was the only person,

> with the Sure enough touch—and the one who loves him well enough to do it as it should be done—for it would take worship & appreciation & homage and [illegible] a strong rare brain—and friendship. All those things it would take to make the man who could most fittingly describe the mighty soul who would be the subject of that biography. He has in him the forces of many men—many men of many kinds. And he is so magnetic—that you can feel his presence in a room when you dont hear him enter.

Twain's magnetic presence aside, Isabel worried that a biography just might derail the edition of letters Twain wanted her to edit, and she defiantly asserted: "Letters would be the best kind of biography anyway." Twain tried to enhance his invitation to Howells to write his biography by cultivating his favor for several months. He had begun "writing an appreciation of Mr. Howells" in March, sending the completed manuscript to Frederick Duneka at Harper and Brothers in April. Later that same month, Twain and Howells dined at 21 Fifth Avenue with Isabel, who gleefully listened to their extravagant expressions of admiration for each other: "That they lay Their homage at Each others' feet—a noble gift—& are the more lovely for the giving—They look into Each others' eyes & their speech is—'Oh noble you—' and it is enough."

Despite Twain's sweet talk, Howells ultimately declined the biography project. In early June, after discussing the matter with his daughters, Twain had Isabel write to Duneka, asking him not to bother Howells about editing his letters as now Clara and Jean had expressed interest in the project (even though in January he had suggested that Isabel should edit them). Two weeks later, he wrote Clara at her Norfolk, Connecticut, sanitarium saying he had appointed "you and Jean to arrange and publish my 'Letters' some day—I don't want it done by any outsider. Miss Lyon can do the work, and do it well . . . and take a tenth of the royalty resulting." Just three months later Twain changed his mind again, telling Isabel that Clara would be the principal editor and she could assist in the project. Jean was out. Visions of royalties danced in Isabel's head:

> Tonight as Mr. Clemens lay on the wicker couch reading Macauly's *Life & Letters* edited by his nephew Sir Trevelyan & I was playing to him; he . . . said—"There's one Thing I wanted to say to Clara. In fact I have said it—& that is that she is to edit my letters when I'm dead. You can do the drudgery but she can do editing, & it will be principally striking out."

Twain's maddening fickleness in assigning the editorship would come back to give whiplash to everyone involved. The monetary value of his letters was already high. In April 1906, a single Mark Twain autographed letter to Thomas Nast, dated November 12, 1877, was sold for $43 at auction in New York City. This was a considerable sum of money, and there were thousands of letters. Twain's fetched a higher price than the letters of all the other authors and public figures of the day, including those of Ulysses S. Grant. An edition of Twain's letters would be a guaranteed best seller.

Choosing to ignore Twain's inconstancy, Isabel hungrily realized the potential financial promise this project would hold for her. Lack of money was her constant enemy. While she must have gained a measure of relief from her monetary pressures by living with Twain, the benefit was limited because she paid for her mother's room in a nearby board-inghouse. And while her duties had significantly increased over the past year, she had not received a raise. Feeling increasingly pinched, she sewed and sold pincushions to offset her inadequate salary: "All the days . . . are sprinkled with pin cushions—They're pretty little creatures—& best of all they sell—Teresa [the housemaid] calls them my boys." In October 1905, she proudly "piled up 172 little pincush-ions on the bed to-day—172."

Isabel was struggling to maintain the self-image of a lady, while she was simultaneously a sewer of handcrafts, a seamstress. Indeed, her only compliment on her piecework came from the housemaid. Now, to be named an editor of Mark Twain's letters by the author himself, that was a befitting occupation and certainly a leap in elevation of her status! If Twain allotted Isabel a share in a posthumous publication from which she would receive a portion of the royalties, this could generate a sub-stantial income. It seemed that the financial security Isabel had been searching for since her father's death was nearly at hand. She reflected on the rosy publishing history of General Grant's memoirs:

> Away back when General Grant was about to publish his memoirs, & he asked Mr. Smith of the Century Co. $25,000 for the ms. Mr Smith said it wasn't possible to pay such a price—& so McClure was just about to get the publishing when Mr. Clemens happened to be at General Grants house at the time that he was about to sign the agreement. And he told Gen. Grant that the price was ridiculous—& that he would give him his own check then for $50,000\00. But Gen. Grant wouldn't con-sent to that. Finally Mr. Clemens offered to publish the book. Giving Gen. Grant 3/4 of the profits—& that he would pay the expenses out of his fourth. An arrangement was finally made—& the Grant family got five or six hundred thousand dollars out of a book that the Century Co had refused to pay $25.000 for.

Clearly Twain's own story was a highly marketable commodity, and Isabel recognized its value when she repeated a comment that the author and abolitionist Thomas Wentworth Higginson made to her in August 1905, "that really if publishers had any sense they would be approaching me on the subject of 'writing up' Mr. Clemens." Isabel had modestly declined: "How terrible. And just because I know Mr. Clemens in his strongest best silent beautiful self. That is the very reason why it would be an impossible thing for me to do. It wouldn't be possible for me to do him justice in any one of his characteristics."

And yet Isabel was disingenuous, at the very least, in her response to Higginson: she had begun "writing up" Twain from the first moment of her employ with the family. Timing, though, is everything, and Isabel probably viewed Higginson's tempting possibility as a liability. After all, why risk Twain's good favor when she was going to coedit his letters? Isabel wasn't about to compromise her winning hand. Sewing pincushions as quickly as she could, she decided that waiting to publish Twain's letters was the best investment she could make for her future, and she reminded herself, " 'Our maker himself has taught us the value of silence by putting us speechless into the world: if we learn to Talk later we do it at our own risk.' (Who of us thinks enough to remember the risk—)." In 1906, Isabel scribbled a cryptic note and dropped it between the pages of her daily reminder: "Mr Clemens closed the matter & it is not my place to open it again." Apparently the debate about who would edit Twain's letters had ended—but only for the time being.

## 10

With their similar childhoods, their shared evenings of cards and music, and Isabel's supplanting of his daughters, Twain and Isabel had formed a multilayered intimacy. Isabel constantly exulted about the "solemn joy of living in the same house with Mr. Clemens who grows ever sweeter with the white white years." She found him quite physically attractive, noting in her journal "his great—very great beauty." For his part, an energized Twain effectively returned to his creative life. He had read news reports describing attacks ordered by the Czar against strikers in St. Petersburg, and quickly completed his story "The Czar's Soliloquy," which he read to Isabel and Jean at the end of January. Isabel wrote, "He is at his best then. Today he was wonderful. Thrilled with the Tremendous interest of the naked Czar's soliloquy. His voice shook with emotion." Her enthusiastic reaction to Twain's prose would be repeated anew with each piece he produced.

Twain was pleased by the warm reception from Isabel and Colonel

*Colonel George Harvey*

George Harvey, editor of the *North American Review* and president of Harper and Brothers, and "The Czar's Soliloquy" was published in the March edition of the *North American Review.* Twain then began "another Soliloquy King Leopold's—who is gloating over & excusing to him-self the Congo atrocities." Susan Crane, Twain's sister-in-law, who was visiting, was treated to multiple readings, along with Isabel and Jean, from his latest horror-inspiring effort: "Breathless we sat. & were weak with emotion when he finished the bald . . . truthful . . . statements that rolled from Leopolds vicious lips—Horribly—too horribly picturesque it is, & Mr. Clemens . . . will . . . cut out some of it—It's a pity too—but I suppose it would be too strong a diet for people & governments." (Twain subsequently blamed Frederick Duneka's Catholicism for Harper's refusal to publish "King Leopold's Soliloquy.")

While Isabel's perceived experience of living with Twain may have been all sweetness and light, bleakness was pervading Twain's writing. His work during this period can easily be described as reformist—obvious examples are his essays demanding that injustices perpetrated by the Czar and Leopold immediately cease. Yet lurking beneath his calls for ending oppression was a constant note of misanthropy, a hopeless refusal to believe that mankind could ever be anything but cruel and inhuman. Isabel was soon treated to another work in this same vein, *What Is Man?,* a philosophical essay relating a dialogue between Young Man and Old Man, examining questions of free will and the existence of God. In early May, Twain sent the manuscript to Frank Doubleday to publish anonymously. Doubleday arranged for publication by the Manhattan-based De Vinne Press, and in August, 250 copies were printed. The book was copyrighted under the pseudonym J. W. Bothwell. Twain hoped it would create a literary sensation; instead, it fell flat. The arguments were not particularly new: Shaw and Nietzsche had already plumbed these topics. Years later Isabel recalled, "The disinterested reception was a keen disappointment to Mr. Clemens, and he wanted to burn the 240 volumes left." Isabel chose to love the piece, and she reiterated superlatives about Twain: "He is so wonderful—so ennobling." Jean was not quite so forgiving (or perhaps self-deluding); she hated the manuscript and made her disapproval clear to her father. Isabel was most disappointed in Jean's inability to appreciate *What Is Man?,* or, as Isabel called it, his "Gospel":

This morning I played for Mr. Clemens. & Then he said "Now Come up stairs." We went up to the study. & he read aloud to me a part of his

*Frank Doubleday*

Gospel—his unpublishable Gospel. But Oh it is wonderful—Always I've been afraid of it—but that was because my only knowledge of it was through Jean who hates it. & if you hate a thing you can't see any of its good. This is full of wonderful thoughts—beautiful Thoughts, Terrible Truths—oh such a summing up of human motives—& if it belittles . . . does it belittle?—every human effort. It also has the power To lift you above that effort. & make you fierce in your wish to better your own conduct—such poor stuff as your conduct is—

Practical Jean was much more interested in dealing with the daily realities of life than in the spinning of nihilistic fantasies. She took it upon herself to find a suitable place to vacation for the summer, traveling through heavy snow in early 1905 to Dublin, New Hampshire, to inspect the home of the author Henry Copley Greene. Jean loved the heavily wooded area and Twain gladly signed a lease.

Five days after reading *What Is Man?* to Isabel, Twain completed his short piece "The War Prayer," continuing his increasingly shrill cries for justice, an ideal he ultimately believed unachievable. He was angered by the Spanish-American War and the Philippine-American War, both of which he considered unjustified, and "The War Prayer" was a pacifist indictment of war. He took particular aim at those providing patriotic and religious justifications for it. Isabel defended "The War Prayer" as Twain's "eternal Slap at the human race—'All machines' we are—not responsible for any action of ours." Twain sent his "Prayer" to Elizabeth Jordan, the editor of *Harper's Bazaar,* who politely responded that while she liked it, she "didn't think it would do for a woman's magazine." Twain's friends, family, and publisher all advised him not to publish it, due to its inflammatory subject matter, and "The War Prayer" was withheld from publication during his lifetime. It was finally published posthumously in *Harper's Monthly* in November 1916, during World War I.

By the end of March, words were still pouring from Twain's pen, and he busily worked on a sketch disavowing the notion of a universal brotherhood:

Tonight Mr. Clemens read a very interesting unpublishable sketch. Unpublishable because it is what an old darkey says of the universal brotherhood of man—& how it couldn't ever be, not even in heaven— for there are only white angels there. & in the old darkey's vision the niggers were all Sent around to the back door. It's a wonderful little sketch but it wouldn't do for the clergy—They couldn't stand it. It's too true.

Twain's misanthropic universe now included heaven, and in his hellish version, racist epithets were part of the landscape. In the midst of all this bile, Isabel was the picture of cozy contentment, writing in her daily reminder: "Life in this way is so vitally interesting—The hours are like [crossed out: strings & strings] of pearls and in a string I hope The cord that holds them is a strong one."

The tie binding Isabel and Twain was still strong, primarily due to Clara Clemens's continued absence from home. Clara spent the fall and winter under Dr. Parry's care in New York City, allowed to communicate only with her nurse and specialist. Word reached Twain that she was finally allowed to sit upright for brief periods and read. Isabel reported that Clara had "gained 5 1/2 pounds" and was asking for copies of "Plato & Byron & the Iliad & dry essays." Clara continued to improve, and she was allowed to take brief walks outside. At the end of March, it looked for a time as though her arrival at 21 Fifth Avenue was imminent. Isabel worried about Clara's effect on the relatively stable environment she had established. She knew that Clara tended to take out her frustrations on the staff and her family, and that once she rejoined the household, she was sure to challenge Isabel's new importance and access to her father. Wounded, arrogant, and insecure, Clara was engaged in a lifelong battle to develop a sense of personhood apart from her dominating father. Isabel, venting her nervousness, scribbled a heavily coded note:

A Little change has taken place in The routine of my life. And it has unbalanced me—I cannot yet arrange my forces. Oh, Santissima—you who make a shrine of any house you inhabit—You who are a gift to Every one who falls under your Sweet Thrall—Oh Santissima—

I bend my head in silent worship of your flower soul. & of the white white soul—the rainbow Soul backed by the black clouds of experience—of your father.

Isabel was granted a temporary reprieve from the "flower soul" when Clara decided to delay her return to New York and to summer in Norfolk. In early May, Isabel, Jean, Katy Leary, and Jean's dog Prosper relocated to Dublin, New Hampshire. Isabel loved the summer retreat and found a measure of peace there.

> The view is wonderful wonderful—Far far distant hills—hoary Monadnock to the South East—and forever the singing sighing breathing pines & hemlocks . . . close to the very windows—And so silent—except for the songs of the pines & the birds—You see a glint of the Lake too. The restfulness of it is beautiful—The house is charming—I find it all in exquisite taste, because it has the lovely plasters & casts & books & colorings & pewters & Things that I love.

Twain remained behind in the city because on May 10 Clara had to have an emergency appendectomy, a very serious operation at the time. After making such excellent progress in regaining her health, this was a significant setback. Twain was terrified about the prospect of losing a third child, and the time he spent waiting for news while Clara was still under ether must have been torturous. When he saw his daughter after the operation, he was extraordinarily relieved to have "found her plump & oh so pretty." The day after Clara's procedure, Isabel wrote, "Oh the anxious hours for Santissima's safety"; though this concern for Clara did not keep Isabel from complaining just two days after the operation about Twain's decision to delay his trip to Dublin in order to keep watch over his daughter's recovery. When Twain did arrive at the end of May, Isabel was ecstatic:

> Today Mr. Clemens arrived.
> Today the sun burst through the clouds just after the telegram came saying that he would arrive in Harrisville at 11:35
> Today the aeolian came. Seven New England men unpacked it—Such nice soft speeched gentle New England [men]. Something sweet about them. I like them. It was dear to see Mr. Clemens arrive Today with a furtive searching glance at Things & people—as he drove up to the house.

Twain delighted in his summer accommodations. Typically self-centered, he appropriated Isabel's room for his bedroom and Jean's room for his study, and immediately immersed himself in writing. During the last part of May and through June, he worked with such ferocity on a new short story, "Three Thousand Years Among the Microbes," that Isabel worried he'd make himself ill: "Mr. Clemens spends too much Time over his work. Hours & hours & hours he sits writing with a wonderful light in his eyes, the flush of a girl in his cheeks—and Oh the luster of his hair." Isabel had established Twain's ideal writing environment: quiet surroundings, a regular routine of cards and music, and an appreciative audience. Rising early in the morning and sometimes working until after sunset, Twain was obsessed with his latest project. Nightly readings of the day's production were given to Isabel and Jean.

> This evening after dinner Mr. Clemens read the ms. he worked on all day. A cholera microbe's own story of microbe life in a human being. It is a marvelous imaginative scientific little story—With his acute eye that little microbe sees undreamed of wonders & kingdoms in the body of the dirty Russian Tramp that he inhabits. I asked Mr. Clemens how long he'd been turning those marvelous imaginings over in his mind, & he said that the idea had been there for many years—he tried to work it up from a drop of water, & a Scientist with a powerful microscope; but it wasn't right—He had to be-come the microbe, & see & think & act & appreciate as a microbe. He truly said to Jean that it isn't a story for babes—But it will delight physicians & bacteriologists—Oh he is such a marvel. Such a marvel.

In the midst of all this creative ferment, Isabel received a letter from Clara in Norfolk, asking her to write with family news and sharing her recent religious conversion. Clara eventually embraced Christian Science, a religion her father caustically attacked in a 1907 publication, *Christian Science: With Notes Containing Corrections to Date,* that Harper's only reluctantly published. (Clara had the final word about Christian Science in her book *Awake to a Perfect Day,* published in 1956.) Isabel deduced that because Clara could not find comfort for her continuing grief in her family, she had sought refuge in religion.

> A great faith has come to Santissima. She had to reach out to some-Thing in her grief—a woman has to. She can comfort others perhaps, but she cannot comfort herself. & she has to reach out for the help that is in the eternal—Perhaps a man doesn't need it—I don't know—He can

shield & comfort & protect a woman—he's shelter & comforter & protector by his right & instinct—& the woman who hasn't that human protector has got to turn to the spiritual one—and Santissima Turned.

Despite Clara's newfound religiosity, her health travails continued throughout the summer. She was disappointed with the diagnosis by her throat specialist, who told her that she could not sing for at least four months as her vocal cords had been affected by the appendectomy.

At the end of June, Twain switched to another writing project that he had begun in Florence but never completed. He dropped the unfinished manuscript in Isabel's lap and asked her to read it "when I had leisure." An incredulous Isabel joked, "Leisure? You'd boil it out of midnight if you couldn't find it anywhere else." Twain spent the next six weeks reworking *No. 44, The Mysterious Stranger.* Of course, Isabel thought it brilliant.

On the evening of Independence Day 1905, Twain mused to Isabel about how "the world is full now of young writers who admire each other." Twain confided that he did not feel such a group of people had existed when he came of age as a writer, although it had for the generation that preceded him—Holmes and Emerson principal among them. Twain divulged to Isabel the unexpected admission that he had never had much fruitful interaction with male writers: "For himself there are only Mr. Howells and Mr. Aldrich—and he surprised me into recognizing the truth by telling me that he hasn't had much of a literary friendship with men. And he hasn't—Hartford is presumably between New York & Boston—but it isn't."

In mid-July, Twain wrote the lyrical "Eve's Diary," a short story consisting of diary entries chronicling the relationship between Adam and Eve. The writing went quickly, with Twain reading drafts to Isabel every night; the story was completed in a week. In it, Adam and Eve are together for forty years, and Eve hopes that the more resilient Adam will outlive her because she could not bear life without him. Her wish is granted, and the closing line is one of Twain's most memorable: "Wheresoever she was, there was Eden." Isabel was overcome with the beauty and sentimentality of the text as well as with her own happy existence:

> This summer is so exquisite that sometimes I am afraid to speak into the silence fearing to break the magic spell—Oh don't let me break it—

Let it be broken by sounds from other lips than mine. "After the Fall"—
Mr. Clemens read Tonight & Eve sums up all the reasons why she could
love Adam—but doesn't—It's Something Else. It's because he's hers.
Dear little Eve.

Isabel thought Twain had created "a lovable creature & So innocent
& So human—'The Same old Sex'—he said—when I said 'Oh, but she's
a woman.' " "Eve's Diary" is Twain's most insightful piece presenting a
woman's perspective, and the narrative touchingly explores the beauty
of a cherished relationship. The story was published in the 1905 Christmas issue of *Harper's Monthly Magazine*. "Eve's Diary" has always been
considered Twain's endearing tribute to Olivia, and appropriately so,
although considering the contentment he was enjoying with Isabel, he
may have been acknowledging her as well. While Twain struggled for
years composing *Extracts from Adam's Diary* (beginning in 1891), he
wrote "Eve's Diary" in just six days (July 12–18, 1905). Contained
within "Eve's Diary" is a line that sounds strikingly similar to a senti-
ment expressed by Isabel about Twain: "I study to be useful to him in
every way I can, so as to increase his regard."

### 11

While Twain was putting the final touches on "Eve's Diary," Isabel read
a story by Rudyard Kipling, one of her favorite authors, which also
delved into a loving couple's growing intimacy.

> This afternoon I read Kipling's new story. "An Habitation Enforced."
> And it has some darling strokes in it. The spinster who heard the swear-
> ing & felt that she had lost her virginity because of it is one of the best
> Ever. And I feel as if it must have originated with Mr. Clemens.

Isabel's enjoyment over the spinster's lost virginity is illustrative of
the sexual allusion in her journals. Here is at the very least the suggestion that her rhapsodizing over Twain had a libidinous dimension,
emerging in its least carnal form in the appreciation of the attractiveness
of the man, but bursting forth at times in more explicit identifications.

Kipling's story "An Habitation Enforced" culturally and personally
held immense meaning for Isabel. Turn-of-the-century middle-class
women were actively encouraged by magazine advice columns and self-

improvement manuals, good-naturedly titled *What Books Can do FOR YOU,* for instance, to practice "reading up." That is, readers were advised to read books with plots and characters they could identify with and were told that through their engagement with the text they could remake themselves through both material and intellectual "cultural acquisition." Readers were assured that their lives would be "vividly enlarged and clarified through [this] experience." To take this notion of self-improvement one step further, readers were encouraged to practice a kind of active wish fulfillment, meaning that the more intense their connection with the story and characters, the more likely they were to be rewarded with class mobility and consequent material wealth.

Kipling's story begins with protagonist George Chapin's nervous breakdown. His doctors recommend living in Europe for at least two years and abstaining from all work. Millionaire George and his devoted wife, Sophie, spend months drifting through various continental capitals until they meet the prescient Mrs. Shonts, who sends them to southern England to stay at Rocketts farm. George and Sophie are enchanted with the quaint ways of the British country folk and begin to explore their surroundings, discovering a semi-abandoned colonial home named Friars Pardon. Sophie impulsively bows to the structure and declares to George: "We began here." The elderly caretaker shows them the house and grounds, and George realizes with a start that he has not thought about himself for an entire two and a half hours. The two learn that five farms surround Friars Pardon.

George and Sophie become increasingly infatuated with the beauty of the area, and George offers the London solicitors $68,000 for the house and all the farms as a business venture. Sophie, moved and pleased by George's purchase, bursts out, "We're two little orphans moving in worlds not realized, and we shall make some bad breaks. But we're going to have the time of our lives." George and Sophie shyly inform the tenants that they are the land's new owners, and they are heartily welcomed. The next day in church George and Sophie feel the stares of all their tenants on the backs of their necks:

> Here was nothing but silence—not even hostility! The game was up to
> them; the other players hid their cards and waited. Suspense, she felt,
> was in the air, and when her sight cleared, saw, indeed, a mural tablet of

a footless bird brooding upon the carven motto, "Wayte awhyle—wayte awhyle."

The two immediately begin reconstructing Friars Pardon and caring for the dilapidated farms. Sophie soon becomes pregnant, and persuades George, whose first impulse is to set sail immediately for America, that they now belong to their land and to leave would be "desertion." After their son's birth, Sophie learns that Friars Pardon is actually her ancestral home when their neighbor delivers a silver christening mug. "The mug was worn and dented: above the twined initials, G.L., was the crest of a footless bird and the motto: 'Wayte awhyle— wayte awhyle.' "

It is hardly surprising that the theme in "An Habitation Enforced" would resonate with Isabel. Sophie had achieved the social climber's ultimate dream—the goal of upward mobility with a baby and an English title thrown in. The narrative was evocative of Isabel's past and current life experiences: the emotional paralysis of a nervous breakdown, the feeling of being culturally adrift, the art of maintaining an intimate relationship, and the reestablishment of family status.

It must have come as a rude shock and quick return to reality when, just two days after reading "An Habitation Enforced," Isabel received a letter from Clara containing a thinly veiled threat. "Santissima has given me a creed. No—a watchword—'Never take anything for granted.' " Apparently, news had reached Clara about Isabel and Twain's domestic bliss. In retrospect, Isabel may have been a bit too effusive in her letters to Clara, regaling her with happy tales of life at home with her father and his renewed zeal for writing. Surely Twain's friends would not have been particularly surprised to see him wed again; he certainly required an enormous amount of devoted care and undivided attention. Clara, however, with plenty of time to ruminate while summering at the sanitarium, had no intention of allowing this mere secretary, obsequious and pleasant though she might be, to usurp her mother's place as Mark Twain's wife.

Undeterred, Isabel divided her journal page in two and countered Clara's warning:

Kipling has given me another in his [crossed out: Dear] story "An Habitation Enforced—" or rather he has forcibly put into two words

what I say often to myself in many words—"Wayte A. Whyle." It's the
only True way to live. When you're lying at night with weary wakeful
eyes waiting for the dawn. Just say "Wayte A. Whyle—"

Isabel had her dreams and was prepared to fight for them.

In mid-October, an increasingly suspicious Clara wrote Isabel reminding her a second time: " 'Never take anything for granted—' A
pretty good watch word—& when C.C. reminded me that it was a good
one, she didn't know that I'd learned it when I was a pretty young
'Freshman'—Oh a very young one . . . that was nearly twenty five years
ago—and I'm nothing but a rusty 'Soph' now." If Clara was going to try
to take away Isabel's winning hand, she had better play her cards carefully. Isabel was carefully scripting the plotline to her life story, and she
was willing to sacrifice everything to risk a happy ending.

Toward summer's end Jean visited the recovering Clara in Norfolk,
and upon her return she confided in Isabel about her sister's travails. In
a daily reminder entry, Isabel seemed to recognize a certain predilection
for unhappiness within the Clemens family:

> Jean has told me much about C.C. [crossed out: I wish I didn't suffer a
> little over other people's griefs, and distresses other than griefs.—]
> There seems to be a tragic something hanging near; [crossed out: & who
> can say. Oh to be able to protect the ones that you love. I have the feel-
> ing that I must scream at the] Some Fate that is Coursing along in their
> blood, & waiting to drop with a clutch at their hearts. [Crossed out:
> Really I don't sleep.]

Isabel knew that her fate was bound up with Twain's, and she understood that Clara would oppose any kind of arrangement that made her
affiliation with the family permanent. This realization left her sleepless
with worry. In reaction, she became hypercritical about her performance, chastising herself for any perceived missteps: "It's terribly Thin
ice I'm walking on, for watch as I will, I cannot cure myself of my
capacity to make mistakes—It isn't any consolation to know that
I . . . make Them unintentionally—and it isn't any excuse That other
people make mistakes Too—Those Things don't make it any better."

While much of Twain's attention was directed toward Clara's health,
a frustrated Jean was having her own struggles. From May to July

1905, Jean averaged one seizure a month. Isabel understood that Jean needed close supervision and with typical hyperbole referred to her responsibility as "my Sacred charge." Jean spent the summer studying French, German, and Italian, as well as busying herself birding, hiking around the lake, riding (astride) through the woods to Mount Monadnock, and reading to Isabel in the evenings: "Now it is a book by Madame Laschovska—a Viennese friend of the Clemenses—on Transylvania—and now it will be a little French History—and now it is Heine—Dear Child that She is—Such a Complex nature. & yet so entirely simple—Consistent—yet so inconsistent. There is a power in that young nature."

Isabel's greatest challenge with Jean was helping her find a purpose for her life. Jean despaired after an overnight visit from the strikingly handsome Gerome "Gerry" Brush, a successful sculptor and painter eight years younger than she and son of the well-known artist George de Forest Brush. He made her "feel the uselessness of the days she is living—doing nothing of value—Everything to be called a 'whim.' " Jean was now twenty-five years old and because of her health, she had no prospect of ever being allowed to marry and bear children.

With oversight of Jean safely delegated to Isabel, over the course of the summer Twain indulged himself by flitting from one writing project to the next. He insisted on reading to Isabel everything that he wrote and eagerly solicited her predictably positive comments. In September Twain became engrossed with his latest piece, "A Horse's Tale." This story was the last transvestite tale Twain would write, thirty-five years after his first, "A Medieval Romance." Written at the urging of Minnie Maddern Fiske, a leading American actress and animal-rights advocate, the story follows the adventures of nine-year-old Cathy Alison (modeled on Twain's daughter Susy) and her horse, Soldier Boy. After the death of her parents, Cathy is sent to live with her uncle, General Alison. She travels from Rouen, France (the site of Joan of Arc's trial and execution), to the American western territory, where she pretends to be an officer and routinely inspects her soldiers while dressed in military clothing. Twain worked for hours on the manuscript and while reading the piece to Isabel he would signal her to make bugle calls on the Orchestrelle at the appropriate intervals. Isabel pronounced the maudlin tale "a prodigious piece of work." While Isabel freely criticized other writers in her journal, when it came to Twain's work, if she held a contrary opinion about its literary merit, she never expressed it. Nearly thirty years later, Isabel recalled watching Twain compose during that magical summer of 1905:

> A calm dreamlike concentration with eyes wandering on far beyond . . . when he was working on Eve's Diary or Some purely fictional fancy . . . liked the Mysterious Stranger [crossed out: (a child of his fancy)] But Captain Stormfield's Visit to Heaven held an amused concentration. Then he would . . . leave his chair to . . . knock out the ashes of his pipe with Sharp quick taps & against the fireplace or the . . . porch rail. But when he was letting his lovely dream life flow along he would knock out the pipe ashes in slow deliberate dreamlike fashion sitting down stairs you could gauge his mood by those pipe knocks.

At this stage of his life and career, Twain was less interested in being critically challenged than he was in being comforted and reassured, and Isabel had become the crucial person in keeping his demons at bay. Twain needed to believe that he was still productive, and Isabel was there to reassure him that he was. At summer's end, Isabel totaled up the number of manuscripts Twain had written:

> This morning Mr. Clemens called me upstairs & read the last—the end of the beautiful story—"The Horse's Tale." It is so lovely & so touching.
>
> > Mr. Clemens's output this Summer has been
> > a remarkable one.
> > The Microbe Story—
> > The wonderful Poem to Death.
> > Adding to the "Mysterious Stranger" some
> > fine imaginative chapters.
> > The beautiful Eve's Diary.
> > Revising the Gospel.
> > The Deity Article.
> > The Freedom of Speech article
> > & now this exquisite story ["A Horse's Tale]

For a troubled man in frequent poor health on the eve of his seventieth birthday, this was a record of which he could justifiably be proud.

On November 1, 1905, Jean, Isabel, and the household staff bid farewell to pastoral Dublin and returned to New York City. Twain would join them a few days later. As the group arrived in a horse-drawn carriage at 21 Fifth Avenue at 9:30 in the evening, they saw the light in Clara's room dim. A minute later they saw silhouetted against the light a "black figure" in the front doorway; Isabel realized that the prodigal daughter had finally returned. She and Clara had not seen each other for over a year.

# TWO

# THE GATHERING STORM

## FALL 1905–FALL 1908

I am the only person in the world who sees the King in his sorrow;
& when he sings loudest, then I know his loneliness & sorrows are
weighing most heavily upon him. . . . If you could know the King
just a little, you'd find in him all the exquisite colors of the world.
You'd find in him an ice storm & a thunderstorm, & the deeps of
night, & the granite crags, & the great song of the wind, & the
sweetest flower.

—ISABEL VAN KLEEK LYON

*Insert card issued by the Mogul Egyptian Cigarettes Company,
summer 1909–fall 1910. It reads, "To woman: a parodox who
please when she puzzles and puzzles when she pleases."*

Twain had last lived in Manhattan with his family in 1900. During the intervening five years, the city had been transformed. New York City now boasted the world's busiest harbor, the biggest ships and longest bridges, the worst slums, and overwhelming prosperity. There were elevated trains that crossed rivers and twenty miles of newly completed New York subway; the fare was just a nickel. Traffic was thick with people, pushcarts, horses, cars, and trolleys all jostling for a place in the crowded streets. The largest conglomeration of millionaires in history, who had accumulated gigantic tax-free fortunes, lived in massive homes on tree-lined boulevards. An enormous wave of immigrants from Eastern Europe and Italy was passing through Ellis Island, changing the city's ethnic makeup and culture and creating tremendous social and political stresses. New York was the largest Jewish city in the world, the largest Irish city, one of the largest German cities, and home to more than seven hundred thousand Russians. This was Mark Twain's city and he was its most celebrated citizen, popularly recognized as the "Belle of New York," a moniker his friend Jamie Dodge had given him.

The fall of 1905 found all the surviving Clemenses and Isabel living under one roof at 21 Fifth Avenue. The year before, extensive remodeling had been done on the house to prepare it for the family's residency, and over the summer, while Twain, Jean, and Isabel had been in Dublin, Clara, with Katy Leary's assistance, had completed an extensive redecoration. Clara spared no expense in her efforts to create a beautiful environment, and the house stood ready to receive its occupants, gleaming walls freshly plastered and painted and rooms stocked with new furniture and linens. Surely this might prove to be a propitious time when father and daughters, comfortable in their new home, could rebuild their lives together. Yet families, unlike buildings, are not so easily repaired. Even the house, despite its solid and well-maintained appearance, seemed to reflect the stresses of its new residents. As part of the lease agreement, over the summer a heating system had been installed. But the new radiators, with their banging and rattling, made such a constant racket at night that everyone's slumber was ruined.

In the midst of their luxurious New York City surroundings, Clara, Jean, and Isabel, three short-tempered, sleep-deprived women, were constantly ill with psychological and physical ailments. Despite having made a full recovery from her appendix surgery, Clara was consumed by a multitude of ailments that kept her bedridden. In September, she had a minor sinus operation that left her "weak & tired & discouraged." She also suffered from sore throats, forcing her to cancel concerts in November and December. Her voice problems continued despite frequent visits to throat specialists. Twain halfheartedly supported his daughter's singing ambitions, viewing her efforts primarily as a good way to keep her busy, although his ambivalence likely contributed to Clara's pattern of sudden illnesses and abrupt cancellations. Friends of the family, like the poet Witter Bynner, described her voice as "queer." (After listening to a performance Clara gave circa 1930, Russell McLauchlin, a professional music critic for *The Detroit News,* was more blunt. Clara "was not a good singer," McLauchlin opined. "Her vocal gifts were several kilometers short of great.") Even the dutifully politic Isabel euphemistically referred to Clara's voice as being "strongly individual."

In any case, potential patrons rarely heard it. Clara's desire to perform could have been related to wanting to succeed in public as her father had, yet her fear of not measuring up to the standard of excellence expected of Mark Twain's daughter muted her time and again, to her utter frustration. Moreover, she had to fight to avoid the charge that it was only because of her father's fame that she was given engagements.

Isabel shared Clara's health woes. She suffered from depression, and the decorous mask she wore around the family slowly began to slip. She complained in a journal entry she later inked through, "Some breath of life is gone." In December, she confessed (an admission she later tried to obliterate): "My brain is so brittle these days. I feel it could snap so Easily." While she felt seriously unwell, she tried to hide any visible signs of illness from the family because she feared negative repercussions. When Teresa Cherubini, the Italian maid, fell ill with a stomach ulcer in February and was hospitalized, Isabel and Twain visited her. In his usual fashion, Twain exaggerated the severity of Teresa's affliction, in effect writing her off, saying to Isabel that Teresa should be shipped back to Italy posthaste. He claimed that he could not be held responsible for allowing Teresa to remain "against the doctor's advice and warning. If I allowed her to stay I should feel that I was treacherous to her people, who are trusting me and believe me worthy of their trust." Despite Twain's prediction of her imminent demise, Teresa recovered after an extended convalescence and returned to work. To Isabel, Twain's message was clear. If she wanted to avoid being stuck on an express train back to Farmington, Connecticut, she had better appear to be the very picture of robust health.

Jean was by far the worst off of the three women. In the years after her mother's death, Jean's seizures dramatically increased in their frequency and severity. Isabel carefully charted the occurrences of the seizures throughout 1905 and 1906, in effect creating a medical history, and her record shows an alarming acceleration beginning in spring of 1905 and continuing into the fall of 1906.

By this time Jean had been suffering from epilepsy for approximately a decade. At the disease's onset, she had only petit mal seizures. This kind of seizure, most often observed in young people, involves a brief lapse of consciousness lasting seconds or a few minutes. After the "absence" seizure concludes, normal activity can resume. Jean described the effect of the petit mals as leaving her tired and "not any too clear-headed." About half of the children who suffer from this kind of seizure outgrow the malady. The other half will develop much more serious grand mal seizures, and that is what happened with Jean.

A characteristic of her illness was that, as she grew older, she often experienced a cluster of seizures, sometimes as many as three a day. On a single day in August 1905, her multiple seizures prompted Isabel to observe: "one at 11.30—1.20—& 5.30 very droopy all day." Over the next few months Jean's health continued to worsen, and in November there occurred an episode that would affect the course of her life for years to come. Three days after Thanksgiving, Jean experienced cluster seizures at three o'clock in the afternoon and eight o'clock in the evening. Sometime that evening she physically attacked Katy Leary. While the attack was unprecedented for Jean, prevailing medical opinion at the time held that there existed a direct connection between epilepsy and violence. In fact, epilepsy was commonly accepted as a source of criminality. Obviously, that theory has since been debunked, and there is no evidence that a patient can make an intentionally motivated act of aggression during a seizure.

Recent research, however, has identified the existence of a postictal psychotic state (a state of altered consciousness) in which physical acts of aggression against other people and "behavior disturbances" do occur in epileptic patients. Psychosis usually develops in patients ten to fifteen years after the onset of epilepsy. Today postictal psychosis is widely regarded by experts as "the most common of the episodic epilepsy-related psychoses." According to Dr. John Milton, a professor of neurology at the Claremont University Consortium, during "the postictal period, the patient becomes psychotic, and in this case, the aggression against another person is not intentionally motivated violence. The other person just happens to be in the wrong place at the wrong time. . . . These acts are not intentionally planned by the patient, but are the response of the psychotic patient to a stimulus."

During the month of November 1905, Jean had a total of six seizures, with three of them occurring on the same day, six days before her attack on Katy. Immediately following a seizure, a patient suffering from postictal psychosis will experience a period of lethargy and confusion. This confusion resolves into an "interval of apparent normality" lasting hours or days before the onset of psychosis. Patients then enter a psychotic state, typically lasting at least fifteen hours and not more than two months, during which they experience one or all of the four main forms of the disorder: "confusion, visual and auditory hallucinations, and paranoid ideation." Jean's medical history is consistent with a diagnosis of postictal psychosis.

In Isabel's papers, there are two mentions of the post-Thanksgiving attack. On November 26, 1905, she noted the times of Jean's seizures and underlined Katy's name. Directly underneath, Isabel quoted the last stanza of William Blake's poem "The Fly."

> Jean. 3–pm 8 pm <u>Katy</u>
> Then am I
> A happy fly.
> If I live
> Or if I die.

In her cryptic fashion, Isabel's quoting "The Fly" deftly defines the temporality of her and Jean's peculiar existences; they were both caught in a place on the margins of life as they dreamed of living it. Both women were frustrated in their attempts to create futures for themselves and both were subjected to circumstances they were powerless to control: Isabel was ensnared in a trap created by circumstance and dependent upon an elderly man's whims, and Jean was mired in a downwardly spiraling illness.

It makes sense to consider Jean's epilepsy as a barometer of the Clemens family's discord. Unlike Clara, Jean did not retreat to a sanitarium after Olivia's death. Instead, she remained at home and was the primary witness to a growing intimacy between her father and Isabel. Of all the Clemens children, Jean had been the daughter closest to and most dependent upon her mother. When Olivia was alive, she was the parent who bore direct responsibility for managing her daughter's treatment, and she was Jean's greatest comfort. After her death, Jean's care was relegated to Isabel. The loss of her mother created a wound that would never heal, and the sight of her father happily accepting Isabel's overtures must have caused her extraordinary anxiety. The continuing trauma left by Olivia's death, combined with the change in Jean's physical surroundings from country to city, must also have been enormously stressful for her. While she was safe from public scrutiny in Dublin (a location she infinitely preferred to New York City), at 21 Fifth Avenue, with its endless parade of visitors attempting to gain access to her father, she had nowhere to hide and nowhere to heal from the loss of her mother.

Living in such an incendiary household was proving to be too much for Twain's fragile youngest daughter, Isabel realized: "Not only has her malady increased—but her whole physical condition is at a low ebb. And the child calls . . . for great waves of love from those of us who care. . . . In these last few days a sadness has settled over her, a gentleness that is pitiful—& you long for the masterful young creature whose powerful moods . . . spread consternation. But always back of these moods there [is] an individuality—a frankness of a very high order." Jean was desperately calling for help, but the people around her were absorbed by their own needs and no one understood her illness well enough to effectively answer. Tragically, Dr. Edward Quintard, the family's personal physician, regarded Jean as a physical threat and dangerous to those around her; he warned Isabel "never to let Jean get between her and the door, and never to close the door." Assuming that Isabel at least in part heeded Dr. Quintard's advice, one can only imagine what signals she might have sent Jean through changes in her behavior toward her.

The friction between Clara and Isabel that had been simmering over the course of the summer now reached a slow boil with the two of them living in the same space. When Isabel arrived at 21 Fifth Avenue in the fall of 1905, five days before Twain, Clara immediately told her that she could no longer live with the family. Most likely the two argued, with Clara insisting upon the living-out arrangement that her mother had enforced and Isabel countering that Twain always wanted her instantly available. In a victory for Clara, Isabel began looking for accommodations the next day. Isabel chose not to write about their exchange and the next six days in her daily reminder were left uncharacteristically blank. Isabel's search for housing was immediately terminated upon Twain's arrival. This contesting between father and daughter over where Isabel would live was a difficult situation for Isabel, of course.

Clara and Isabel next clashed over who would assume responsibility for managing the household. All had proceeded peacefully under Isabel's direction while Clara was away. Now that Clara had returned, she made it clear to everyone that there was a different mistress of the house. Twain vainly attempted to mediate the situation. He had assured Clara prior to his return that 21 Fifth Avenue was under her "full and sole authority," and that no one other than she would be allowed to "scold or correct a servant." Isabel fumed about Clara's victory in that skirmish and wrote in her journal about the servants' unhappiness under Clara's direction. On one occasion, according to Isabel, Clara impulsively decided that the cook should be fired and demanded that Isabel dismiss her. A reluctant Isabel did her bidding, indignantly noting that "Mary the good little cook" had a mother to support. Upon finding Isabel weeping over what she had been forced to do, a furious Clara declared: "After this I'll do my own dirty work." An appalled Katy Leary warned Isabel, "In time she'll do the same to you & worse. She hates you and don't you forget it."

Isabel was made sorely aware of her inferior status, especially on those rare occasions when she was included in highly fashionable public events. She was thrilled to be invited to the September society wedding of Colonel Thomas Wentworth Higginson's daughter Margaret, although she was disappointed by the seating arrangements: Twain "sat in pew 16—in the middlest aisle." She and Jean "were only 'Common or Garden' folk. & sat on the side."

A few months later, on December 4, 1905, Isabel was overjoyed to learn that she had been invited to Twain's seventieth birthday fête at Delmonico's Restaurant just two days later, on December 6. Delmonico's was New York's finest dining establishment and the first New York restaurant to have a separate wine menu. Its stylish décor was the height of Gilded Age excess, and the columns flanking its entrance reportedly had been imported from the ruins of Pompeii. Rather than being directly invited by Twain to accompany him, social decorum once again reared its tiresome head so that Twain passed along a message from Colonel George Harvey, the party's organizer, informing Isabel that the Colonel "would be glad if I would go." She cautiously celebrated her good fortune: "I'm afraid to breathe lest I find that the permission be nothing more than a . . . thistle-down of a thought to float away into . . . clear air."

At what point Isabel would be allowed to arrive during the festivities was apparently a very sensitive point of etiquette for Clara, who was opposed to her coming at all. Isabel hoped to be allowed to sit quietly in the public reception room until "speech time"; however, it was deemed socially inappropriate for Isabel to enter Delmonico's with the Clemenses. She could only arrive later, alone, when the ceremonial part of the evening was about to commence. Isabel was furious at Clara over the slight, and she despaired that her time at such a socially prestigious event would be so limited. She bitterly noted in her journal that Twain thought she would be accompanying him to make an entrance: "That was the reason why he called out to me as he passed my door—'Clara's just about ready!' "

Twain's party would later be remembered by the newspapers as "the most notable festive occasion in New York literary history,"—a "cultural Everest." *The New York Times* reported the next day, "There were 170 of his friends and fellow-craftsmen in literature gathered in the Red Room at Delmonico's for the celebration." Guests entered the Red Room serenaded by forty musicians conducted by Nahan Franko, concertmaster of the Metropolitan Opera Orchestra. Twain led the procession of guests into the dining room, with the novelist Mary Wilkins Freeman on his arm. The banquet lasted an astonishing (and indigestion-causing) five hours, with fifteen speeches given and nine poems read to the distinguished audience. The first speech of the evening was given in absentia by President Roosevelt and read by Miss Cutting, the president of Vassar College's Alumni Association.

I wish it were in my power to be at the dinner held to celebrate the seventieth birthday of Mark Twain—it is difficult to write of him by his real name instead of by that name which has become a household word wherever the English language is spoken. He is one of the citizens whom all Americans should delight to honor, for he has rendered a great and peculiar service to America, and his writings, though such as no one but an American could have written, yet emphatically come within that small list which are written for no particular country, but for all countries, and which are not merely written for the time being, but have an abiding and permanent value. May he live long, and year by year may he add to the sum of admirable work that he has done.

At the end of the evening, after a toast by William Dean Howells, Twain rose and proclaimed:

The seventieth birthday! It is the time of life when you arrive at a new and awful dignity; when you may throw aside the decent reserves which have oppressed you for a generation, and stand unafraid and unabashed upon your seven-terraced summit and look down and teach—unrebuked. You can tell the world how you got there. It is what they all do. I have been anxious to explain my own system this long time, and now at last I have the right. I have achieved my seventy years in the usual way: by sticking strictly to a scheme of life, which would kill anybody else. It sounds like an exaggeration, but that is really the common rule for attaining old age. When we examine the programme of any of these garrulous old people we always find that the habits which have preserved them would have decayed us. I will offer here, as a sound maxim this: that we can't reach old age by another man's road.

Twain's speech was so well received that newspapers printed large portions of it in the days following the event. Photographs were taken of the invitees, to be assembled in an album that was given to Twain as a souvenir of the occasion. As a party favor, everyone in attendance was given a foot-high plaster bust of the honoree. By the evening's close, there were 171 Mark Twains in the room.

Among those invited were Twain intimates Reverend Joseph Twichell, William Dean Howells, Andrew Carnegie, Henry Rogers, and Richard Gilder. Unlike Whittier's seventieth birthday party, when women were allowed to enter only after dinner, *The New York Times* noted that there was a plethora of women: "They were not present as mere appendages of their husbands, but as individuals representing the art of imaginative writing no less than the men. An observer looking over the host of diners, after having scanned the list of guests and noticed that every feminine name in it was familiar to all readers, could not but wonder that the women he found corresponding to those names were all young and pretty. The whole gathering did not seem to include half a dozen women with streaks of gray in their hair." These impressive individuals included the authors Willa Cather, Ruth McEnery Stuart, Louise Chandler Moulton, and Frances Hodgson Burnett.

While initially expected, the socially incandescent novelist Edith Wharton declined to partake in the festivities and sent her regrets. The African American author Charles W. Chesnutt was invited and took his seat at a table with John Kendrick Bangs. Colonel Harvey could not resist the opportunity to publicize *Harper's,* and he had packed the guest list with minor contributors to the magazine. When Twain

*Mark Twain's seventieth birthday dinner at Delmonico's Restaurant. Left to right: Kate Douglas Riggs, Reverend Joseph Twichell, Bliss Carmen, Ruth Stuart, Mary E. Wilkins Freeman, Henry M. Alden, Henry H. Rogers*

*Mark Twain's Seventieth Birthday Dinner
program cover, 1905*

finally rose to speak, he faced an audience that contained many people
he had never met. Nearly six weeks after the party Isabel remarked,
"Col. Harvey is being much criticised for giving the kind of dinner that
he did for Mr. Clemens on his 70th birthday—for it was shameful to
sacrifice Mr. Clemens to what is regarded as a great advertisement for
Harper." Colonel Harvey continued his promotional efforts, claiming
in an interview published on March 3, 1907, in *The Washington Post*
that he held an exclusive contract with Twain making him the highest
paid writer in history, receiving thirty cents a word ($7.10 in 2008).

Isabel's frustration increased when Clara began treating her as her
personal maid, sending her to pick up purchases at Tiffany's. A sulky
Isabel "mooned about" looking at jewelry that would remain forever
out of her reach. Clara often included Isabel in her visits to various
dressmakers and hatmakers, which served to hammer home the message that Isabel was a servant, nothing more. Isabel's role was to admire
what Clara had, never to buy anything for herself. A proud woman,
Isabel was pained by her plain appearance. She owned three dresses, two

for day and a formal dinner gown. While this was typical for women in service, Isabel never viewed herself as the average employee; rather she saw her working status as a temporary inconvenience to be ended as quickly as possible. On one occasion, in an unusually generous act, Twain came to Isabel's room and gave her $50 to buy a dress, saying, "Not that I don't like the ones you have but I like variety." Isabel asked Twain to choose a color for her new dress, "Brown? Gray? Blue." He responded, "I'd like you to get all the colors of the rainbow." In his next breath, he reminded Isabel how different her orbit was from Clara's: "You can't get as good a dress as Clara gets because she spends much more than $50.00." Not to be outdone, thrifty Isabel purchased four colors of silk, including turquoise blue and frosty pink, and she and her mother sewed her a new wardrobe. Twain loved bright colors and liked Isabel's vibrant new appearance "very much." The King's gesture meant so much to Isabel that for the rest of her life she kept a precious scrap of fabric, "frosty white & pink with a small black dot," from what Twain called her "watermelon dress."

Isabel took to heart a comment by Mrs. Freeman, a friend of Twain's, who said that "living as I am with the greatest human being, there can be no danger of my ever over dressing the part, the danger will be in my failure to dress up to it. The King would love to have me in rich soft clinging silks of splendid or delicate colors; & when I told him what Mrs. Freeman had advised me to do, he said that she was a wise woman." Twain, though, sounded a warning note about women's dress in marginalia he left on his personal copy of Edith Wharton's *The House of Mirth:* "It is almost as stupid to let your clothes betray that you are ugly as to have them proclaim that you think you are beautiful."

Isabel resented and blamed Clara for her various slights, and her humiliation began to translate into extreme sensitivity about her age and dress. On December 15, 1905, Isabel turned forty-two. She spent a miserable birthday, weeping in her mother's embrace so that their "tears mingled." But Twain's uncustomary financial generosity continued, with Isabel's mood decidedly improving on Christmas Day, when she awoke to discover on her breakfast tray an envelope "from Mr. Clemens" containing a bonus.

Twain was ill equipped to deal with his daughters' problems and Isabel's anxiety, and for the most part he deliberately removed himself from his household's histrionics, spinning a cocoon of social engagements to insulate him from the fray. During the fall of 1905 he had come and gone, first to Boston to visit the Aldriches and Higginsons and on to the Cambridge Author's Club for a speaking engagement. Jean was to have accompanied her father to Boston—a trip that would have been beneficial for her by cheering her spirits—but he dodged her company by claiming that she was "too much responsibility."

He then traveled to Washington, D.C., twice with Colonel Harvey to lobby for copyright reform and to dine with President and Mrs. Roosevelt. Isabel reported, "Mr. Clemens found [the first lady] charming—simple—& without any shred of self consciousness—a lovely woman." Returning home in time for the gala seventieth birthday celebration, he delighted in being showered with telegrams, tributes, and flowers. Isabel celebrated his homecoming, proclaiming in her daily reminder: "Mr. Clemens's 70th birthday—But he is only a young & beautiful 50." Her fantasized connection to the great man was fueled by the swirl of the social season that followed.

Between his travels, Twain received Booker T. Washington at home, lunched with Howells, dined with Mary Elizabeth Mapes Dodge (an author and the editor of *St. Nicholas: Scribner's Illustrated Magazine for Girls and Boys*), met and dined with the members of the Astronomical and Astrophysical Society, was honored with a banquet by the Society of Illustrators, was welcomed back and made an honorary member at the Players Club (healing a rift created three years earlier when he had been cited for nonpayment of dues), and had tea with Poultney Bigelow. Isabel was especially delighted with Bigelow's return visit, as she found him extremely attractive.

All in all, Isabel was thoroughly incapable of faulting Twain. Given the power asymmetry of their relationship, her lot was to applaud and to forgive. He was the show; she was the animated audience. She was caught just like the hapless fly in Blake's poem: "Such an impulsive man he is. . . . He'd have to have a history [crossed out: men & women with] temperaments like his are pretty apt to spring over Conventionalities. I think they cant help it." Twain complained to Isabel about his constant social engagements, saying that he missed the quiet of New Hampshire, as his days were so busy "that there isn't much chance for work or rest." As the author of his own manic schedule, Twain seemed most determined to avoid writing and parenting.

With the public ever clamoring for his presence, Twain gladly made

*Mark Twain and Booker T. Washington,*
*January 22, 1906*

a number of local public appearances. On December 19 he spoke at
Sarah Bernhardt's benefit for Russian Jews at the Casino Theater, an
event Isabel attended. To Isabel's delight, the great Sarah stopped by
Twain's box to have a word with him before she went onstage. Isabel
basked in the twin glow of their presence: "It was a delight to watch
those rare geniuses chat." After describing how Twain sauntered out
onstage "amid giant applause," Isabel concluded (and then tried to
obliterate): "& that is my daily bread. Bread!"

Twain faced his largest audience on January 22, 1906, at Carnegie
Hall, where a packed house had gathered to celebrate "the great 25th
anniversary of the founding of the Tuskegee institute in Alabama." An
ebullient Twain, who enjoyed a three-minute "wave of applause,"
stepped onto the stage and took his seat next to Booker T. Washington.
Isabel was beside herself with enthusiasm: "I was so excited—that I
wanted to cry & laugh & sing." That evening a different social unfortunate would have to sit with the " 'Garden' folk"; Isabel would reign
over a box with other guests including her mother and the Reverend
Twichell. At long last, Isabel faced New York society front and center,
unencumbered by the nettlesome presence of the Clemens daughters.

Nothing could have kept her from her social triumph that evening, including a terrible accident Jean had suffered earlier that day. That morning Jean was gripped by a seizure so violent that she fell and severely burned her arm on a hot radiator. But daughters and illness be damned, Isabel and Twain would have their evening in the spotlight. When they visited the bedridden Jean two days later in her room to show her the illustrations for his book *A Horse's Tale,* she was only "half aware" of them.

At the very time when Jean was most in need of her father's ministrations, he turned away and chose the stage of public acclaim. Rather than extending himself to his family, Twain withdrew into again considering his biography. While Howells had politely refused to write the authorized biography of his old friend, Twain had not given up the idea. A minor Harper's writer who had been in attendance at the Delmonico's fête was about to make Twain's ardent desire for hagiography a reality.

## 2

Albert Bigelow Paine was forty-four years old, the author of a book of verse, and two years earlier had published a well-received biography of the political cartoonist Thomas Nast. Paine's portrayal

*Albert Bigelow Paine*

of Nast emphasized his humble beginnings and his reformist perspective in politics, most famously demonstrated in his Boss Tweed cartoon series. Paine was an enormous admirer of Mark Twain; he later confided to Isabel that "it had always been his dream, ambition, to write Mr. Clemens's biography, but he never came close to the prospect of it until Mr. Clemens said to Mr. David Munro that Paine's book on Thomas

Nast was 'damn good'—& Munro told . . . Paine." In an odd coincidence and one that would endear him to Twain, Paine was also the father of three little girls: "Louise aged 11—a little poetess—Frances aged 7—& Tiny Joy aged 3."

Paine visited Twain at his home on Saturday, January 6, 1906, nearly one month to the day after seeing him at Delmonico's, to speak with him about writing his biography. Apparently the morning meeting went well, because later that same day, according to Isabel, Paine immediately started the "collecting of the many notes from the Ms. Trunk." Twain could now literally direct the stories of his life: while Paine wrote his official biography, Twain continued writing his autobiography. Paine persuaded Twain to hire a secretary to take shorthand as he dictated his autobiography, a move Isabel applauded, as she was uncomfortable with the audio "Columbia graphophonic" recordings that had been made of Twain's voice (none of which has survived), finding them macabre: "There is something infinitely sad in the voice as it is reproduced from the cylinders, and how strickening it would be to hear the voice of one gone."

Twain's chosen biographer began work on Tuesday, January 9, arriving promptly at eleven o'clock in the morning with Josephine Hobby, a stenographer. Twain dictated for an hour, talking about his early days out west with his friend Joe Goodman and the Big Bonanza mine, and Isabel watched "his wonderful rising color—& his brilliant eyes—as he warmed to the subject." This new arrangement, Twain exclaimed, was "enchanting & an inspiration—'I would like to have relays of shorthanders—& keep them at it for six hours on a stretch.'" His ideal dictation audience had been assembled—nonjudgmental, interested in every utterance, each word recorded for posterity—and since he owned every word, Twain would have the power to vet everything before it was published.

Paine fell to his twin tasks with equal enthusiasm. He began assembling all of the papers Twain had intended for his autobiography that had been amassed over the years, as well as organizing and researching material for his intended biography. A little over a week after Paine had started coming to 21 Fifth Avenue, Twain ruminated to Isabel about the kinds of biography that had been published, thinking out loud about just how candid he planned to be: "he drifted into the Biography chat, as is his wont in these days—& he said that so few—no autobiographers—were ever very frank. Bayard Taylor was . . . 'so self satis-fied—& sat back & licked his chops'—but it was all delightful. and then Mr. Clemens said that he was going to be frank—not once but many times—(There were Rousseau confessions—but [crossed out: Mr. Clemens was] I am going to leave that kind alone, for Rousseau had looked after that end—)"

Seven months after these initial bold thoughts, a more restrained Twain concluded, "A man can't tell the truth about himself—He couldn't write it, for he wouldn't dare read it if he could—& no one could stand the strong truth of it." Any surprises to be found in Twain's autobiography or Paine's biography would be manufactured by Twain in much the same fashion as he had written his stories. He had success-fully invented a fictional Eve to tell the story of human creation through the pages of her diary, and his persona, Mark Twain, would tell his life story through the pages of his autobiography. Twain had devel-oped a creative medium through which he could give a fictionalized account of himself that would enlarge his already larger-than-life pres-ence in American mythology.

Paine surely understood the conditions under which he would be allowed to write the story of Twain's life, and Isabel was initially thrilled with the King's biographer. She viewed him as a faithful, obe-dient employee who shared her adoration for Twain. With Paine as a loyal member of the household, Isabel could rest assured that no painful revelations would emerge to besmirch the Mark Twain legacy, and, she hoped, her own presence in Twain's story would be recognized.

The mornings typically saw the energetic Paine, the machine-like Miss Hobby, and the watchful Isabel encircling the nightshirt-clad Twain propped up in his bed. Twain had long enjoyed the comfort of remaining in his nightclothes and relaxing in his magnificent bed, and he had now found a way to combine work with pleasure. The morning's dictation completed, Twain would rise and dress. The precious after-noons and evenings at home away from Twain's public amusements belonged to Isabel. Her desire had intensified, and Twain returned her affection. One early winter afternoon in mid-January, the two shared their mutual feelings. After luncheon Isabel went to Twain's room to give him a sentimental poem about the Mississippi River sent to him by a southern admirer, Caroline Stern. After reading it through silently, Twain walked over to Isabel, stood next to her, and read her the poem:

*Who speaks of Care, of toil, of time?*
*The night-wind cools the heated deck,*
*The minstrel river sings in rhyme,*
*And gathers largesse in our wake.*
*And like a refrain, Solemn, Slow,*
*The leadsman's chant comes from below—*
*Ma-a-r-r-k Twa-a-ain*

Looking her in the eye, "his voice thrilled," Twain said to Isabel, "There ought to be the echoing cry from the deck." This intimate moment meant so much to Isabel that, overjoyed, she poured out her feelings at the end of the day: "Oh the richness of his nature, & his brain, & his soul—He sounds the awfulest depths of the tragedies of earth & heaven & hell————he bubbles over with gaity—he melts with grief into silent sobs—he slays with satire your beliefs—he boils over into profanities that make you feel the terror of the thunderbolts that must come—& he is the gentlest, most considerate most lovable creature in all the Earth—Yet how he covers his true self away from most!" She is in the inner sanctum, an intimate of a lesser God. It is, for her, at this moment in time, the most secure place on earth or in heaven.

But the lives of the other Clemens family members were less felicitous. Jean and Clara were decidedly less pleased than Isabel with the new arrangement of the mornings taken over by Paine and Hobby. At his daughters' expense, Twain had gathered a coterie of people to keep him distracted. Clara dealt with her father's rejection by physically removing herself from his presence for most of the winter and spring, shuttling between New York City, Norfolk, and Atlantic City. Jean remained at home and her health soon took an awful turn.

### 3

On January 1, 1906, Jean had had a cluster of three seizures: "Jean— 11—1.20—7 P.m. very severe." Following the typical trajectory of postictal psychosis, immediately afterward she entered a brief lucid state followed by increasing troubling signs of emotional distress. Four days later, Isabel noted "Jean is not well—Not only has her malady increased—but her whole physical condition is at a low ebb." Psychosis assumes different forms and among them are "marked and varied mood changes." Twelve days after the cluster attack, Twain tried to read a transcribed autobiography dictation to an unappreciative Jean. Isabel exclaimed about his aborted attempt in her daily reminder: "But oh a disturbing element stopped it. (A mood of Jean's)." The month would culminate in an episode on Saturday, January 27—one not witnessed by Jean's father, who had absented himself, this time to Washington, to attend a banquet "full of pretty women in beautiful garments" held in his honor.

> This was a tragic day—I came in from a shopping expedition for Jean & others—& when I went into her room for Tea, she told me that a Terrible thing had happened. In a burst of unreasoning rage she struck Katy a Terrible blow in the face—The significance of it is what is so terrible, for now she has done what I have seen in her [crossed out: unescapable] & feared she would do. [Crossed out: She is distressed poor child]—She described the wave of passion that swept over her as being that of an insane person. She knew she couldn't stop—she had to strike. & she said that she wanted to kill. /& was sorry she hadn't—to her mind it doesn't seem right not to finish any job you have begun & she had wanted to kill Katy/

Isabel's attempt to characterize the episode as somehow being a long-standing personality trait may not be terribly productive. What is clear is that Jean, in behavior consistent with that of one enmeshed in the throes of a postictal psychotic state triggered by the cluster of epileptic seizures she suffered at the beginning of the month, had attacked Katy Leary a second time. Isabel's interpretations of Jean's desire to "finish" any "job" and kill the housekeeper was in keeping with the delusional state of postictal psychosis. Isabel's use of the phrase "unreasoning rage" is descriptive of the fact that sufferers in such a condition do not experience intentionally motivated acts of aggression. Katy was again in the wrong place and the unfortunate recipient of Jean's response to internal stimuli of which she alone was aware.

Jean's repeated attacks must have been terribly upsetting for the devoted Katy, who had begun working for the Clemens family the year Jean was born. For twenty-six years, Katy had cared for Jean and had, along with the family, helplessly watched as her health disintegrated. If, indeed, the anger and aggression of the sufferer of the disease is stimulated by the emotional attachment between attacker and victim, then it is understandable why Jean, who was enormously fond of Katy, struck her. In a conversation with Doris Webster in 1948, Isabel spoke about Jean's affliction and "how at times she was really dangerous. . . . The epilepsy seems to have been inherited from Livy's [Olivia's] side—some relative of hers had it. Livy was very much surprised to find this out. You could tell the day before when an attack was coming—She would begin picking at her dress."

The next day, January 28, Jean experienced another cluster of seizures, for a total of six seizures in a month's time. Susan Crane, Olivia Clemens's older sister, arrived soon after from Elmira to help care for her troubled niece. Twain did not return home until Tuesday, January 30.

At the beginning of the week, with Twain still en route, a worried Isabel visited Dr. Quintard, Jean's physician. On Friday morning, February 2, Isabel finally spoke to Twain about his daughter. Confronted with the urgent nature of Jean's situation, Twain unleashed a torrent of angry rhetoric:

> I had a very plain talk with Mr. Clemens this morning about Jean's condition. & told him how on Tuesday I had talked with Dr. Quintard. The dreadfulness of it all swept over him as I knew it would and with that fiercest of all his looks in his face, he blazed out against the Swindle of life—& the . . . treachery of a God that can create disease & misery & crime. create things that men would be condemned for creating—that men would be ashamed to create. [Crossed out: And you agree with him—you have to]

Later that same day, Jean had another cluster of three seizures. Her father, once again, was not there to witness them. He was having dinner with Dorothea and Richard Gilder, wearing a white tie and what he laughingly described to Isabel as a "pair of ratty old daylight pants—but when I tell the Gilders they'll overlook it." Twain would also have had little time to check on Jean over the weekend, as he visited Frank Fuller and his wife, Mary, on Saturday (Frank, one of Twain's oldest friends, was the ex–acting governor of Utah and president of a health-food company), lunched with Mr. and Mrs. John W. Alexander and Maude Adams (one of the most well-known stage actresses of her time,

famous for her signature role as Peter Pan) on Sunday, and entertained
Mr. Montague and Mr. and Mrs. Loomis (Olivia's niece and her spouse)
at teatime the same day. Isabel absolved Twain, explaining that he
"keeps away from anything that wrings his heart. He has too many
speeches to make, too many people to see in these days & he must
remain cheerful."

On Monday, February 5, 1906, outside of the regular consultation
days of Tuesday, Thursday, and Friday, Isabel and Jean went to visit Dr.
Frederick Peterson, "who is going to have charge of her case—her pitiful malady—if he feels that he can benefit her. She has been running
down rapidly & looks badly—& is ill—really very ill—" Peterson was
forty-seven years old and stood an imposing six feet four inches tall. He
was the first professor of psychiatry at Columbia University and was
widely recognized as the most prominent epilepsy specialist in the
country. Well known as a pioneer in psychiatry and neurology, he was
also regarded as a mental-health advocate. He served as chairman of
the Section of Neurology and Medical Jurisprudence of the American
Medical Association from 1898 to 1899, as president of the New York
Neurological Society from 1899 to 1901, and was president of the
American Neurological Association in 1924. Peterson considered the
social ostracism of epileptics as cruel and undeserved, and he founded
Craig Colony, located in Sonyea, New York, the first comprehensive
epilepsy center established in the United States, where severe epileptics
could receive treatment and lead full and meaningful lives. Peterson
was appointed president of the board of managers at Craig Colony in
1895.

Peterson's research on epilepsy and insanity was voluminous, with
over two hundred publications, including one work that would prove
particularly apt in relationship to Jean's affliction, *Epileptic Insanity.* His
best-known book, *Nervous and Mental Diseases,* published in 1911, five
years after Isabel and Jean's visit to him, would become a standard for
generations of physicians. In his chapter "Epilepsy," there is a discussion concerning "psychic equivalents of the epileptic attack" where
"immediately following the fits, we may have a variety of acute mental
disturbances." These disturbances included homicidal acts; however,
"as a rule, [patients] have no knowledge of such acts." In addition,
"sudden wild, maniacal outbursts, in which the patient may be destructive and dangerous to others, are encountered, and these may terminate

suddenly or be protracted for several days." Peterson may have been the first physician to recognize what is now identified as postictal psychosis, without actually naming it as such.

While Peterson was well published as a medical writer, he also had a literary side that would have appealed to his new patient and her father. He was an accomplished poet with a special interest in Chinese poetry and art and had published four books of poetry under his pseudonym, Pai Ta-Shun.

The visit to Peterson proved to have a palliative effect upon the household; Jean went for over a month without a seizure. Isabel's spirits also improved and she once again dwelled on the joy of being part of the Clemens home in an entry she later tried to obliterate:

> All these days are full of interesting doings—A steady flame of delight burns through every hour; it burns—but Sometimes the fog of little trying circumstances will obscure it until the wit comes to make you see right through the fog to the wonderful wonderful flame— I don't want any Earthly Thing outside of this house—And it is such a com-fort to have Mr. Paine full of the love of the daily dictation, missing not a gesture—not a word—not a glance. but treasuring it all in his good heart.

She added a more calculating note the next day (which she later crossed out), musing, "As I grow older I marvel more & more over the fact that anything I long for with a strong steady silent desire, comes to me in Time. It never fails." At the end of February Isabel and Twain went day-tripping: "Mr. Clemens he suggested that the joys of a trip in the subway from Astor Place to the Northern terminus would be considerable, for he loves the Subway. I said doubtless he would enjoy it. Then he asked me if I'd like to go. It was a [crossed out: dear] & happy suggestion." A white-suited Mark Twain delightedly riding along in a subway car must have been quite a sight for the average New Yorker.

Yet this happy, confident mood would prove short-lived. On March 21, Jean left to spend a week or two in Lakewood, New Jersey, fifty-eight miles away, at a well-known winter resort for the wealthy located on fourteen acres. Jean wrote Isabel that she had become unwell once again, and Isabel recorded three seizures: at 9:00 a.m., 11:00 a.m., and 4:00 p.m. on March 25: "Lakewood, very bad day." Jean unexpectedly returned home on March 27, looking ill and "quite pale." During Jean's absence, Twain grew increasingly melancholy, and he erupted in a tirade to Isabel on March 24:

> This is the wretched day when Mr. Clemens went down to the living room & there wasn't anyone there—For a half hour he waited for a human being & none came to stay. C.C. [Clara] looked in upon him as she passed out of the house—& then a blast of cold and bedeviled loneliness swept over him & made . . . him hate his life—C.C. was late for luncheon—& Mr. Clemens loathed the meal. He dropped his 2 hard water biscuits with a bang on the mahogany Table. in . . . a cursing wave of . . . bitterness. [crossed out: reached me & made me wretched too.] These are the agony days when he [crossed out: misses] knows Mrs. Clemens is gone.

## 4

Had Isabel chosen to, she would have realized that there were ominous auguries in the events of the fall and spring of 1905 and 1906. While her earlier reading of Kipling's story "An Habitation Enforced" buoyed her upwardly mobile hopes, a second fictional work sank them. Edith Wharton's novel *The House of Mirth* was published on October 14, 1905, and became an instant literary sensation. Wharton's realism captured the zeitgeist of a generation with her insider's depiction of New York's upper class, inciting the reading public's obsession with wealth, ritual, and status. Demand for the book far outstripped its availability. An astounding thirty thousand copies were sold within three weeks of its initial printing, and an additional sixty thousand copies were ordered after the first month. For many of the one hundred thousand readers who had purchased the book within seven weeks of its publication date, the novel's inherent tragedy had less to do with Lily Bart's sad ending than with Wharton's detailing her heroine's failure to succeed in her quest for class mobility. Wharton had penned the feminine antithesis to *Ragged Dick,* and this cautionary tale about the upper class held an irresistible appeal for the fascinated public.

Isabel was completely traumatized by Wharton's novel. Repelled, yet obsessively drawn to it, she attempted to read it on three separate occasions. The experience proved so upsetting that she stopped reading altogether for months: "Perhaps I'm discouraged from attempting anything more felicitous, by the great horror left [crossed out: within me] by 'The House of Mirth.'" Each time she tried to read the book, she had to "dash it aside full of pain over its dread-fulnesses." Deeply depressed by Wharton's narrative, Isabel found no succor even in sleep. At the end of the paragraph in her reminder in which she decries Wharton's text, she wrote and then crossed out, "Oh such tragic dreams— Such devastating dreams All day I drag myself along for the sadness they create."

*Edith Wharton, 1905*

What could Wharton's story have provoked within Isabel to create such an emotional furor? *The House of Mirth* traces the life of a single woman from a distinguished, although financially ruined, New York family who possessed a particular kind of wealth, namely her striking physical attractiveness. But Lily's riches, her singular beauty, prove ephemeral, and her social and economic capital decreases with each birthday. On the verge of turning thirty, Lily realizes she is no longer a brand-new freshman and is quickly becoming, as Isabel said, a socially unacceptable, "rusty 'Soph.'" Lily's awful awareness that her shelf life is running out fails to save her, and her ambivalence about marrying into the very class that would allow her to lead a financially and socially advantaged life ultimately proves fatal.

Through the actions of the hapless and ultimately hopeless Lily, Wharton exposed the upper layers of New York's Gilded Age society. This was an era when the city's traditional upper class, consisting of old Dutch families (like Isabel's mother's parents the Van Kleeks) and Yankees dating back to the Revolutionary War, had given way to the showy excesses of the nouveaux riches, such people as Mark Twain. The newly affluent, their fortunes made in business, railroads, real estate, stocks, banking, and publishing, forced the elite set to open its ranks, and the new members swaggered in with impunity. Ostentatious displays of wealth became the currency for status. Social life was no longer restrained behind the walls of private clubs and homes; instead, enormous residences, opulent hotels, and expensive restaurants were built where showy celebrations were held as the newly rich paraded their finery up and down the fashionable arteries of the city. Old and new money mingled and married, and changing one's social class upwardly must have seemed within the realm of the possible. In this environment, wealthy widowers like John Kendrick Bangs marrying their secretaries must have confirmed what the public so desperately wanted to believe, that fairy tales do come true. Yet with every plucky success story that gave women like Isabel hope, there were plenty of other, much darker, tales that Wharton's novel made visible. "Never take anything for granted," Clara's advice to Isabel, could have been a Greek choral refrain in *The House of Mirth*.

Wharton's realism threatened Isabel's ambition. Isabel found far too much to identify with in the novel—indeed, Lily was Isabel's doppelgänger. Both women had come from formerly well-established families; both had long passed the ingénue stage of life as well as the socially acceptable age for a first marriage; both were pressed into playing endless games of cards to humor their benefactors (Isabel had the additional duty of pumping away for hours at the Orchestrelle); both worked as secretaries to the wealthy; and both had their share of ene-

*Mark Twain at a dinner at Charlotte Teller Johnson's house, nicknamed "A Club,"*
*April 11, 1906. Among those present, Robert Collier and Arthur Brisbane*

*Charlotte Teller Johnson*

mies. Ultimately, Lily makes a fatal social gaffe, for which the upper class would prove unforgiving. She sinks beneath a storm of sexual innuendo, having been falsely accused of having an affair with her benefactress's oafish husband. Would the same fate await Isabel?

*The House of Mirth* ends with Wharton's Lily dying alone in a poor tenement room, abandoned as a formerly attractive object that had lost its appeal. Isabel's great horror was the ugly possibility that the same fate might await her. But she refused to accept that her life could imitate fiction, wanting so much to believe that she was secure and central to the life of Twain's household and needed by him. Isabel, like others in Wharton's reading audience, blamed authorial malfeasance for Lily's tragic death, instead of interpreting the ending as the logical outcome of a novel critical of materialism and the fantasy of upward mobility.

Spring brought a new threat to Isabel's peace of mind in the form of another, much younger woman. At the end of March, Twain made the acquaintance of thirty-year-old Charlotte Teller Johnson, author of a novel, *The Cage,* and two plays, *Mirabeau* and *Joan d'Arc.* Charlotte lived with her grandmother just down the street from Twain, at Number 3 Fifth Avenue, which she called the "A Club" house. Charlotte paid an unexpected call on Isabel and asked if she could introduce a Nikolai Tschaykoffshi, a Russian revolutionary agitator, to Twain. Twain agreed. Charlotte returned later that same afternoon with Tschaykoffshi in tow and made the introductions. As she prepared to leave the two men alone, Twain asked Charlotte who she was, and when he discovered that she was the author of *Joan d'Arc,* he asked her to return the next day and read it to him. She did, and he was greatly moved by her as well as by her subject. Shortly afterward, on April 11, Twain attended a dinner at Charlotte's home with "her revolutionary tribe," including Maxim Gorky, Zinovii Peshkov (Gorky's adopted son), and Ivan Narodny. Isabel noted that the dinner party, which she was not invited to attend, totaled "13—such a hellish superstition it is." To Isabel's great consternation, over the course of the next three months the vibrant Charlotte visited Twain almost every day. Isabel's disdain for Twain's talented new friend grew to the extent that after one visit, she uncharacteristically swore, saying Charlotte "paid me damn compliments."

By May, Isabel felt such an overwhelming sense of panic about Twain's new relationship that she visited a palm reader. The seeress, Miss Hyde, only upset her more when, after gazing upon her overworked digits, she forecast "calamity for me a great hence. & the ghost—the demon of that Calamity is ever beside me." For a woman as high strung and nervous as Isabel, Miss Hyde's prediction was enough to drive her to near collapse. Yet she still refused to believe that all her efforts to secure a future with Twain might be in vain. The next day she was forced to resort to extreme measures to ease her tension during a rare visit by Clara.

> [Crossed out: I am sitting here at 2.30 in the morning. I couldn't cant sleep.] Down stairs. I hear Mr. Clemens cough. I have taken 2 heavy drugs—but they dont effect—a terrible anxiety weighs—up Fifth Ave—drays drag themselves—Horses I suppose are in front of them— [Crossed out: I feel a calamity—] The Valley of the Shadow Mr. Clemens called this house—Trunks are around [crossed out: but the terror is heavy upon] me—[Crossed out: When Santa started for Gilders tonight I told her I'd go for whiskey—but there was no whiskey to quiet me—Foolish for me to think it would—it doesn't]

Undoubtedly, what drew Twain to Charlotte Teller Johnson was the combination of her youth and her talent. She probably reminded him a great deal of his lost daughter Susy, an aspiring writer. The two discussed their various writing projects, and Twain assured Charlotte that she possessed "greatness"—indeed, "more of it than you suspect, I think." The admiration was mutual, and Charlotte appeared to inspire Twain to finally complete his "Gospel," *What Is Man?,* which he had been working on for years (he claimed in his preface to the 1906 edition that he had begun the work "twenty-five or twenty-seven years ago").

## 5

The season in New York was long and wearying for the Clemens family, with tensions exacerbated by the public's adulation of Twain and his private friendship with Charlotte Teller Johnson. Jean's suffering, Twain's frequent absences, Clara's antagonism, and Charlotte's flattering attention to Twain all proved too much for Isabel. A seeming reprieve arrived in May, however. On a Monday afternoon, after Twain and Charlotte had a morning farewell chat, Isabel and Twain left New York for the distant climes of Dublin, New Hampshire, arriving on May 15 at the house Twain was leasing, called Upton House. Jean had happily abandoned New York for Dublin two weeks earlier with the devoted Katy; her maid, Anna Sterritt; and Mary, the cook. Thomas Bigelow Paine and Miss Hobby (Miss Hobby had been talked into quitting her job at *The Century Magazine* by Isabel and Paine so as to come and work for Twain) joined them on May 20, with the massive Orchestrelle arriving a few days later.

But unlike the restful and pleasing Copley Greene house, Upton House was much smaller and more isolated. There exist two dramatically different narratives about the quality of the time spent there that summer. Paine (with whom Miss Hobby shared a nearby cottage) claimed years later in his introduction to *Mark Twain's Autobiography* that Upton was a "perfect setting" for Twain's dictations. Isabel vigorously refuted Paine's halcyon recollection in a scribbled note on the margin of the page, in which she declared that Upton was absolutely "not a 'perfect setting,'" that it was "out of the world, & an ugly house." Apparently the living room was too small for Twain's taste and he took a particular dislike to a marble-topped table located in the center of the room, ordering that it be moved to the side to create more space: "Katy the maid put it back in the morning, & when Mr Clemens saw it, he roared 'Take that damned thing to the cellar.'"

Jean's epilepsy continued to worsen despite the quiet, pastoral surroundings. She became practiced at predicting the onset of her seizures, at times experiencing nausea shortly before an attack, although the severity of her illness and its capriciousness continued to frustrate her best efforts to keep it at bay. Over the summer, she recorded in her diary the frequency and severity of her seizures as well as her unease over her forgetfulness. When one reads the tally that Isabel and Jean kept in their personal journals, it becomes clear that at minimum Jean suffered more than thirty-two seizures from May to mid-October (this did not include all her petit mals, which sometimes occurred up to twenty times in a single day).

On at least six separate days she experienced cluster seizures, in Jean's words "petit-mals . . . fearfully long, many of them," the precursor of postictal psychosis. In her journal entry for May 3, Jean wrote: "My memory about where the various friends live here in Dublin, is terrible. Yesterday, I felt decidedly vague about which road to turn up to go to the Thayers' house. Nothing could be more idiotic than that, considering where I lived all last summer." During the first two weeks of May, she recorded how her multiple petit mals ("little short touches of absentmindedness," in her words) made her "wretchedly tired" and "afraid." On May 4, she described a particularly difficult day:

> As soon as I wakened, by five o'clock, I realized that I was going to be ill, but I hoped, after yesterday's result, that the attack would pass off in a few petits-mals early in the morning. I didn't take the pills quite as promptly as perhaps it would have been well to do so, because I hate to get into the habit of taking drugs like that when I feel a thing coming on. The petits-mals were fearfully long, many of them, but toward eleven o'clock I went down the hill with Anna & was fairly well during the walk. I had times of being very bad indeed & fairly well, all day long. After lunch I took a nap & when I first wakened felt well. . . . Katy really tho't the danger of an attack was over, & so did I but we were wrong. It finally came right after my supper, about eight o'clock. It was a medium one.

During the early summer, Isabel wrote to Dr. Peterson several times informing him of Jean's worsened state. At the end of June, Peterson wrote back to Isabel in response to her inquiries as well as Jean's. He was disappointed to learn that Jean's "mental and nervous improvement do not keep pace with the physical change for the better," and included a stronger prescription of bromides. Yet despite the increased dosage, Jean continued to deteriorate. She was enormously discouraged about being forced to live in what she considered to be a state of limbo, neither child nor adult woman, and on July 4, she confronted the depressing nature of her existence:

> Why must I live on aimlessly, with nothing to do, utterly useless, all my life? I who long so for the love and companionship that only a man can give, and that man a husband. The affection of friendship between man & woman does not suffice; & of course the love between two women cannot even be considered in the problem of this hunger. Am I never to know what love means because I am an epileptic and shouldn't marry if I had the chance? I seem never to be attractive to men. . . . Will I have to go on indefinitely leading this empty, cheerless life without aim or real interest?

Adding to Jean's pain was her disappointment about failing to establish a romantic relationship with Gerry Brush. When she learned in July that the Brush family was intending to live in Italy for two years, the news made her "ill." "Two years!" she exclaimed. "I shall be twenty-eight then and all the young Brushes will begin to regard me as a stolid old maid; too old for them to bother about. Why can't they jump forward seven or eight years, or I jump back???" In October, she wrote at length about her growing feelings for Gerry:

> What can I do? I have a decided feeling that I love Gerry and yet I ought not to. I'm much too much older than he and to show real affection, I ought to force it to become merely a quiet, warm affection such as a boy & girl can perfectly well have for each other. The hard part of it is that the older I grow—the nearer & nearer to old-maidhood—I get more & more anxious to marry. I know perfectly well that while my illness flourishes I ought not to think of any such a thing, but the idea of spending all of my older years practically by myself—Clara & I won't want to live together very much and we aren't especially sympathetic, anyway—is perfectly hideous. . . . I believe that the desire to marry is so strong in me that no matter what man, provided he was at all nice, were

to propose to me & seem to be in love, that I should almost at once fall in love with him, or at least imagine myself to be in that state. Of course father would at once raise every objection, no matter whether I were better in health, or who the man might be, but if I could believe myself in love & loved, I should pay no attention to his desires . . . so tremendously hungry for love—marriage—makes me fear, almost believe, that I shall never have it.

AS WELL AS BEING ATTRACTED to Gerry Brush, Jean developed an attachment to Gerald "Gra" Thayer, son of Abbott Thayer and brother of Gladys (called Galla) and Mary. Twain had known Emma Beach, Abbott Thayer's second wife, for decades, having met her when they were both passengers on the *Quaker City*. Abbott was a well-known artist, celebrated for his idealized portraits of women as well as for being one of the first artists to design military camouflage. He was joined in his camouflage efforts by his friend George de Forest Brush and his son Gerry. Thayer's son, Gra, was an exceptionally handsome young man, who told Isabel and Jean about his impulsive, naked sprint up Mount Monadnock. "I think it was a glory of a thing to do," Isabel enthusiastically wrote, "Think of that strong young naked white creature dashing along through the winter woods. Think of him standing alone among the mighty rocks on the top of that mountain. It is the great primeval call of the wild—& there seems to me to be something akin to a religion in it."

To try to divert Jean's attention from naked young men and unhappy thoughts of spinsterhood, Isabel urged her, with little success, to pursue an interest in carving and to complete a decorative box as a gift for one of her cousins. A weary Isabel wrote that "Jean's insolences—poor child—& the great lonely hours" drove her and Twain to distraction.

While Jean and Isabel enjoyed a close and warm relationship, Jean was often verbally abusive to those around her—"venomous" was Isabel's adjective—and her behavior had become increasingly erratic. Isabel feared that Jean's physical attacks upon Katy Leary might be repeated with her: "In Jean's present condition it isn't safe for me to be alone with her—She could easily lapse into the violence the doctors fear may come in time." In one despairing entry (later crossed out), an exhausted Isabel dramatically compared herself to Prometheus: "I cast my thoughts toward the ones with whom I would willingly be—but I am Prometheus—& am chained to the rock & daily my Soul is Torn out of me—No—not my Soul—not my Soul." Isabel ignored her personal physician's orders to leave Jean and go away for a rest cure, deciding instead to "take hold of the condition mentally—I must heal it from within—& in my own lame way I shall do it. I did quiet the quivering nerves."

Twain hated life at Upton House and left whenever he could find an excuse to do so, absenting himself for over a month to make various visits to friends. While it might be tempting to view Twain as a neglectful father because of his deliberate absences from his stricken daughter, a likelier explanation is that he could not abide watching her suffer. He had confessed to Henry Rogers in 1902 that he rarely witnessed his daughter experiencing seizures: "I have seen it only three times before, in all these five fiendish years." Seizures can be terribly frightening to observers. When a grand mal seizure strikes, the individual may shriek as the air from the lungs is expelled. Jean had a distinctive cry that signaled the onset of a seizure and she would vomit. Sufferers will typically become rigid and fall, and then the muscles will relax and tighten, causing convulsions. Typically Jean's convulsions would render her unconscious and she would become incontinent. After the seizure had concluded, she would be left confused and bruised. Usually people who experience grand mal seizures have no memory of what occurred. Being a passive observer to his daughter's affliction was more than Twain could stand; indeed, a gloomy Twain disliked his living circumstances so much that he gave the house various descriptive titles including Wuthering Heights and the Lodge of Sorrow. Yet the last nickname Twain chose could not possibly have given Isabel less comfort—the House of Mirth. Whatever Twain called the house, the months spent there were an unmitigated failure.

Jean's physical and mental condition had so deteriorated by September that Isabel insisted that Twain return to Dublin, something she was loath to ask him and he was equally reluctant to do. After a weeklong siege in mid-September when Jean suffered multiple seizures, an exhausted Isabel, in her words, "went to pieces." As Jean's primary caretaker, Isabel was overwhelmed. Throughout her months sequestered in Dublin, a depressed Isabel smoked cigarettes (an utterly taboo act for a woman—just two years earlier a woman had been arrested on Fifth Avenue for smoking in an automobile) and drank sherry alone late into

*Bromidia, a popular all-purpose patent medicine*

the night, on one occasion lingering, "waiting for the electric lights to go out at midnight." She also began to dose herself regularly with Bromidia, a popular all-purpose patent medicine. Bromidia was an extremely potent tonic containing extract of Cannabis indica (marijuana), 10 percent alcohol, chloral hydrate (a sedative and hypnotic), extract of hyoscyamus (a powerful narcotic and hypnotic), and potassium bromide (a salt used as an anticonvulsant and sedative). The recommended dosage was a stout eighth of a fluid ounce every hour until sleep occurred. With the volume of alcohol and narcotics contained in the mixture, it is little wonder that people taking it felt dramatic relief from their aches and pains. Patients quickly grew dependent upon its restorative powers, increasing both the frequency and the amount of dosage. The Clemens family, with their host of illnesses, also regularly availed themselves of this miracle elixir. Yet despite Isabel's determined attempts at self-medication, she was unable to find peace: "[Crossed out: I have to sleep on Bromidia. The loneliness here this year is enough to do one a damage. And the loneliness is not because one is alone, either]."

While dealing with Jean, Isabel also increasingly worried about her status with "the King." Someone Isabel had thought she had come to know quite well was proving to be frustratingly enigmatic. While she kept determinedly pretending that Twain was much younger than his chronological age, claiming at one point in her daily reminder that "he is overflowing with a buoyancy belonging to a man of 45," in truth he felt and looked every day of his hard-fought seventy years. Although his health was relatively stable, he suffered frequent bouts of bronchitis and gout. A return of the gout to his feet would guarantee irritability on his part and require Isabel to kneel and repeatedly paint the offending area with iodine. In an October daily reminder entry that she later tried to obliterate, she expressed her frustration: "Now I'm not sure that I understand the King at all. Or, rather, there is such a deep side to him that I know I don't understand him, & that I never can. But I don't want to. It's the side of him that is unfathomable that helps to make his Sweet greatness."

While it was thrilling to Isabel that Twain freely shared his thoughts with her, it did not seem to increase their personal intimacy. Twain's constant swearing was disconcerting to everyone within earshot, yet Isabel tried to ameliorate the effect of his language. The "lovable" one would launch into tirades about religion so frequently that Isabel had become indifferent to "his disgust at those who worship 'a Tarbaby of a Jesus Christ—' or the 'dangling carcass of a virgin.' " She laughed away Miss Hobby's horrified reaction to his mocking the idea of Immaculate Conception, noting that when it came to sex, "discussion of the Immaculate Conception doesn't leave much uncovered—Not if Mr. Clemens is doing the discussing." Even Isabel's capacity for the denial of Twain's dark moods failed upon occasion. At the conclusion of another bleak session when he proclaimed the failure of the human race, her benign mask finally slipped: "After a talk like the ones he gives me I grope all the rest of the day with my soul spirit weak with the terrible mental weeping that is with me, & then when every one is sleeping the real tears come—It's always like that. Ever since the night in June when he read the *Apostrophe to Death*—one of his best values is that he doesn't ever pay you a compliment, but helps you to see your raw quivering faulty self."

Some measure of relief from Twain's increasing bitterness was granted Isabel when he waxed nostalgic about his youthful romances with two Missouri women, Laura Wright and Laura Hawkins. The reminiscing had been brought on when he picked up a newspaper and read the date, May 26, 1906, whereupon he announced that this was the anniversary of when "48 years ago I said goodbye to my little sweetheart"—proving, Isabel hoped, that he was a sentimentalist at heart. Romance, however, did not appear to be on Twain's agenda when it came to the woman he was living with. Isabel's awareness of this lack of interest on his part took a heavy physical and mental toll. In September she wrote and then crossed out, "My soul is not moored to anything. I can't keep it up where it ought to be—& so I cry & cry."

While Isabel's spirits were fading and Jean's health was eroding, Twain appeared to be flourishing. Amused by the scarlet stockings that Isabel had purchased for him and Witter Bynner to wear while dressed as Siamese twins at a party, Twain told her that he wanted to wear them all the time as an accent with his white suits. He proclaimed that he loved "gaudy things—In fact he'd 'like to dress like a nigger.' " Continuing in the same vein while speaking of the supposed proliferation of the Jewish people, Twain, waving his hands expansively, pronounced: "The jews are increasing so, & increasing so, that soon there'll be enough of an audience for another crucifixion." Whether Isabel found this last statement amusing is left unrecorded in her journal. Less than two weeks before his return to the city, Twain decided that he would defy "Conventionalities" and wear "his Suitable white clothes all winter, so he has bidden me order 5 new suits from his tailor; the suits to be ready against the time we arrive in N.Y." One can only imagine his tailor's panic at the sudden order.

Adding to her growing portfolio of duties, Isabel had become Twain's personal valet and was responsible for maintaining his eccentric haberdashery. On one occasion she pointed out that he had forgotten to button his pants. "Darlingly he cocked his head at me & said 'I don't, always; but since you are so particular I'll do it this time,' " a bit of overtly sexualized repartee. In response to Twain's inquiry as to why he could not have a cloak like Richard Gilder's, Isabel assured him that he could and ordered one. In return, he expected her to constantly hold his new black velvet cape at the ready in the event that he might need it spread "on a mossy bank or a stone—or to throw around him." Twain also thought that a white velvet cape would look striking with his white suits and asked Isabel why he could not have one of those. She again responded in the affirmative, and he ordered two. By the fall of 1906, Twain owned seventeen white suits and would insist upon taking six of them with him when he went to visit Henry Rogers (the total number of

*Mark Twain with his white velvet cape in Tuxedo Park,*
*New York, 1907*

white suits would increase to twenty-four by June 1909). According to Isabel, he "often went off on R[oger]'s boat & he couldn't stand a spot on his clothes." As his personal life became increasingly messy, Twain became obsessed with eliminating the dirt and grime on his clothes.

Such was his confidence in Isabel that he entrusted to her care the physical asset of which he was most proud—his hair. He anointed her his personal stylist:

> I've just been cutting the King's hair; he sitting up in his sunshiney room, & teaching me how to use the flat shears that clip the back of his neck. And it was a successful cutting too. He has just come down to say

that I'd beaten the barber at his own trade. How much of happiness that means.

Always particular about his hair, Twain relied upon Katherine, one of the house servants, whom he had nicknamed the Librarian, to rub his head dry after his bath. Whenever Katherine was unavailable to perform her styling responsibility, Isabel took her place "& rubbed his damp hair into a glory of a white & beautiful fluff."

## 6

One glimmer of hope for Isabel amid all this fluffing and fussing came with the possibility of acquiring a home of her own. In March 1906, Albert Bigelow Paine had casually mentioned to Isabel that he knew of a parcel of land for sale, seventy-five acres total, with an old farmhouse on it, near where he had recently purchased a place in Redding, Connecticut. Isabel told Twain about the conversation, and he impulsively gave Paine $100 as a down payment on the property (Twain eventually purchased approximately 248 acres). Isabel expressed a surprising measure of resentment about Twain's willingness to purchase:

> [Crossed out: I didn't think he would want it—because I couldn't think he would want anything that I want—with an aching heart I reached out for that farm for I dont ever want to go back to Farmington again. I want & want & want to sell Choisy [her mother's home] & so be able to settle where there is more room—you can see for 20 miles—Life is such a tiny bubble—that why we reach out for material things I don't know; but we do it—& that old beamed farm-house on top of the hill held out its arms to me.]

Isabel sensed a potential ally in the twice-married Albert Bigelow Paine and initially trusted him. Over the course of the summer, the two took frequent walks during which they talked endlessly about Twain and shared intimate details of their lives. Paine presented himself as a sensitive man, deeply moved by poetry and prose, and the emotional Isabel was an appreciative audience. In September, she described how Paine had been brought to tears during one of their country tête-à-têtes:

> But in the afternoon AB [Paine] came out & found me near the quivering white birch trees—& after a good talk he read aloud to me from Madame Butterfly—the darlingest saddest movingest little story in the world. Dear ABs voice shook & broke & stopped & he wept. How sweet it is to see a man weep—

At this stage in their relationship, Paine and Isabel probably believed that there was enough of Twain to satisfy both of them, and the two forged an unspoken alliance. Another possibility gleaned from reading Isabel's journal entries is that, if necessity demanded, she figured she would be able to outmaneuver Paine. If so, she greatly underestimated her convivial hiking partner. At the end of a June 1906 daily reminder entry exclaiming upon how wonderful she found Paine's life story, Isabel years later added a caustic editorial note: "Old Fraud."

Later in August, the two walked to the upper pasture in Dublin, speaking again of the King's virtues: "That is our ritual" and together they began measuring off rooms for the new house Twain wanted built in Redding. Isabel ecstatically recorded, "if I am good—very good—I am to have a Strip of land in Redding to build me there a little house—AB. will let me use the strip from his own property. Oh I must be good—monotonously good." Paine's generous offer bought him Isabel's confidence for a time.

In August, Isabel traveled from Dublin to New York City, where she met Clara, and together they dined with William Dean Howells's son, John Mead Howells, an architect. The three discussed plans for the new Redding house and the next day they took the train to Connecticut. After an eight-mile carriage ride, Twain's land lay before them. Isabel thought the location beautiful, albeit remote, with an excellent building site for Twain's new residence. She placed her confidence in John Howells, whom she described as "the most polished of young creatures," remarking that it was "a pity he is so small. & with a face like a Greek mask." In the distance she could see the chimney of an old shingled farmhouse. At that moment Isabel believed she had glimpsed her future, a vision of a safe haven that would belong only to her. The planning for Twain's new house would proceed throughout the winter and spring of the coming year.

The cost of the new dwelling quickly became an issue, as did the family's overall spending. According to Twain, after 1906 the amount of royalties he would be paid would be substantially reduced. An annual payment of $25,000 from Harper's would end, and the coming year would see a 60 percent decrease in the previous year's royalties. This meant that Clara and Jean would have to make do with a mere $25,000 for living expenses during the coming year—an economy neither one would tolerate well. This sum must have represented an unbelievable luxury to Isabel, whose annual salary totaled $523, $77 more than the average American's annual income in 1900.

Twain set a budget of $25,000 for construction (the final cost was $60,000). Financing would come from his $30,000 agreement with the *North American Review* to publish chapters from his autobiography in serial format in twenty-five issues from September 7, 1906, to December 1907. Once the decision to move forward with his new home had been made, Twain wanted nothing to do with its actual planning and construction. This was a repeat of his behavior when Olivia had taken charge of completing their Hartford home a few years after their marriage. When friends came to visit and inquired about his new Redding home, Twain refused to discuss it. Isabel marveled: "He won't allow himself to be informed or Consulted; he will pay the bills & that's all he will do—but when the house is finished then he will go to it. It astounds his questioning friends to hear him answer 'I don't know.' To Every question they ask about the house or property. He doesn't want to see it—or hear anything about it." Once Clara approved the plans, Twain turned the details of the construction over to Isabel. With building proceeding apace, Isabel had reason to believe that while her efforts to secure Twain as her husband might come to naught, she would be successful in obtaining a home of her own with a healthy income—but only if she continued her "monotonously good" behavior. She was still counting on the future royalties that she would earn from the publication of Twain's letters. There were other people, however, who had also become interested in Twain's future earnings.

## 7

Isabel returned with Jean and Twain to 21 Fifth Avenue in the chilly October of 1906, with the demon of Calamity by her side. Try as she might, she had been unable to entirely dismiss Miss Hyde's dreadful prophecy, and it seemed as though much that had happened in the

Twain family during the summer only confirmed her prediction of doom. Isabel's best hope for her future income lay in keeping Clara appeased, an unenviable task for anyone. In the fall of 1906, the restless Clara had decided to restart her singing career. Her voice was deemed strong enough for the rigors of touring and she embarked upon a series of concerts. Her "début" as a concert singer took place on September 22 in Norfolk, Connecticut, in the Norfolk Gymnasium, and served to underscore the difficult dynamics of her relationship with her father. Twain wanted to attend, but Clara rebuffed him, fearing that he would steal her spotlight. She finally agreed that he could be present, although he was not allowed to lead her out and had to agree to sit quietly in the third row.

Twain, aware only of his need for attention and not his daughter's desires, sprang to his feet at the concert's conclusion, gained the stage and proceeded to make a twenty-minute speech. The next day *The New York Times*'s article proclaimed, "Miss Clemens in Concert. Mark Twain Makes a Speech at His Daughter's Debut." The *Times* reported that Clara "is the possessor of a rich contralto voice" and was "enthusiastically received" by her large delegation of New York friends. Clara's success was somewhat mitigated when a newspaper article appearing two days later in the *New York Sun* covered Twain's performance and mentioned Clara's singing only in closing. Clara's manager, knowing what the public wanted, encouraged Clara to be photographed with her father for publicity shots. She refused. After playing several dates in October and November, she canceled the remaining performances and fled the city for a two-month rest in the country.

One of Clara's singing dates happened to coincide with one of the most difficult moments of Jean's life—her departure to Hillbourne Farms, an expensive, well-appointed sanitarium for patients with what was politely called at the time "nervous disorders." The facility was located approximately an hour north of New York City by rail, in the hamlet of Katonah within the township of Bedford in Westchester County, New York. After her awful country summer, marked by the worsening of her disease and the sting of unrequited love, Jean had returned to New York City in an ill humor because Gerry Brush had not come to see her off at the train station in Dublin. Desperate for a cure, upon Peterson's recommendation Jean had begun to consider the possibility of treatment at Hillbourne Farms. Jean was well aware of her family's complicated emotional dynamics and knew that Dr. Peterson, with his strong opinions about placing her in an epileptic sanitarium, must have appeared as a godsend to her sister and father. To Jean's utter astonishment, Katy informed her that when Clara had heard of her "Katonah plan," she became upset in "the same way as [at] Mother's death" and had taken to her bed for three days. Jean had assumed that Clara was indifferent to her fate because of her preoccupation with her singing career. Shortly after returning to the city from New Hampshire, Jean and Isabel had paid a visit to Hillbourne Farms.

While the trip north was brief, a distressed and anxious Jean had still managed to count seven cemeteries along the way. Hillbourne Farms was located half a mile east of the Katonah train station and village, at the top of a hill, occupying forty acres, with beautiful wooded groves and fields dotted with dairy cows. A published pamphlet used for advertising purposes described Hillbourne as "a private Health Resort where Exercise and Occupation are employed as a therapeutic agent in treatment of functional nervous disorders." Hillbourne promised that "no expense has been spared," and the first building Jean and Isabel glimpsed was proof positive of that statement. The Club House, located at the bottom of the hill just inside the stone entrance gate, boasted a sitting room with a fireplace, a piano and pianola, a solarium, bowling alleys, a squash court, a billiard room, a well-outfitted carpenter shop (of particular interest to Jean, as she intended to continue her carving), an arts-and-crafts shop, a greenhouse, and seven living rooms.

As the two women continued on their way up the hill, standing on a knoll was the grand main building, a three-story wooden structure with twenty-four rooms, including "a large solarium, reception rooms, dining rooms, medical office, clinical laboratory, hydrotherapeutic and electro-therapeutic equipment." Two separate living residences were located on the property, the Iris and Wisteria Bungalow and the Orchard Lodge, for patients who desired more private accommodations; and Jean would occupy one of these bungalows during her stay.

All this luxury and privacy came at a premium. The minimum cost for a week's stay was $50.00, the equivalent of what Isabel earned in a month. Jean's average expenses at Hillbourne would be much higher than the published rates: from March 1907 to January 22, 1908, her Hillbourne bills would average $274.00 per month, with her personal spending an average of $51.00 per month over the same period. All

*The wood shop at Hillbourne Farms, Katonah, New York*

together Twain would be supporting his ill daughter to the tune of $325.00 per month. By comparison, the mean daily pay for a male worker in the building trades in 1906 (such as the bricklayers, carpenters, laborers, lathers, painters, paperhangers, plasterers, and plumbers who were building Twain's Redding house) was $2.06, for a mean monthly pay of $41.20.

Dr. Edward A. Sharp, originally from New York City, had founded the Hillbourne Farms in 1905, purchasing the property in 1904 and expanding it in 1905. After their tour, Jean decided that the place was acceptable and remarked on the beautiful trees growing on the grounds. The two women returned to the city that evening. The next day Isabel helped Jean pack her things, with her departure planned for October 24, but Jean was delayed by a day due to a seizure cluster. On October 25, 1906, when Jean was twenty-six years old, she left home:

> It was desperately hard to leave Father and Clara in order to come out
> to a totally strange place. I tried my hardest not to cry before them, but
> as the time of departure began to approach I found it growing more and
> more difficult to restrain myself, especially when Clara began to cry, too,
> then it was really hopeless. Poor little Father seemed to feel badly, too,

and the whole business was perfectly horrible to me. I wanted to cry hard whenever I spoke to anyone and yet at the same time I wanted to refrain from showing my feelings too plainly.

Isabel accompanied a weeping, despondent Jean to the train station, and with Jean's personal maid, Anna Sterritt, in tow, secured their luggage and saw them off safely on the 11:40 a.m. train. The sadness of the scene deeply affected Isabel, who called it "heart stretching to have her so & to see her go." Father and sister did not accompany Jean and Isabel to the station, choosing instead to remain at home. Despite her hysterics before Jean's departure and her tears that afternoon, Clara quickly recovered and performed that evening for an audience in Irvington, New York. Her little sister would be a resident at Hillbourne Farms for fifteen months.

Encouraged by Clara's visit two days after her arrival, Jean entered the sanitarium with the best of intentions, determined to be a good patient. For the first time in years, she finally had hope: "I began this morning by obeying carefully every one of Dr. Hunt's instructions, namely to stay out of my room half an hour before going to work and of taking a bath & cold shower. The latter he wants me to take every day instead of every-other-day as I have been doing. I walked half an hour in the bright, cold air & I am sure it is good." Yet the routine quickly became stultifying: "Today nothing of importance has occurred—Life wanders on its way pretty regularly up here." A highly intelligent, formal, and assertive woman, Jean chafed at the leaden pace and close supervision she was forced to endure. Coming from an indulgent life, she found the adjustment to the strict regime nearly impossible. Every morsel of food and exchange with other patients was scrutinized and required approval by her doctors. Doctors considered diet to have a direct connection with epilepsy, and they debated the dangers of Jean's eating fish in the evening and encouraged her to eat milk toast and cereal instead of eggs. Lard was feared and salt entirely banned.

Despite Jean's best efforts to follow the regime, she continued to have seizures. After a difficult day on December 8, 1906, when she awakened feeling ill but decided against sending for her doctor only to suffer a grand mal seizure at eight-thirty (she would not be fully conscious until nine o'clock), doctors began to consider a much more radical course of treatment. Sadly, Jean blamed herself for the severity of the attack, attributing it to "my own stubbornness and unwillingness to send for Dr. Sharp. He might have warded it off again, but there is no use in discussing the possibilities, now. The deed is at present in the past and I can only hope to control myself more sensibly in the future." While Jean had been dosed with bromides for years, the next day Dr. Hunt spoke with her about trying "a certain kind of hyperdermic." Dr. Sharp, Hillbourne's director, was convinced that Jean's epilepsy was the result of poor circulation, and he thought his "hyperdermic" might prove successful. He did, however, want to hear back from Dr. Peterson first on the subject. Dr. Peterson must have answered affirmatively to Dr. Sharp's inquiry because on December 16 Jean had her first treatment.

> I dreamed last night of Dr. Sharp and of his being in my room & attending to me. As soon as I sat up to eat my breakfast I began to have many and long absent-minded turns, so that as soon as Anna returned from her own breakfast I sent her to get Dr. Sharp. It was then about eight o'clock & by half past eight he gave me my first hyperdermic in my shoulder. He froze the shoulder first, but it was fearfully painful & ached all day long. In the course of the day I had three injections and at one time—last in the afternoon—both the doctor & I thought the danger was over, but that proved to be a mistake, because just after I had finished my supper—in bed—I had the attack. . . . It was a distressing and monotonous day.

Jean was no better the next day, receiving an injection in her leg early in the morning and another at eleven o'clock: "a pretty violent injection in my hip which made me jump." Despite her discomfort, Jean was grateful that at least she "didn't have to have the soap & water injection to move the bowels that had been given me yesterday." The painful treatments failed to produce a cure.

In January 1907, after having been gone from 21 Fifth Avenue for nearly three months, Jean made a startlingly candid assessment of her family's mind-set concerning her absence and her feelings toward them:

> I had often felt that it would be a relief to the family to have me out of the way, because I often caused trouble by being unmanageable when I was ill, etc. I laid no blame on Father or Mother and I said quite recently I had begun to have the above feeling less because of his &

Clara's sweetness that is true, but still, while I know that neither one of them would admit being glad to have me away & therefore relieved of the presence of an ill person, I am sure that they must feel so. That is in no way against them, it is only absolutely human. I don't for a minute believe that I was sent out here for any such reason, but since it is better for me to be here it at the same time must be a relief to them. Also the idea that they miss me is absurd! Clara's interests are too absolutely different for us to be necessary to one another even if we are fond of each other & Father can't possibly find any entertainment or interest in me. I am sure he is fond of me but I don't believe that he any more than Clara, really misses me. It seems a heartless thing to say, but now that I am accustomed to this place, I don't really miss either of them. I far more often feel a desire to see Father, than I do to see Clara, which is only right & natural. I do often have a sort of hunger to get hold of him & hug him, but if I were to say I missed him or Clara steadily I should be lying. I love both of them devotedly, but my love seems to be of a curiously passive sort. When I am with people that I am fond of, I grow more & more so, but when I leave then I often go days without even thinking of them!

By this point, Jean was having "two or three petits mals per day." Rebelling against all the restrictions she was supposed to follow, she defiantly ordered three pounds of triple vanilla chocolate from Maillard's chocolate shop in New York City, followed by a second order for five pounds ten days later. Further aggravating her, patients were only allowed to eat in pairs, because doctors believed that an increase of the number of diners might cause nervousness and excitability that would negatively affect their health. Jean objected to what she regarded as a specious rule, because she wanted to eat with two of her fellow patients, women with whom she had become friendly, but in the end Dr. Sharp overruled her.

On another occasion, Dr. Sharp demanded that Jean's maid accompany her when she left the grounds to play squash at a local club, despite her being part of a larger group where there were other women present. Mercifully for her, her doctors were convinced that physical activity and movement would have a beneficial effect on her illness, and it was recommended that she engage in up to five hours of exercise per day. Thirty-two kinds of exercise were available, including lawn tennis, medicine ball, croquet, tetherball, and riding. Patients could go boating and canoeing at a reservoir within walking distance. A fierce competitor, Jean did not take losing well. On one occasion while playing squash, she struck her male opponent with her racket after he had won a play: "Of course, the minute I had done it, I realized what a disgusting thing I had done and apologized."

In winter, Jean was allowed to ski, skate, toboggan, and sled. In search of additional activity, she asked her father to have her beloved horse, Scott, sent to her. To her joy, Scott soon appeared, and because she was no longer allowed to ride horseback, Twain purchased a carriage for her to ride in. Jean had her driver, George O'Connor, regularly take her around the countryside on carriage rides. Her dream was that someday her disease might be either cured or stabilized so that she could live independently. She also wanted to earn her own living in order not to have to rely upon her father for financial support. To that end, Hillbourne boasted impressive facilities for leatherwork, metalwork, wood carving, basket weaving, rug and tapestry weaving, pottery and clay modeling, printing, bookbinding, and stained-glass work. The good doctors of Hillbourne Farms sanctioned Jean's continuing her wood carving, and on January 30, 1907, she was thrilled to receive a letter congratulating her on becoming "a professional member of the National Society of Craftsmen!"

## 8

Although Isabel had certainly gained a measure of relief at no longer having to be Jean's primary caregiver, she still had Charlotte Teller Johnson to fret over, and her terrible anxiety about establishing a permanent place in Twain's life was heightened by Twain's continuing attachment to Charlotte.

Twain and Charlotte had maintained their correspondence over the summer of 1906, and he had become an ardent advocate of her writing. In June he wrote Clara a "special letter," urging her to accept Charlotte's forthcoming invitation to dinner, even though he openly acknowledged his daughter's dislike for Charlotte. Twain was convinced that Charlotte was a great talent, and even the reluctant Isabel regarded her play *Mirabeau* as a "prodigious piece of work and a remarkable one." But by the end of June, Isabel had convinced herself that Charlotte was endangering Twain's health: "He is often animated by a devastating something in these days—a Something destroying his peace of mind—The drama of life I suppose it is—Charlotte Teller."

In July Twain journeyed to the city to meet with Joseph Sears, the president and manager of Appleton and Company, a New York publishing firm. Twain apparently persuaded Sears to publish Charlotte's book manuscript *The Cage,* and on July 10 he gleefully wrote Isabel, telling her that the evening before he had made Charlotte "one of the happiest persons in America" when he informed her that Sears would publish her novel and that the serial rights would be sold to the magazine that made the best offer. Isabel expressed her feelings about Charlotte's publishing triumph in her journal shortly after receiving Twain's news. Her entry is rife with references to Charlotte, describing her rival's manipulation and control over Twain.

It is only by means of fertilization that any best in us can be brought to full flower & fruit; & unlike the growing plants we can partake of the fertilization of many minds—Utterly under the power of one mind or personality, we can be drawn away from it by a counter force of mind or personality, & our malleability is wonderful & beautiful: Being drawn away from one influence does not mean that we are dead to that influence; if we are, in a measure, balanced, it must mean the better perceptions of the power & benefit of that influence. & the preparation within us to receive even greater good from it.

When Isabel returned to New York in October, she believed the time had come for her to use her "counter force of mind" and wield her influence to draw Twain away from Charlotte. Thanks to Albert Bigelow Paine and his propensity to gossip, she would have the perfect opportunity. Just four days after she, Twain, and Jean had moved back to the city, on October 22, a Miss Doty from Number 3 Fifth Avenue (Charlotte's address) came to call. Miss Doty was greatly displeased when Twain declined her visit and refused to grant her permission to publish the stories that he told when he had dined at Number 3. After Miss Doty's huffy departure, Isabel informed Twain that Paine had told her rumors were circulating about his relationship with Charlotte. Twain immediately sent for his comely neighbor, whereupon he "repeated the gossip to the one gossiped about." Charlotte demanded to know who had told him. Twain sent for Isabel, who confirmed that a member of the Players Club had asked Paine about Twain's relationship with her. Although Charlotte tried to dismiss the incident as idle chatter, Twain was alarmed that propriety had been breached and asked Charlotte if she would be willing to move away from Fifth Avenue, a rather melodramatic response considering that he already had a single woman living in his home.

Charlotte, outraged by Twain's request, abruptly declined. The next day Isabel rejected Charlotte's request to come to Number 3 to speak privately with her. On October 24, Charlotte visited Twain again to discuss the matter, and Isabel "gave what I dared" (details of the gossip) to the enraged Charlotte. Later that same day, Charlotte sent Twain a message telling him that she had contacted Sears and asked him not to print Twain's foreword to *The Cage*.

In the spring of 1907, Charlotte again demanded a meeting with Twain and Isabel; Twain ordered Isabel to see what she wanted. Isabel did as requested and went to Number 3 Fifth Avenue. An angry Charlotte told Isabel that Miss Doty had informed her that Isabel had said Charlotte was "an adventurer & planning to marry Mr. Clemens." Isabel's reaction to this news was to laugh "with relief & amusement over the impossibility of such a thing." A "grey and savage-looking" Charlotte was furious at Isabel's reaction, and when Isabel turned to leave she swore: "I'll get even with you for this!" Clearly Isabel proved the willing messenger for Paine's gossip, likely thinking that it could be used for her advantage, but then, the messenger's fate is often one that is unenviable.

Twain and Charlotte's relationship was finished. Charlotte never saw Twain again, although she made a few attempts to reconnect with him, on one occasion asking if he would speak at a benefit, an invitation he refused. Nearly two decades later, in the foreword to a privately printed volume containing Twain's personal correspondence with her, Charlotte disingenuously claimed that she had had no idea that Twain had met with Joseph Sears, and she vehemently denied charges of opportunism in the very edition of letters intended to parlay her correspondence with Twain into profit.

Twain's response to the ending of his relationship with Charlotte and seeing his weeping daughter leave home was to escape. He began planning a trip to Egypt with his old friend Leigh Hunt. Isabel was "stunned" by Twain's announcement and confided to her journal, "I am desolated." Hunt told Twain he could take anyone he wanted with him, and he chose Ralph W. Ashcroft, the treasurer of the Plasmon Company of America, and Joseph Twichell. Isabel would have to remain in New York "at this base of action." A few days later Twain suffered a sudden bout of bronchitis, and an enormously relieved Isabel was "so glad—So selfishly glad" that Twain had to cancel his trip. Instead of sailing down the Nile, Twain contented himself playing billiards with Paine on his new Brunswick-Balke-Collender Company "Warwick" model billiard table, an early Christmas present from Henry Rogers. He hosted various dinners, including a "buck dinner" in early November for Thomas Bailey Aldrich, William Dean Howells, Andrew Carnegie, and Colonel Harvey, and listened to Isabel play the Aeolian.

The cumulative emotional toll of the previous six months finally caught up with an exhausted Isabel, and she departed for Hartford on November 24 for a two-week rest cure. She returned on December 10 to an empty house, as Twain had left for Washington, D.C., with Paine in tow, dressed in white sartorial splendor, to lobby for a new copyright law. He explained to Jean that the trip was all for her and Clara's sakes because of his concern about their future income. On December 12, Twain returned to New York, and an emotional Isabel declared in her daily reminder that while he could go away from her, she would "not go away from him again unless he sends me."

## 9

Over the winter, Twain had been lobbied by Paine to include him in his estate planning. The various changes Twain made in response to Paine were guaranteed to inflame all parties. A copy of a document authorized by Twain, dated December 10, 1906, states his expressed desire that the autobiography be edited and prepared for publication by Paine and, most strikingly, appointing him as the official "Editor and Executor of my literary remains, it being understood such executorship shall not interfere with the collection & publication of a volume of my letters by my daughter, Clara, and Isabel V. Lyon, the said Isabel V. Lyon to have ten percent of the royalty returns of such book." While this document was certain to overjoy Paine and to reassure Isabel, it was highly unlikely to please Clara. Not entirely coincidentally, just three days after this document was written, Paine moved into 21 Fifth Avenue.

Now, in addition to acting as Twain's real estate agent (conveniently locating him as his neighbor in Redding, Connecticut), Paine could ostensibly assist Isabel in caring for Twain and act as his live-in billiards partner. Of course, Paine's decision to move out of the home he shared with his wife and three daughters had more to do with ensuring his own financial future than with any altruistic motives, and Mrs. Paine was openly displeased about her husband's new living arrangements.

Four days before Christmas, Twain announced his latest plan for an adventure to Isabel, and it proved to be the perfect present. The two would sail to Bermuda in January and take Twichell with them. This proposed vacation surely displeased Paine, who wanted to keep his quarry within easy reach. An elated Isabel and Twain spent a cozy Christmas together. Jean was in residence at Katonah and, after a quick visit that morning, Clara chose to spend the day with the Gilders. On Christmas Day, Twain confided to Isabel that he had asked his lawyer, Samuel M. Gardenhire, to draw up the papers making Paine his literary executor. Isabel, perhaps sensing that Paine's reach was extending too far into her territory, delicately demurred, contending "that isn't the place for AB. & C.C. would not wish him to occupy it—so he will be surprised to learn of an annulment of that situation." In taking sides Isabel created an in-house enemy, and Paine would not forget or forgive what she had done. The next day Gardenhire arrived to make the change. John Larkin, Twain's New York attorney, later arrived to finalize Twain's will, which gave Clara "full authority over all literary remains." Any role Jean might have played in her father's literary estate had been forgotten. Isabel was convinced she had made the right move: "Oh King—you are so wonderful, as you sit in bed leaning on one elbow, & reading the new clause of your will—the clause making C.C. library executrix." The deed was done.

On the morning of January 2, after a flurry of packing, the three travelers set sail on the *Bermudian*. Isabel found the slower pace on board ship most appealing. To occupy himself, Twain had taken portions of his autobiography to edit. In an extended conversation with Isabel on their first full day at sea, he explained his idea of publishing excerpts from the autobiography in future editions of his older works in order to preserve his copyright on them. By this time, Twain's daily stint of autobiography dictations had dramatically decreased and his ebbing recollections had begun to be replaced by commentary about contemporaneous news items; by the spring of 1907, he would be

*Rev. Joseph Twichell and Mark Twain posing for Isabel Lyon en route to Bermuda, on the* Bermudian's *deck, January 2, 1907*

describing the parties he had recently attended. The dictations would continue until 1909; however, 1907 was a watershed year, with Twain recognizing in a March autobiography dictation that he had "completed the only work that was remaining for me to do in this life and that I could not possibly afford to leave uncompleted—my Autobiography. Although that is not finished, and will not be finished until I die, the object which I had in view in compiling it is accomplished: that object was to distribute it through my existing books and give each of them a new copyright life of twenty-eight years." Isabel's appropriate reaction was to call Twain's plan a "scheme" and regret that he had shared it with reporters. She apparently found Twain's monetary interest base and believed it sullied his art.

On board the ship to Bermuda, this bracing talk of posthumous profit whetted Twain's appetite, and on their last day at sea he enjoyed a hearty luncheon of "baked beans & bacon & cabbage & milk," that left him with awful indigestion. For Isabel the voyage was actually a return trip to Hamilton, Bermuda, a place she had visited for the first time eighteen years earlier with the Claghorne family when she was governess to their daughter Juliet. The Bermuda idyll was brief, just four days long, but it proved rejuvenating for both Twain and Isabel. The natural beauty of the island was soothing and Isabel delightedly attended to Twain's every wish, unencumbered by hordes of strangers seeking access to him or by the demands of his two daughters. Twain

*Mark Twain and Isabel Lyon's trip to Bermuda, February 22–April 11, 1908.*
*Left to right: H. H. Rogers, Grace Watson Freeman, Josephine Dodge Bascom Bacon,*
*Mrs. Peck's mother, Elizabeth Wallace, Mark Twain, Mrs. Peck, Isabel Lyon,*
*Zoeth Freeman*

contented himself by complaining about various friends and expressing his impatience with Twichell's deafness. As for the insightful Twichell, Twain's close friend for decades and the minister who had officiated at his wedding to Olivia, he took advantage of the opportunity during a walk with Isabel to give her some subtle advice. Twichell felt that Isabel did far too much for Twain, he told her, saying that made him "lazy." He described the profound effect Olivia had had on "remodeling" his friend over the course of their marriage.

> Of course there couldn't ever be anybody who could Train him so that he wouldn't drop away a little back to his wildnesses, & his strengths—But Mrs. Clemens did more than anyone else in the world could do—Mr. Twichell said that Mr. Clemens was so grateful to Mrs. Clemens, & so humbled because she married him. She was this Great Guiding Star.

In his gentle ministerial way, Twichell was trying to help Isabel realize that lavishing care on Twain was unhealthy for them both, and, more important, to understand that no woman could ever take the place of his friend's departed wife. Isabel rationalized her smothering in her journal, explaining that it was her express responsibility to keep Twain calm: "He mustn't be harassed, he mustn't have unnecessary matters brought to him to fret over, he must be saved in all ways [so] that he can be saved from anxiety—for he has had enough of it in his life." She was also concerned that the stress Twain felt could endanger his health; "I'm worried since once or twice recently he told me of a vertigo that Surged over him because he was harassed. Years ago it happened too; in Hartford, he got up to turn on the gas, & the vertigo that surged up into his brain made him fall on the floor. When he is tired he is so grey—his face is quite without color." Isabel's self-interest, both personal and monetary, was doomed in this environment. Twichell wanted Isabel to understand that the time had come for her to retreat from Twain's life. This would have been best for Isabel and probably for Twain as well. Yet where was Isabel to go? She had no interest in resuming her former capacity as a governess. By this point she had made such a great investment in a presumed future that she could not turn away. The sad truth was that while Isabel could copy down Twichell's words, she was deaf to his message.

Immediately after their return, Twain again threw himself into the social whirl. Between dining with friends, including Helen Keller and Henry Rogers, Twain played ceaseless billiards, some days spending upward of ten hours at the game. Dressed in his white silk coat, made for him at A.A. Vantine's, and smoking constantly, Twain joked that his main partner, Paine, had vastly improved as a steady companion since he had begun swearing. Isabel played the enthusiastic audience, perching on the arm of a red sofa. After she commented on the delectable quality of the smoke from Twain's pipe, he happily gave her her own little meerschaum to smoke along with him, joking, "The secretary can do anything she wants to, provided it's proper." When Katy Leary witnessed Isabel contentedly smoking, she paused aghast at the sight. But then Katy recovered and commented that Isabel might as well enjoy herself, seeing that she had "missed so much." After a lifetime of being in service, Katy knew well what it meant to sacrifice personal pleasures in order to appease one's employer.

Twain's interest and energy for the daily dictations had ebbed, and he busied himself with organizing the autobiography material he wanted printed in the *North American Review.* His winter days stretched long before him and he was often lonely, as his coterie of friends had left town for warmer climes. Isabel scrambled to organize a steady stream of amusements and the two planned what Twain called a "Doe luncheon" for January 14, which included old friends Mrs. Stanchfield, Mrs. Doubleday, Mrs. Collier, and Dorothea Gilder. For his enjoyment as well as theirs, Twain drew pictures of deer for the place cards. Isabel felt a personal sense of failure whenever Twain became restless and bored, and she empathized with his frequent lonesomeness: "When I go to his room to tell him that these people are all otherwise employed—he says 'It doesn't matter' but it does matter; it matters very much indeed."

The pressure of her living situation continued to mount for Isabel, and at the end of January she had a graphic and frightening nightmare, which she referred to as her "earthquake dream end of the world." (She later tried to erase mention of it.)

It was that remark of his which set me dreaming last night & went this way: I'd been dining alone at the Brevoort, & as I started to leave the place, the floors began to heave & slant away up to the night, so that I had to hurry along in the angle made by the meeting of the wall & floor. But I couldn't hurry, for it suddenly became dark—a blue black dark—with flashes of blue light & crashing of falling buildings all about. I got into the street—& leading north was a very narrow path—& up that I flew struggling to get my breath, for the air seemed to be going & terrible gas filled its place—up & the path I went—calling "Oh the King—the King—" (I seemed to know that mother was all right.) & in the blue blackness & the Terrible crashing I saw in the distance the Times Building & the Flat Iron, topple toward Each other—(they alone were white in the Terrible black-ness) & strike each other with a terrific crash & then came blackness again & wakeful I was awake.

Isabel's vision of Armageddon reflected her deepest fears and insecurities. Her failure to find her King in the ruins of New York underscores that on one level she knew that her time with Twain was nearing its end. Yet, again, she refused to heed the message. The one source of security in this menacing darkness is her mother, Isabel's one constant in terms of love and acceptance. With her dream world in ruins, feeling attacked on all sides and with her King lost, her year had the bleakest of beginnings.

Isabel was not the only member of the household having visions. In January, Twain visited two psychics to have his future read. On the twenty-third, he sat with a clairvoyant by the name of Professor Bert Rees, who informed his skeptical client that he would live to be "98 years ten months & 2 days old." Twain responded that he'd be willing to "Swap off some of those years & months & days." Three days later, he visited "Fletcher," a palmist, who assured him he would reach the century mark and advised him that he should hang on to two investments "connected with the Ground," for at least two years. Twain received Fletcher's savvy instruction in high humor, thankfully disavowing any intention of following his advice.

The circle of people around the King shrank that winter with the departure of Paine in February to spend four months researching Twain's early years out west. Clara spent six weeks on the road, resuming her singing tour on February 19, with stops including Elmira, Hartford, and Utica, and concluding the tour at the end of March. When she returned home, Isabel marveled at her improved spirits: "She is a made over creature with happiness & Success & music running rampantly through her veins. What a creature she is. & how beautiful." Clara believed that her career was finally proving to be successful. However, while she might have triumphed in terms of personal esteem and confidence building, financially the tour was a loss. Twain, normally hypersensitive around money matters, when told by Isabel that the deficit for Clara's tour was at least $2,500, resignedly responded that the bills should be paid and that Clara could go ahead with her plan to continue touring for another month. While scraping away at his face during his morning shave, he rationalized the tour's cost to Isabel saying that Clara was "learning her trade. & the only way she can learn it is to know how to sail her ship in adverse winds—he said that if she had come home with twenty thousand dollars in her purse it would not be of the value to her that this experience has been; the big enthusiastic audiences are not the ones that are of greatest help—but the smaller cold audiences that you win over are the ones that help you most." Twain's generosity meant Clara's immediate departure, and she spent her time that spring traveling from place to place, occasionally visiting Jean in Katonah.

After a second lightning-quick visit with Isabel to Bermuda in mid-March, where they spent only one day ashore before returning to New York, Twain displayed more typical wallet-tightening behavior in his bargaining for a summer lease on a home in Tuxedo Park, New York, a resort community for the wealthy on the Ramapo River approximately thirty miles from Manhattan. Twain refused to return to desolate Dublin, New Hampshire. After an extended negotiation with William Voss, the owner of the Tuxedo residence, the cost of the lease was reduced from $2,400 to $1,500. As summer approached, Isabel was kept busy managing the household at 21 Fifth Avenue as well as organizing their upcoming stay in Tuxedo and planning the construction of the Redding house. She noted in her daily reminder how much of her time was spent trying to appease the needy members of the Clemens family:

> Here am I missing the Sweetest of all Sweet Chroniclings—the daily life of the King. But I have been so busy, for there is . . . Santa to love & be with when she was here & do for—& Jean to be anxious over & to help if I can, & her doctors to see, & the King's social life to look after. for in these days he is very [crossed out: lonely] & reaches out for people— & people he must have—so now I'm planning parties for him.

Disinterested in the dictations, personal friends away, daughters gone, and his billiards partner absent, the easily bored Twain determinedly set about creating a set of new relationships to occupy his time. He had always delighted in the company of children and in his autobiography openly mourned the maturation of his daughters. He claimed that one day when Olivia was still alive, the two had discussed how their children had been lost from their lives forever—"as little children." He made it clear that he preferred his daughters as girls, rather than as the estranged, ill, and disagreeable women they had become. Twain reflected that after Olivia's death he felt a terrible loneliness that his daughters could not alleviate, disingenuously excusing them as being "busy with their studies and their labors." He found his salvation with the realization that he needed grandchildren: "I had reached the grandpapa state of life; and what I lacked and what I needed, was grandchildren. . . . In grandchildren I am the richest man that lives today: for I select my grandchildren." And that was just what Twain did, beginning in December 1905, when he met fourteen-year-old Gertrude Natkin as he was leaving Carnegie Hall. He and Gertrude struck up a friendship, and Isabel jealously noted in March 1906 that before Twain went onstage to speak to an audience of "Y.M.C.A. men" at the Majestic Theater the only thing he appeared to care about was whether Gertrude would be there to see him.

The two regularly visited and corresponded, and when Gertrude turned sixteen in April 1907, she was crestfallen to learn from Twain that he had decided that this birthday marked her departure from childhood and therefore she had to exit from her "grandfather's" life. The under-occupied Twain, however, wasted no time in locating several replacements. Over the next three years, he developed friendships with a dozen little girls (including Paine's oldest daughter, Louise) whom in 1908 he nicknamed Angelfish, and who had their own club manifesto and angelfish pins. (Clara was also given a pin.) He apparently seized upon the name Angelfish because he liked the idea of having a bright and colorful aquarium of girls and because he had met several of them while vacationing in Bermuda. He composed approximately three hundred letters during this period, and the last letter of his life was to thirteen-year-old Helen Allen, written while returning from what would be his final trip to Bermuda. Twain delighted in the innocence of these little girls, and they proved deeply comforting at a time when he was often lonely and depressed.

Isabel's reaction to Twain's Angelfish friendships was mixed. While she definitely preferred that he spend his time with females who were not her rivals, it fell to her to organize the logistics of the girls' travels to visit Twain and to entertain them while they were in residence. In August 1907, Dorothy Quick came with her mother to visit Twain in Tuxedo for a few days. Upon her arrival, after a seventy-mile car journey from her home in New Jersey, Twain swept his pretty little angelfish off to tea at an acquaintance's home, while Isabel was left to serve tea to Mrs. Quick and awkwardly engage her in small talk. It was with considerable relief that Isabel "dispatch[ed] those people [Mrs. Quick and her driver] off to Plainville again." She was equally pleased four days later when she saw eleven-year-old Dorothy off at the train station with her new turtle, named Lyon, to return to her mother in New Jersey.

Isabel's anxiety about keeping Twain occupied abated in early May when he received a cable from his old acquaintance the novelist Whitelaw Reid, former editor of the *New York Tribune* and current ambassador to Great Britain, forwarding a message from Lord Curzon, Oxford University's chancellor, inviting him to receive an honorary doctor of letters (D.Litt) degree at the end of June. An awed Isabel pro-

*Mark Twain and Dorothy Quick, July 1907*

nounced the award "too splendid," and an ecstatic Twain immediately began pouring his energy into planning his triumphant return to England.

Four days after receiving the notification, Twain and Isabel relocated to Tuxedo. Twain was most pleased with his choice of residence for the summer, and on his first afternoon Mr. and Mrs. Harry Rogers, the son and daughter-in-law of Henry Rogers, held an afternoon reception to honor him. Isabel marveled at Twain's enthusiasm for his new surroundings: "He is in love with Tuxedo—Today as well as yesterday when we were driving around making calls, he was like a young Creature who had been caged for years." For the same reason that Twain found Tuxedo appealing, namely its bountiful social distractions and the plethora of wealthy, well-known people who welcomed him into their midst, Isabel was dissatisfied. She did not like having to spend her summer among New York society, forced to abide by all the rules demanded by that elite stratum and constantly reminded of her inferior status.

Mr. Clemens is carried away by the loveliness of this place—He says he has never seen so beautiful a place in all his travels. To me it is the expression of artificiality & great wealth. And I'm beginning to feel a hampering—a great quiet longing for Dublin & the upper pasture & the road leading to the Raynor Cottage. There I was almost-a-free creature of the hills—Here I am a gloved & card-cased thing.

Despite the snobbishness of Tuxedo, Isabel believed that her relationship with Twain was strengthening, and she was allowed extraordinary access to him in all his most revealing moments. At the beginning of June in the early morning, Twain slipped up to her room wearing only his "silk underclothes . . . such a beautiful man he is" to share with her an invitation he had received from Mary and Harry Rogers. More significantly, shortly after he and Isabel had arrived in Tuxedo, an astonishing legal document was drawn and witnessed by Ralph S. Hull, an attorney, giving Isabel complete control over Twain's affairs and the authority to manage his property:

POWER OF ATTORNEY

S.L. CLEMENS

to

S.V. LYON

May 7, 1907

Know all men by these presents, that I, Samuel L. Clemens, of the city and state of New York, have made, constituted and appointed, and by these presents do make, constitute and appoint Isabel V. Lyon of the same city, my true and lawful attorney for me and in my name, place and stead, to exercise a general supervision over all my affairs and to manage all my property both real and personal and all matters of business relating thereto; to lease, sell, and convey any and all real property wheresoever situated which may now or which may hereafter at any time belong to me . . . to make repairs to any buildings thereon . . . to demand, collect and receive all dividends, interest and moneys due and payable to or become due and payable to me; to satisfy and discharge all mortgages; to sell, assign and transfer any and all stocks, bonds and mortgages belonging to or which at any time belong to me . . . to draw checks or drafts upon any banks, banker or trust Company. . . . In witness thereof I have hereunto set my hand and seal this 7th day of May, 1907 Samuel L. Clemens

In presence of:

(signed) SAMUEL L. CLEMENS.

(signed) Ralph S. Hull.

Isabel now held the financial reins for all the Clemenses firmly within her gloved hands. There is no record that Twain discussed this document with either of his daughters before drawing it up to be signed, and they go unmentioned in it. Isabel's lot improved even more a month later when, on June 8, the same day Twain sailed to England, he informed her that he was giving her a parcel of land and a house from his Redding, Connecticut, property. Eureka! Isabel's dreams of financial solvency and security had finally been realized. The demon of Calamity appeared to have been vanquished.

## 10

Good fortune should have been Isabel's constant companion during the spring of 1907—a welcome friend offering a rosy future filled with security and plenitude. Yet by the third week of June, she presciently scribbled in her daily reminder, "It is going to be a Strange Summer." She seemed to sense that something was in the air, something intangible and unsettling, even though many of her greatest desires seemed to have been realized: a future 10 percent share of the royalties resulting from coediting Twain's letters, financial control over his affairs, property ownership in Redding, and an apparent rapprochement with Clara.

But Isabel's uneasy premonition proved true just days later, on July 1, with a single question asked by a curious reporter at the Halifax Hotel in Nova Scotia, where she and Clara were staying on their first vacation together. The reporter had received a telegram from *The New York Herald,* a large-distribution newspaper based in New York City, "linking the name of the King with that of his secretary." Shocked by the reporter's inquiry, Isabel tartly commented, "the King would be as pained as his secretary to hear of any such report." Isabel's adamant denial only served to whet the reporter's appetite for sensational news. Three days later the *Herald* claimed that there would be a marriage. The following day it ran Twain's emphatic refutation, sent from London. "I have not known, and shall never know," Twain thundered, "any one who could fill the place of the wife I have lost. I shall never marry again." Halifax was intended to be a stopover on an excursion to Newfoundland. The reporter's question and the subsequent newspaper report, however, halted the women's journey, and five days later Isabel noted that the two had "decided to go home by rail," forgoing the remainder of the trip. In Boston, they parted.

Who could have shared such incendiary gossip with the *Herald*? Two possibilities came immediately to Isabel's mind. Albert Bigelow Paine, alone in New York City at the time, was a likely candidate. Paine and she had been jockeying for months to win Twain's favor, and while they had not yet suffered a total break in their working relationship, fissures had surfaced due to Isabel's persuading Twain not to name Paine as his literary executor. Paine had engineered Charlotte Teller Johnson's banishment when Twain heard his gossip linking the two together and perhaps he thought he would repeat the same ruse. (Paine may have suspected that the bright, literary Charlotte might have designs on becoming Twain's executrix.) Another likely suspect is Charlotte herself. Her last furious words to Isabel at the end of May were "I'll get even with you for this!" Perhaps she had figured out a way to settle the score. Years later, Isabel told Samuel and Doris Webster that she thought the rumormonger had been Charlotte, that Charlotte had initially spread the story that Isabel and Twain were intending to marry; apparently Charlotte then made her tale more salacious by telling mutual friends that the two were *not* going to wed, instead implying that they were having an affair.

Ironically, a little over a week before the reporter's inopportune question, Isabel and Clara were having apprehensions about Twain's behavior in England. When he was notified about the Oxford honor at the beginning of May, Twain decided "Colonel Harvey is the mensch to go." Although by the time of the voyage Ralph Ashcroft accompanied the honoree instead. Paine had lobbied hard to be the one to go along with Twain on his triumphant journey, and as he was the King's personally selected biographer, his desire to accompany his subject made eminent good sense. Yet Paine suffered from a speech impediment, which Twain apparently considered a handicap in dealing with the British press. "It was a blow to Paine" to be usurped by Ashcroft, and he believed Isabel had promoted Ashcroft over him.

On the day of Twain's sailing, Paine exacted his measure of revenge. Distraught over Twain's leaving, an emotionally overcome Isabel had already returned from the pier and was "lying weak and sick" at home. Paine hastened to 21 Fifth Avenue from the dock to tell her that he had seen the King being roughly treated by "a hideous lot of people & a man 1/2 drunk threw his arm around the King's neck & said he'd known him 40 years ago." Paine's upsetting news had its desired effect. "I do hope Ashcroft will brace up & take care of him," Isabel fretted, "It's all wrong to let him go off that like—He is going for honors, but he ought to go with the proper protection too."

Despite Paine's alarming report, Twain managed to arrive safely in England. Shortly after his landing, to the consternation of Clara and Isabel, disconcerting stories surfaced in the New York newspapers that he had strolled through the lobby of his London hotel wearing only his bathrobe and slippers out into Dover Street to a public bathhouse. Twain " 'scares us to death' with his inclination for the unconventional," Isabel fussed. With only Ashcroft to advise him, Isabel was convinced Twain would be prone to do "thoughtless things" that would result in his being "severely criticized" in the press. Clara was so concerned about the situation that she telegraphed her father: "REMEMBER THE PROPRIETIES—AM ANXIOUS." A defiant Twain cabled back: "THEY ALL PATTERN AFTER ME."

The Oxford ceremony took place on June 25; the other honorees included General William Booth, Auguste Rodin, Camille Saint-Saëns, and Rudyard Kipling, who was further honored in December of that year with the Nobel Prize in literature. The day after the ceremony, Twain deliberately taunted Clara in a cable: "TRY NOT TO BE JEALOUS. FATHER." Isabel chose to interpret his message as representative of a "gay little rivalry between them." Clara returned the volley with an answering cablegram: "MORE WORRIED THAN EVER DOCTOR, REMEMBER THE PROPRIETIES." Having a distracting newspaper story linking him romantically to his secretary after being fêted by the cream of British aristocracy and receiving the greatest honor of his career must have been viewed by Twain and his daughters as a humiliating social embarrassment.

Twain bid an emotional farewell to England and sailed into New York Harbor on July 22, six hours earlier than expected, on the Commodore ship *Minnetonka.* Standing at the end of the pier, Isabel spied her King on the lower deck at the end of a long line of passengers. She was relieved by his safe homecoming, and the next day the two left New York City for the peace and privacy of Tuxedo Park. Despite Isabel's naïve hope that her relationship with Twain would be left unaffected by the very public exposure of their connection, she could not escape the fallout from the *Herald*'s report.

Within a week of his return home, Twain asked Isabel if she had

*Mark Twain receiving his honorary doctorate of letters
degree at Oxford University, June 1907*

heard anything from Charlotte Teller Johnson. Isabel responded that
she had not, but that she blamed Charlotte as the newspaper's source for
the story about their supposed upcoming nuptials. Twain responded
that he suspected the same, and that they could count on hearing "more
yet from that devil." Even while dismissing the gossip, Twain insisted
on taking a Miss Herrick with them as a chaperone when he and Isabel
went for carriage rides. Twain remarked that he liked "the 'protection'
of it," much to Isabel's dismay. Although the notion of these two need-
ing to be overseen by a chaperone is ludicrous, it is worth contemplat-
ing why Twain felt it was necessary. He may have been troubled about
public opinion, his daughters' reaction, or Isabel's true intentions.
Whatever his concerns, Isabel chafed under the constraint and complained in her daily reminder that a subsequent drive the two had taken
with Miss Herrick was a "very tiny drive—a thin drive you may say, for

the talk was that kind." Isabel need not have feared, as the chaperoning did not last long. Just a month later, at the end of August, she exulted: "It was Sweet to drive along these lovely roads beside him. Sweet to have him Silent & Smoking. He was tired—the steady roar of the luncheon table exhausted him as I knew it would. & as soon as we reached home he went to bed & after my solitary dinner, I found him lying with his beautiful feet uncovered, & reading Macaulay's life & letters."

Despite returning to their companionable drives together, a new distance began to insert itself into their interactions, and over the course of the next few months Isabel would bemoan the absence of the King she knew and loved. This change in their personal intimacy was underscored in January 1908, when she noted with surprise that in conversing with Twain during dinner "he was very Sweet, very delicate, & like his old self before warring outside things came in to harshen him up— & make him rude to me."

### 11

An additional worry for Isabel was the continuous starting and stopping of the construction of Twain's Redding home. After approving spending for the planning of the estate in August 1906, just five months later Twain panicked and halted all efforts when he learned that the *North American Review* was reducing its total number of pages for each issue. He feared that this reduction might lower the amount he would be compensated for the twenty-five installments from his autobiography, and doubted that he would be able to support the expense of construction. Nevertheless, four days later, on January 20, 1907, he felt confident enough to sign a construction contract after receiving a personal visit from Colonel Harvey, who pledged that his friend would be paid $2,000 a month "until the one hundred thousand words [of the autobiography] have been turned in, & that will provide the needed amount to build the house at Redding."

Clara accompanied Isabel on the train to Redding for the informal groundbreaking in May 1907, but had turned back due to spring rain. Isabel continued with H. A. Lounsbury and Mr. Turner, two construction contractors, and met a group at the site consisting of John Howells, Paine, and William R. Coe (husband of Mai Rogers, Henry Rogers's daughter). After an elegant luncheon prepared by the Brevoort

Hotel and delivered to the site, each person had in turn dug a small shovelful of earth; then, to Isabel's surprise, "they poured in some whiskey—I wonder why?"

While Isabel welcomed their impending move to the country, the King was now less sure about living so far away from friends and society. Possibly the idea of being trapped in a grand hall with the servile and high-strung Isabel constantly fussing over him gave Twain serious pause. In August 1907, just a month after his return from England, construction of the Redding house was halted at his order. Ever sensitive to public opinion, he may also have been reluctant to contribute to the possible perception that he was constructing a home where he would live openly with his mistress. He realized that it was highly unlikely that Clara would ever opt to spend much time with him and that Jean's illness might prevent her from ever returning home. Twain directed Isabel to contact John Howells to determine if there was a way to abandon the project without losing money. After numerous phone exchanges with Howells, the upshot was that the house would have to be finished for rent or sale, otherwise "the loss would be a big one, fully fifteen thousand dollars, or half of the price of the finished house."

Twain's decision not to live in the house meant that Isabel's rosy future was threatened, and her health spiraled downward in consequence. While grimly attending to the Angelfish Twain kept inviting to Tuxedo Park to keep him company, she suffered from frequent headaches that rendered her nearly insensible. In Isabel's view, the King's health (and hers) would best be served if the Angelfish were banned. Twain, on the other hand, in the midst of a social afternoon's discussion about the pleasures of hobbies, gleefully announced to Isabel and assorted guests that his intention was to collect schoolgirls. By February 1908 Isabel resignedly observed, "The King's interest in children increases—his interest in little girls. He can spend hours & hours with them & finds them such good company." Apparently Twain was finding Isabel a bit of a bore compared to the fun he was having with his bevy of little girls.

Declining both physically and emotionally from the strain of trying to keep Twain and his Angelfish amused, as well as from uncertainty about her future, by the end of August Isabel felt "savagely ill" with "crashing, crackling pains in the back of my head." After suffering from a painful bout of "neuritis in my left neck & arm & shoulderblade," earlier in the summer, she began to rely upon the painkiller Phenacatine (commonly spelled phenacetin) for relief. Phenacetin had become available in 1887 and was widely used as an analgesic. Her health and her utility to Twain were always Isabel's twin worries, and she was very much aware of his harsh views concerning illness and his staff's concomitant usefulness to him.

On one occasion during the summer of 1907 when Twain witnessed Isabel feeling poorly, he expressed his "entire dissatisfaction in my condition." Visions of his casual suggestion of discarding of Teresa Cherubini when she was sick must have passed through Isabel's head, and she often wrote about having to continue her duties despite feeling unwell. In January 1908, Isabel wrote about receiving an irritated message from Twain when she didn't emerge from her bedroom. In a note he gave to Katherine the maid to deliver to her, Twain demanded to know if she was ill. If she was not, she was expected to immediately start telephoning people. Isabel instantly "hopped out of bed, & put on a wrapper & a shawl & went down. He was crossish—as the King has never been before—& pounded the bed."

Isabel would have to wait five long nerve-wracking months before Twain would finally begin to "feel that he wants to live" in his new Redding home. Her dream of having a home of her own and of having Twain to herself might be realized after all. Certainly his changed attitude brought a measure of relief; however, as might be expected, the planning and construction of the house provided its own drama. On a quick trip to Redding in June 1907 to check on the progress, Isabel found to her horror that someone had moved its location. She found the change unacceptable and immediately halted work. She returned to Redding a week later with John Howells, and the two decided that the house had to be moved back to its original site.

Tiptoeing around Clara and Jean's competing needs and egos concerning the size and location of their rooms within the new residence also took its toll. Although the amount of time Clara had actually logged under her father's roof during the previous few years had been minuscule, it would have been a fatal mistake to infer that a smaller room would be acceptable. An alarmed John Howells told Isabel that when he had met Clara for dinner to discuss the plans, she had made clear her expectation that a suite of rooms would be installed for her express use. Clara's demands (the second-story bedroom suite, a music room with Japanese burlap and grass cloth for the walls, and a ground-floor wing added for her pleasure, featuring a loggia) resulted in a $4,100 increase in the overall project cost.

Jean, too, was ever sensitive about how her presence would be represented in her father's new home and was quick to find personal slights in the planning efforts. She had initially opposed the entire project because the idea of a country location other than Dublin meant she would no longer be in close proximity to Gerry Brush. However, she gradually warmed up to the idea, and Isabel gladly noted that by spring 1907 she was finally "full of plans for the future home in Redding." Twain's youngest daughter was instantly offended by any indication that she was an afterthought, as she already felt distanced from her father with her self-imposed confinement at Hillbourne Farms. Distressed, she raised objections after seeing from the blueprints that she had been provided with a small bedroom that the maid would have to walk through in order to exit from her quarters. She commented bitterly that neither her father nor her sister had noticed the inconvenience and lack of privacy, and she credited Isabel with correcting the problem.

The turmoil the project generated was reflected in the multiple names suggested for it. Isabel had initially called it Autobiography House, and in March of 1907 the *Sun* newspaper published a clever letter signed by an anonymous "Scrivener" suggesting various sobriquets.

TO THE EDITOR OF THE SUN —

Sir: I notice that Mark Twain is going to build a country house at Redding, Conn. What name will he give it? Will It be "The House of Mirth," or "The House of Seventy Gables," or "Freak House," or "The House with the Green Candles," or "The House of a Thousand Shutters," or "The House on the March," or—maybe somebody else can suggest a better name. A house anywhere along the Sound without an appropriate name isn't a house at all. It is merely a residence. P.S.— What's the matter with "Twain Towers"? He does, doesn't he?

SCRIVENER.
NEW YORK, MARCH 26.

Twain entered the naming fray long enough to change the name from Autobiography House to the (unintentionally) satiric Innocents at

Home. Clara rejected Innocents because of what she perceived as a reference to the Angelfish. Twain sarcastically remarked that the name had to be changed because "the task of providing enough innocence to justify the name fell entirely upon him and proved a burden beyond his strength. None of the other members of the family had any!"

Ultimately Clara had the final say. She christened the residence Stormfield, arguing that it was thanks to the *Harper's Magazine* publication of Twain's essay "Extract from Captain Stormfield's Visit to Heaven" and its accompanying revenue that the house could be completed. (The revenue from "Extract" covered the cost of the additional suite that Clara had demanded for her personal use.) Twain acquiesced; he agreed to calling the house Stormfield because, due to its location at the summit of a hill, the view allowed him to see any approaching storms.

Twain's decision to move to Redding meant that Isabel could actually take possession of the house located on the piece of property that he had given to her. Overjoyed with Twain's gift, an act of rare largess, Isabel understood that this house would afford her and her mother a permanent home. "She could do what she like[d] with it," Twain said in reference to his gift, and while Isabel wished he would officially deed her the property and asked him if he would be willing to do so, he responded, "Nothing needs to be in writing between you and me." It appears though, that at a later date Twain did deed the property to Isabel. Five days after Twain informed her that he was giving her the land and house, Isabel visited Redding and surveyed her assets. Upon entering the two-hundred-year-old farmhouse, she was dismayed to find a dead swallow on the floor. "Poor prisoner—I had a strange little sense of fear."

Shaking off her foreboding, Isabel declared her property "the mos' bes' nize house in the world." The view from the hill was beautiful, and Isabel was "filled with happiness over it—Real happiness." The farmhouse would prove a welcome distraction from Twain's maddening vacillations and his daughters' incessant demands. Over the course of 1907 and 1908, Isabel would happily describe in her daily reminder all the work taking place. In September 1907, she reported that Eugene Adams, who was renovating the farmhouse, and H. A. Lounsbury, in charge of heavy labor, had installed "triple windows" and that "the shingling is 2 parts done & when Adams tore off the plaster from the ceiling in the long room, he revealed what will be a most beautiful oak ceiling, for beams are splendid & the flooring above is a darling color. It is going to be glorious." A wing was added for a new kitchen, and the old kitchen with its big fireplace had been turned into the living room. The farmhouse also boasted a study and an upstairs bedroom, for a total of twelve rooms.

In the midst of all the names being tossed around for Twain's residence, John Howells good-naturedly suggested that an appropriate title for Isabel's abode would be Lyonesse. Isabel appreciated the literary allusion and described Lyonesse as " 'the magic land' that went down into the sea." While the well-intentioned Howells was obviously playing off Isabel's last name, a more disturbing name would have been hard to imagine. According to Arthurian legend, the land Lyonesse reeked of tragedy. In Tennyson's epic poem *Idylls of the King,* Lyonesse rises from the depths of the ocean upon King Arthur's return. It is the location for the final battle between King Arthur and his deceiver Mordred. In the end, the King slays his enemy and Lyonesse sinks once again beneath the moaning ocean waves. Suggesting land appearing and disappearing, and a murderous battle between a King and his betrayer, the nickname for Isabel's new home would prove prophetic.

Clouds began gathering over Stormfield even before its completion, and they arrived in the form of Clara's fury about Isabel's control regarding the decoration and furnishing of the residence. It was obvious to Isabel that her security was fully dependent upon Twain's satisfaction with his future home and his willingness to take possession of it. The stakes were extraordinarily high, as was the pressure for a woman already on the verge of an emotional and physical collapse. Her reaction was to expend all her energy finishing Stormfield and to personally approve every detail. At the beginning of May 1908, Isabel wrote that she had wept for hours due to exhaustion and Clara's criticism:

> Santa misunderstood all my efforts in working over the house—My anxiety over the furnishings, my interest in my search for the right things for the King's house has all been misinterpreted, & the child says I am trying to ignore her. All my effort has been to please her, to keep her from the dreary search of hours & hours to find the right thing, or shape or color. The King has resented my being out of the house so much, until I've told him that I only seem neglectful—& that all my days are only for his interest, & that when he thinks that I am out frolicking, I am only trying to save his money.

Actually, Clara had read Isabel exactly right. While Isabel would not openly admit it, she loved buying all the beautiful, luxurious furnishings for Stormfield as well as for Lyonesse. Her new purchasing power was certainly a welcome change from her days of enviously watching Clara make purchases at Tiffany's or going window-shopping at Schriners jewelry store. Isabel now fancied herself a member of the group of "leisured, urban women who shopped." She had never before experienced the pleasure of having her bankroll equal her taste, and the stores in New York City offered an abundance of goods from which to choose. Stormfield boasted Persian rugs (Khiva and Bokhara), heavy carved furniture, ornate draperies, beautifully upholstered furniture (including a daybed in the library for Twain to lounge upon), and wicker chairs for outdoor seating. John Howells took Isabel to look at gas fixtures at Caldwell and Company, the preeminent designer of lighting fixtures in America. Isabel described Caldwell's as a "wonderful place on 15th Street where they have most exquisite reproductions from all nations. These men (Mr. Von Lossburg among them) spend their lives searching museums & excavations . . . & palaces for the most beautiful, perfect lamps & chandeliers & lanterns—& their place is as comforting—more comforting than a museum."

Paine accompanied her to "Bogagian's" "to look at rugs—& bought one—a Khiva" for Lyonesse. And despite the awkward encounter with the reporter in Halifax, Isabel had not departed Nova Scotia before purchasing an enormous four-posted bed for herself with posts measuring seven and a half feet high that she had had shipped to Redding. As angry as Clara might be, Isabel was determined that Stormfield would be her sole creation, and she would not be deterred from fulfilling what she regarded as her right and responsibility to create a home for the King as well as for herself. Nevertheless, Isabel's turning a deaf ear to Clara's objections would prove dangerous.

Twain had spent the winter and spring of 1908 traveling back and forth to Bermuda, the first trip at the end of January for twelve days with Ashcroft and the second trip with Isabel and Henry Rogers for nearly six weeks (February 22 to April 11). His first visit to his property took place on the same day he moved in—June 18, 1908. He delighted in his new surroundings. His first two guests were Louise Paine, Albert Bigelow Paine's oldest daughter, who lived nearby, and Dorothy Harvey, daughter of Colonel Harvey. Twain's two daughters were absent that day. Twain was openly appreciative of Isabel's efforts,

*Isabel Van Kleek Lyon, ca. 1908–09*

writing Angelfish Dorothy Quick a few days before seeing Stormfield, "Miss Lyon is working very hard, these days, getting the new house up-country ready. . . . She has been at it night and day, the past week, and has gotten all the furniture and the Orchestrelle and a billiard table in, at last."

Isabel had designed a home whose sole purpose was to entertain the King. She chose to believe that if she created a pleasure palace for Twain, he would become so dependent that he would be unable to live without her. The Ayton Castle mantel from the Hartford house was installed in the living room along with the Orchestrelle. The house, designed after an Italian villa, featured on its ground floor a grand hall, a living room, a dining room, a kitchen, a billiard room, Isabel's office, and an outdoor terrace that provided sweeping views of the grounds. The second floor included Twain's master bedroom and bath, Jean's room and bath, Clara's suite, Isabel's bedroom (the room originally meant for Clara, which she had rejected), two guest bedrooms, and servants' rooms. The first-floor billiard room had pictures of Twain's Angelfish hanging on the walls and a Hawaiian koa-wood mantelpiece (a gift from an admirer) with the word "Aloha" carved on its face. Indeed, Stormfield was a grand space, eighteen rooms in all and over 7,600 square feet. A steam generator supplied the heat and an acetylene-gas system provided light. For the vast majority of Americans, this degree of luxury was unimaginable. In 1908, 90 percent of Americans lived without indoor lighting, and indoor plumbing was

*Louise Paine, Mark Twain, and Dorothy Harvey
on Twain's first day at Stormfield*

considered "a pipe dream." Outside the house, under the porte cochere, the closed carriage that Twain's father-in-law had given his daughter and son-in-law on their wedding day nearly forty years earlier stood waiting to receive its passengers. By 1908, the carriage showed its age, as did its owner, and the inside wood was autographed by the hundreds of matches Twain had struck against the varnish to light his cigars.

When Twain took up residence at Stormfield, he declared to Isabel that it was his desire to have one Angelfish under his new roof at all times. Isabel was less than pleased with this aspiration, as it meant an increased workload for her. Clemens's friends found his Angelfish hobby a puzzling, yet harmless, occupation, although Clara had never felt comfortable with her father's attachments to little girls. Nevertheless, Twain took great pleasure in his newest, and youngest, friends.

Despite having finished Lyonesse's renovations, Isabel did not choose to live there. Instead she lived with her King at Stormfield. Her efforts to please brought only a fleeting respite from the external and internal pressures that disturbed her. She concluded at the end of June 1908,

> I shan't ever be able to write any thing again, for all my time—my strength are given over to the finishing & furnishing & installing—the King in this beautiful home. I am savagely interested in it—not tenderly; because although in a way much of it is my creation, I have no sense that any corner of it belongs to me. Not even my own cluttered room.

The pages for the next thirty days in her 1908 daily reminder were left blank.

Twain was so delighted with Stormfield that while sending crowing letters to his friends Howells, Twichell, and Rogers, he unthinkingly

*Mark Twain at Stormfield*

*Mark Twain at Stormfield*

threw gasoline on the fire when he wrote Clara that "the thought of ever going back to that crude and tasteless New York barn, even to stay overnight, revolts me." The "tasteless barn" happened to be the place Clara had personally renovated and decorated. By August, Twain had declared Stormfield his permanent residence.

During the month of September, Isabel was in charge of clearing out the family's remaining possessions from 21 Fifth Avenue. Twain had ended his lease, and the brownstone had been let for five years to a medical doctor who planned to turn Twain's billiard room into his consulting office. Writing down her thoughts in the quiet of a Stormfield evening, Isabel found the "packing & clearing out the dreadful rubbish of many years' accumulating" brought back memories, both pleasant and ill, of her years with the family.

The burden of this house is heavily upon my shoulders. Being on my shoulders it is an alien weight & has all the chances of being shifted to other props. I keep it there rather than in my heart too securely for if it were, or when it is taken from me, all the bleeding heart of me would be torn out with it. It's because I've been down to the N.Y. house working hard all day, & because Paine was there & was sad at leaving it. Sad at seeing the dismantling of the rooms where we've had charming times, & gay times. But for me they have been sadder than gay I think, or more agonizing—for in that house I saw the terrible sorrow & grief of the King, after Mrs. Clemens's death—& I saw the crying rage of servants dismissed by Jean & Clara. I saw Jean in her convulsions. & I saw Clara in her agony & in her illness, & in her strugglings with her career, & in her hates and fierce lovings. And while my heart was full of loving for all of them, there was a long long lack of peace, & the stairs I climbed were often pitifully weary ones—But against it all was the great joy of living close to the King & of learning his ways & his moods. & of holding my spirit arms about him, & of having my life fuller than I thought it could be.

BIDDING FAREWELL to 21 Fifth Avenue meant that a chapter of Isabel's life with Mark Twain had ended. Twain, too, seemed to realize that a fundamental change was taking place, although it had nothing to do with his change of physical address.

"I wish he wouldn't talk quite so often of his death," Isabel wrote. "It is terrible just to think of it. But when he speaks the word, all the world is hung with black, such terrible black & the pillars of the temple are shattered." Mark Twain had become increasingly preoccupied with his demise, only half facetiously complaining to Charlotte Teller Johnson two years earlier that he was tired of being interrupted "every time I try to arrange about my funeral." Isabel panicked whenever Twain brought up the topic: "The King talks so much about his death in these days— [crossed out: His death—what can that mean to those of us who live only as he lives]." Isabel's concern was not unwarranted, as Twain's health was steadily eroding.

Over a year earlier he had begun to lose "track of the hours of the day" and had suffered a number of dizzy spells since then. On multiple occasions when he had overexerted himself, his skin assumed a grayish cast. During a long celebratory evening at the Lotos Club in January 1908, halfway through dinner a visibly tired Twain announced that he was temporarily departing the festivities to take a nap. After dessert was served he returned, feeling refreshed, and gave a brief speech. Two months later, while Twain and Isabel were vacationing in Bermuda, a horrified Isabel found him hunched over the billiard table, where he had been playing with a young German tourist, looking "pale as death." The young man was trying to comfort him by rubbing the back of his head: "[Crossed out: A terrified sickness ran through me, stayed through me & I dragged myself into the room to] I heard . . . him say 'Do you feel better now?' Then the King straightened himself up & said he did, he thought—It had been just a sudden 'crick in his neck,' & the pain . . . is always so acute with him that it makes him weak. [Crossed out: All day my terror did not leave me.] All day I too was weak with the memory of the look on his face."

While Isabel fretted about Twain's mortality and the implications for her own future, the King seemed to view his demise as a once-in-a-lifetime opportunity for self-promotion. Twain thought the pageantry he had witnessed at Oxford during the ceremony granting him the honorary doctorate in 1907 provided a fitting template for his funeral procession, which he was busy "planning on a large scale." Yet even more important to Twain than the style with which he would be ushered into the grave was how he would be remembered. He was determined to depart this earth with a reputation as unstained as his white suits, universally recognized as a literary lion, highly regarded as an icon of integrity, and widely remembered as a loving husband and devoted father—and woe to anyone, including his daughters, who might stand in his way. (His determination to achieve this grand legacy was so obvious that after his death, his published obituary insightfully recognized him as the "architect of his own reputation.")

Not only did Twain cultivate and shape his public persona, but he spent those years dictating his autobiography with the intention of creating a particular narrative of his life that would prove immune to critical scrutiny and also continue to generate royalties decades after his death. The autobiography was Twain's vehicle for presenting his life as he wanted it to be—the facts were entirely beside the point. Telling this version of his life, Twain believed, was the most effective means of accomplishing literary and historical immortality. He defined his purpose in a letter to Howells: "An autobiography is the truest of all books; for while it inevitably consists mainly of extinctions of the truth, shirkings of the truth, partial revealments of the truth, with hardly an instance of plain straight truth, the remorseless truth is there, between the lines, where the author-cat is raking dust upon it which hides from the disinterested spectator neither it nor its smell (though I didn't use that figure)—the result being that the reader knows the author in spite of his wily diligences." Twain—and no one else—would decide just how much dust would be raked.

Paine understood that his purpose was to construct an official biography portraying Twain's life in its most flattering light. And if he ever lost sight of that goal, when the facts did not agree with his subject's version and he became tempted to deviate from the approved storyline, Twain, Isabel, and then Clara were waiting to reinforce with Paine the reason he was there. At the end of January 1908, Isabel asked Paine to account for some letters that she could not find, explaining that Twain and Clara would hold her responsible if they were misplaced, and she was appalled by his reply: "He was cross, & answered in a burst of ill temper that he had many letters & would take them when he wanted to—This is not quite right of Tino [Paine]—& is a new & regrettable attitude—[crossed out: & my anxiety over it is making me ill]." Contained in this note was a thinly veiled threat. Isabel wanted control over Paine's sources and she would not hesitate to involve Twain in order to get her way. Doubtless she must have informed the King about this "regrettable attitude," because two days later Paine sent her an extensive rationalization and apology.

> I have no desire to parade the things he would wish forgotten—to hold them up to the world saying, "See how weak a strong man may be," but it is absolutely necessary that I should know all there is to know, whatever it may be, in order that I may build a personality so impregnable that those who, in years to come, may endeavor to discredit and belittle will find themselves so forestalled at every point that the man we know and love and honor will remain known as we know him, loved and honored through all time.

On August 2, 1908, death struck close to Twain with the tragic drowning of Samuel Moffett, his favorite nephew, at age forty-seven.

When Twain learned of Moffett's death, which occurred while swimming in the ocean in full view of his hysterical wife, Mary, and their two children, Anita and Clemens, he was devastated. The horrific episode was chronicled in a lengthy *New York Times* article that Twain doubtless read. With Ashcroft accompanying him in the intense late summer heat, Twain attended the funeral service, held on August 4 in Mount Vernon, New York. Grief-stricken and physically spent, Twain collapsed upon his return to Stormfield. The episode was so serious that Isabel sent for two doctors and Colonel Harvey to assist in his treatment and recovery.

Isabel blamed Paine for causing Twain's alarming condition. Just ten days earlier, Twain had suffered a fainting spell and Paine had not thought to inform anyone about the incident until after Moffett's funeral, when Twain became so ill. Taking in Twain's increased fragility as well as his remote country location (approximately sixty miles from New York City), the doctors and Colonel Harvey appealed to Isabel never to leave "the King alone again." Isabel received their charge with utter seriousness and dramatically proclaimed to Harriet Whitmore that "some days I feel as if I were moving through this house with my spirit hands folded in prayer that I may be the right woman in the right place. Ashcroft will stand by me, & with me, for to him the obligation is the Same. The King is very much better now, but I will not go even to N.Y. for a day unless Ashcroft can be here, & he is in Canada for a fortnight."

The shock of Moffett's death made Twain even more resolute to get his affairs in order. What Twain could not have known at the time was that whatever semblance of order his life currently held was about to be snatched away.

# THREE

# "ANOTHER STRIPPED & FORLORN KING LEAR"

Rumble thy bellyful! Spit, fire! spout, rain!
Nor rain, wind, thunder, fire, are my daughters:
I tax not you, you elements, with unkindness;
I never gave you kingdom, call'd you children,
You owe me no subscription: then let fall
Your horrible pleasure: here I stand, your slave,
A poor, infirm, weak, and despised old man:
But yet I call you servile ministers,
That have with two pernicious daughters join'd
Your high engender'd battles 'gainst a head
So old and white as this. O! O! 'tis foul!

—SHAKESPEARE, *KING LEAR*, ACT 3, SCENE 2

*Mark Twain at Stormfield with Ralph Ashcroft, W. E. Grumman (stenographer), and Isabel Van Kleek Lyon, 1909*

Having outlasted most of his contemporaries and immediate family members, Mark Twain was encircled in his last years by individuals with vested interests who wanted a piece of his person, his fame, his possessions, his writings, and his wealth. Clara later rhapsodized that the last years of her father's life could be characterized as a constant "atmosphere of adulation," with "the most sensational kind of cordiality from the public, press, and friends." The happy result, according to her, was that every day resembled a kind of "great festive occasion."

Celebratory though it might have been in her halcyon reminiscences, in actuality, Clara's and Twain's temperaments were incompatible, eliminating any possibility of a peaceful life together. Father and daughter had argued for years over Clara's choices and what Twain regarded as her indecorous behavior. Theirs was a history of long-fought battles, with one argument in the summer of 1905 resulting in Twain's writing to his absentee daughter demanding that she return home while assuring her that he had "broken my bow and burned my arrows."

As a result, they were unable to remain for any prolonged period within the same physical space. For years now Clara had absented herself from her father's presence. She politely excused her exits as fulfilling the wanderlust that she had inherited from him. She declared that she loved the luxury of "being in one place in the morning, & then suddenly making up her mind to go to another place," and rationalized her constant departures as "like having a wishing carpet."

Her incessant travel away from her father in effect constituted a magic carpet of escapism, all of which her father grudgingly underwrote. While initially compliant with his daughter's absences and requests for travel funds, by the end of 1907 Twain complained to the always sympathetic Isabel that "he didn't get much good out of Clara. When she is in N.Y. he never sees anything of her & when he goes to her rooms he feels like a stranger making an untimely & unwelcome visit. Poor King! It is all Too True."

In addition to their personal friction, Clara found it onerous to be the daughter of such a renowned man. In a 1908 interview with *The New York Times,* she was shockingly open about how burdensome she found it to be his child: "I have just come to the conclusion that things want readjusting in this old world of ours. Need I mention the fact that I refer to the glaring injustice of having to go about labeled 'Mark Twain's daughter' when I am doing my best to pursue a musical career? Father is, of course, a genius—and that is what makes me so tired. My fatigue is directly caused by the incessant strain—prolonged over some years and induced by trying to find a secret hiding place where I can shroud my identity."

Part of Clara's drive to establish a singing career can be found in her desire to earn her father's respect as well as to create a sense of purpose for her life. What also contributed to her professional resolution was an individual new to Clara's circle, the handsome pianist Charles Edwin (nicknamed Will) Wark. Wark was highly desired as an accompanist for opera singers, and *The New York Times* noted on November 10, 1907, that Wark would be playing piano at a recital by the internationally famous Myron W. Whitney, Jr. Wark had begun accompanying Clara on piano during the winter of 1906 and quickly became her constant consort. Twain thought very highly of Clara's new friend, telling his daughter in February 1907 that he liked "Mr. Wark and his honest blue eyes ever so much. I think you are fortunate to be in his guardianship."

By this time Clara was leading a determinedly bohemian lifestyle, and Will Wark made the perfect companion. Will was Canadian, born on December 1, 1877, in the village of Cobourg, east of Toronto, situated along Lake Ontario. Cobourg's clear Canadian skies were advertised as having the "highest quality ozone" in the world, a delightful change from the sooty surroundings of the industrial northeastern United States, and the town quickly became one of the most popular resort communities for wealthy Americans. Enormous homes were constructed on huge estates, and elaborate summer parties, regattas, and horse shows were held throughout the season.

Amid this heady atmosphere of Gilded Age wealth and status, Wark came of age. The contrast between his working-class family and the glamorous life led by the summer visitors left a deep impression upon him. One of eight children and already described at age five as a piano prodigy, he left Coburg in 1898 to seek his fortune south of the border. Two years after he came to the United States, Wark stayed for a time at the Jackson Sanatorium, located in Dansville, New York. While it is unknown what ailed Wark, male patients were treated there for various kinds of dissipation, including alcoholism. It appears that Wark moved to New York City sometime in 1901; in the 1901 edition of the American Guild of Organists, he is listed as "Teacher of Piano, Accompanist, Coach. Concert Direction."

In addition to his exceptional talent at the keyboard, Wark's special gift lay in his ability to charm and attract patrons. In March 1907, Isabel expressed her gratitude to Wark for giving her and her mother passes to attend a performance of Verdi's *Requiem.* By the summer of 1907, Wark was shuttling between New York City and Tuxedo Park to see Clara. In the softness of an early summer's evening on June 1, Isabel heard singing from her third-story room. Going downstairs to the second floor wearing "a long thin black gown that made a little swish," Isabel found Twain standing in the hallway wearing only "his underdrawers in the 2nd hall, to hear & . . . [he looked] up at me with his eyes shining with delight." Rather than being shocked, Isabel enjoyed the view: "So there he stood in the hall listening to Santa—He had slipped off his trousers & stockings—& he had his yellow calabash pipe in his hand—It is so true—that the ruts people complain that I am in because I don't holiday more, are far higher than their greatest heights." Standing in the hallway side by side, Twain and Isabel listened to Clara and Wark make beautiful music together.

By the end of the month, Wark was dining with Clara at Tuxedo Park "every night," and Isabel bore witness to their romantic relationship. "I have been dreaming a wonderful love story in these days," Isabel mused wistfully, "A story all of beautiful colors, and it makes me so very lonely and so sad." Isabel understood only too acutely that her moments of human connection were limited to happenstance, late-night meetings in hallways listening to the sounds of life taking place at a considerable remove.

After an August visit to Boston, where Clara and Wark were staying, Isabel observed that Clemens's daughter "is beautifuller than she had ever been for Boston agrees with her & her intense happiness in her life

*Mark Twain, Clara Clemens, and Marie Nichols at the piano, 1908*

& in her art, are making for her an existence that is ideal." Wark sent word to Twain that same month informing him of the good news that Clara had gained weight, and how he wished Twain "could hear Clara's voice and notice the great improvement—it has the true ring and I am confident she will do really great work this coming winter, and the dear child gains confidence with every new work she undertakes." No longer a child at age thirty-three, Clara was three years older than her beau.

During the early months of 1908 Clara gave several performances in New York, one, as *The New York Times* reported, at the home of Dr. Edward Quintard, where she was accompanied, in addition to Wark on the piano, by Miss Lillian Littlehales on the cello. By spring Clara and Wark were full of plans for a European tour. On May 16, 1908, Clara, along with Wark and Marie Nichols, a Boston violinist, sailed from

New York on the *Caronia* bound for England. Over the summer, both Clara and Wark would regularly send ebullient letters to Isabel, assuring her of their musical success while simultaneously asking for additional funds. Shortly after the trio had arrived in England, Isabel received notification from the bank that "the fourth letter of credit for Miss Clara Clemens" had been issued in response to her request.

Clara made her English singing début in early June at Queen's Hall and Bechstein Hall, now known as Wigmore Hall. Wark wrote a chummy letter to Isabel at the end of the month from the Grand Hotel in Broadstairs, Kent, using the nickname the two had bestowed upon her, Nana. He explained that his exhausted songbird had spent the past week in Kent recovering from her recital. Wark informed Isabel that he and Clara were planning to travel to France "very soon" because "London is more than expensive." The two would "settle down in some cheap country place (probably Barbizon) in about two weeks." He noted that Clara's weekly expenses averaged approximately twenty-two pounds, and he asked Isabel to "please tell me frankly if you think Clara is spending too much." Before closing, Wark excitedly noted that a concert was being planned near London the following year, "on shares so that Clara won't be under any expense," and that the two of them missed "Nana" terribly "and would give anything to have you here— several times a day one of us will say, 'Now I'm sure Nana would like this place or Nana would like that'—or 'Nana must have some of these cigarettes.' "

Wark was ideally suited to attend to a woman of Clara's enormous emotional needs. Indeed, a newspaper profile later underscored his sympathetic playing, reflecting his accommodating personality:

> He understands perfectly how best to accompany the prima donna. He knows what volume is required, what shading is desirable, how much of it, and he follows every motion of the singer to detect her next require-ment in the manner of piano support. He not only knows these things, but he does them. That is why he is such an excellent accompanist.

HELPFUL, CLEVER, AND GOOD-LOOKING, Wark had found himself a fragile little heiress and quickly realized that with the right amount of pampering and coddling he could accompany her in more ways than just musically for a long while. Will and Isabel were simpatico in that they were both trying to accomplish the same end by appeasing their more affluent partners. By the time of their European idyll, Wark and Clara were certainly enjoying more than a professional relationship, and they most likely were sexually involved. In July Clara sent Isabel a letter in which she confided that "dear old W. is more wonderful all the time but I can't bear the many many months still that separate us from freedom and frank expression of the truth." What Clara did not mention in her letter was that the chief impediment between the two and the "truth" happened to be none other than his wife, Mrs. Edith Cullis Wark. Edith had married Wark five years earlier, on October 10, 1903, at Grace Church Chantry in lower Manhattan, just a few blocks away from 21 Fifth Avenue. On her wedding day the bride wore a lovely white crêpe de chine dress with a long tulle veil and carried a bouquet of white anemones. Will's best man was Francis Rogers, a well-known baritone soloist. The couple was blessed with twins.

*Charles Wark and Edith Cullis's wedding day, October 10, 1903.*
*Francis Rogers is at top left, beside Charles Wark. Edith is seated*
*between two flower girls.*

Clara's tour with Wark did not go unnoticed by either his wife or the press. Shortly before the two were due to sail into New York Harbor, the papers were full of news about them. On Monday, September 7, 1908, the *World* reported to curious New York City readers:

> Miss Clemens will give a reception in her old home on Saturday to her many friends. It is expected that at the reception her engagement to Mr. Wark will be announced. After his daughter's marriage, a friend of Mr. Clemens said yesterday, the novelist will be virtually alone; and this, it was said, influenced him strongly in deciding to make Redding his home throughout the year.

An appalled Isabel read the story in the morning paper along with the rest of the public; later that same day she met with reporters and vehemently "contradicted that & many things." Either Isabel was not very convincing or the story was just too good to let die, because the next day *The New York Times* elaborated.

> Miss Clemens . . . has been traveling abroad with friends. With the party is Charles Wark of New York, whose engagement to Miss Clemens has been rumored. Mr. Clemens will come to town from Redding today to be on hand when the *Caronia* comes in. . . . Miss Clemens will give a reception at the old house on the evening of her arrival. It has been suggested that her engagement will be announced at that time.

There was no party. Immediately after docking on September 9, Clara departed for Stormfield with her father and Isabel.

Clara's artistic and sexual affair with a married father contained all the lurid characteristics that New York newspapers craved. For the previous two years, the press had provided hysterical daily accounts of what was popularly called the "Crime of the Century," the murder of New York's most prominent architect, Stanford White, by the deranged Pittsburgh millionaire Harry K. Thaw; the public was obsessed with the scandal. Thaw claimed that the reason he shot White three times in the head in front of nine hundred witnesses was that White had "ruined" his wife, the gorgeous nymphet Evelyn Nesbit. Martin Littleton, Thaw's head counsel for his second trial, kept his friend Mark Twain well informed about the details. Thaw's second trial commenced at the beginning of January 1908, with Littleton providing a spirited defense. In early January, Twain complained about having to spend a listless night without his billiards partner because "Mr. Littleton is submerged in the Thaw trial, & has to work Every Evening." Littleton's schedule was more accommodating later in the month, and Twain and Isabel enjoyed lunching with him and his wife just ten days before the end of the trial. On February 1, Littleton won his case. Thaw was acquitted of murder by reason of insanity.

Twain's path crossed in other ways with the "Crime of the Century." On January 12, he was an honoree at a dinner at the Lotos Club, which he frequented in celebration of his Oxford degree. On that evening members feasted on Innocent Oysters Abroad, Roughing It Soup, Fish Huckleberry Finn, Joan of Arc Filet of Beef, Jumping Frog Terrapin, Gilded Age Duck, Hadleyburg Salad, Life on the Mississippi Salad, Prince and the Pauper Cakes, Puddin'head Cheese, and White Elephant Coffee. In his brief after-dinner remarks, Twain announced to the assemblage that he had embarked upon a new hobby of collecting compliments directed toward himself. On proud display at the Lotos Club was Frederick Church's painting of an underage, nude Evelyn Nesbit, in which, as she described it, she was portrayed as "an Undine [water nymph] with water lilies in [my] hair, running down my bare limbs, [with] two striped tigers at [my] flanks." In an interesting coincidence, Twain and Evelyn Nesbit had been photographed by the same prominent New York photographer, Gertrude Käsebier.

Careless and rebellious, Clara was on very dangerous ground. While no murder had been committed, if the unforgiving newspapers caught wind of the facts of her complicated love life, as the daughter of America's most famous citizen, her reputation would be ruined. Isabel did not record in her daily reminder any particular reaction or concern voiced by Clara or Twain over the newspaper articles, and it is unclear how the story reached the press. Twain's silence is particularly curious as it stands in stark contrast to the prim stance he took regarding Maxim Gorky's rather complicated marital arrangements just two years earlier. Unable to divorce his wife in Russia, Gorky had secured a decree in Finland. The American press declared that his Finnish divorce was not legally binding and reported the sensational story that Gorky had traveled to America in the company of his mistress. Despite the social reformer Jane Addams's urging that Twain should ignore Gorky's tangled personal relationships for the greater good of helping the Russian people, Twain immediately distanced himself. He rationalized that because Gorky had come to the United States as a diplomat and not a revolutionary, the niceties of social etiquette bound him. Isabel's insightful analysis of Gorky's situation, coming just two months after Stanford White's murder, was that Americans "are readier to wink at the horrors & debaucheries of men who live as Stanford White is said to have lived; they will condone immoralities, but not illegalities." The operative word here is "men." Women at the time were allowed no such leniency when it came to the issue of morals. It is impossible that Wark would have passed Twain's litmus test as a suitable escort for Clara if he had known about Mrs. Wark and the children.

The lurid newspaper details of Stanford White's dalliances with underage chorus girls likely influenced Clara's vehemently negative reaction to any mention of her father's Angelfish and was, in part, the reason that she rejected the name Innocents at Home in favor of "Stormfield" for the Redding house. White collected "protégées" by the dozens; he elaborately seduced them, wrote loving letters to them, and kept their names in a little black book. Clara's skin must have crawled at the sight of her father's Angelfish billiard room at Stormfield.

At long last supremely happy both personally and professionally, Clara was in no mood to pay attention to her father's standards of decorum, if indeed he expressed concern. The likeliest scenario is that Twain did not know that Wark was married, and Clara was not about to tell him. Based on Isabel's personal interactions with the two and the nature of the confiding letters that Wark and Clara sent her, it seems clear that she knew they were intimately involved, and that she was also aware of Wark's marital status. Isabel thus possessed powerful information that placed her in an extremely tenuous position: if she informed Twain about the true nature of the situation she would earn Clara's undying enmity; if she kept the information secret and Twain eventually discovered that she had known it, he would consider her a traitor. The dilemma was in her knowing it, not his discovering it.

2

A distinct pattern had gradually emerged over the previous two years with gossip bedeviling the members of the Twain household and those in close contact with them. It is doubtful that Isabel would have been the source for this latest rumor, since over the summer Clara had forgiven her for her role in the construction and decoration of Stormfield, and Isabel would have been reluctant to rekindle Clara's wrath. At times it is useful to look where there is silence, and the one individual not mentioned in the press or gossiped about during the same period is Paine.

Twain's biographer may have been spreading rumors about Clara and raising questions about her behavior as payback to Isabel. His frustration over Isabel's influence with Twain had reached the boiling point, and the two had been arguing for months about his lack of access to Twain's private papers. Isabel wanted to restrict Paine's usage of any letters in his biography because of Twain's promise that she could edit an edition of his letters and receive a percentage of the royalties. Previously published letters would diminish the value of her volume. Paine was equally unwavering about his absolute need to use them in order to add to the authority of his work. Printing excerpts from the letters in his biography, Paine argued, would amount to publicity for Isabel's edition of the letters and could only enhance her future sales. Isabel, in Paine's opinion, was being shortsighted and selfish. Isabel was unconvinced by Paine's argument, displeased about the deleterious effect prepublication could have on a future edition, and alarmed that Paine refused to inform her when he had solicited letters from individuals to whom Twain had written. These letters were precious, not just because of their possible inclusion in a future edition, but because they also possessed a distinct monetary value. Isabel was determined not to let any letters slip through her fingers and demanded accountability from Paine in order to safeguard them.

In January 1908, when Isabel discovered that Paine had asked Samuel Moffett for letters without first asking Twain's permission to do so, she immediately informed the King. Twain's reaction was to write Samuel and tell him not to comply with any such request. Also at Isabel's urging, Twain wrote to Twichell and to Howells urging them to resist Paine's requests to see any letters. "Paine could have killed me," Isabel remarked, "because he told me how he had asked for & obtained from Mr. Howells a lot of the King's letters when we were in Dublin in 1906. [Crossed out: the King wrote to Mr. Howells at that time asking for some of the letters & Mr. Howells to let him have them] but Paine managed to get them—He said I must not tell the King, when I told him that the King & Clara would be hurt. Angry."

YEARS LATER, Isabel wrote to William T.H. Howe that by January 1908 Twain had begun to lose confidence in Paine. The situation reached its climax when Katy Leary found Paine going through private papers and letters and told Twain about her discovery. Twain apparently responded by asking Isabel to "lock the Ms. Trunk and the box . . . containing all the letters he had written Mrs. Clemens (always kept in his room . . . just as Mrs. Clemens had kept them close to her.) and to give the keys to him. [Crossed out: He had been a little annoyed by Paine for some reason I do not remember now.]" A frightened and upset Paine approached Isabel and beseeched her to intercede on his behalf with Twain. Isabel told Paine that she would lobby for him. Twain agreed that while he would allow Paine to continue his work, any "letters must first be submitted to him before Paine could use them." Paine was infuriated that Isabel had such clout with his subject.

On the eve of Clara and Wark's return to New York, the tension over Paine's right to freely view Twain's letters and manuscripts had resurfaced. A livid Paine and Isabel argued, with Isabel receiving an additional tongue-lashing over the phone from Mrs. Paine regarding her husband's lack of access to "the red Ms. Trunk." An enraged Mrs. Paine insulted "the King & Benares [Ashcroft] & me." If it was Paine who had talked to the press about Clara and Will's relationship, his purpose might have been to create additional rancor between Clara and Isabel, in the hope that Clara would suspect Isabel of betraying her most personal secrets and consequently convince Twain to fire her. With Isabel gone, Paine would have his choice of Twain's letters and manuscripts, and he would be the logical choice to compile an edition of his letters. But no matter who was doing the talking, the newspaper stories failed to separate the singer from her accompanist and the secretary from her King. Clara's European tour had done her a world of good, and she now declared Stormfield "very beautiful."

After spending a long weekend at Stormfield, the energetic Wark returned to New York City on September 17 and rented an apartment on the eastern edge of Stuyvesant Square. Just two and a half weeks later, Clara rented an apartment in the same location. Rejecting appearances, Clara left her father in order to be with Will. Clara found a "very pretty" apartment in the Stuyvesant building, located at 17 Livingston Place (since renamed Nathan D. Perlman Place), also on the eastern edge of Stuyvesant Square. The Stuyvesant was New York City's first apartment building in the French style, built in 1869 by the architect Richard Morris Hunt for Rutherford Stuyvesant, one of the most respected men in New York. There were twenty suites and four artists' studios on the top floor. Rents for the suites ranged from $83.50 to $125.00 per month, too expensive for any but the wealthiest New Yorkers. The four studios rented for $76.00 per month; Clara rented one of these. Tenants' needs were attended to by a full-time concierge, and the city's most "varied and free-spirited" elites resided there, including the publisher George Putnam, founder of G. P. Putnam's Sons; Elizabeth Custer, the widow of the general (Twain published her memoir of her late husband, *Tenting on the Plains, or General Custer in Kansas and Texas,* in 1889, under the auspices of Charles L. Webster and Company); and Elizabeth Jordan, the editor of *Harper's Bazaar,* as well as an editor of and contributor to the collaborative novel *The Whole Family.*

Clara moved into her new abode on October 2. Four days later, Isabel came to visit her and that night enjoyed a "wonderful sleep in Santa's little apartment." Clara and Wark were keeping very close physical company, something Isabel doubtless noted. In having a sexual liaison with a married man, smoking cigarettes, living in a studio apartment, flitting from place to place, singing before strangers, and associating with musicians, Clara had deliberately chosen a lifestyle that her socially astute mother never would have tolerated.

The two music lovers were together constantly throughout the fall, making frequent weekend trips to Stormfield. On September 17, 1908, robbers broke into Stormfield. Wark, along with the French butler, Claude Joseph Beuchotte; the contractor H. A. Lounsbury; and the sheriff gave chase and captured the two thieves. The day after the two men were taken into custody, Wark accompanied Clara and a white-suited Twain to a court hearing to watch justice take its course.

3

With Clara preoccupied with her accompanist, the only dark cloud in the sky was a conversation she and Isabel had at the end of October regarding Twain's finances and Clara's allowance. Twain was worried about the expiration of the copyright from *Innocents Abroad* and anticipated that this would mean his annual income of $25,000 would be reduced by 20 percent within a year. Isabel explained to an angry Clara that this meant she would receive "only 800 a month instead of 2000." Clara's churlish response was that "she had supposed that her father was very rich & that he had a million saved." Twain's daughter was not one to live on a budget, and she deeply resented being told to limit her expenses by her father's secretary. Clara's angry retort also might have been aggravated by the likelihood that she was supporting Will and did not want to explain any extra costs to Isabel or to her father. As a professional musician, Will's income was meager. With Clara's assistance, he had money available to travel constantly, to maintain an apartment separate from his family and provide them with living expenses.

Like Clara, Jean found her attention frequently occupied with romance and money. Jean resented what she regarded as Twain's parsimonious attitude toward her requests for funds (never mind her expensive treatment at Hillbourne Farms), and, unlike Clara, she despaired over ever finding anyone who would love her. Although she called Isabel the day after leaving 21 Fifth Avenue, telling her that she liked Hillbourne Farms and had already "been fishing with the doctors," it did not take long for Jean to become bored with this slow, cautious, and repetitive way of life. A little more than a month after her arrival, Jean began forming a romantic attachment to Dr. Hibbard, a physician on staff. At the beginning of December 1906, she started to accompany Dr. Hibbard while he was making his patient rounds in the area. During the course of their drive, the two amiably conversed about a multitude of subjects, and on one occasion in early December, on a freezing-cold morning, they engaged in a remarkably frank exchange about female and male relations.

Very soon we got out onto forbidden grounds and talked openly. There was no occasion for embarrassment. Dr. Hibbard is a nice, clean young man and when he said he thought it decidedly wrong for girls to be brought up in such absolute ignorance of the real facts, that they believed their men friends were as clean as they themselves, I agreed absolutely. He said he had never known anything at all until he went to the grammar school, and only a little, then, but that when he went to the Medical College his eyes were opened. Almost without exception the students were bad. At last I vouchsafed what I have so often heard made as an excuse for the immorality of men: that the desire is actually a physical need and very difficult to withstand. I asked Dr. Hibbard if he believed that to be true. He said "no" most emphatically and backed it up by adding that he didn't believe any physician could be found who would hold that as a possible thing. Therefore, most men are weak, dirty brutes. And the reason for that? The willingness of women to overlook the former character of men that they wish to marry and whom they hope to reform after marrying them. What idiots! Men demand that their wives be clean, moral women, but of course they have the privilege of belonging to the stronger sex and believe themselves without fault, or, that no one would dare find a fault in one of their loose and moralless [*sic*] number. More than ever before, I liked Dr. Hibbard. I have liked him from the beginning, but I especially liked the way he talked today.

Having a conversation of this nature for the lonely and longing Jean was tantamount to adding gas to a fire. A week and a half later, when Dr. Hibbard casually mentioned that he doubted he would remain at Hillbourne beyond June, an emotionally distraught Jean swore that the place would become "absolute Hades to me" with him gone. "I don't in the least hope to win him, fond as I am growing of him," she wistfully wrote, "but I can't help wishing that if he is engaged I didn't have to be thrown with him so incessantly as I am. If there could only be some other nice young man here it would be a relief to me & doubtless to him. I wonder if he considers me a fearful burden? He always seems mighty nice & cordial & friendly, & I think he likes me but I must try & not force myself onto him too much. . . . Doubtless for that very reason no one will ever care for me and I shall have to drag my useless, empty life out by itself. Oh! Is there no hope whatsoever for me? What can I do! I feel as tho' I must find some means to prove attractive to a person that I can also learn to love."

Jean confided in Clara about her feelings for Dr. Hibbard, but her sister proved unsympathetic. An appalled Clara demanded that Dr. Sharp to put an immediate end to Jean's drives with the young physician. Clara then lectured Jean "that what I do is just the kind of thing a fiancée would do and that if it were known in the city people would be likely to remark on it." A horrified and defiant Jean responded that she did not care in the least about gossip. "I am here to regain my health as best I can & one of the principle methods is being out as much as possible," Jean reports that she retorted, "besides which being out in that way is my chief source of pleasure. I know that . . . doesn't improve the situation any, but while, to quiet her, said I would not go quite so often, that really was a lie." Jean supposed that Clara feared she would "fall in love with Dr. H. and wishes to ward it off & she feels, as mother did, that I must never marry."

Considering that Clara was having an affair with her married pianist, this directive seems hypocritical at best and cruel at worst. Jean was furious with her sister, writing that her "action was low, I think, & I don't feel that she had any right to do as she did. And I told her too, that she wasn't my mother & that I didn't consider that she had the privilege of doing as she had done. However, it will be some time before I forgive this performance of hers—this breaking up of about the only real pleasure in life I had been getting & even more than that her speaking of it to Dr. S. & not telling me is what I consider the worst part of it." Clara's attitude left Jean "cold & that her own idea was to stick to all rules & not regard—where it concerned me—my comfort or pleasure."

Twain's visits to his ill daughter were rare; he made the trip to Katonah only three times during Jean's entire fifteen months there. His first trip came during the second week of January 1907, three months into her stay, when an agitated Jean was "in a Torrent of impossible moods & distressed her wonderful father until he was ready to weep." He did not return until May 21. Jean's letters complaining about her life and inadequate living situation were poorly received by her irritated father, who harshly criticized her: "Jean's making out a bad case about herself—Bees wont [*sic*] sting an idiot—"

When Twain finally visited Jean again, on August 12, 1907, the conversation quickly turned acrimonious. She asked for $16 so that she could continue to board her dog Prosper and was appalled by her father's callous response. Twain told his daughter that Prosper should be "destroyed," as he had never found dogs to be of any value. An infuriated Jean "squelched the idea" by telling him that Prosper had been her mother's last gift to her. Twain eventually sent the money. In an attempt to attract her father's attention, Jean insisted that he pay her special favors not given to either Clara or Isabel. When he journeyed to England to accept his Oxford honor, Jean made him promise that he would cable only her when he arrived. Isabel sighed, "Jean may or may not bother to let us know," and she asked Ashcroft to send her a cable as well.

Clara at least saw her little sister more frequently. After her first visit, she left greatly affected by "the place & the Great pathos of the Situation." Clara promised Jean that she would try to see her on a weekly basis, and to Jean's joy kept her pledge into the winter. On December 14, 1906, during a Saturday call, Clara told Jean that her doctors had decided she was improving under their care and should remain over the summer. Jean was profoundly disappointed, as a summer spent at Katonah meant no chance of seeing Gerry Brush in Dublin. On Christmas Day Clara was the only member of the Clemens family to visit Jean—her father preferred to stay in the city, spending the day with Isabel at home and in the evening dining out with Henry Rogers and his family.

Isabel also frequented Hillbourne Farms to speak with Jean and consult with her doctors. Twain had relegated to Isabel the responsibility for making sure Jean was well cared for as well as assuming financial control over her needs. This situation created considerable tension between Jean and Isabel, because Jean knew that any requests that might cause her father concern would immediately default to Isabel. On occasions when Jean would ask for a magazine subscription or a second new lap robe and receive a negative response, her anger would be immediately directed toward Isabel. But it was not difficult for Jean to figure out that Isabel was being used as Twain's shield. Twain simply chose not to say no directly to his daughter and used Isabel to do it. Nevertheless, despite the awkward circumstances, Jean and Isabel did manage to share a congenial relationship, and during a March visit the two spent a happy day together, with Isabel noting that Jean was improving both in health and outlook and was very excited about the plans for Stormfield.

Jean possessed remarkable self-awareness when it came to analyzing her situation and where she stood in regard to the time and consideration her sister and father were willing to devote to her. Nevertheless, having their attention was important to her. By the summer, Clara's regular visits had ceased as she became more interested in developing her voice and her relationship with Wark intensified. Jean was "distresse[d] beyond words" on the occasion of her twenty-eighth birthday when her sister sent a $10 check as her present. An insulted Jean returned the money with a note explaining why she was offended by the impersonal gift—as a patient, Jean had no access to stores where she might spend the money. Oddly, Clara responded by sending a "chilly note & second check for ten dollars." Jean returned the check again, and by August 5, her older sister finally managed to get the message and sent her a strand of "lovely pinkish-red" beads.

Jean's sharp tongue and temper were inherited from her father, and she would frequently take out her loneliness and frustration on her maids. Anna Sterritt had originally accompanied her to Hillbourne Farms to help care for her. After six months, Anna could endure no more of Jean's verbal abuse or the isolation of Hillbourne, and at the beginning of April, Isabel brought a new maid, named Therese, to Hillbourne Farms, where Isabel made the simple observation "Poor Jean—and poor Therese." Two months later, Therese could endure no more of Jean's many "unkindnesses" and returned to New York, weeping as she told Isabel about the harsh treatment she had received. Isabel then took another maid, Blanche, to Hillbourne in mid-June to care for Twain's increasingly angry and resentful daughter. In October 1907, after Jean had spent a lonely and seemingly endless summer picking wildflowers and going bird-watching, to Isabel's consternation she expressed her anger directly to Twain.

> Oh Terrible—Terrible that his children cannot come under the spell of his glories, his subtleties, his Sweetnesses. For this morning there was a cruel letter from Jean damning me—finding fault with him—with him. Always he says that she is not to blame, it is the God who can create such natures such maladies as hers—& in the creating, run them into a . . . mould as inflexible as bronze.

Jean apparently sent the letter after a frustrating conversation with Dr. Hunt. She was desperate to leave Hillbourne Farms at this point and furious that her feelings were not being taken into consideration. Three days later, Isabel met with Dr. Peterson, and afterward told Twain that Peterson felt Jean was making good progress despite "hating the sanitarium viciously" and that he was reluctant to change her care facility. What Dr. Peterson also told Isabel, which she wrote down but did not tell Twain, was that "the epileptic temperament rarely improved, but that it grew worse, & that Jean must never live with her father again, because her affection might easily turn into a violent & insane hatred & she could slay just by the sudden & terrible & ungovernable revulsion of feeling. The one bounding out of the other & the person never knowing that he is passing from one condition to the other."

Dr. Peterson's account of Jean's prognosis as an epileptic patient suffering from postictal psychosis constitutes a remarkably accurate contemporary description of the disease. After all, neurology was much more advanced than psychiatry at this time. Evidently Isabel decided that the description of a hopeless future for a twenty-eight-year-old woman would be too upsetting for a seventy-one-year-old man to hear, especially a man already prone to periods of depression and melancholy. Dr. Peterson felt strongly that Jean belonged in some kind of supervised institutional setting, and the only other one found appropriate was located in Greenwich, Connecticut. Jean had heard that the Greenwich sanitarium was not as nice as Hillbourne Farms and so she rejected that option. Jean spent her second Christmas away from family in Mount Vernon, New York, with friends she had made at the sanitarium. Her father's Christmas present was sent through the mail—a check for $10.

*Hillbourne Farms exterior*

On Christmas Day, the Cowles sisters, Edith and Mildred, visited Twain to inquire if he would be willing to allow Jean to leave Hillbourne Farms, and to offer their assistance in a new living arrangement for her. The sisters had met Jean when a suicidal Mildred had entered Hillbourne Farms as a patient in November 1907. Edith had accompanied Mildred to watch over her. Isabel recorded Twain's rather melodramatic response. "When the dear Cowles girls came here on Christmas day to see if Mr. Clemens would be willing to have Jean change from Katonah to Greenwich (& fearing to come) the King could not speak for a moment, & with his dear voice shaking he said 'Anything, Anything you can do to make that dear child happy first, & then comfortable, you are privileged to do. I am a man. I can do so little for her.'" Isabel telephoned Jean with the promise of a wonderful Christmas gift and described the Cowleses' idea. Jean was ecstatic: "Dr. Peterson is glad, she [Isabel] & Father delighted with the cottage idea & Clara is overjoyed too. She said she didn't see how I had stood it as I had, etc. If they are happy, what am I." Other patients shared Jean's dislike of Hillbourne Farms, and there seems to have been a toxic air of hopelessness about the place. Considering what people were under treatment for and the futility of finding a cure for their affliction, it is hardly surprising.

Jean's departure finally came on January 9, 1908. She moved to Greenwich, not to the sanitarium, but rather to a private home at 57 Maple Avenue with Edith and Mildred as well as Marguerite Schmitt (nicknamed Bébé), a close friend. The plan was that Edith and Bébé would serve as Mildred and Jean's nurses and Twain would underwrite their expenses. Twain and Isabel went to the train station in Katonah to bid farewell to Jean and were shocked by her appearance. Isabel described her as looking "very very ill. She is so white & her once beautiful face is so drawn; her fingers have a curious movement. She is like a drooping lily." "Enraged" that her father had shown up unexpectedly, Jean told Isabel that seeing him had made her forget everything she needed to tell Isabel. The next day Jean suffered five seizures.

While glad to have finally departed from Hillbourne Farms, Jean soon found her new living situation to be unmanageable. Mildred was still suicidal and occupied a great deal of her sister's patience and time. Jean began to lobby for spending the summer in Dublin, and while Dr. Peterson initially thought well of the idea, his opinion ultimately changed. One reason might be found in a conversation Twain had in

January with Mrs. Norman Hapgood, an old friend of the Clemens family, whose husband was the editor of *Collier's Weekly.* Mrs. Hapgood told him that Jean had been heavily "criticized in Dublin when no one knew of her incriminating malady." The insinuation was that had people known about her epilepsy, perhaps they might not have been so harsh in their judgment of her. Isabel also received a letter in February sent by Gra Thayer condemning Twain's supposed neglect of Jean. Gra wrote: "We have been sore, though, at your King, for what has looked from outside like indifference about lonesome and afflicted & often misunderstood (??) brave pitiable beautiful Jean. That is butting in where sacred satyrs fear to butt; yet you know that Jean is fond of us & we of her, & that she doesn't grant us quite the position of outsiders." Isabel defensively responded to the Thayers: "The things that are merely seen from the outside are the things that are never understood. And that you should be sore with my king whose great wealth of love for Jean was never understood by her, could make me sad, but I rush to explain only this, that we who know the real inside, know that the misrepresentations are a part of Jean's malady."

Twain might not have been anxious for Jean to return to Dublin and to be surrounded by wagging tongues, as well as to open himself up for criticism regarding her care. In the end, Dr. Peterson favored Gloucester, Massachusetts. He planned to visit the area during the summer, which would allow him to personally check on Jean, and he had confidence in a local physician. Peterson also thought the climate was healthy. At the end of March 1908, Peterson sent a letter to Twain with his Gloucester recommendation; Twain cabled his affirmative response. But when Jean, Mildred, Edith, and Bébé arrived in Gloucester in May, the situation continued to worsen, as Mildred's self-destructive tendencies intensified, and Jean began to suspect that some of the money her father had been providing for their support was being used to mollify Edith. Another plan had to be devised for Jean, who probably felt at this point that she was condemned to wander for the remainder of her life.

When Jean learned over the summer that Twain had decided to make Stormfield his permanent residence and that Isabel would live in the main house with him, she wrote to her close friend Nancy Brush with great excitement about the possibility of moving into Lyonesse: "Now Father thinks it would be a good place, anyway, because by being out of our house, I should have no difficulty in avoiding late entertainments & unhealthy goings-on & yet I could be near enough to see Father as often as permitted & have a healthy country life such as I need and want to have." Yet Redding was not to be, as Dr. Peterson thought that, instead, expert treatment could be found in Berlin, Germany, with a Dr. Hofrath von Reuvers. Although initially conflicted, pleased about her upcoming voyage yet sad about not living near her father, Jean wrote Nancy that she was "wildly excited at the idea of going abroad again & of seeing Berlin—I saw it last when I was only eleven years old."

Jean's surprise about going to Berlin was compounded by the fact that it was her father who had sent her the message: "Yesterday the news came like a thunderbolt from a clear sky. I came back from a long sail, just before lunch & found a letter from father. . . . When I read the opening sentence, I fairly gasped—if he had crawled out of the envelope, himself, I couldn't have been any more amazed." Fluent in German and a lover of all things European, Jean grew increasingly excited about her upcoming trip. At eleven o'clock in the morning on September 26, 1908, the *Pretoria* sailed for Germany. Isabel, Twain, and the Angelfish Dorothy Quick waved farewell to a "pathetic & wan" Jean, who was accompanied by her maid Anna Sterritt and Bébé Schmitt. While Jean found it a struggle to live within a budget of $50 a month—the amount allocated to her by her father—she was very happy in Berlin, and felt she was making excellent progress while under treatment by Dr. von Reuvers. After such a difficult and trying series of living arrangements over a nearly two-year period, to all appearances a workable circumstance had finally been identified for Jean. In Berlin, she had found her treasured measure of independence, all the while being cared for by her friend and maid and under constant supervision by a world-class physician. And perhaps most comforting for her father, Jean was also far away from embarrassing gossip about her illness.

### 4

Redding's newest and most famous resident quickly grew lonely and bored. Henry Rogers never visited his friend's new home, as he had been in poor health for years. Twain was cheered by constant invitations from Rogers to come visit him in Fair Haven, Connecticut, where he kept his luxurious yacht the *Kanawha,* yet Twain's fondness for Stormfield as well as his own sick turns kept him close to home. Despite the distance, the two men corresponded regularly and managed to maintain their close friendship, and Twain usually stayed with Rogers on his infrequent visits to New York City.

By 1908, Twain's attention to matters literary had begun to wander and the dictations for his autobiography had become infrequent, with only thirty-five in total for the year. In August, Josephine Hobby, the stenographer, was replaced with Mary L. Howden, and "Miss Mollie's" primary responsibility was to tend to the enormous amount of mail that Twain constantly received, rather than to record his recollections. To bolster his spirits, Twain required continual entertainment. With both daughters absent, Isabel played hostess and saw to his every social desire. Over the period of just one month, October 1908, the following individuals made their way to Stormfield to enjoy Twain's company and Isabel's hospitality: Ashcroft; Margaret Blackmer (an Angelfish); Captain Dow of the good ship *Caronia* and with him his favorite steward, Billy; Wark; Clara; Twain's sister-in-law Susan Crane; Mrs. Laura Frazer (Twain's first sweetheart) along with her niece, Ethel Newcombe; Isabel's mother; a Mr. Phayre; and the cartoonist Thomas Nast. Twain also left Stormfield several times during October: to open the town's library (named after its most prominent citizen—Mark Twain), and to dine with Leigh Hunt, meet Lord Northcliffe, and visit Colonel Harvey. In all, an impressive 180 visitors came to see Twain during his first year at Stormfield.

Along with arranging the comings and goings of guests and their entertainments, Isabel had a major workforce issue to resolve. The servants were already dissatisfied with living so far out in the country, and after the September break-in they became convinced their very lives were at risk. On October 1, Claude Beuchotte, the butler, announced that he was leaving and that all the female servants were going to follow him. True to his word, Claude left, and a week later so did the maids and the cook. Isabel spent the remainder of the month hiring a new staff.

On October 8, Teresa Cherubini and her husband, Giuseppe, agreed to move from New York City to Stormfield and were rehired, and the next day a young local man, Horace Hazen, came to inquire about filling the position of Twain's butler. While Hazen had never been in service before, Isabel was not in a position to turn down any interested parties and felt that the eighteen-year-old Horace, all six feet one inch of him, just might work out. A few days later Elizabeth Dick, a young woman of seventeen, arrived to assist Teresa upstairs. Elizabeth was very sweet, although quite homesick for her mother. A little over a week after her arrival she told a sympathetic Isabel "that she cannot stay unless she is able to go home nights to sleep with her mother. The quaint wee Soul! I'm letting her go home to her mother's bed tonight; but also she goes to talk to her mother, & to herself to try to make herself & her mother believe that she will get over her homesickness— Poor wee soul! I . . . remember my own misery—& the same agony can creep over me even now." Elizabeth Dick filled out the corps needed, and by October 11, Isabel had hired "2 Italians, & 2 natives, & the washing is to be sent to the laundry in Bethel on trial."

Running an estate like Stormfield was no trivial undertaking, and having a staff that was well trained and working satisfactorily together was crucial for Isabel's peace of mind as well as to her King's well-being. In order to allay everyone's concerns about personal safety, an alarm system was installed on October 20. Much to Isabel's relief, the gong was located just outside her door and the indicator in her bathroom. That night she enjoyed her best sleep in five weeks, "for there has been no night since Sept 18th without a terrified mental shriek in it. It is not fear, it is a pathological condition."

Unfortunately, Isabel would enjoy only a momentary respite because Clara, who had come to spend only a few days at Stormfield, decided once again that she should give the servants their instructions—not Isabel. "There is such a confusion over the servants—& the confusion lies not in the servant department, but in a part of the house that gives itself credit for a high line of conduct," Isabel complained, "I was to go with the King to Irvington yesterday—but I dared not leave this house to a certain derangement, & a possible clearing-out of the present working force. The servants do not want more than one head—hence the wearying wearying confusion." The two women exchanged ugly words, and, furious, Isabel fled the next day on the "earliest" train.

5

Waiting for her at the station in New York was a sympathetic Ralph W. Ashcroft. Ever since Isabel had supported Ashcroft's accompanying

Twain to Oxford, relations between the two had been most cordial. The day before his sailing with Twain, Ashcroft had thanked Isabel by giving her "a great pink rose." An English native, Ashcroft had been a practical choice as Twain's escort. Born in Rock Ferry, Cheshire, on March 22, 1875, Ashcroft had made Twain's acquaintance in 1903, when he was working as the treasurer of the Plasmon Company, in which Twain was a major shareholder. Plasmon was a food supplement, and Twain believed it possessed the power to eradicate starvation, to cure disease, and to make him a tycoon. The company's headquarters were located in England, and Ashcroft was the secretary of the American branch. With a well-established track record of disaster, Twain was in no position to invest; however, true to form, he could not resist what he thought was a sure-fire investment. Plasmon proved to be no exception to Twain's unbroken record of investment failure, and all the money he had put in, over $25,000, was eventually lost when Plasmon collapsed at the end of 1909.

Isabel's first mention of Ralph Ashcroft came on January 9, 1905, when he visited 21 Fifth Avenue to speak with Twain about business affairs. Ashcroft was thirty years old at the time, slender and good-looking. He came from a quality family, his father having been a Congregational minister, and he had a taste for the finer things in life. Twain quickly grew to like and trust Ashcroft, and admired his overt aggressiveness in business matters. By 1907 Ashcroft had become a regular guest at 21 Fifth Avenue, joining in games of Hearts with Isabel and Twain. Isabel regarded their new "third hand" as "pleasant, bright considerate & properly appreciative."

Yet likable as he may have been to his card-playing companions, Ashcroft was not without his detractors. In October 1907, an article in *The New York Times* described a libel suit between Ashcroft and John Hays Hammond, a wealthy Plasmon investor and mining engineer who had helped found the De Beers diamond company. Ashcroft claimed that Hammond had libeled him by sending a telegram to Twain describing him as "incompetent, or worse." This legal unpleasantness, however, did not weaken Twain's confidence in Ashcroft; to the contrary, it had the opposite effect. Twain became convinced that Ashcroft, along with Henry Rogers, would always act on his behalf with the best of intentions.

By the beginning of 1908 Twain, Isabel, and Ashcroft had become quite a merry trio, much to Paine's dismay. In mid-January, Ashcroft arrived at 21 Fifth Avenue for an evening of fine dining and playing Hearts with Twain and Isabel. At three o'clock in the morning, after a quart of Scotch had been polished off, the game broke up, according to Isabel, with Twain stumbling, "trying to reach the door & landing up in the corner. . . . He . . . cast a gay little eye over at me in his unsteady gait, & said 'I'm just practicing'—as he sailed with light footsteps over to the door—& up to the bath room—Ashcroft began to spill his cards on the floor, & I picked up a discard of 27 cards & tried to arrange it as my hand."

The next day saw a repeat of the previous evening's antics; however, this time it was Paine's turn for dinner and billiards. After watching the two men play until eleven o'clock, Isabel retired to bed. She was awakened at half past two in the morning by the sound of billiard balls hitting into one another. Isabel found Twain,

> playing in a drunken haze . . . & couldn't move without reeling. It was a great thing to see— P—was furious with me & told me to clear out but I sat down & said I'd stay until the King started for bed. P didn't like me—but I didn't care. It was wonderful to see the King pick up a ball & fondle it—& then try to hit it with his cue & be unable to touch it; but he swore splendidly. AB left the room & I gently took . . . the King's cue away, & led him to his room. He staggered & hit his head against one of the little angels on his bed post. & grabbed his dear head with a volley of oaths. Then I left the room but waited to hear his shoes drop.

Taking stock of her situation and the players involved, Isabel decided that her best ally was Ashcroft. Playing Hearts had taught her to carefully plan her next move, and with the addition of Ashcroft to Twain's circle, she believed that she now had some excellent hands remaining. In January 1908, Isabel and Ashcroft began colluding about restricting Paine's access to Twain's letters. When Isabel told Ashcroft how she had managed the Howells letters "episode," she was pleased to find that "he approved of my method of procedure with Mr. Howells for I wrote him of the fact that the King is quite unaware that Paine sent for the letters. [Crossed out: Ashcroft is so good.]"

By June, Isabel had bestowed upon Ashcroft the nickname Benares. The name came from one of Twain and Isabel's favorite writers, Rud-

yard Kipling, who had written a story, "The Bride's Progress," about
the city of Benares. (Isabel had an affinity for Kipling, in particular his
stories about loving couples.) Benares, now known as Varanasi, is one of
the oldest inhabited cities in India as well as the holiest Hindu city. It
is located on the banks of the Ganges in the state of Uttar Pradesh.
Twain had visited Benares when he was on his around-the-world-tour
in 1896, and recounted the afternoon he spent there with a Hindu holy
man in *Following the Equator*. "The Bride's Progress" is a portrayal of
Benares through the eyes of a young, naïve English newlywed, referred
to only as The Bride, and her wealthy husband. Appalled by the
strangeness of the city and unimpressed by its two thousand temples,
The Bride begs her spouse: "*Must* we do it, if it smells like this?" After
briefly touring, the couple makes an early retreat to their hotel. In the
morning they set out on the river to take in the dawn breaking over
Scindia's Ghât, a particularly beautiful setting with a Shiva temple partially submerged in water. Nearly alone on the river the young couple
survey the scene:

> Day broke over Benares, and The Bride stood up and applauded with
> both her hands. It was finer, she said, than any transformation scene; and
> so in her gratitude she applauded the earth, the sun, and the everlasting
> sky. The river turned to a silver flood and the ruled lines of the *ghâts* to
> red gold. "How can I describe this to mother?" she cried, as the wonder
> grew, and timeless Benares roused to a fresh day.

"A Bride's Progress" clearly resonated with Isabel, with her longtime
hopes for marriage and a romantic's appreciation of natural beauty, and
she echoed Kipling's lush prose to describe a sublime summer sky at
Stormfield in 1908:

> The King wandered out from dinner tonight to look at a wonderful sun-
> set & he called Benares & me to look at the mighty show. . . . We cut the
> meal short to go out & sit in the archway & watch the sunset that had for
> its top a great spray of white thin strip-like clouds, & we watched it
> until the moon came riding up high enough to call the west from the
> sun to herself. . . . A few stars were glimmering away up toward the
> Zenith, & the King said "The sunset is like some Brobdingnagian fire
> Company that is trying to put out the stars."

Ashcroft's supportive presence and keen understanding of the complicated dynamics of the Clemens household must have appeared to Isabel like a godsend. Navigating this uncharted and emotionally rocky terrain had exhausted her over the years, and the continued bickering with Paine had also taken its toll. Isabel valued Ashcroft not just for his intelligence and savvy, but also for his ability to manage Twain.

By the fall of 1908, Ashcroft had become indispensable to Isabel because Twain was simply too mercurial a personality to manage by herself. Clara had proven impossible to please for any extended period, and Jean did not hold any real power when it came to deciding important matters. Also, by that fall Isabel needed an ally because her trust in Paine had utterly deteriorated. She had questioned his motives for some time, and her suspicions were confirmed over the summer, when Ashcroft told her about a conversation that Paine had initiated with him. In July Paine and Ashcroft had been traveling together by train on their way to Stormfield. During the trip, Paine told Ashcroft that Isabel was "ruining [her] mentality etc with drugs." Isabel recorded that after their arrival, Ashcroft asked about her feelings regarding "Paine's friendship for me," and told her that while on the train Paine had "sat with him & talked against me." Isabel was outraged by Paine's betrayal: "fenacetine [the drug]—Why I cant even spell the word."

Isabel had probably told Paine about the medication she had been using, not realizing that Twain believed his nephew Charles L. Webster had been addicted to the drug and (wrongly) blamed it for his ruination and subsequent death. Paine knew about Twain's views regarding phenacetin, having heard his version of Charles's death in an autobiography dictation. It would not be much of a leap to assume that in addition to telling Ashcroft, Paine had also told Twain about Isabel's phenacetin usage in an attempt to weaken his confidence in her. Less than two weeks after this trespass, Isabel did some quiet lobbying of her own, telling Colonel Harvey how Clara had come to be appointed her father's literary executrix. Isabel shared with the colonel how "nearly Paine had culled that for himself," and triumphantly noted in her daily reminder, "now Col. Harvey is to do the editing of the Biog." This latest development was certain to infuriate Paine. Taking stock of the situation, Isabel realized that although she had planned to accompany Jean to Berlin to help her settle into her new surroundings, she had best remain at Stormfield to protect her interests: "Benares & I have a moral obligation now in looking after the King. I shall not leave him for an hour unless Benares or another as good is here to look after him. & Together we must uphold him in our spiritual arms." The ranks were closing against Paine.

The infighting between Isabel and Paine continued well into the fall. On October 15, Isabel discovered that for the past year Paine had had in his possession letters from Olivia Clemens to her sister Susan Crane without her or Twain's knowledge. She immediately informed Twain; furious, he ordered her to telephone Paine and "demand those letters." Isabel did what she was told and Paine immediately sent "Sanford the Grocer" to deliver them to the house. Isabel, though, did not make the call alone. She gratefully acknowledged that "Benares" had stood by her when she was on the phone "to courage me up." With this newfound support, Isabel had become "unafraid, for always there is Benares to be near me—& to help me."

Isabel began to regard Ashcroft as a potential partner in more ways than just helping her diminish Paine's influence. Mixed in with her gratitude was a new note of emotional involvement, expressed with her typical hyperbole:

> In the late twilight Benar & I wandered down to the Pergola. The soft light, & the dim trees . . . put a spell over the place—like that of Debussy music. It was all soft grey harmony. The only pin was the Sound of Benar's voice, in the still green grayness. And now I know why the Earth was so lonely when he was in Canada, & it seemed as if he never would come back. He is strong. & by his calm judgment he carries me through difficulties, he gives me a support & a knowledge of the values of things.

With her affection for Ashcroft increasing, it was only natural that Isabel would turn to him when she would quarrel with Paine, and that she would run to him after clashing with Clara. Waiting for her at the train station in New York on that morning in late October, Ashcroft possessed the ability to dispel the "gloom that misunderstandings frequently put into my heart." Glimpsing him standing at the platform, Isabel immediately brightened and the pair spent a contented afternoon shopping in the city. Strolling together down the streets, they entered a new store at 424 Fifth Avenue, located on the corner of

Thirty-eighth Street, to purchase an out-of-the-ordinary present for their King.

6

The Arnold Electric Company had opened a shop to sell to the public the latest innovation in home health care. Isabel and Ashcroft purchased the company's newest invention, an electric handheld vibrator. At first blush the Arnold electric vibrator might appear to be an odd choice for an elderly man frequently under the weather. Twain, however, always had a fondness for gadgets and his curiosity was sure to be piqued.

As is still the case today, vibrators then were marketed as an aid for relieving sexual tension as well as soothing sore muscles. It was also believed that electricity possessed healthy properties the vibrator was an ideal conduit. This invention came complete with plentiful testimonials from satisfied users avowing its health benefits with attached photographs showing happy users in states of rapturous ecstasy. The vibrator was part of a whole series of electrified machines newly made available to the public for purchase. With the introduction of the electrified home at the turn of the century, labor-saving devices had begun to be developed and marketed. Steam-powered and battery-equipped vibrators had been in use since the 1870s by physicians, largely for the treatment of female "neurasthenia" or "hysteria." In the nineteenth century, neurasthenia was considered a new disease afflicting women, caused by the stresses of modern life. Treatment for this disease included massage by electric vibrator of the pelvic area and sexual organs. The electric vibrator could be self-applied and was much less expensive than the cost of multiple visits to a physician. By 1900 more than a dozen manufacturers had begun producing both battery-powered vibrators and models that operated from line electricity.

Vibrators were primarily marketed in such women's magazines as *Modern Woman* and *Woman's Home Companion.* Advertisements proclaimed: "Relieves all Suffering" and "American Vibrator . . . can be used by yourself in the privacy of dressing room or boudoir, and furnish every woman with the essence of perpetual youth." Men, though, were also determined to be a viable market and the men's journal *Popular Mechanics* ran ads for the Arnold electric vibrator touting its glorious benefits.

Snap, ginger, punch in every
thought and action! The joy of glorious health, strength, power, life—
yours through vibration.
Wake up that sluggish circulation! Send the rich, red blood leaping
along through every vein and artery!. . .
Flood your whole body with health!
Don't be satisfied with mere existence! Begin to live!

Isabel and Ashcroft understood that their highest priority was to
keep Twain in good health. Perhaps this miracle invention would also
keep Twain in high spirits. More calculatingly, the longer Twain lived,
the more time the two had to position themselves to financially and
socially benefit from their association with him. The Arnold vibrator
must have seemed the ideal treatment; Ashcroft and Isabel hoped that
its "magic" would revivify Twain. Returning to Stormfield that evening, the twosome "drove home in the twilight, along these darling
roads & through the woods made so stately by their naked trees."
Before sharing their gift with Twain, Isabel and Ashcroft "tested it on
me—& on him—Benar." The results were apparently satisfactory, as
Isabel recorded in her daily reminder: "We had a most lovely evening."

Twain loved his slightly used Arnold electric vibrator. The contrap-
tion weighed approximately ten pounds and was expensive, costing
around $20. Included were four massage heads made of various materi-
als and profiles. Two days after being presented with his electric handheld vibrator, Twain raved about it in a letter to Emilie Rogers, Henry
Rogers's wife:

> I want Mr. Rogers to buy and try the Arnold electric vibrating
> machine . . . and you must try it too. It seems to do all that the human
> massageur does with his hands—and more, and better, and pleasanter,
> and simpler, and more effectively. It stops headaches for Miss Lyon and
> cures and limbers lame and stiff backs for me. It claims to ease all sorts
> of pains, and I judge it can do it, for it stirs up the circulation quite
> competently and tones up the nerves—and that is really the essential
> function of osteopathy and kindred treatments.

Twain was so enthralled with his gift that he subsequently purchased
a second vibrator that ran on batteries. Could Twain have known about
the vibrator's most common use, namely as a masturbation aid for

women? It seems almost impossible that he would not. As a faithful user of "odorless" condoms in his early thirties and as the author of "1601," an ode to masturbation and other ribaldry (published anonymously in 1880), he would have appreciated the "capital-labor substitution innovation" aspects of the device.

## 7

With the residents of Stormfield seemingly well massaged and refreshed, it appears reasonable to expect that some measure of peace would follow. Peace, however, would prove to be in very short supply that year. Isabel attempted to view the hurtful "misunderstandings fired" at her by Clara as what she had to endure in order to "hold so great a Treasure as the King," and that meant, "the price one must pay can never be too high a one. It will be a high one. But to know that you know the King is to send big roots down to support your tree." As for the "mud of criticism," she rationalized that "mud can clarify things in time—& can build a foundation from which I'll be the better able to see the King." And while she had undoubtedly entertained thoughts of a possible marriage to Twain immediately after Olivia's death, by this time she had shifted her affections to Ashcroft. On October 28, Isabel wrote an eloquent response to a request by a Mrs. Furnas for her thoughts about Olivia. Isabel's message was lyrical in its unconcealed appreciation for the deceased:

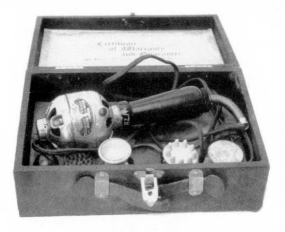

*Arnold electric vibrator,*
*manufactured by Arnold Electric*

Dear Mrs. Furnas:

Your letter was answered while I was ill, or I Should have tried to tell you a few of Mrs Clemens's very remarkable & beautiful characteristics. To begin with, she was not an "unknown" wife, for her qualities were such that wherever Mr. Clemens was personally known & loved, she had her full share of the love & admiration that were bestowed upon him. From the time of the publishing of his first book, she was his only critic, & edited Everything that he wrote. She was a brilliant woman, highly Cultivated & Educated; & the house that she was queen of, was the rendezvous of the great literary lights of all Countries, who came to do honor to her, as well as to Mr. Clemens. There never was a woman more universally loved in this Country, in Europe, India & Australia, than Mrs Clemens was; & she was entertained at the courts of Europe when she & Mr. Clemens were living abroad. There was never a more perfect wife, & mother of 3 beautiful daughters, than Mrs Clemens was. It is impossible for me to do her justice, but I am glad to pay this tribute to her memory.

When Isabel showed Twain the letter before sending it, he responded emotionally: " 'That is *good! Very very!*' & his Dear voice shakes."

Although Twain and Isabel appeared to have settled into an agreeable routine at Stormfield, conflict with Clara was always looming. Stunned and upset by Clara's criticisms, Isabel visited Dr. Quintard and received his recommendation that she "was badly in need of rest & change." Yet, despite his warning, she stubbornly refused to take a break. Instead, Isabel and Twain spent the first weeks of November attending the trial of the men who had burgled Stormfield and stolen the silver, and they both testified on November 6 and 10. On the eleventh, after another "trying and terrible" day spent in court, Isabel finally "went to pieces" at dinner. She spent the next few days ill in bed. On November 14, possibly in response to Isabel's fraying nerves, Twain asked that a new legal document be drawn up to replace the previous power of attorney, dated May 7, 1907, which had granted her sole control over his affairs. With his daughters continuing to be excluded from their father's legal agreement, Twain now legally appointed Isabel and Ashcroft his "true and lawful attorneys for me and in my name, place and stead, to exercise a general supervision over all my affairs and to take charge of and manage all my property both real and personal and all matters of business relating thereto; to lease, sell and convey any and all real property wheresoever situated which may now or which may hereafter at any time belong to me." The document was signed and sealed by Twain.

Why would Twain continue to exclude his daughters from such an agreement? A reasonable explanation is that neither one had the slightest experience in managing money, nor did they understand what his annual income was nor how long his royalties would extend. They were primarily interested in the spending of money, and Twain likely thought that trusted employees with financial acumen would best administer his estate. His actions were also influenced by his knowledge of the awful fate that befell Bret Harte's only surviving daughter, Jessamy Steele, who was reduced to living in a poorhouse because her father had given up the rights to his royalties, leaving her penniless after his death, in 1902. The close partnership that Twain had now formed with Isabel and Ashcroft was symbolized in the Christmas card mailed to his close friends in December 1908. It featured a photograph of Twain sitting in the window at Stormfield, with Isabel and Ashcroft protectively hovering at each side. This was Twain's family now, the photograph seemed to say, and his daughters had become invisible.

*Photograph used in Twain's 1908 Christmas card,*
*with Isabel Van Kleek Lyon and Ralph Ashcroft*

A little over a month later, after the power of attorney had been revised, another legal document was drawn up and approved by Twain. As early as October Isabel had noted how "very nervous, very worried," Twain was in anticipation of the expiration of copyright for *The Innocents Abroad.* Twain likely viewed the expiration of copyright on his first publishing success as a precursor of his own death. After much planning and consultation with Ashcroft throughout the previous year, on December 23, 1908, the Mark Twain Corporation was formed. The purpose of incorporating his nom de plume, *The Washington Post* reported, was to allow Twain's "two daughters Clara L. and Jean L. Clemens, to receive the financial benefits of his works for the greatest possible length of time," instead of permitting them "to be filched away by strangers." Incorporating the Mark Twain name would be "the surest way to keep the earnings of Mr. Clemens' books continually in the family, even after the copyright on the books themselves expires."

Twain assigned his existing copyrights and his pen name to his new corporation. *The Washington Post* reported that the officers of the corporation included Twain as president, Ashcroft as secretary and treasurer, and Clara, Jean, and Isabel as the three directors. In the article about the corporation that appeared in *The New York Times,* Ashcroft was quoted:

> The knowledge that the copyright of his works would soon expire and that strangers instead of his own kin would reap the financial benefit from his literary works has troubled Mr. Clemens for a year. He has been in consultation with Mr. Hobbs and myself practically every week. We finally hit on the plan of incorporating the Mark Twain name itself. We believe that when this name is the property of a perpetual corporation Mr. Clemens's heirs will be in a position to enjoin perpetually the publication of all of the Mark Twain books not authorized by the Mark Twain Company, even after the twenty-year first copyright and ten-year secondary copyright have expired.

Twain, however, was interested in more than just protecting the copyright on his books. He was the first important author-celebrity immediately recognizable worldwide with a resoundingly positive popular association. Since the beginning of his writing career, his pen name and face had been frequently used to sell products without his permission and without remuneration. During his lifetime, the image and pseudonym Mark Twain sold playing cards, Oldsmobile cars, Pullman train passenger cars, baking flour, jumping-frog mechanical banks, scrapbooks, photograph albums, cookbooks, postcards, sewing machines, shaving soap, fine china, decorative silver spoons, and, of course, whiskey and cigars. Twain was quick to credit Ashcroft for the formation of the Mark Twain Corporation. He was now an official commodity and possessed the right to control the usage of his likeness. And Twain applauded Ashcroft's zealousness in enforcing his copyright with those who would dare to use his image and words without compensating him.

## 8

Connected to a genuine desire to provide for his two feckless, unmarried daughters was Twain's insatiable desire for his name to live in perpetuity. He was determined that his fame and wealth would exist beyond the grave, and he undertook this quest with utter gravity. The root of his obsession can be found in the nineteenth century's veneration of the self-made man. Twain came of age during a time in America when to fail did not merely describe one's lack of business acumen; it characterized the totality of one's being. The dark side of the self-made man was failure, and failure had become synonymous with having a deficient self. The poor, it was commonly held, deserved their lot because they possessed insufficient character. People who failed did so due to a "problem native to their constitution," and it was believed that their children would inherit "the particular biological identities of both parents."

By the latter part of the nineteenth century, failure had become defined, much as it still is today, as "the most damning incarnation of the connection between achievement and personal identity." This widely held belief was even expounded from the pulpit. The Reverend Russell Conwell, famed orator and educator, directly linked the pursuit of capitalism with the pursuit of God in his well-known speech "Acres of Diamonds," delivered over six thousand times to enthusiastic congregants:

> The opportunity to get rich, to attain unto great wealth is . . . within the reach of . . . almost every man and woman who hears me speak tonight. . . . I have come to tell you what in God's sight I believe to be

the truth. . . . Never in the history of the world did a poor man without capital have such an opportunity to get rich quickly and honestly. . . .

Some men say, "Don't you sympathize with the poor people?" . . . But the number of poor who are to be sympathized with is very small. . . . there is not a poor person in the United States who was not made poor by his own shortcomings. . . . It is all wrong to be poor anyhow.

To describe the salvation of one's soul, the clergy had appropriated the language of business.

The specter of failure had a particular resonance with Twain. As has been mentioned, while a young child he had watched his father repeatedly fail in his business endeavors, and the family was eventually forced to move into a small apartment above the office of a successful physician in Hannibal. Upon John Marshall Clemens's death, his family was plunged into poverty. The fear of failing like his father tormented Twain throughout his life, and his appetite for success was insatiable. His brother Orion, a decade older than Twain, tried many different ventures—journalism, printing, politics, law, chicken farming, and writing—all unsuccessfully, and was considered to have inherited his father's "aptitude for failure."

In 1862, when Twain was twenty-seven and living out west, he sent this chilling message to his older brother:

> I shall never look upon Ma's face again, or Pamela's [his sister's], or get married, or revisit the "Banner State," until I am a rich man—so you can easily see that when you stand between me and my fortune (the one which I shall make, as surely as Fate itself,) you stand between me and home, friends, and all that I care for—and by the Lord God! You must clear the track, you know!

After Twain had achieved a level of financial sustainability, he subsidized Orion for nearly thirty years.

Forced to declare bankruptcy at age fifty-nine as the result of bad business investments, Twain must have felt that he had finally shown what he had most feared—that the father's deficiencies would surface in the son. The only possibility of salvation, according to the prevailing ethos of the Gilded Age, lay in embracing a capitalist identity. Max

Weber's argument in *The Protestant Ethic and the Spirit of Capitalism* (1905) was that "striving for success is a compulsory virtue, even a sacred duty in American culture." To be successful meant "the rational pursuit of profit, the perpetual increase of capital as an end in itself, the development of an acquisitive personality, and the belief that ceaseless work is a necessity of life."

Twain proved a receptive audience to the message, and he ultimately regained financial solvency by embarking upon his worldwide lecture tour and continuing to publish. But more important, he left the management of the bulk of his business affairs to Henry

*Henry Rogers*

Rogers. Twain's method of thwarting his biological destiny was to sign over power of attorney to Rogers just months after meeting him for the first time, in the fall of 1893. Rogers ably managed Twain's business investments, negotiated his book contracts, and reestablished his positive financial position, allowing Twain to pay off his creditors in full, which earned him a worldwide reputation for integrity. This experience might help explain why Twain later granted power of attorney to Isabel and Ashcroft. By that time, Rogers was in failing health. Twain's belief that financial failure might be his family's biological destiny included the fear that his daughters were vulnerable to the same failing and therefore needed to be protected.

Rogers's influence upon Twain extended far beyond the positive effect he had on his bank balance; Twain's mood was always lighter when he was in Rogers's presence, and he looked forward to their increasingly infrequent outings together. Isabel was so pleased (and probably relieved) to see the cheerful effect Rogers had that she was inspired to compose verse:

*The King last night went gambling.*
*With the Lord of Standard Oil.*

*He came rolling home this morning*
*With his pockets full of spoil.*
*He had played with Mrs. Rogers*
*'Gainst her Lord of provenience,*
*And Melville Stone {general manager of The Associated Press} so naughty—*
*And won, by five & seventy cents.*
*It makes him proud & happy,*
*Till his face is fair to see.*
*And Dorothea Gilder said*
*She could have hugged he!*
*(But she took it out on me.)*
*So there's no Such Thing as*
*headache—*
*There's no Such Thing as grief.*
*And I'm on my knees a-worshipping—*
*A-worshipping my Chief.*

Since their initial meeting, Rogers had become Twain's most trusted friend. "His wisdom and steadfastness saved my copyrights from being swallowed up in the wreck," Twain gratefully acknowledged, "and his commercial wisdom has protected my pocketbook ever since." Without Rogers's help, Twain was convinced he would have died a ruined man. Yet even with Rogers's firm guidance, Twain still could not entirely resist the lure of quick money and he continued to speculate—always at a loss.

During the fall of 1908 at Stormfield, guests arrived one after the other, and everyone was expected to conform to Twain's particular daily schedule. He was a late riser and typically enjoyed breakfast in bed shortly before noon. When he was feeling well, billiards was a daily event. Dinner started at eleven o'clock at night and was always accompanied by wine (despite the fact that Redding at the time was legally dry under a local ordinance) and "a big dish of radishes" (Twain believed radishes warded off heartburn). During the third week of November, Mr. and Mrs. Doubleday visited, Judge Case and Mr. Styles Judson dined, and Lord Northcliffe and Colonel Harvey spent the night. By the twenty-first, when Captain Dow arrived for his visit, even Twain had finally become "very very tired."

What bed rest or doctor's orders could not improve, however, was the increasingly obvious break between Clara and Isabel. When one is playing the game of Hearts, the player to the left of the dealer leads first. The following players must play in suit if they can, and the highest card of the suit led wins the trick. The winner of the trick leads to the next trick. A player cannot lead with a heart until a heart has been "broken," or played in the game. Clara, Twain, and Isabel would soon commence playing their last game of Hearts, but this time they would not be playing with cards; instead, the tricks would be people.

**9**

The first hand was dealt by Twain. On November 25, 1908, Thanksgiving Day, an ill Isabel wrote a brief note in her daily reminder: "Will came early & Santa came later." This simply worded entry, innocuous at first glance, actually signaled that many changes were afoot. By November 1908, Clara and Wark had been involved for nearly two years. But Thanksgiving Day 1908 signaled a watershed moment because after that date Wark seemingly vanished from the Clemenses' lives. The rumors about Clara and Wark and the nature of their relationship had intensified after the newspapers covered their return from Europe, and Twain must have finally discovered Wark's marital status. Exactly how he found out is unknown, but he did, and Twain made it clear to Clara that Wark would no longer be her intimate. For a family who maintained such active correspondence with friends and relatives, the silence around Wark's disappearance is deafening. There survives one mention of Wark after Thanksgiving; in February he wrote his name in the Stormfield guestbook, a day after Clara and Ossip had arrived. That same week, an overwrought Isabel wrote from her sickbed: "There is a heavy heavy fog—I'm wondering if it extends out to sea—" Clara never made reference to Wark in any of the writings she published after her father's death.

Already antagonistic toward each other, father and daughter shared volcanic tempers, and the two must have had an epic battle. In the end Twain prevailed (after all, Clara was totally financially dependent upon him) and Clara's freewheeling life of magic-carpet travel and free love was over.

In addition to Wark's sudden disappearance, Twain played two other hands over the next four weeks. After settling into her new life in Berlin, Jean had eagerly become part of the regular social circuit of teas and luncheons. Dr. von Reuvers had given her newfound hope that her epilepsy could be cured, and on December 11, 1908, she happily purchased Christmas presents for her family and Isabel, and mailed them to Stormfield. Six days later, a shocked Jean received the following terse telegram:

> YOU SAIL JANUARY NINTH STEAMER PENNSYLVANIA
> PASSAGE PREPAID. SEND MARGUERITE HOME. DONT CABLE.
> FATHER.

Jean had expected to remain abroad for at least six months. Twain offered no explanation for his change of mind, and the pages in Isabel's daily reminder for December 13–17 were left blank. Isabel's only reference to Jean's homecoming was on December 30, 1908, when she mentions in passing that she will go into the city the next day to speak with Dr. Peterson about finding Jean housing. After an extended voyage due to bad weather, Jean sailed into New York Harbor on January 25, 1909. She was initially placed in a group home called Unkeway Farm in Babylon, on Long Island, although that quickly proved not to be to her liking, and she moved to a more palatable facility, Wahnfried, in Montclair, New Jersey, in March.

The final hand was played on December 18, 1908, when an old friend of Clara's suddenly reappeared at Stormfield. A piano prodigy, Ossip Gabrilowitsch (his birth name was Osip Salomonovich Gabrilovich) was born in St. Petersburg, Russia, and had studied piano and composition at the St. Petersburg Conservatory with Anton Rubinstein, Anatoly Konstantinovich Lyadov, and Alexander Glazunov. After graduating, in 1894, he had traveled to Vienna, where he spent two years studying with Teodor Leszetycki. He successfully débuted in Berlin in 1896 and subsequently toured the United States and Europe.

Gabrilowitsch met the Clemenses in April 1898, while they were living in Vienna. Clara was four years older than the talented Russian, but the two became close and remained in touch over the years. In April 1902, Clara traveled to Europe with a chaperone, and visited Gabrilowitsch in Paris, where he was living. Much to her parents' consternation, she remained abroad until August 12. On July 5, 1902, in *Harper's Weekly,* Twain published an article entitled "Why Not Abolish It?" The "It" he was referring to was the age of consent: "Why should there be an age at which a member [of a family] may help a criminal to destroy that far more valuable asset, the family's honor?" The timing of

*Ossip Gabrilowitsch and Clara Clemens
at the piano*

the article and of Clara's extended absence might be sheer coincidence, but it is noteworthy.

Isabel's first mention of Gabrilowitsch came shortly after beginning her employ with the Clemenses. On January 1, 1903, while she was visiting with Clara "his voice rang out in happy laughter," and Gabrilowitsch thoughtfully volunteered to "run this morn for scissors" for Isabel. Clara put a red carnation in his buttonhole, and Isabel commented, "The year began well for him." After Olivia's death the two drifted apart, although they continued to correspond. Isabel's next mention of Gabrilowitsch came four years later, on January 19, 1907, when she and her mother went to an afternoon concert and heard him play selections from Arensky along with a Chopin sonata. That same evening, he dropped by to see Clara. Clara had just started her relationship with Wark. Over the next three months Isabel recorded three visits from Gabrilowitsch: in February, when Clara was not at home, and in both March and April, when he played for Clara, Twain, and Isabel.

For the next two years Gabrilowitsch went unmentioned in Isabel's writings—until December 18, 1909. "Such a rich personality," Isabel effused. "He has a fortnight holiday & must spend it . . . somewhere in studying & perhaps will stay here." Gabrilowitsch was encouraged by

Twain to pursue Clara during his stay, although the first few days of his visit certainly did not prove propitious. Just two days after his arrival at Stormfield, *The New York Times* reported that tragedy had been narrowly averted on the morning of December 20:

> Miss Clara Clemens, daughter of Samuel L. Clemens, (Mark Twain) was saved from serious injury and possible death this morning through the action of Ossip Gabrilowitsch, a Russian pianist, who is a guest. . . .
>
> M. Gabrilowitsch, who is making a tour of America, and Miss Clemens went for a sleigh ride this morning, leaving the Clemens residence at 10 o'clock. While passing through Redding Glen, about three miles from Miss Clemens's home, the horse took fright at a wind whipped newspaper and bolted.
>
> Mr. Gabrilowitsch, who was driving, lost control of the horse. At the top of a hill the sleigh overturned, and Miss Clemens was thrown out. At the right of the summit of the hill is a drop of fifty feet. When the sleigh turned over the Russian leaped to the ground, and caught the horse by the head, stopping it as it was about to plunge over the bank, dragging Miss Clemens, whose dress had caught in the runner.
>
> In leaping to rescue Miss Clemens he sprained his right ankle. Miss Clemens was picked up uninjured, but suffered greatly from the shock of the accident. The injury to the pianist's ankle was painful, but he helped Miss Clemens into the sleigh, and drove her to her home.

Oddly enough, this traumatic incident goes unmentioned by Isabel: the entry for that date in her daily reminder is left blank, and there is no surviving correspondence by anyone in the family that refers to it. Clara recovered with lightning speed from her "shock," leaving Stormfield by herself on December 21—the same day the *Times* article was published—to return to her studio apartment at the Stuyvesant.

If Twain's plan was to reunite Clara and Gabrilowitsch at Stormfield for the purpose of encouraging a union, he must have been annoyed about the lack of time the two spent together. After Clara's departure that evening at 9:30, Gabrilowitsch, despite his reportedly sprained ankle (perhaps he sprained his left ankle), gave Isabel and Twain a private concert. "Gabrilowitsch played to us for an hour," Isabel wrote, "He is a darling musician & it is so good to have him in the house." Two days later Gabrilowitsch traveled to New York City and returned with a truculent Clara the next day. The next mention of Gabrilowitsch by Isabel comes on December 29: "Gabrilowitsch & I walked down to the gorge in the Early moonlight." Clara apparently was not present. In fact, Clara would not resurface in Isabel's record until January 25, 1909, when she was in the city waiting for Jean to sail home from Berlin.

The sleigh accident story handily served to link Clara's name publicly with another man, someone of appropriate social status, unencumbered by a spouse and children. To try to strengthen the perception that Clara and Gabrilowitsch had been romantically involved over a period of years, Twain wrote in 1909 to one of his Angelfish that the two had been engaged in 1901 but "the engagement was broken twice in 6 months." In a written statement to *The New York Herald,* Twain told the same story about the engagement being broken twice but gave the year as 1903. Twain's claim regarding Clara's supposed engagement is suspect, not just because he could not seem to remember the year when she was twice engaged, but also because the bohemian Clara had long been vehemently opposed to the proposition of marriage, having declared to her parents years earlier that she intended never to marry.

Gabrilowitsch's abrupt reappearance after such a long absence and Jean's curt order to return home were not unrelated. Faced with possible public embarrassment over Clara's behavior, Twain decided to circle the wagons, and *The New York Times* story about the miraculous rescue certainly could not have hurt. Yet it did not seem to help much, either. Just three weeks later, on January 11, 1909, Isabel nervously remarked that when the Reverend and Mrs. Twichell came to visit Twain at Stormfield, Mrs. Twichell confided in her that "all the Hartford world is talking about Clara's reported engagement to Wark—saying that she is only waiting for Mrs. Wark to get a divorce from him, when the marriage will take place. It is a sickening report. The Country people around here have got hold of a similar Tale." This kind of scandal, horrifying to polite society in 1909 and ruinous to Clara's reputation, was enough to give the old man a stroke. Knowing Twain's extreme sensitivity regarding propriety and his obsession with his image, this "sickening report" confirmed by two of his oldest friends must have inflamed all of his worst fears and insecurities. Sexual scheming, adultery, and licentiousness on the part of the King's daughter were, in a word, forbidden.

Twain, with Isabel a participant, hatched a plan, as convoluted as any of his fiction, to save his daughter's honor. The framework can be found in the plot of Twain's short story "Wapping Alice," written in 1898. The basis for "Wapping Alice" was an actual event that occurred in the family home in Hartford in 1877. Twain had discovered that the English maid, Lizzie, had been seeing a young mechanic, Willie Taylor, late in the evenings. Willie had been sneaking into the house after hours through the basement to have sex with Lizzie and kept tripping the burglar alarm. After Twain confronted her, Lizzie confessed. He ordered her to bring Willie before him and gave the incredulous mechanic an ultimatum: he had to marry Lizzie immediately to keep her from being ruined. A reluctant Willie finally agreed and Twichell immediately performed the ceremony. Twain decided to launch a similar effort in early 1909 to force Clara into giving up Wark and, instead, to choose a life of respectability with Gabrilowitsch.

Isabel collapsed under the strain caused by Twain's plotting. Two days before the Twichells came to visit, during the second week of January 1909, Isabel was diagnosed with neurasthenia and advised by her doctor "to stay right in this room & never move from it for a week & I'm not to know anything about anything in, or out of the house." Over a month later, a still indisposed Isabel wrote (and then crossed out) lines about her and Ashcroft's feelings for Twain in her date book: "He knows that we love him—we too; he knows that we couldn't find happiness anywhere in the world while he lives, but with him, & he knows that he couldn't drive us away without filling our lives with desolation. The 2 men walked to the gorge, & played billiards, & the King read more Macbeth to us. & we had a very sweet & placid day. My little bed is a blessed place to live in."

This is quite a scene to envision. While Clara's fury mounts and Jean's loneliness grows, Twain, tucked away in his ersatz Italian villa in Connecticut, performs a dramatic reading to his two-person audience about betrayal, murder and guilt. Perhaps Twain read his rapt listeners these lines from Act 5, Scene 1:

> *Foul whisperings are abroad. Unnatural deeds*
> *Do breed unnatural troubles; infected minds*
> *To their deaf pillows will discharge their secrets.*

Tone-deaf Isabel was delighted by Twain's literary choice: "His reading of Shakespeare is the individual presentation of each character, & the . . . masterly, conscious, worship of the superb English of the matchless plays. [Crossed out: Ah, we are rarely treated by Fate; and we are aware of it. We do not hold cheaply any hour of any day; not any act, or presence of the King. To have him walk into this room where I lie in bed, is to have the place suddenly filled with the flash of human beauty, & wit flash upon flash of the Sweetest wit ever lodged in any mind.]" This entry, from February 13, 1909, is the last surviving one from Isabel's 1909 date book.

It was at this time that Isabel and Ashcroft made the momentous decision that they would marry, presumably as a way to further protect Twain's reputation and to insulate themselves from Clara's anger. If Isabel is to be believed, Twain was, in effect, playing puppeteer with the lives of those closest to him under the guise of safeguarding the Clemens family honor, and Isabel entered into a sham marriage to Ashcroft to help him achieve his end. If this is true, Isabel was not entirely selfless in doing so. Her daily reminder entries reveal that Isabel regarded Ashcroft with considerable fondness (calling him "good Benares") as well as recognizing him as a crucial ally. She likely thought that in marrying him, both her emotional desires and her financial needs would be fulfilled. Ashcroft also possessed a strong personality, and with his thorough knowledge of Twain's business matters, Isabel was convinced that he would protect her. There are, however, multiple competing narratives, as revealed in journal entries and personal correspondence, and none is easily separable from any other. While Isabel later claimed—over three decades after the fact—that she had never loved Ashcroft and married him only because of a "deal" she had made with Twain, she gave friends contrary accounts.

On February 16, while still bedridden, Isabel wrote to Hattie Whitmore, her close friend and the daughter of Harriet Whitmore, that she would be traveling to Hartford the following Tuesday, February 23, to stay for a week at the elegant Heublein Hotel to recuperate. Isabel confided to Hattie that she and Ashcroft were going to wed, although "the psychic moment hasn't come yet for telling the King." Isabel was quick to reassure Hattie that her upcoming marriage "won't make any difference in my life work with the King—I'll stay right here, & Benares will come when he can to be with us both." Isabel explained to Hattie that it was her preference that the ceremony be private, without "any engagement announcement, & there isn't going to be any public wedding. It will be quiet as a whisper." Certainly this was an odd request coming from a woman acutely aware of etiquette and who had long been interested in reclaiming her family's position in society. Isabel's ambivalent tone was evident on January 21, 1909, a few weeks before she wrote her letter to Hattie, in a date-book entry: "Plenty of time there is now, for thinking over conditions that are grave, that are important—that seem trivial, but in reality are most weighty." After departing Stormfield, while at the Heublein, Isabel apparently felt the "psychic moment" had arrived and wrote to Twain about her nuptial plans.

Dear Mr. Clemens,

I've been thinking it all over—this, about Benares & me; & I know that I can't go on alone carrying the dear weight of wonderful Stormfield direction. Together we can work for you. . . . And you won't ever know anything different from the present plan, except that I will have one with the right to watch me, & keep me from breaking down. So I think, dear beautiful King, that before I come back to you, we'll go quietly to New York & be married, & the announcement can follow a little later. I haven't spoken of this to Benares, but I do want to hurry & get strong, & he can help me better than any one I know. . . . In fact, Benares has listened to my plan in this minute, & agrees that I am right. Dear King, I shall feel so much securer & of more value to you, & I'm so grateful for your sweet sanction.

In 1950, in her elder years, Isabel told Doris Webster an alternative version of the story. She explained that Ashcroft had taken her to Hartford to recover her health. Once they were there, an old friend of hers inquired if she was interested in marrying Ashcroft. Isabel said she was not, although Ashcroft "wants me to but I wouldn't think of it." Isabel's friend responded that she had better do it because "there was a good deal of gossip around Hartford about her and M.T. because she had stayed on as his secretary after Mrs. C.'s death, and when the girls were away [she] was sometimes alone with him. The friend said rumors were going around that she was M.T.'s mistress." Isabel told Doris that was the reason why she had wed Ashcroft; in effect, Ashcroft was an unwitting cover to protect her and Twain from errant gossip. Doris expressed to Isabel that this reason struck her as "a little unfair to him." Isabel returned: " 'Why, it was what he . . . wanted.' " Supposedly it was only after her convalescence that Isabel told Twain about her plan: "she told M.T. that she was going to marry Ashcroft and he was furious.

She said 'Mr. Clemens, you once asked me, if I heard anything harmful to your reputation to tell you about it, and I said I would.' She then told him the situation. She said he must come to her wedding. He was still very angry (and never really forgave her) but said he would come." Isabel also told Doris that she had voluntarily offered to resign her position instead of marrying Ashcroft and that Twain "wouldn't hear of it."

Twain wrote yet another account of the story, claiming that upon Isabel's return to Stormfield a "shamefaced, embarrassed, hesitating" Ashcroft told him about the impending marriage. Twain's response was that "it was an insane idea, & unbelievable." Ashcroft supposedly assured Twain that if he found the idea so repugnant they would delay their nuptials or cancel them entirely. However, Twain responded that he was unwilling to be "party to the freak in any way." Ashcroft then offered that they could marry secretly, a suggestion that Twain not only brushed aside but thought "could get us all into hot water presently." The veracity of Twain's account is highly questionable because a secret marriage would refute Isabel's claim that a wedding had to occur in order to allay gossip about her being his mistress. Twain's response was also bizarre when considered in the context that it seems reasonable that two single people who obviously had common interests might want to wed. How could the secrecy have put them into "hot water"? The likeliest explanation is that Twain was writing a fictionalized account. Yet marrying Ashcroft must have held some appeal for Isabel, and she probably believed at the time that she had played a perfect hand and won the trick.

Whether Isabel's decision to marry Ashcroft was what Twain had told her to do or her own idea, in the end it was of no consequence to Clara. Isabel might have been holding up her end of Twain's "deal" in marrying Ashcroft, as she later insisted, but Clara refused to willingly sacrifice her happiness on the altar of her father's vanity. Clara was convinced that Isabel had informed Twain about Wark's marital status. And thus enraged by this betrayal of her confidences, Clara also suspected Isabel of rumormongering, telling people in Hartford and Redding that she was insane as well as an adulteress. While Clara would be unable to sway her father from imposing sanctions against her, she could blame and seek revenge against Isabel, and did so with a furious energy.

At the same time that Isabel was ensconced at the Hotel Heublein, dithering over what explanation to give people for marrying Ashcroft, Clara began pressing her case to her father that Isabel had fraudulently misappropriated funds. A regrettable personality trait that Clara shared with her father and with her grandmother Jane Clemens was the tendency to form unforgiving personal grudges. Once condemned, former friends would rarely be reinstated into her good graces. Denied permission by her father to be with the man she loved, Clara directed her full wrath toward Isabel and no amount of punishment could ever prove adequate.

With Isabel absent in Hartford, Clara, along with her decidedly offbeat friend, the professional stage actress and psychic (two endeavors considered quite risqué at the time) Mary Lawton, paid Twain a visit. The two accused Isabel of embezzlement and argued that Clara had been shorted in her allowance because Isabel had stolen it. Twain considered the charges ludicrous, as did Mrs. Paine, who knew about the women's visit. Mrs. Paine, no friend of Isabel's, still found Clara's claims preposterous and wrote her husband on March 8 that Twain was

being driven almost crazy, and he said that until three weeks ago he thought he was happy and well off, but since then it has been h—— and that if things did not get better he would cut his G—— D—— throat—It would not be surprising what he might do—

Mr. Ashcroft and Miss Lyon are to be married!!! And it's a sworn secret just now, but I suppose soon, what can he be thinking about but I suppose they think that is the only way out and the only thing to do since they have criticized Clara.

To cast doubt in her father's mind and to have a plausible explanation for what would become a very public, vituperative attack, Clara claimed that Isabel had been stealing from Twain over an extended period. Isabel told Doris Webster years later that she had been accused by Clara of "taking various things from the Clemens house, getting away with money, taking rake-offs on things she bought for the house, etc. Clara and Paine and [John B.] Stanchfield [Twain's Elmira-based attorney] were the prime movers."

Isabel was not particularly surprised by Clara's accusations, telling Doris that she had noticed Clara becoming increasingly unfriendly toward her "before the break came." Clara objected to the quality of Isabel's wardrobe, suspecting that she had been spending unapproved amounts for clothing purchases. Then there was a contretemps over the location of some "Carnellian beads" that had belonged to Olivia that

Clara was convinced Isabel was intending to steal. What would become the largest and most serious point of contention, however, was the amount of money Isabel had spent on the renovation of Lyonesse. Twain asserted that he only became aware of the additional expenses after a chance conversation in early May with H. A. Lounsbury, the construction foreman, who supposedly informed him that the renovation of Isabel's house had cost in excess of $3,500, not the $1,500 Twain claimed Isabel had told him. (A few months later, Ashcroft told John Stanchfield that Isabel had actually told Twain that the cost was $2,700, not $1,500.)

Twain rejected his daughter's accusations in a letter written to Clara on March 11, 1909, reminding her that when Olivia originally hired Isabel she had agreed to a $50-per-month salary and had never asked for an increase. Isabel's character, Twain argued, was well known to him: "I have no suspicions of her. She was not trained to business and doubtless has been loose and unmethodical, but that is all. She has not been dishonest, even to a penny's worth. All her impulses are good and fine." If Twain hoped his spirited defense would appease Clara, he underestimated her desire for revenge. Two days later, Ashcroft and Twain held a business meeting of sorts. "General Clean-Up Day," as Twain would later term it, was intended to clarify both Ashcroft's and Isabel's standing in the household as well as their involvement in his business and legal affairs. Twain may have thought that if he adopted a more businesslike approach to dealing with Isabel, Clara would drop her allegations of graft. In the course of their meeting, Twain read and agreed to sign several legal documents. Two new contracts between Twain and Isabel were signed and notarized, the first stating that Isabel would "compile for publication the manuscript of a book or books to be entitled: 'Life and Letters of Mark Twain' " with total compensation "in consideration of the sum of One Dollar, lawful money of the United States, each to the other paid." The future royalties Isabel had been dreaming about were erased by a a stroke of Twain's pen.

A second document, also dated March 13, delineated that Isabel was Twain's "literary and social secretary" and would receive a monthly payment of $100 for services rendered, double the amount of her previous salary. Isabel's duties would be sharply restricted to matters social and literary, "and not to those of any member or members of his family; she shall not be required to supervise, direct or attend to, in any way whatsoever, his household or any part thereof, or the affairs of any member

*Isabel Lyon's home before renovation*

thereof." The Clemens daughters would no longer have to discuss the amount of their allowances with Isabel. Ashcroft also had Twain sign two agreements defining his responsibilities as an officer of the Mark Twain Corporation. Last, Ashcroft presented a "Memorandum of Understanding" to Twain stating that Isabel had been given permission by him to purchase clothes and make renovations on Lyonesse, with her promising to repay a portion of the funds. Twain read and signed all the documents. Again, if Twain thought these agreements would mollify Clara, he greatly underestimated his daughter's ire. Five days after "Clean-Up Day," Isabel and Ralph Ashcroft were married.

In the end, the decision about whether or not to make a public announcement was rendered academic by *The New York Herald* in its article published March 18, 1909.

> Cupid has been active in the ranks of the Mark Twain Company (Inc.), and two of the directors are to form a subsidiary corporation. They are Miss Isabelle Van Kleek Lyon, private secretary, and Ralph W. Ashcroft, business agent for Mr. Samuel L. Clemens. The romance dates from the time Mr. Ashcroft became associated with the author. Friendship ripened into love, and without taking Mr. Clemens into their confidence the couple became engaged. . . . Mr. Clemens came to New York yesterday from his country place at Redding, Conn., to be present at the wedding. He is a guest at the home of Mr. H. H. Rogers, at No. 3 East

*Isabel Lyon's home after renovation*

Seventy-eighth street. He declined to see reporters last night, but Miss Clara Clemens, his daughter, told of the plans for the marriage. She said that both Mr. Ashcroft and Miss Lyon would remain with the Mark Twain Company, which was organized last December by Mr. Clemens, his two daughters, Mr. Ashcroft and Miss Lyon.

The marriage took place on March 18, 1909, just a few blocks from 21 Fifth Avenue at the Church of the Ascension, at Fifth Avenue and Tenth Street, with the Reverend Percy Grant officiating. Present were friends Mr. and Mrs. Zoeth Freeman; Mrs. Martin W. Littleton (her husband was Harry K. Thaw's lawyer); Isabel's mother, Georgiana; Ashcroft's brother John; and Twain. Clara, Jean, and Paine were not in attendance. At long last Isabel was married, at age forty-five. The bride was twelve years older than her groom. After the wedding Twain said to Ashcroft, supposedly in jest: "The first one of you people who gets pregnant is going to get fired."

There was no pregnancy. However, less than a month later Twain severed the last tie that had enabled him to enjoy any semblance of normalcy.

On April 13, Clara sang at Mendelssohn Hall in New York City. Noteworthy is the fact among her musical selections that evening, Schubert, Schumann, and Strauss, she also sang a Gabrilowitsch composition. The *New York Times* reviewer thought it "a pity that a singer

*Isabel Van Kleek Lyon and Ralph W. Ashcroft's wedding day, March 18, 1909, in front of the Church of the Ascension, at Fifth Avenue and Tenth Street*

with as good a natural voice as that of Miss Clemens, who sings with so much feeling, should not use her voice to better advantage. Her tones last night were too often uneven and muffled." The critic was more generous in his praise of Clara's accompanist, Miss Littlehales. Playing a sonata by Johann Ernst Galliard and the obligato to Vannuccini's "La Vision" on her cello while Clara sang, Miss Littlehales showed "good technique and true feeling," according to the critic. "The audience was moderately enthusiastic." Clara's roughness in sound may have been because she had not yet grown entirely used to her accompanist. Twain had banished the person Clara cared for the most, and in return she would extract her pound of flesh.

On April 15, Clara sent her father a note demanding he "give Miss Lyon her notice right away." That same day, Twain sent a notice of termination to Isabel, via a housemaid, which was delivered to her in her bedroom in Stormfield. In a moment, their relationship ended. Everyone ran about in mutual states of confusion and anger. Doris Webster recounted that Isabel told her that upon opening the envelope, "she found it was a very kind letter discontinuing the secretaryship, and enclosing two months pay." That would be the last generous word Twain would ever offer her.

### 10

Despite his initial defense of Isabel, Twain ultimately decided to succumb to his daughter's need for retribution. Tellingly, he warned Isabel shortly after her marriage, "Remember, whatever I do is because of a promise I have made to Clara." What Isabel failed to fully appreciate was that Twain would always be primarily concerned with protecting his daughter's social reputation as well as his own, and that she herself was utterly expendable. After receiving her notice of termination, Isabel moved from Stormfield into her renovated farmhouse while Ashcroft continued his employment with Twain. That Isabel was fired and Ashcroft was not certainly underscores the supposition that Clara's animosity was initially directed at just one individual: Isabel. However, in Clara's mind—and soon in Twain's—Ashcroft had joined forces with the enemy, and he would enjoy just a temporary reprieve.

The only person who appeared to benefit from these tumultuous events was Jean. Isabel's leave-taking resulted in Jean's finally being reunited with her father. On April 26, 1909, just eleven days after Isabel's ouster, Jean came to Stormfield from Montclair. A reluctant Dr. Peterson tried to limit her to only a week's visit; however, despite her physician's misgivings, Jean remained. With Clara refusing to live with her father, Jean was the only family member willing to attend to him. Ecstatic about finally having a purpose to her life, Jean happily assumed her new duties as mistress of Stormfield. Twain gave his youngest daughter a farm, called the Italian Farm, with an accompanying 150 acres. (Ashcroft had purchased the Italian Farm on behalf of Twain as part of Stormfield's total acreage just a few weeks before their falling out.) Twain hailed Jean's return, and he marveled to friends and family about her excellent heath. "Wisdom, judgment, penetration, practical good sense," Twain crowed in a letter sent to Clara, "like her mother—character, courage, definiteness, decision; also goodness, a human spirit, charity, kindliness, pity; industry, perseverance, intelligence, a clean mind, a clean soul, dignity, honesty, truthfulness, high ideals, loyalty, faithfulness to duty—she is everything that Miss Lyon isn't."

Although Twain chose to represent his daughter's disease as cured, this was only wishful thinking on his part. Writing to Nancy Brush in July, Jean expressed her longing to see her; however, she recognized that doing so would entail taking an attendant who could mind her during her seizures: "They would not want me to go far alone. Now if it is going to be in the least inconvenient for you to have two people when you asked one, be absolutely outspoken in saying so." Certainly Jean's return to her father and to the countryside, which she loved, had a soothing effect upon her health, but her dreadful affliction would continue.

Just over a week after Isabel's dismissal, Clara paid a visit to Henry Rogers to alert him to "her troubles" and to ask him to become personally involved in the situation. This was a bold move in that it meant Clara's enlisting Twain's closest and certainly most powerful friend to become part of her vendetta. Evidently terminating Isabel's employ-

*Jean Clemens with Prosper le Gai*

ment was not enough to satisfy Clara. A sympathetic Rogers agreed to look into the matter, writing an enigmatic letter that he sent to Twain the same day:

> I had a call this morning from Clara, when she told me of her troubles, and after she had said you knew of her coming to me, I ventured to say that I would be very glad to take up the matter, if you desired it, and see if I could straighten it out to your entire satisfaction.
>
> I think I have read between the lines. In the last two or three years I had my suspicions of things, which you in your good natured way have overlooked. You may be sure I shall be glad to serve you, as ever, if you will but give me your approval. My judgment is that you should call in a competent lawyer and accountant to overhaul your entire affairs. This should be done with but little annoyance to you, and if you will but say to those people that you have decided to ask me to look into things, I am quite sure you will not have further trouble.

Rogers's politic comment about reading "between the lines" indicates that the most desirable outcome for everyone would be the silencing of "those people." To effect that end as quickly as possible, a week later Rogers summoned Ashcroft to his office for a private conversation. But if Rogers's intention was intimidation, he failed. After his meeting with Rogers, Ashcroft sent Twain, still his employer, a letter imploring him to do the impossible: turn against Clara, publicly disagree with her, and openly support Isabel. Ashcroft maintained that Rogers concurred with their circle of friends, that Isabel had received "ghastly— treatment," and reminded Twain that he had already privately volunteered that Clara's "charges emanated from a brain diseased with envy, malice and jealousy, and it is only when one forgets this fact that one views them seriously." Ashcroft urged Twain to "exercise your prerogatives of fatherhood and manhood in a way that will be productive of the greatest benefit to yourself." He closed by recognizing that the contents of his letter might have an adverse effect upon the relationship he had previously enjoyed with Twain.

Ashcroft could not have imagined the enormity of the effect his words would have. If his intention was to bring Twain to his senses and convince him that he should drop the matter, he profoundly underestimated the old man's vanity. Ashcroft and Isabel were both left incredulous by Twain's following hysterical and utterly irrational response.

Infuriated about being lectured by an employee about restoring his "manhood," Twain received additional dismaying news at the beginning of May. Rogers had turned over the responsibility for an audit of the books to a woman in his office, his "second secretary," Miss Watson. Twain had expected that Rogers would assign the audit to "a man who had been in his employ twenty-five years." Twain bemoaned this unexpected development because he was convinced that Miss Watson would support Isabel in sympathy with her sex (the fact that Clara was also a woman undercuts his argument). His fears about Miss Watson were heightened when an audit document indicated that the total amount of money used to renovate Isabel's farmhouse was $3,435.24, with only $281.01 not traceable to checks. Twain then decided that the time had arrived to take matters into his own hands.

By this point Twain realized that Clara's vindictive accusations might cause repercussions. Ashcroft's aggressiveness in business matters, a trait Twain had once found admirable, now was a serious liability. Clara's destructive agenda might just prove to be the factor that would make Ashcroft and Isabel decide to disclose to the public the details of her adulterous affair as well as the true nature of Jean's illness. To ensure that the two would never step forward with tales certain to disgrace himself and his daughters, Twain relied on his best weapon of all, his writing, to mute them. He wrote the "Ashcroft-Lyon Manuscript" over the course of five months, beginning on May 2, 1909, and concluding on October 21, 1909. The manuscript is 429 pages long and contains letters (both sent and unsent), newspaper clippings, and various exhibits of "fact." The manuscript, in effect, is a poison-pen epistle dedicated to destroying any credibility Isabel and Ashcroft might ever claim.

The first lines Twain composed were directed toward William Dean Howells in the form of a letter (thankfully never sent—one can only imagine what Howells's appalled response would have been). Writing from Stormfield, Twain told his old friend that thanks to Clara the Ashcrofts' perfidy had finally been exposed. Falsely claiming that such good friends as "Harvey, Dunneka, Major Leigh and David Munro" had been aware for at least a year of underhanded dealings, Twain also threw his support toward Paine, telling Howells that Paine had known about them for "two years—but Clara & I remained peacefully asleep." In a mention surely intended as the final stroke, Twain declared that no one less than "H. H. Rogers read 'fraud' all over Ashcroft the first time, he saw him." Why such a large group of supporters had never bothered to alert Twain or his daughters about such "rotten eggs" in their midst apparently was a bothersome detail best left unexplained. Recollecting a fictional, halcyon past, Twain declared that Clara and Isabel had once been so close that they "were like lovers," although despite their bonhomie all it took for Clara's suspicions to be aroused a few months earlier was Dr. Quintard supposedly telling her that he suspected the pair of skimming. Twain mockingly refers to Ashcroft's "manhood" letter and demands that his friend agree with his estimation of Ashcroft's character: "I suppose you see he is a cad? He is 34 years old & a cipher in the world; I am nearly 74 & a figure in the world, yet he blandly puts himself on an equality with me, & insults me as freely & as frankly as if I was his fellow-bastard & born in the same sewer."

Ashcroft's penchant to go for the jugular was now of enormous concern, and Twain expressed his uneasiness to Howells: "But I know about this, for he fell upon John Hays Hammond two or three years ago, with his pen, & rained filth & fury and unimaginable silliness upon him during two or three weeks—daily? No—almost hourly." Twain was convinced that he and Ashcroft had entered into a rhetorical battle: "Man, let me tell you, Ashcroft would consider himself quite competent to carry on a literary war with me. Now that is true; I am speaking seriously. He is clever—& in many ways, too—but not with his pen. He does not suspect this." The "Ashcroft-Lyon Manuscript" became Twain's trump card and would top all the best hands Ashcroft could muster.

After a year of infrequent and unfocused autobiography dictations and the embarrassing extended essay "Is Shakespeare Dead?" (a manuscript Isabel had hoped in vain that Twain could be persuaded not to publish due to its poor quality), Twain's creative juices were flowing once again. The words, in fact, gushed—after all, Twain had a "literary war" to win. Having permitted himself free license to say anything he pleased, he proceeded without compunction to cast Isabel as an unscrupulous alcoholic, a hypnotist, a thief, a drug addict and an embezzler. He accused her of spreading a rumor that Clara was insane, and he claimed that Isabel's "one great crime, cruel & unforgivable crime" was deliberately keeping Jean "exiled in dreary & depressing health institutions a whole year & more after she was well enough to live at home without damage to her well-being."

While all of these charges were sensational in kind, the most fantastic was the accusation that Isabel had made unwanted, sexually aggressive advances. Isabel had repeatedly tried to seduce him, Twain confided to Howells, although he swore that he had refused to succumb to her licentious ways:

> She would . . . stretch herself out on her bepillowed lounge in her bedroom, in studied enticing attitudes, with an arm under her head & a cigarette between her lips, & imagine herself the Star of the Harem waiting for the eunuchs to fetch the Sultan & there she would lie by the hour enjoying the imaginary probabilities.

Here Twain borrowed the language of yellow journalism from William Randolph Hearst's *New York Morning Journal* and Joseph Pulitzer's *The World;* all he needed to do was mention a red velvet swing and he could have been describing the infamous seduction of Evelyn Nesbit by Stanford White, rather than of himself by his emotionally overwrought, forty-five-year-old former secretary. Indeed, this supposed description of a coquettish Isabel would have stood perfectly for any number of photographs taken of Evelyn Nesbit in her heyday. Much of the vitriol contained in the "Ashcroft-Lyon Manuscript" could have been directly lifted from the melodramatic and sensational press coverage of White's murder and Thaw's subsequent trials. Twain, at certain points, reflexively caught himself and confessed to William Dean Howells just how much like fiction his entire tale was.

> Doesn't it sound like print? Isn't it exactly the way it would happen in a book? Howells, the whole great long Lyon-Ashcroft episode is just as booky as it can be; so booky that sometimes its facts & realities seem more cheap commonplace shopworn artificialities to me & as if they hadn't ever happened, but had straggled into my half-asleep consciousness out of some paltry & fussy & pretentious old-time novel of that hallowed ancient day when. . . . well, you see, yourself, how dam stagey the whole thing is!

The genesis of the "Ashcroft-Lyon Manuscript" is not entirely surprising. For some time, Twain, having run out of experiences from his life to include in the dictations for his autobiography, had resorted to commenting on daily events depicted in the newspapers. He had, in a sense, lost his subject: himself. His deciding to create a fiction about his family's squabbles while drawing upon the sensationalistic prose employed by the press was a fusion that he hoped (strangely enough, considering the subject) would provide gripping and convincing reading. Truth in the "Ashcroft-Lyon Manuscript" was abandoned for impact.

Any possibility of a quiet, negotiated resolution between the angry parties was extinguished when Henry Rogers died suddenly from a stroke on May 19, 1909. Twain received the news the next day from reporters when he arrived with Clara at Grand Central Terminal from Redding. He had come to the city to spend the day with Rogers. "This is terrible, terrible, and I cannot talk about it," Twain burst out when told. "I am inexpressibly shocked and grieved. I do not know just where I will go." Emotionally devastated, Twain served as a pallbearer at Rogers's funeral service and returned to Stormfield a broken man in ruined health. His chest pains were increasing in frequency and intensity, and doctors diagnosed angina pectoris, which Paine tried to ease by placing hot-water bottles on his chest. As a distraction from his grief over losing his cherished friend, Twain pursued Isabel and Ashcroft with even more fervent zeal. To his dismay, Rogers's son, Harry, quite rationally declined to continue the investigation of Isabel's financial records, so Twain hired John Stanchfield's accountant, W. J. Weiss, to conduct an audit.

By the end of May, Twain had decided that he wanted Isabel to return her farmhouse with its accompanying twenty acres to him. He had convinced himself that the amount agreed upon for Lyonesse's renovation had been maliciously and deliberately exceeded. At the same time, Clara and Paine discovered that Isabel and Ashcroft held the power of attorney over all of Twain's affairs and demanded its immediate revocation. Twain devised a unique twist that absolved him of any need for honest explanation of why he had excluded his daughters from the legal document. According to Twain, it was Clara who offered him the reason why he gave his employees so much power: "Clara finally said—'It's hypnotism! It accounts for it all.' " This rationale was certainly convenient: "I had never thought of that. The suggestion looked reasonable—particularly since no other plausible way had been discovered of accounting for the enslaved condition I had been in for the past two or three years."

Twain argued in the "Ashcroft-Lyon Manuscript" that he had been held in a hypnotic trance since approximately 1906. Ignoring that a person cannot be hypnotized if he does not wish to be and that hypnosis cannot make a person do anything he does not want to do, Twain claimed that he was rendered helpless before the power of suggestion and that his free will had been taken over by Isabel and Ashcroft. Saved by the kind intervention of his loving daughter, he was finally able to regain his senses—that would be his story, no matter how implausible. What made this assertion utterly senseless is that on December 1, 1906, in an autobiograpy dictation, Twain recalled a mesmerizer's visit to Hannibal in 1850, when he was fifteen years old. "I had a burning desire to be a subject myself," he asserted, although, despite attending the show three nights in a row, all his efforts failed. Longing to be selected to come onstage and perform the mesmerizer's commands, on the fourth night Twain faked that he was under hypnosis.

Nevertheless, in mid-June, the Clemenses started a letter campaign to friends representing their version of events. In a letter sent to William R. Coe on June 16, Twain declared that the November power of attorney was the "most amazing document that has seen the light since the Middle Ages. . . . Until June 1st I had never heard of that paper—yet I signed it. Come—match me this mystery if you can."

Jean wrote a long explanatory letter to Twichell on June 14, declaring that Isabel "took large quantities of whiskey & bromide, reducing herself pretty close to insanity at times." She also backed her father's claim that he knew nothing about the power of attorney: "Father swears he never saw [the power of attorney document] which was put on file here & in New York last November." The controversial document was finally revoked on June 1, 1909, signed by Twain and notarized by John Nickerson, the same notary who had signed the November power of attorney. Twain could spin as many stories as he liked, yet the incontestable fact was that Nickerson swore in writing that on November 14, 1908, "before me personally came Samuel L. Clemens, to me personally known to be the individual described in and who executed the foregoing instrument, and he acknowledged to me that he executed the same."

Throughout the summer, the squabbling continued over the cost of Lyonesse, as did Twain's determination to claim it. After Ashcroft's April meeting with Rogers, Ashcroft contacted Clara and warned that doing an open audit of expenses would expose the large amounts of money her father had invested in "papering" her tours to make them appear successful as well as the excessive sums of money she had paid out to Wark. Ashcroft's threat was real. Twain had repeatedly complained about the cost of Clara's concerts. In the audit report, prepared by Weiss, under the heading "Clara's Expenses," it is noted that in 1909 Wark was paid $100 on January 29 and $400 on April 21. Judging from the amounts Wark was being paid, in just four months he had earned $54 more than the average American's annual income, making him the most well paid accompanist in the country. The totals are especially curious since he was apparently not accompanying Clara during the month of April. In a recital Clara gave on April 13, Miss Littlehales, a cellist, was her accompanist. Clara was possibly still secretly supporting him.

Ashcroft's warning only made Clara more determined to strike back. She began making her case to the press, falsely claiming that Isabel had stolen $10,000 in cash in 1907 and 1908. Clara repeated Twain's story that he had never "knowingly" signed the November power of attorney and that "two witnesses [a] former gardener and stableman, when shown the document, said positively they had never seen it before." Naturally Clara excluded mention of Nickerson, the notary.

By the beginning of June, John Stanchfield had placed a lien on Lyonesse, and, in an extraordinarily malevolent move, he attached Isabel's mother's home in Farmington. Isabel, having accompanied her spouse on a Plasmon-related business trip to England, was informed upon landing on June 9 that Twain had obtained a lien of $4,000 against her farmhouse. Panic-stricken, Isabel returned to New York on July 14 and gave an interview to *The New York Times:* "I believe the whole trouble is caused by his daughter. Miss Clemens is of the artistic temperament, but in this affair I believe that she has been wrongly advised into taking a step she would never have taken had she the right understanding of the case." The fight was now very public and the newspapers were only too willing to print article after article. *The New York Times* alone published five headline stories over the summer, and there were articles in the *New York Telegram,* the New York *American,* the *New York Sun,* the *New Haven Union,* and the *Connecticut Courant.*

On July 17, Isabel and her mother were confronted by Charles Tressler Lark, Twain and Clara's lawyer, with Jean as a witness, at her farmhouse and informed that a complaint would go forward to the grand jury unless Isabel signed over the deed to Twain. When Isabel asked for time to consult with her lawyer, Lark refused to allow her to do so. A horrible scene ensued, leaving Isabel and Mrs. Lyon in hysterics. That same day an utterly intimidated Isabel, near collapse, signed the agreement and also wrote a check to Twain for $1,500. Mark Twain stole Isabel Lyon's home. Three days later, Lark returned, demanding that Isabel sign a lease agreement binding her to vacate her home by September 1. This time Clara accompanied Lark to enjoy Isabel's distress. Twain recorded all these events in the "Ashcroft-Lyon Manuscript," exulting in the extreme misery he was inflicting upon Isabel.

When Ashcroft returned to the United States at the end of July, he sent Stanchfield a furious letter expressing his amazement at how Isabel had been "inveigled into transferring her cottage and land at Redding to Mr. Clemens." He noted that Isabel had not been charged with "moral turpitude, embezzlement or defalcation," and threatened that if "any such charge be made by any responsible person, please consider the after part of this letter withdrawn, and we will immediately prove to the satisfaction of a court or jury that not $1. was ever misappropriated or misapplied by Miss Lyon, and will justify her reputation by holding those responsible for the defamation, in addition to enforcing whatever rights she may have in the matter." Displaying an impressive grasp of detail and legalistic jargon, Ashcroft provided ledger entries and a copy of the agreement he and Twain had signed on "General Clean-Up Day" about costs and payments connected with the farmhouse, remarking that he doubted Stanchfield knew of its existence.

Ashcroft asserted that a total of $3,000 was "paid in cash to Miss Clara Clemens for her accompanist, Mr. Wark, her manager, Mr. Charlton, part of the expense of her concert trips, a trip to Nova Scotia, and many other items." His not so very subtle intimation was that this information might become public if a quiet and quick conclusion could not be reached, and the undesirable attention of the press would expose not only Clara's profligate ways, but also her connection to Wark. Ashcroft expressed the couple's desire to settle the matter without further public attacks or legal action, although seven conditions would have to be met in advance. Stanchfield likely found Ashcroft's letter equally insulting and menacing. Yet Ashcroft's threat proved effective and the parties, through their lawyers, commenced working on a settlement.

However, even though an agreement was in the offing, Ashcroft went public a final time. Perhaps he thought that this last interview might gain him leverage in achieving a more profitable resolution. He also could not resist extracting a measure of revenge against Clara for orchestrating the attack that resulted in the couple's losing Lyonesse, their most valuable asset. The *New York Times*'s headline shouted: "Ashcroft Accuses Miss Clara Clemens. Says Mark Twain's Daughter Made Charges Because She Was Jealous of Her Success. Quotes Humorist's Letter. In It He Praised His Secretary and Rebuked Daughter." In the course of the lengthy article, Ashcroft made available to the reporter passages from a personal letter Twain had sent to Jean two years earlier in which he defended Isabel. The excerpt included mention of Dr. Peterson and Dr. Hunt, referencing them as "nerve specialists," in effect revealing to the public Jean's epilepsy, the scourge the Clemens family had tried to keep a secret for so many years.

Ashcroft was not finished in exposing what he considered to be the hypocrisy of the Clemenses. He dismissed to the reporter Clara's latest gambit, namely the accusation that Isabel had stolen large amounts of cash, and he was also contemptuous regarding her supposed singing talent: "One's vocal ambitions, however, sometimes exceed one's capabilities in that direction, and the bitter realization of this has, in this instance, caused the baiting of a woman who has earned and kept the admiration and respect of all of Mark Twain's friends. . . . Miss Lyon is in a position to prove that the bulk of the money was paid to Clara Clemens herself for the expenses of concert tours and the delightful experience of paying for the hire of concert halls destined to be mainly filled with 'snow' or 'paper,' " Ashcroft grimly continued, "for the maintenance of her accompanist, Charles E. Wark, and to defray other cash expenditures that an embryonic Tetrezzini is naturally called upon to make."

Ashcroft pointed out that legally he was still the manager of the Mark Twain Corporation, with two years remaining on his contract. The public mugging was so hostile that the *Connecticut Courant* delicately declined to publish his full statement (*The New York Times* was not so diplomatic), explaining to its readers: "It involves an attack on the two Misses Clemens, put in the way to hurt these sensitive young women most keenly."

Another letter to Stanchfield by Ashcroft, sent on August 18, 1909, itemized in detail Clara's musical expenses (excluding the thousands of dollars paid to her manager) for the years 1907 and 1908. Ashcroft wrote, in summary, that during those two years Clara "and her troupe [Will Wark and Miss Nichols, the violinist] received $13,220.48 by check." What his account reveals is that along with checks cut for Clara, Miss Nichols, and Will Wark, there were numerous large cash disbursements paid directly to Clara. Noteworthy were two checks for

222 · MARK TWAIN'S OTHER WOMAN

$50.00 each, made out to the Hotel Brevoort in November 1907. Clara was covering Wark's living costs.

An agreement was finally reached on September 7, 1909, in which Twain, his daughters, and Paine agreed to a "discharge of all indebtedness and obligations of Ralph W. Ashcroft and Isabel Lyon Ashcroft from the Mark Twain Company." The matter appeared, finally, to be concluded. Yet to Twain's fury, on September 13, 1909, another headline in *The New York Times* blared, "Mark Twain Suits All Off. All Litigation Between Him and the Ashcrofts Is Finally Dropped":

> The differences between Mark Twain and his daughter, Miss Clara Clemens, on the one side, and his former secretary, Mrs. Ralph Ashcroft, and her husband, have been settled without an appeal to the courts. All criticism of the conduct of Mrs. Ashcroft has been withdrawn and all suits have been dropped. . . .
>
> Mark Twain has agreed to drop his suit against Mrs. Ashcroft for an alleged loan of $3,050 and has removed the attachment which he had caused to be placed on the property of his former secretary at Farmington. Reparation has also been made for the hard things which the Ashcrofts alleged had been said of them by the author and Miss Clemens. Mark Twain has signed a document acquitting Mrs. Ashcroft of all blame for her conduct of his affairs while she was in his employ as his secretary. Miss Clara Clemens has also to the satisfaction of Mr. and Mrs. Ashcroft retracted the criticisms she is alleged to have made on Mrs. Ashcroft.

Enraged, Twain wrote a letter to Adolph S. Ochs, publisher and owner of the *Times,* accusing him of bias with his sympathetic coverage of the Ashcrofts:

> The facts in my case are simple; the matter is a private one, the public has no concern in it, and not the least right to know anything about it. . . .
>
> None of the interview was up to the standard of matter fit to print in *The Times* without examination as to their truthfulness, since they assailed the private character of a respectable family. That examination should certainly have been made, but for two quite apparent reasons: the interviewer had a personal grudge against me, & the sub-editor who

accepted the interviews without verification of their alleged facts had also a personal grudge against me.

Eventually, Twain decided not to send this rebuttal but to drop the matter. For someone usually enamored with the press's attention, *The Times*'s coverage must have been particularly galling. The next day Clara insisted that her father prepare and send a news release to Melville Stone at the Associated Press representing their side of the issue, which Twain reluctantly did.

The end result of all this squabbling and legal positioning was that Ashcroft resigned from the Mark Twain Corporation and retained his position with the Plasmon Company, which would collapse before long. The officers for the Mark Twain Corporation then included Twain; Jervis Langdon, Olivia's nephew (for the period 1909–43); Charles Lark (1910–43); Edward Loomis, the husband of Twain's niece Julia Langdon Loomis (1909–37); and Paine (1909–13).

As for Isabel, her hopes of editing Twain's letters were dashed; her dream house, Lyonesse, along with twenty acres of property, had been lost; she had entered a marriage which years later she would call "a mistake"; and she had lost her King forever. Albert Bigelow Paine, who survived the falling-out, became Twain's secretary and nurse; he entered into an agreement with Twain at the end of July 1909 specifying that he would edit and publish an edition of Twain's letters in cooperation with Clara. (In keeping with earlier contracts, Jean was excluded.)

At some point during this long summer of contentious newspaper stories and malicious exchanges, Twain decided to enlist the newest form of media to assist in making his case to the public: he allowed the Edison Company to come and film at Stormfield. With the approval of the Clemens family, a short silent film was made, entitled *Mark Twain (Samuel Clemens) Photographed by Thomas Edison 1909* (now accessible on YouTube). Twain, dressed in his white suit and smoking a cigar, stands in the doorway of his new home and then strolls around the back of the house. The second portion of the film is titled "With Daughters, Clara and Jean, at 'Stormfield,' Redding, Connecticut, 1909." All three family members sit in the loggia calmly sipping tea and politely chatting with one another. Claude Beuchotte enters the frame carrying Clara's hat, which he gives to her, and he quickly departs. Clara puts it on, using three hat pins to anchor it, and the family then rises and exits the scene. This was the only film Twain appeared in, and the idyllic tableau of peace and genteel elegance was the image he wanted seen and remembered. The carefully cultivated projection of a happy family, an elderly father with his patrician daughters (both looking well and pretty), was an opportunity for the media-savvy Twain to recapture some of the credibility he must have felt he had lost in his battle with Isabel and Ashcroft.

## 11

An exhausted Isabel and Ashcroft quickly disappeared from public view. With the two of them dispatched, and with Clara based at the Stuyvesant and Jean living at Stormfield, Twain might have finally found a measure of peace. Yet nothing could have been further from the truth. The real story was deliberately suppressed by Twain, Clara, and Paine; as a result, it has been unknown for the past hundred years. The events of the fall of 1909 were so shocking and resulted in such extraordinary turmoil that considering his frail health Twain was fortunate to have survived the month.

Along with fighting with Ashcroft and orchestrating press coverage, over the summer Twain welcomed a seriously ill Ossip Gabrilowitsch back to Stormfield. Gabrilowitsch had long been ailing, plagued by a number of health issues that, according to Katy Leary, finally culminated in "a terrible operation." He was diagnosed as suffering from an infection of the mastoid process (also known as the mastoid bone, located behind the ear), and was forced to undergo three separate operations. Such an infection occurs when an untreated, severe ear infection spreads from the middle ear to the bone. It is excruciatingly painful. Symptoms include difficulty in hearing, severe tinnitus, fetid discharge, headache, and an increase in temperature. Treating an infected mastoid process in 1909 required a grisly operation, involving slicing open the back of the ear. The operating physician would chisel out a section of the mastoid bone, and ream out the infection, after which the ear would be reattached. A large, unsightly scar ran the length of the ear. Postoperative complications included deafness, cranial nerve palsies, infection, and death. Based on the number of operations Gabrilowitsch underwent and their invasive nature, it is certain that he suffered significant hearing loss in one ear. As a professional musician, he must have been enormously concerned about the effect his illness would have on his career. Years later, when Gabrilowitsch was the conductor of the Detroit Symphony Orchestra, local music critics wondered how he was able to endure Clara's singing. Ralph Homes, the music critic for the *Detroit Times,* observed, "I've always heard that love was blind. But I never knew it was deaf." He did not realize at the time just how right he was.

When Gabrilowitsch first arrived at Stormfield, according to Katy, "he was pretty near dying." She nursed him back to health, regularly massaging his head, "just as I used to rub Mr. Clemens's" (to encourage Twain's hair growth). By Tuesday, September 21, 1909, just over a week after the *New York Times* article declaring a truce had been struck between the Clemenses and the Ashcrofts, Gabrilowitsch had recovered sufficiently to be able to perform with Clara at Stormfield to raise funds for the Mark Twain Library in Redding. The program lasted nearly two hours and the encores added a half hour. A profusion of guests traveled to Stormfield, 525 in all, according to Twain, and the press reviewed the evening positively. When Twain rose to make a brief speech he managed simultaneously to recognize and insult his daughter. While acknowledging how fortunate everyone was to have the well-known pianist Gabrilowitsch and the internationally famous baritone David Bispham from the Metropolitan Opera Company there to entertain them, Twain concluded, "We shall now hear from my daughter Clara. . . . She is, they tell me, a mezzo-soprano. She is not quite so good a musician as Mr. Gabrilowitsch and Mr. Bispham, but she is much better looking." Good-looking Clara certainly was and she was also unquestionably a contralto, not a mezzo-soprano, as her father undoubtedly must have known.

The concert would prove to be the least exciting event that evening. After the concert Clara and Gabrilowitsch took an evening stroll. In her memoir *My Husband Gabrilowitsch,* Clara melodramatically recounted that when Katy Leary was bidding her goodnight that evening in her bedroom Clara told her,

> "Katy, the date is set." Cautiously she approached my bed. "Miss Clara, is it set to stay?" "Yes, indeed." "God be praised!" Then, fervently seizing my hands, "When—when?" "In ten days." I said. "No waits this time, because the stars are with us!"

While certainly dramatic, Clara's version is, at best, doubtful. Katy offered an entirely different account of the conversation, saying that upon Clara's return to the house that evening, she had a "funny look on her face." When Katy met Clara in the city several days later, Clara told her not to prepare her apartment for the opera season because " 'I'm going to be married next week!' " The engagement stunned everyone. Jean expressed her astonishment in a letter to her friend Bébé Schmitt, saying Clara "will wed Gabrilowitsch next Wednesday and leaves to reside at Potsdam or at Berlin the 12th of October!" Even *The New York Herald*'s story the day before the event mentioned its weird suddenness:

> News of the wedding will come as somewhat of a surprise to most persons except the close friends of the family, for although the names of the pianist and Miss Clemens have been linked at various times, no formal announcement of the engagement has been made. Stories have been printed of a romance dating from the time when Mr. Gabrilowitsch went to the rescue of Miss Clemens, who met with a sleighing accident while driving near her father's house last winter. . . .

Twain attempted to defend the abruptness of the wedding to *The New York Times* by claiming that the rush was necessitated because the beginning of Gabrilowitsch's European season was imminent. In his biography, Paine echoed the same explanation, that Gabrilowitsch "had signed for a concert tour in Europe, and unless the marriage took place forthwith it must be postponed many months." On the surface a reasonable explanation, but no one had informed Clara's tour manager, R. E. Johnston, who upon reading about Clara's wedding in the newspaper wrote to Twain complaining that thirty-one of her engagements had to be cancelled. Johnston told Twain he expected him to explain the situation in a public letter. Five days later, on October 12, Twain wrote to Johnston that the two needed to marry in haste because

> Gabrilowitsch was leaving for Europe; and as the wound in his head (from the surgical operation of a month or two ago) was not yet healed; and he was weak from his long illness, the sudden marriage was decided upon in order that my daughter might go with him and continue to nurse him. They will spend two or three months in retirement in Italy, for rest and recuperation, by order of the physicians. Also, by their order, Gabrilowitsch has cancelled his European engagements by cable.

Two months later, Twain offered a third version of the leave-taking. He claimed that after arriving in Europe, Clara "had been nursing her husband day and night for four months and was worn out and feeble." Twain was having trouble keeping his stories straight. Years later Clara wrote that Gabrilowitsch had taken the year off from performing and that the two were "free to go wherever we wanted to." These conflicting explanations for why they had to decamp so quickly indicate that there was another, more urgent, reason for their sudden engagement, marriage, and departure. Clara and Twain must have known that there was trouble brewing and decided that the faster Clara became a married woman and left the country with her new husband the better.

Katy recalled the flurry of activity that took place in order to prepare Stormfield for the impending nuptials. Oddly enough, on October 5, the night of the wedding rehearsal, Twain refused to participate. He insisted that he could not be distracted from his billiard playing. The agitated bride dispatched Marie Nichols, her violinist, to convince her father to come downstairs and join the wedding party, but Twain refused her entreaties. Miss Nichols said she "argued with him in vain, and finally he put the mortar board on my head and the robe over my arm and told me to go in and take his place." On what would typically be a joyous occasion, Twain's refusal to participate in the preparations certainly leaves a downbeat impression, particularly considering the pleasure he normally took in donning his Oxford regalia whenever an opportunity presented itself.

Before the wedding, Clara directed Joseph Twichell to omit the word "obey" from the vows, an unheard of request for the time. Stranger still, the day before the wedding, Twain prepared a statement about the impending nuptials. The Associated Press was duly notified, and when its representative arrived at Stormfield the next day he was handed a typed copy of Twain's remarks. *The New York Herald* reported that Twain's explanation for preparing the press release in advance was that "he wished to 'avoid any delays at the wedding.' " There would be no spontaneous and open exchange with reporters. While a little more than two weeks earlier Twain had invited to Stormfield over five hundred people for a library fund-raiser, the guest list for his daughter's nuptials was tiny by comparison, with only thirty-two people present, including the wedding party. Mr. Charles Edwin Wark was not among those invited.

According to Katy, the bride looked lovely, although her father overshadowed her in his scarlet Oxford robes and mortar board. Once the morning nuptials had concluded, Twain changed into his white cashmere suit and all retreated for a wedding breakfast. Afterward, instead of riding to the train station in the carriage that had been her parents' wedding present, the bride and groom departed Stormfield in an automobile. Clara had finally married, and Twain could congratulate himself for having engineered the outcome. The day after the wedding, newspapers across the country carried the rather inauspicious headline " 'A Happy Marriage is a Tragedy'—Twain," with Clara and Gabrilowitsch's photographs printed beneath. Twain was quoted as saying that he could count "two or three tragically solemn things in this life, and a happy marriage is one of them, for the terrors of life are all to come."

Clara's abbreviated betrothal and rushed marriage were utterly inappropriate during this era of codified etiquette: every rule dictating behavior for polite society had been violated. Twain, a lifelong lover of ceremony and spectacle, and a frequent attendee of society weddings, had married off his daughter in almost total privacy out in the boondocks of rural Redding. This was hardly the socially acceptable ceremony that would have been expected for America's most famous writer and his daughter. The extraordinary speed of events proved indicative of troubling outside circumstances. A headline appearing just over a week after the wedding added to any speculations people and the press might have had about Clara's dash to the altar. On October 13, 1909, *The New York Herald* printed a small notice on page one:

Mrs. Edith Wark, wife of Charles E. Wark (formerly accompanist to Miss Clara L. Clemens), is requested to send her present address to Charles J. Campbell, attorney, 346 Broadway, New York City.

That same day Twain wrote a friend, Augusta M. D. Ogden, saying that Gabrilowitsch had done him a "service for which I am most thoroughly grateful: he has squelched Clara's 'career.' She is done with the concert-stage—permanently, I pray. I hate the word. I never want to hear it again." But through the newspapers he would be reading plenty about his daughter's career.

The Associated Press issued a release on October 14 explaining the circumstances of the notice published the day before, which had been carried by newspapers from New York to California. The New

*Clara Clemens and Ossip Gabrilowitsch's wedding day, October 6, 1909, at Stormfield, in Redding, Connecticut. Left to right: Mark Twain, Jervis Langdon II, Jean Clemens, Ossip, Clara, the Reverend Joseph Twichell*

York *American*'s headline shouted "Clara Clemens in a Mysterious Case." According to the accompanying article, a "mysterious suit, which promises to involve the names of a number of prominent people in sensational developments is concealed behind the following advertisement, which appeared in several of yesterday morning's papers. . . . Every effort was made yesterday to conceal the object of the advertisement, but it was reported that Mrs. Wark, who is now establishing a residence in a Western State, had started a suit against the former Miss Clemens."

Charles Campbell, the lawyer who had posted the notice, refused to state what his interest in the case was or whom he was representing: "He would neither admit nor deny that he was Mrs. Wark's counsel in any litigation, and took the same attitude when asked if any suit against the former Miss Clemens had been started, or papers served upon her." Campbell declined to tell the reporter "by whom I am retained or the purpose of discovering the whereabouts of Mrs. Wark." The New York *American* reported that Charles Wark was currently separated from his wife and children. Campbell promised the eager reporter that he expected that there would be more information soon, "which would make interesting reading for the public." The lawyer was most anxious to know the date on which Clara and Gabrilowitsch were due to set sail for Europe. The dogged reporter also called Jean at Stormfield to inquire if she or Twain knew anything about the potential suit and received this icy response:

> No suit that I know of has been started against my sister . . . and served on her. I do not believe the story about the starting of a suit, and if such a story is in circulation it is probably the work of malicious persons. I have one woman in particular in mind who is taking every opportunity she can get to trouble us and who would be likely to start such a rumor.

Gone, but not forgotten, Isabel was still being blamed for any ill fortune that came the Clemenses' way. The Oakland *Tribune* reported that Mrs. Wark had in fact started a suit against Clara. The suit the newspapers were referring to was for alienation of affection, a commonly invoked legal action at the time. A cursory reading of *The New York Times* at the beginning of the twentieth century reveals such lawsuits routinely appearing within its pages, with sums for damages ranging from $25,000 to $500,000. It may be that Mrs. Wark's inspiration for the lawsuit had come from reading *The New York Times*'s article in which Ashcroft alleged that Clara had given Wark money. Mrs. Wark could sue for damages through the daughter and gain access to Twain's assets. The basis for an alienation of affection tort was that there had been a "willful and malicious interference with marriage relations by a third party." Causes of action elements included "wrongful conduct of the defendant, plaintiff's loss of affection or consortium of spouse, and a causal connection between the two."

*The New York Herald* published the most shocking story of all. The headline read "Mystery in Quest of Pianist's Wife." In the article, R. E. Johnston, Clara's former tour manager, expressed great surprise over the revelation that Charles Wark was not a bachelor: "He is an excellent man, but until I saw the advertisement I did not know he was married." Johnston noted that Wark had "played all Miss Clemens' accompaniments during her last concert tour." After inquiring at the Brevoort Hotel where Wark "had lived at intervals during the last two years," the reporter was told that the hotel was unaware that its frequent guest was married.

Three days later *The New York Herald* announced "Pianist's Bridal Trip Deferred," due to Gabrilowitsch's continued ill health. The couple had been booked to depart on October 16; however, Gabrilowitsch was suddenly struck ill with appendicitis. When he was asked about the Campbell advertisement of the previous week, his response was peculiar. He said he believed that an individual "who does not feel kindly toward my wife may be attempting to stir up trouble, but I doubt even that." If he was referring to Ashcroft or Isabel, he appeared to immediately retract his statement. But if not to them, then to whom? A slightly different slant was presented in a story in the New York *American* on October 17. Under the headline "Denies Daughter of Mark Twain Is Sued: Gabrilowitsch and Bride Cannot Understand Rumor of Alienation Action," Gabrilowitsch rejected the rumor "that Mrs. Wark had brought suit for alienation of affection against [Clara]." Yet the newspaper found his protestations to be suspect:

> Mr. Gabrilowitsch's statement only served to surround the rumors of a suit with deeper mystery. . . . Last Tuesday an advertisement appeared in the morning papers, in which Mrs. Wark was requested to send her address to Attorney C. J. Campbell. . . . The next day an anonymous letter was sent to the newspaper offices, saying that every effort was being made to serve Mrs. Gabrilowitsch . . . with papers in an alienation suit. . . . "My wife and I are at a loss to know what it all means," said Mr. Gabrilowitsch. . . . "Mr. Wark is a personal friend of both of us, and I am sure he has nothing to do with it. The report has evidently been circulated through maliciousness." Mr. Gabrilowitsch also denied that the expected suit had any thing to do with the postponement of their honeymoon on which he and the former Miss Clemens were to have started yesterday. He said that he was suffering from appendicitis and would undergo an operation tomorrow. . . . R. W. Ashcroft . . . declared yesterday that neither he, nor his wife had anything to do with the circulation of the rumors of Mrs. Wark's suit. This had been suggested by Jean Clemens.

What ultimately happened regarding the suit and its circumstances might never be known. No newspaper stories quoting either Will or

Edith Wark have surfaced. A search of court cases for Manhattan yielded nothing. During that period a suit could have been filed, but if it was settled or abandoned, the outcome might not have been recorded. It is possible that the threat of a suit by Mrs. Wark might have been enough to force a monetary settlement from Twain. The same day on which the New York *American* article ran, Jean wrote to Twichell begging him not to show anyone the copy of the letter to Adolph Ochs that Twain had written and included in the "Ashcroft-Lyon Manuscript." Twain apparently had been "troubled for fear it might possibly be quoted by some unthinking person, which quotation reaching the ears of certain charming friends of his, might give them an excuse for starting an action." Apparently Twain did not want to derail any settlement that had been reached. The next day a check for $1,000 was made out to John B. Stanchfield, Twain's attorney, signed by Jean and countersigned by Twain.

Twain finished the "Ashcroft-Lyon Manuscript" less than a week later and told Clara that she was free to use it however she liked in order to protect herself. If Ashcroft or Isabel ever tried to come forward and offer the newspapers the full explanation for Clara's adulterous affair and subsequent marriage to Gabrilowitsch, Twain's manuscript would suffice to rob them of all credibility. Twain and Clara were confident the two had been permanently silenced. Twain left a warning note in his 1910 notebook, ordering Clara, after his death, to retain his lawyers at $1,000 a year to maintain constant vigilance over his assets: "At this very day Ashcroft is manufacturing forgeries to rob Clara with when I am dead. Keep Lark & Stanchfield always, to be ready for him."

As for Will Wark, he and Edith divorced, and on October 16, 1912, he married the New York socialite Ruth Sands at the Church of the Ascension. The happy couple permanently relocated to France. In 1913, Ruth was named as primary beneficiary of her uncle's $600,000 estate. For a poor man's son, Will Wark had done very well indeed, with an independent income and entrée to New York's social register.

While Albert Bigelow Paine omitted any mention of the threatened lawsuit and newspaper headlines in his biography of Twain, he did briefly mention *Letters from the Earth,* which Twain wrote during the period when his daughter was publicly identified as an adulteress. Twain's topic in *Letters,* a discussion of traditional theological orthodoxy in a comic vein, was in part a continuation of ideas he had earlier explored in "Extract from Captain Stormfield's Visit to Heaven." Paine claimed that he and Twain laughed "themselves weak" over the manuscript. But while Paine apparently found *Letters* entertaining, he was dismissive of the ideas presented in it, claiming that they were new only in terms of their "phrasing. [Twain] had exhausted the topic long ago, in one way or another." Yet Twain was in fact far more expansive than he had ever been before about one particular topic, namely female sexuality and, most specifically, female adultery:

> During twenty-three days in every month (in the absence of pregnancy) from the time a woman is seven years old till she dies of old age, she is ready for action, and competent. As competent as the candlestick is to receive the candle. Competent every day, competent every night. Also, she wants that candle—yearns for it, longs for it, hankers after it, as commanded by the law of God in her heart. . . . By the woman's make, her plant has to be out of service three days in the month and during a part of her pregnancy. These are times of discomfort, often of suffering. For fair and just compensation she has the high privilege of unlimited adultery all the other days of her life. That is the law of God, as revealed in her make. What becomes of this high privilege? Does she live in the free enjoyment of it? No. Nowhere in the whole world. She is robbed of it everywhere.

This hardly appears to be the stuff for mutual guffawing. Actually, these passages in *Letters* could be interpreted as Twain railing against polite society, along with his felt imperative to force his daughter to uphold its mores, an irony he probably would have had greater appreciation for as the subject of his fiction rather than his life.

### 1 2

Twain lost another old friend on November 18, when Richard Watson Gilder, one of his closest and most trusted companions, died unexpectedly. Twain was asked, along with Howells, to serve as a pallbearer at Gilder's funeral, held at the Church of the Ascension. However, unlike Howells, he declined. *The New York Times* reported that Twain's absence was due to ill health. Quite simply, Twain had lost too much over the previous year to be able to endure another funeral.

On November 20, 1909, the day of Gilder's funeral, Clara and Gabrilowitsch finally sailed to Europe. The newlyweds spent their first weeks in Wiesbaden, Germany, visiting with Gabrilowitsch's family, before traveling to Switzerland and Italy. Twain and Paine had sailed a day earlier for Bermuda. Jean was not invited to join them. Although both ships left from New York Harbor, Twain and Clara did not see each other before they departed. Twain wrote Dorothy Quick the day before the sailing, telling her that he did not want to go to Bermuda, but since he had been unwell for the "past 5 months," his doctors had ordered him to make the trip: "I must obey, I suppose." Paine offered a different version, saying that the voyage had been Twain's decision. According to Paine, Twain "was not at all ill going down to Bermuda," and on the morning of his seventy-fourth birthday "he was looking wonderfully well after a night of sound sleep, his face full of color and freshness, his eyes bright and keen and full of good-humor." Twain and Paine would remain in Bermuda for a month. At Twain's specific request, no news was forwarded to him during that time.

When Twain and Paine returned to New York on December 20, they went directly to Stormfield, where Jean welcomed them. Jean had blossomed in her new surroundings and happily described her daily schedule to friends in great detail. Busy with her chickens and the apple orchard on her property, Jean also acted as her father's secretary, corresponding on his behalf. Yet, despite the pleasing fullness of her days, she remained deeply lonely. Upon receiving Nancy Brush's letter announcing her upcoming nuptials, an overwrought Jean responded that in her view Nancy was rushing, questioned whether she could afford a marriage, and warned her that she should delay starting a family. "Don't begin right off to have a lot of children!" Jean castigated Nancy: "There are harmless ways of preventing such an occurrence and for a girl as young as you . . . it would seem to me too heartrending for words, if she began the cares of a mother before two or three years, at least." Jean's injunctions notwithstanding, at age nineteen Nancy married Robert Pearmain (Jean was twenty-nine at the time).

Jean's attempts to control her friends' lives seemed to alienate them. Bébé Schmitt received a letter in October from Jean demanding to know when she planned to visit her. In the same letter Jean told Bébé that she had felt "real jealousy" when she found out Bébé had spent time with another friend instead of with her: "I don't like the idea that you are much with her." A little over two weeks later, Jean wrote to Bébé again saying, "The principle reason for the existence of this letter is that I want to beg you to come and spend Christmas with me." Although Bébé ultimately declined Jean's pleadings to come to Stormfield for the holidays, Jean was pleased to be celebrating her first Christmas at home in several years, and she busily set about making preparations.

Jean's habit was to wake early and take a cold bath at seven every morning. She had become very sensitive to the nuances of her disease and approached the prospect of bathing with great caution. On one occasion, she described what happened when she began to feel the onset of a seizure: "I began to be absent-minded as soon as I started to take my bath, so I hurried with it & after partially dressing, I lay down on my bed."

On the morning of Christmas Eve, after an early ride to West Redding to collect the mail, Jean went for her customary bath. When she did not appear afterward, Katy Leary went looking for her. To her utter horror, she found Jean lying motionless in the water. After Katy removed Jean from the bathtub and failed to revive her, she ran to roust Twain from his bed, and the two rushed to the bathroom. Twain stood still, gazing at his dead daughter lying on the bathroom floor, and finally said to Katy: "She's happy now, she's with her mother and sister; and if I thought I could bring her back by just saying one word, I wouldn't say it." Eight months after moving to Redding, Jean was dead.

In an account published in the New York *American* on Christmas Day, the examining physician of the county attributed Jean's death to drowning. This initial diagnosis was incorrect; after an autopsy found an absence of water in the lungs, the cause of death was believed to be sudden heart failure. Jean died seven months shy of her thirtieth birthday. Two days later, Twain expressed his utter relief to Mai Rogers over his daughter's demise.

> I am already rejoicing that she has been set free. It is always so with me. My grief for the loss of a friend is soon replaced by gratitude that the friend is released from the ungentle captivity of this life. For sixteen years Jean suffered unspeakably, under the dominion of her cruel malady, & we were always dreading that some frightful accident would happen to her that would stretch her mutilated upon her bed for the rest of

her life—or, worse—that her mind would become affected; but now she is free, & harm can never come to her more.

Writing to Mrs. Whitmore on December 28, Twain managed to combine his sorrow over Jean's death with a condemnation of Isabel's character.

> She is out of it all, dear Mrs. Whitmore—the first kindness that has come to her from the Source of All Kindness in sixteen years. She & I had a long & loving chat the night before the blow fell, & she gave me a commission for you. I said I would write you my side of that matter, & I proceeded to map it out, but she stopped me & asked me not to write in that heated vein—& not to try to write at all, because I would not be able to keep my temper. She told me to ask you to come down here & let me state the case orally. I promised at once. She had been shamefully & criminally abused for three years, through the plots & lies & malignities of that unspeakable person. . . .

Twain's lying to Mrs. Whitmore about not having written an account of "the matter" (his manuscript—all four hundred plus pages of it—had been completed two months earlier) likely was for dramatic effect. The next day Paine and his wife and daughters moved into Stormfield to keep Twain company. The Paines, Twain commented, would "constitute my family henceforth." With Jean's passing, Twain could finally admit the severity of her illness and how her death was a welcome release from her hellish existence. In "The Death of Jean," composed on the morning she died, Twain confessed, as he had reportedly said to Katy on viewing Jean's body, that even if he had had the power to bring her back to life, he would not have: "If a word would do it I would beg for strength to withhold the word. And I would have the strength; I am sure of it." Twain told Paine that "The Death of Jean" signaled the end of his autobiography—this was the final chapter. Twain was convinced that Jean's dying was not ill fortune. Her epilepsy had never been cured, and he had dreaded the thought that she would outlive him. In addition, now that Jean was at last free, so was Twain, from the troubling possibility that she too might become sexual. He would not have to deal with any embarassing affairs as he had been forced to with Clara. He declined to accompany his daughter's body to her final resting place in Elmira, sending Katy in his stead. Clara sent her regrets and remained in Europe.

Twain's health continued to erode, and he departed for a long visit to Bermuda on New Year's Day 1910, with Claude Beuchotte accompanying him. There, despite the best efforts of his hosts, Mr. and Mrs. William H. Allen and their daughter Helen, to distract him, a brooding Twain continued to ruminate about Isabel Lyon. A cover letter dated January 14 sent to Paine with the manuscript "The Death of Jean" included Twain's last piece of writing:

*WHO?*

> *Who loves to steal a while away*
> *From Sinful joys & foolish play*
> *And fold her holy hands & pray?*
> > *The Bitch.*
> *Who loves to watch while others pray,*
> *And hog their assets, night & day,*
> *Wherewith to fat her Ashcroft—say?*
> > *The Bitch.*

Twain could neither forgive nor forget Isabel. Paine apparently found this piece of vulgar doggerel so amusing that he could not resist writing an additional stanza:

> *Who feeds on bromide and on Scotch*
> *To keep her nerves at highest notch?*
> *Who makes of business-books a botch?*
> > *The Bitch.*

While Twain was writing vicious verse about Isabel, she was also reminiscing about him, although her thoughts were far more benign in nature. On January 21, she wrote a note on a piece of paper reflecting on all that had occurred over the previous twelve months:

A year later—No more association with the King except as a strange white weak ghost. And here I am married to Ralph Ashcroft—& those Conditions which seemed grave are trivial—& the trivial ones then are the real strong things of Today.

*Mark Twain in Oxford regalia*

Two months later Twain, still fulminating about Isabel, expanded upon his depiction of her as a scarlet woman in a personal letter he sent to Clara, signed "Marcus," in March 1910: "In your guess of a year ago you were unquestionably & unqualifiedly right; the severalties of that guess being that she was a liar, a forger, a thief, a hypocrite, a drunkard, a sneak, a humbug, a traitor, a conspirator, a filthy-minded & salacious slut pining for seduction & always getting disappointed, poor child." At long last, father and daughter were in agreement.

After suffering from repeated attacks of angina in Bermuda, Twain sent for Paine, who sailed at the beginning of April. Clara later professed that she knew nothing of her father's increasingly serious condition and claimed that she had planned to see him again in the summer (although existing correspondence indicates that she was actually arranging to return with Gabrilowitsch earlier—in March or early April—to try to mediate bickering between Katy and Mrs. Paine as to who was the mistress of Stormfield). Paine arrived in Bermuda equipped with morphine and a hypodermic, which he steadfastly administered for ten days. Twain's condition continued to worsen, and a telegram was sent to Clara. Twain returned to New York with Claude Beuchotte and Paine on April 14, and all went immediately to Stormfield. After a five-month absence from the United States, Clara and Gabrilowitsch arrived from Europe on April 17.

In the late afternoon softness of early spring, on April 21, 1910, with his only surviving child by his side, seventy-four-year-old Mark Twain died. And just as he had hoped, Halley's Comet was once again in the heavens. Did father and daughter have a deathbed rapprochement? Perhaps this detail can provide a revealing glimpse of how things stood between them at the end: despite having had several months to send word from Europe as well as four days spent with him at Stormfield, Clara let her father go to his grave without ever telling him that she was five months pregnant with his only grandchild.

# EPILOGUE

Clemens was sole, incomparable, the Lincoln of our literature.

—WILLIAM DEAN HOWELLS

*Mark Twain*

Just as he had so carefully planned, Mark Twain's death was a defining event, and he was mourned worldwide. His *New York Times* obituary read in part:

We have called him the greatest American humorist. We may leave it an open question whether he was not also the greatest American writer of fiction. The creator of Mulberry Sellers and Pudd'nhead Wilson, the inventor of that Southwestern feud in "Huckleberry Finn," which, with all its wildly imaginative details, is still infused with rare pathos, has certainly an undying vitality. An emotional and quite unconventional sort of man, Clemens was, whose early life was a hard struggle for existence. He obtained his education where he could get it. Presumably his faults were as large as his merits. Intellectually he was of Herculean proportions. His death will be mourned, everywhere, and smiles will break through the tears as remembrance of the man's rich gift to his era comes to the mourners' minds. However his work may be judged by impartial and unprejudiced generations his fame is imperishable.

Twain's corpse was carefully dressed in one of his white cashmere suits and his snowy white hair was fluffed a final time. On the morning of the day of the public funeral, April 23, the pregnant Clara, dressed entirely in black and heavily veiled, descended the staircase from her second-story suite at Stormfield unaccompanied, and entered the parlor to spend a few final private moments with her father. White horses pulled the carriage carrying Twain's coffin through the town of Redding (where businesses were closed in honor of their most famous resident) to the station, where a private train car awaited them. Clara, Ossip, and Katy Leary followed, riding in Clara's parents' wedding carriage. The small Stormfield delegation also included Dan Beard (the illustrator for many of Twain's works and his Redding neighbor), Charles Langdon (Twain's brother-in-law), and Claude Beuchotte. Everyone boarded the train for the trip to New York City.

After their arrival at Grand Central Terminal shortly before noon,

Twain's body was lifted into a hearse. The funeral cortège traveled to the Brick Presbyterian Church, where the service began promptly at 3:00 p.m. Twain lay in his coffin in front of the altar, with his right hand across his chest, and a wreath of laurel leaves fashioned by Dan Beard resting on top of the coffin. The church was full and nearly fifteen hundred people waited outside straining to hear the service. Two pieces of music were played, Chopin's "Funeral March" and Grieg's "Death of Asa." The service was brief, lasting only twenty minutes. Conducting it were the Reverend Henry Van Dyke and the Reverend Joseph Twichell, who managed to say only a few words before he was overcome by grief. Afterward, for two hours, more than three thousand people filed by the coffin to see Twain a final time and to pay their respects.

The next day a private train car carried Twain's body to its final resting place, in Woodlawn Cemetery in Elmira, New York. At 3:30 p.m., the Reverend Samuel Eastman (a last-minute substitute for Twichell, who had suddenly been called home to Hartford the day before due to his wife's grave illness) conducted a brief service in the parlor of the Langdon family home, where Twain and Olivia had married forty years before. The coffin was opened for a final family viewing, and then sealed, and the cortège departed for the cemetery in the pouring rain. Twain was buried in the family plot with Olivia, Susy, Jean, and Twain and Olivia's son, Langdon. While all of the other gravestones in the Langdon-Clemens family plot have inscriptions, Clara left her father's blank.

The notoriety of Clara's sexual liaison and the controversy with Isabel followed Twain to his grave. The official obituary issued by the Associated Press on April 29 contained a bullet-pointed chronology that included these two entries for 1909:

> 1909 — The humorist and his daughter are involved in a humiliating controversy regarding a farm given to his former secretary, Mrs. Ralph W. Ashcroft, when Mr. Clemens attaches the property on his daughter's advice.

> 1909 — Mrs. Charles E. Wark tries to serve Mrs. Gabrilowitsch, the former Miss Clara Clemens, with papers in an alienation suit.

This would be the last public mention of the Wark scandal for a century. As the sole heir to the Clemens estate, Clara would devote the remainder of her life to ensuring that these particular episodes in her and her father's lives were expunged from the official Mark Twain biography.

After the rain-soaked burial ceremony was concluded, Clara and Ossip returned to a gloomy Stormfield to await the birth of their only child. Rather than being appeased by Isabel's abrupt firing, Clara appeared to grow more enraged with the passage of time. Over a year after Isabel's termination, Clara said to Mrs. Whitmore that she had discovered only after the fact that Isabel had been "going about everywhere taking my reputation away from me. I could simply sit and wonder if she wasn't mad.—That seemed worse to me than all the stealing & without any excuse whatsoever." Even more outrageously, Clara lied to Mrs. Whitmore, saying that her mother had never cared for Isabel and "in fact used to speak of her as untruthful, insincere & even dishonest," and that without Clara's kind intervention, Isabel would have been dismissed by her father after Olivia's death.

Clara concluded her character assassination by reassuring Mrs. Whitmore that the Isabel Lyon she had once known no longer existed because "her whole character has been changed by the constant use of drugs & stimulants." Clara swore that Twain had wanted to put Isabel in prison for her multitudinous crimes, however the "poor man . . . got where he couldn't mention her name without having a heart attack & I longed to have him forget it all. The things which have happened in this house since it was built are so terrible that they seem to belong to one long hair-raising nightmare." Clara delivered the coup de grâce when she blamed Isabel for being "the cause of my father's death." After all her bile had been expressed, Clara was careful to assure Mrs. Whitmore in closing that she could "not be thankful enough to the Lord for that solace" her marriage had brought her. Just in case Mrs. Whitmore had not fully received the message that Clara was in marital bliss, she emphasized again that her marriage was the "only happy event that has brought real happiness."

A little more than a month later, just before the baby's arrival, Clara again wrote to Mrs. Whitmore thanking her for a brooch she had sent to "the little creature." After conveying her gratitude for the lovely gift and expressing how "sad" and "hard" a place Stormfield had become, Clara once again tried to persuade Mrs. Whitmore that her version of the fight was the true one:

246 · MARK TWAIN'S OTHER WOMAN

About "Miss Lyon" I can so well understand Hattie's [Harriet Whitmore's daughter and Isabel's close friend] inability to believe this dime novel for even I, who have seen it all, awaken sometimes in the night with the conviction that it must be a dream. And really from the sentimental standpoint merely of friendship the shock was so great to me to learn that such things could happen in the world that for a while it seemed as if nothing much worse had ever happened to me & it was no more surprising than if I had discovered that Jean or Susy was plotting my death.

Finally, Clara could not resist boasting to Mrs. Whitmore about her latest interaction with Isabel and Ashcroft:

I must tell you that only ten days or two weeks ago we had what I hope is our last battle with the Ashcrofts. They had stolen some of father's manuscripts & were offering them to dealers and publishers here in N.Y. which we discovered because the dealers came to us to know if they were genuine. At the same time either Miss Lyon or Mr. Ashcroft sent me a blackmailing letter (which I will tell you about when I see you) apparently thinking that this letter would frighten me into letting them have anything they wanted and thus at least avoid some more of their scandalous talk in the newspapers. But father left me one weapon to use in case they troubled me any more & I used it—He wrote out a full description of their entire story of dishonesty which I was to publish if there was no other way to keep them quiet.—So we sent the lawyer out to Chicago (where they are now), who threatened them with the publication of this M.S. if they did not give back to me all the manuscripts of father's that they had in their possession & desist from annoying me in any way. It was successful. A paper was signed before a notary & I believe that we may for a time lead a peaceful private life. I hope so! Dear Me! For I have written a long letter & could have waited to tell you these things (But do let poor Hattie remain in ignorance!)

Actually, the lawyer had been sent to Racine, Wisconsin, where the Ashcrofts had moved, to threaten them into returning the manuscript of "Is Shakespeare Dead?" The Ashcrofts' "blackmailing letter" has never been found, if indeed one ever existed.

On August 18, 1910, Nina Clemens Gabrilowitsch, Mark Twain's only grandchild, was born at Stormfield. She would not be told by her mother who her grandfather was until she was in her teens. Katy attended to Clara during her last months of pregnancy, and it was to Katy that the doctor handed the wrapped infant. Katy's first thought was how very happy such a sight would have made Twain. Clara told Katy a few weeks after the baby's birth, "I had hoped it would be a boy, Katy, because then it might have been like father." While Nina was not the sex of Clara's preference, she was a picture perfect replica of her father, Ossip Gabrilowitsch. Unfortunately, this similarity was not to Nina's advantage. A friend of the family later remarked that it was "sad that [Nina] inherited her father's cast of countenance, instead of her mother's," as Gabrilowitsch was known for having "strongly-marked features and an outsized nose."

In October 1910, Clara, Ossip, and the baby left Stormfield and departed for Europe, where they planned to reside permanently. Katy Leary also left Stormfield; on her final day she went alone into Twain's bedroom and wept for her lost master. The cooking staff was given the pots and pans from the kitchen and the gardeners all the yard tools. Katy moved to New York City, where she ran a boardinghouse; Claude Beuchotte was one of her lodgers.

After Twain's death, the Mark Twain Corporation officially appointed Albert Bigelow Paine as literary executor, and he exercised almost total control. He had a keen understanding that the key to remaining in such a powerful position was directly related to his ability to placate Clara. To that end, when his mammoth three-volume *Mark Twain, a Biography: The Personal and Literary Life of Samuel Langhorne Clemens* was published, in 1912, he dedicated his work to Clara, expressing his appreciation for her upholding "the author's purpose to write history rather than eulogy as the story of her father's life." Paine's biography was not a critical study by any means, and upon this aspect of his work he and Clara were utterly united. Clara initially had been somewhat lukewarm about Paine's biography, writing Mrs. Whitmore a year after its publication that she thought it "very fine," but wondered "if it struck you as being too long—as it did some people—it was hard for me to judge."

Almost twenty years later, in Clara's memoir *My Father Mark Twain,* her earlier opinion had improved considerably. She, in turn, dedicated her book to Paine, "who understood my father and faithfully demonstrated his love for him." Clara pronounced "Mr. Albert Bigelow Paine's biography of my father a remarkable exhibition of a most exact and truthful picture of his characteristics, general talents, and habits." The subtext to Clara's praise was a warning to future biographers not to trifle with the image of the man that Paine had projected, an image in which she had such great personal investment.

Isabel Lyon was somewhat more critical in a 1936 note she wrote commenting on Paine's opus:

> After 21 years I am scanning. Skimming. . . . I think Paine's *Biography* is very mushy in spots, inaccurate in other spots. Too much like "Good Housekeeping" or "Ladies Home Journal" style of writing—but also in spite of these . . . defects, it is a very grand achievement. He has woven from the rich incidents of Mark Twain's life & from an unusual insight into these early days, a rare & fine fabrick.

Regarding Isabel's existence, Paine set the standard for subsequent biographers by including only a single, offhanded reference: "The building of the new home at Redding had been going steadily forward for something more than a year. John Howells had made the plans, and in the absence of Miss Clemens, then on a concert tour, Mark Twain's secretary, Miss I. V. Lyon, had superintended the furnishing." Paine and Clara had effected the biographical equivalent of *damnatio memoriae.* Isabel's presence in Twain's life had been effectively erased.

Clara approached her responsibilities in caring for the Clemens estate with a kind of manic zeal. She and Paine made an effective team, combining their efforts to suppress any publications about Twain or by him that they deemed inconsistent with his "wholesome" image. Such was Clara's sensitivity about the Angelfish that former Aquarium Club members were actively discouraged from writing about their time with Twain. At Clara's request, Paine contacted Elizabeth Wallace, a former Angelfish, and told her she was forbidden to publish any photographs of her and Twain together in her memoir *Mark Twain and the Happy Island* (1913). Dorothy Quick waited until the end of her life before publishing her reminiscences in *Enchantment: A Little Girl's Friendship with Mark Twain* (1961). Shortly after her book was published, Dorothy passed away on March 15, 1962, and Clara followed her eight months later.

In 1924, Harper and Brothers published *Mark Twain's Autobiography,* a two-volume work edited by Paine. Paine's edition was an abridged version of Twain's transcriptions. Paine wrote to Harper and Brothers in 1926 to say that no one else should ever be allowed to write about Mark

Twain: "As soon as this is begun (writing about him at all, I mean) the Mark Twain that we have 'preserved'—the Mark Twain that we knew, the traditional Mark Twain—will begin to fade and change, and with that process the Harper Mark Twain property will depreciate." Twain was a valuable commercial property, not a person to be examined in depth.

A pair that Clara was resolute about keeping in check was the Ashcrofts, and her constant vigilance became a personal obsession. After moving from Redding to Wisconsin, the Ashcrofts departed the United States for Montreal, Canada, in 1913, where Ashcroft had secured a position as the advertising director of Dominion Rubber Company. During his years in Canada, Ashcroft also worked as the general manager of the Trans-Canada Broadcasting Company and manager of radio station CKGW. While the first few years of the couple's marriage were apparently happy ones, ultimately Isabel had little good to say about the experience. In total, she was married for eighteen years; her divorce decree is dated June 13, 1927. In the cold language of a legal document, the sad story of a failed marriage is laid bare. Ashcroft deserted Isabel on May 24, 1923, and never returned, "with total neglect of all duties of the marriage covenant."

Isabel requested that her married name be dropped and that she henceforth be known again as Isabel Van Kleek Lyon. Permission was granted. According to Doris Webster, Isabel's ex-husband proved to be "very unsatisfactory. He drank, 'never could keep a job,' and was fundamentally dishonest. He even accused her of doing some of the things he had done. He had taken a number of manuscripts and various other things from Twain's house. But they were all returned." Isabel went back to New York City, where she found employment with the Home Title Insurance Company. Ashcroft married a second time in 1927, and died on January 8, 1947, at age seventy-two, in Toronto after a short illness. At the time of his death, he was the Toronto manager of the Canadian Advertising Agency.

In Europe, Gabrilowitsch conducted the Munich Konzertverein Orchestra from 1910 to 1914; however, his and Clara's comfortable life ended in 1914, with the assassination of Archduke Francis Ferdinand and his wife and the onset of World War I. In 1917, Gabrilowitsch was swept up in a pogrom aimed at Jews and was briefly imprisoned in Munich, where he and Clara were living. Once he was released, the Gabrilowitsches returned to the United States via Zurich. After spending some time in New York City and Philadelphia, in 1918 the family finally settled in Detroit, where Gabrilowitsch was named the founding director of the Detroit Symphony Orchestra. He was well liked there and enjoyed a very successful career. Clara insisted upon giving private recitals from time to time, her audience consisting of invited guests with Gabrilowitsch gamely accompanying her on the piano. The family appeared to be fairly happy, with Gabrilowitsch a steadying influence upon Clara. Before dying of stomach cancer at age fifty-eight, on September 14, 1936, Gabrilowitsch requested that he be buried at Mark Twain's feet. At the time of his death Clara was sixty-two years old and their daughter, Nina, had just turned twenty-six. A public funeral, attended by more than fifteen hundred mourners, was held in the Orchestra Hall in Detroit where Gabrilowitsch had conducted. Wife and daughter did not attend.

Over a quarter of a century had passed since Twain's death, and in all that time Clara had never erected a memorial to her father. The year after Gabrilowitsch died, Clara asked the Elmira sculptor Enfred Anderson to create a memorial for her husband. Anderson thoughtfully offered her two different designs, one recognizing Twain and Gabrilowitsch (two public celebrities), and the other memorializing her mother and father. The two models represented an interesting Freudian choice. The first, the memorial for her mother and father, featured a bust of Twain on top, with his birth name, Samuel Langhorne Clemens, beneath it. Olivia was in profile below, with her maiden name, Olivia Langdon. At the bottom, Anderson envisioned a sculpture of a kneeling Huckleberry Finn. The second memorial stood two fathoms high, her father in right profile, with his pseudonym underneath, and Gabrilowitsch's face below in right profile, over his name. Clara chose the second memorial, and the first was forgotten. A model of the memorial to her parents was discovered in 1989 at the Elmira Historical Society. Clara wrote the inscription for the base of the second memorial:

> DEATH IS THE STARLIT STRIP
> BETWEEN THE COMPANIONSHIP
> OF YESTERDAY AND THE REUNION
> OF TOMORROW
> TO THE LOVING MEMORY OF
> MY FATHER AND MY HUSBAND
> C.C.G.                    1957

*Rejected Enfred Anderson design for a Mark Twain monument*

*Epitaph on grave marker erected to Mark Twain and his son-in-law, Ossip Gabrilowitsch, by his daughter Clara Clemens Gabrilowitsch*

Despite Paine's injunction that no one else should ever be allowed to write a biography of Twain, two scholarly works had been published in the two decades since Twain's death: Van Wyck Brooks's *The Ordeal of Mark Twain* (1920) and Bernard DeVoto's *Mark Twain's America* (1932). DeVoto's efforts to complete his manuscript were significantly hampered by Paine's refusal to grant him access to Twain's unpublished papers. Paine died in 1937, and a year later the Mark Twain Corporation named DeVoto "custodian and editor of the Mark Twain papers." Interestingly, the estate did not give DeVoto the title of literary executor, which Paine had held; instead that title reverted to Clara. DeVoto had to seek her permission before any previously unpublished Twain manuscripts could be published.

DeVoto and Clara had a difficult relationship, with Clara wrongly suspecting DeVoto of trying to enhance his own fame through his position as editor and accusing him of wanting to publish manuscripts that would hurt her father's reputation. She proved so intractable that DeVoto resigned in January 1946, after she suppressed his edition of Twain's bitter polemic *Letters from the Earth.* Clara also had her squabbles with the Mark Twain Corporation during this time, when she discovered that the other officers had signed contracts without informing her and had allowed Warner Brothers movie rights to her father's life story without giving her approval rights or requiring the studio to put her on an extravagant salary. She later claimed that the corporation had hired DeVoto without her consent. This bickering led to the resignation of Lark and Langdon in 1943; Thomas Chamberlain, a lawyer, and the Manufacturers Hanover Trust Company replaced them.

The directors of the Twain Corporation, including Clara, next asked Dixon Wecter, an English professor at the University of California at Los Angeles, to succeed DeVoto as literary editor, and he accepted. In December 1946, Wecter moved the Twain papers from Harvard University to the Huntington Library in Pasadena where he had an affiliation, and in November 1949, he took them from the Huntington to the University of California at Berkeley. Wecter and Clara enjoyed a positive working relationship; once he had brought the papers to Berkeley, he persuaded Clara to change her will so that Berkeley would remain the papers' permanent repository.

Resurrecting old battles, Wecter had apparently argued with DeVoto against publishing Twain's letters en masse because Wecter feared that such a volume would usurp interest in a biography that he, Wecter, planned to write. Wecter died unexpectedly on June 24, 1950, and the first (and only) volume of his biographical series, *Sam Clemens of Hannibal,* was published posthumously in 1952. Henry Nash Smith was next appointed literary editor, on August 31, 1953, and signed an exclusive publication contract for Twain materials with the University of California Press. He resigned his position in 1964 to Frederick Anderson, although he remained involved with the papers by serving on the editorial board of the Mark Twain Corporation. Anderson created the structure for the long-term editing projects of the papers and assembled a competent staff. Anderson passed away suddenly in 1979 and Henry Nash Smith returned as general editor until 1980, when Robert Hirst was named editor. Hirst remains editor of the Mark Twain Papers today.

After Gabrilowitsch's death, Clara immediately published the hyperbolic and, in places, fictionalized *My Husband Gabrilowitsch*. She and Nina relocated to Hollywood in 1939, purchasing a home, Italianate in style, on five acres with a pool in the front, located directly beneath the Hollywood sign on La Brea Terrace. Accompanying Clara and Nina in their move was Clara's social secretary, Phyllis Harrington, and her chauffeur, Edgar Glanzer. Looking for a fresh start, Clara named her new residence Casa Allegra, or "Happy Home." Even in her new surroundings, Clara could never bring herself to leave behind her long obsession with Isabel.

In August 1940, Clara asked her lawyer, Charles Tressler Lark, to send someone to spy on Isabel. Clara was still afraid that Isabel might speak publicly about Clara's relationship with Wark and forced marriage to Gabrilowitsch, and she remained convinced that Isabel had stolen some of her father's personal papers. The lawyer arranged for an unnamed individual to get in touch with Isabel, posing as a representative of an anonymous Chicago buyer interested in purchasing Twain's manuscripts. In his "A Report of Miss X," the individual identified himself as "an agent of the enemy" (namely Clara) and regretted that he had been unable to win Isabel's trust. Lark gave Clara his report, and on August 28, 1940, he sent a copy to Bernard DeVoto. In the report, the spy relayed Isabel's explanation about how Twain's daughters and Paine

were jealous of [Isabel's] entirely friendly relation with Mr. [Clemens] and that, "to save the good name of Mr. C" and to avoid further trouble, she had taken a husband without loving him. She stated that her marriage was part of a deal whereby she would thus legitimize her standing in the household in consideration of the breaking off of all relations between C.C. and "Will." This deal, originated by Mr. C., who objected strongly to "Will," was honorably carried out by both women.

The marriage of Miss X to Mr. A., while not precisely of the shot-gun variety, proved to be anything but a happy one. Miss X stated that she soon discovered that she had taken a viper unto her bosom; that her new husband soon learned of her reason for marrying him and proceeded to make her life a living hell. . . . Thus, for offering herself as a martyr to the cause of peace and harmony in the C. household, her character had become eternally damned.

*Nina Clemens Gabrilowitsch*

The report certainly offered Clara little comfort. And while she and her daughter might have hoped that their move to California would be the balm to heal old wounds, sadly that would not prove to be the case. Due to their incompatibility, Nina lived with her mother only briefly before finding other lodgings.

Nina was a lost soul, estranged from her mother and without a sense of purpose. She suffered from severe addictions to sex, drugs, and alcohol; over the decades she was hospitalized multiple times trying to cure herself of her alcoholism. None of the treatments worked for long. Small in stature at five feet two and insecure about her physical appearance, Nina underwent plastic surgery to reduce the size of her nose. Her best friend during the 1940s and '50s, Alice Henderson, described Nina as unattractive and lonely. Nina confided in Alice that when she had been a child Clara had "pawned her off on nannies" and that her mother was "very self-obsessed." According to Nina, Clara had never loved Ossip Gabrilowitsch; Nina told Alice that the only way her mother could bear to have sex with her father was to wear a wig and full makeup.

Clara's entire relationship with her adult daughter apparently consisted of a required daily afternoon tea. Nina and Alice Henderson would drive over to Clara's estate from Nina's apartment, wait by the pool, and at the expected hour Clara, wearing a frilly dress and carrying her purse, would emerge from her house. After approximately thirty minutes of polite conversation, Clara would walk back up the hill. Alice remembered Clara as "being a little lightweight and living in a dream world. . . . There was no love there." Neither Clara nor Nina ever mentioned Mark Twain in Alice's presence. After seeing her mother, Nina, who lived on a monthly allowance provided by Clara, would return to her apartment at 1922 North Highland Avenue in Hollywood and immediately start drinking.

Clara grew lonely in Hollywood, and at age seventy, on May 11, 1944, eight years after Ossip's passing, she was married a second time, to another Russian musician, Jacques Samossoud, who was twenty years younger than she. Clara had been introduced to Samossoud when she was still living in Detroit. Jacques was a gambler, regularly playing the horses at Santa Anita, and he expected Clara to cover his debts. His losses were so great that on one occasion, after he had lost $25,000 playing dice in Las Vegas and had written a bad check, the *Los Angeles Times* published a story about him. With such an ill daughter and troublesome spouse, Clara may have retreated to a "dream world" because she could not emotionally confront the harsh, depressing reality of her life. Just as her father had given over the care of Jean to his secretary, so Clara entrusted Nina's care and personal finances to Phyllis Harrington.

Amazingly, Clara's relocation to the West Coast, her remarriage, her sick daughter, and the passing decades did nothing to diminish her determination to squelch any possibility that Isabel Lyon might somehow reemerge to claim a place in Twain's life and spill her secrets. During DeVoto's term as custodian and editor of the papers, lawyers for the corporation kept an eye on Isabel because of Clara's contention that she had stolen documents belonging to the estate. DeVoto specifically suspected that some manuscripts that Isabel had fully annotated for the collector William T.H. Howe were things she had possession of illegally.

At the end of her life, Isabel Van Kleek Lyon was living quietly in the back half of a basement apartment at 7 Charles Street in New York City's Greenwich Village. Despite entreaties from loving relatives to come live with them in Connecticut, Isabel refused to consider moving. Treasured memorabilia from her time with Mark Twain were kept on a large table in the corner of her small living room, and tucked away in her sewing workbasket was a pair of his colored socks. Dozens of photographs covered all the available surfaces of the room, and books overflowed the limited shelf space and were piled on the floor.

Among her friends and family, Isabel's energy level was renowned. At age sixty-nine she suffered a car accident in New York City, and a close friend joked, "You are certainly a tough human being. I was just thinking about your getting hit with a taxicab, and, as I remember now they were never able to do anything with the taxicab—it was so broken up that I think they swapped it for a new one. You in the meantime went on to work and did an extra day's work just for the inspiration you received from the taxicab." Isabel peered alertly at her world through old-fashioned black pince-nez and possessed a "cultured voice and manner." A lover of hats and colorful dresses in her youth, in old age she wore formerly elegant dresses twenty years out of date. She had retired with a pension from her secretarial position at the Home Title Insurance Company in Brooklyn in 1948 at age eighty-four, but she longed for another job so she would feel useful. Stubbornly independent, she lived unassisted into her mid-nineties despite multiple heart attacks and a painful, debilitating leg condition.

The daughter of the aristocratic Georgiana Van Kleek and Columbia University professor Charles Harrison Lyon, Sr., rarely ventured out, keeping in touch solely with her younger sister's family in Connecticut and a small circle of intimates. The only time she opened her life to outsiders was when select people interested in talking about Mark Twain, her life's passion, contacted her. During her last decade, she declined frequent requests for interviews and agreed to speak with only a few individuals about her time with Twain. There was a curious covert aspect to these meetings, which Isabel used to her advantage. The people with whom she met included Samuel and Doris Webster, of New Milford, Connecticut, coauthors with Isabel of an unpublished transcription of her memoirs; Dixon Wecter, the literary editor of the Mark Twain Papers, who arranged for her memoirs to be housed with the permanent Mark Twain Collection at the University of California at Berkeley; and the actor Hal Holbrook, the creator of a famed stage impersonation and tribute to Mark Twain. In her meetings with these key individuals—the writers, the archivist, and the impersonator—Isabel had a specific purpose in mind.

Although flattered by the attention her visitors paid her, Isabel was very particular that certain conditions be met before appointments could occur. All meetings would take place in her apartment and were required to remain secret, and all conversations would be confidential. No details about her life with Mark Twain or any quotations from her were ever to be released to the public. If she warmed to her visitor, Isabel would begin sorting through her memories, repeating snippets of conversations held over half a century before, speaking about the most important relationship of her life. Understandably, she preferred

*Isabel Van Kleek Lyon in later years in her apartment at
7 Charles Street, in Greenwich Village, New York City, 1950s*

to remember the happy times, yet a steady undercurrent of her dialogue was her trying to explain—perhaps more for herself than for her listener—why everything had fallen apart at the end. Until the day she died, Isabel never stopped trying to fathom how after all her love, dedication, and loyalty, she had come to live as a biographical exile in a basement apartment in Manhattan, defending herself to strangers. With her cat Christopher purring in her lap, she would lead guests back to the beginning, to the day she walked into Mark Twain's life. Isabel, understandably, felt violated by the way Twain, Clara, and Paine had treated her, and she recognized the Websters, Wector, and Holbrook as kindred spirits.

What brought Isabel together with Samuel and Doris Webster was the publication of Samuel's book *Mark Twain, Business Man* (1946). In it, he defends his father, Charles Webster—Twain's nephew, and former general business manager and head of his publishing company—from charges of mismanagement, and he does a thorough job of documenting Twain's own responsibility for many of the company's problems. Twain had removed Webster from the publishing company in early 1888, claiming he was incompetent, even though just two years earlier Webster had published *Personal Memoirs of Ulysses S. Grant,* which sold more copies in less time than any book to date. By the end of 1888, a humiliated Charles Webster died a broken man, just thirty-nine years old.

Both Isabel and Charles Webster, at different times, had been close to Twain, and each had suffered tremendously as a result of his vindictiveness. Isabel was determined that she would not be forgotten, and she joined with the Websters in composing a manuscript drawn from her personal writings with hopes of eventually publishing it. In preparation for the transcribing that Doris would do of her papers, Isabel had severely edited her daily reminders and diary and in some cases ripped out entire pages. A great many of her expressions of affection about Twain were omitted and only oblique references to Wark remained. In most instances, she used a pencil to cross out writing made in pen. At some point over the years, Isabel had made an edited, handwritten copy of her 1906 daily reminder, leaving no explanation as to why; however, there is one intriguing clue. In an undated, handwritten note, Doris Webster recounts Isabel's telling her that during the final years of her time with Twain she feared that her diaries might be stolen. She probably thought that Clara would attempt to destroy them and had made a dummy copy for her to find. Isabel told Doris that she had decided to hide her diary and daily reminders "inside a voluminous dress that hung inside out in her closet." Both the original 1906 daily reminder and the edited copy are housed with the Mark Twain Papers. It may have been during this period that Isabel dispensed with the bulk of her 1909 journal, thinking that the contents were too sensational to be published or believed.

Doris and Samuel spent three years transcribing Isabel's diary and daily reminders. The transcription begins on January 17, 1904, and ends abruptly, on December 30, 1908, with this observation by Isabel about Twain: "Oh, but he is lovable & naughty & good." There are no accompanying notes to the transcriptions and no context for the quoted portions. It appears, based on inspection of handwriting on the typescript, that the Websters shared their transcription with Isabel, who proceeded to edit it further. When Isabel's original materials are compared with the Webster manuscript, wherever Isabel crossed out a section in the original, it is omitted from the typescript; therefore, Isabel edited the materials twice, both in the original and in the typescript. In addition to saving bits and pieces of notes from various conversations, Doris also transcribed three lengthy interviews she had with Isabel—on March 5, 1948; January 5, 1950; and May 17, 1953—which were not included in the transcription manuscript.

Dixon Wecter learned about the Websters' friendship with Isabel and he subsequently visited her. In consideration of Clara's sensitivity when it came to Isabel, Wecter contacted Isabel surreptitiously; had Clara discovered the visit, the Twain Papers might have gone to another archive. After Wecter's death, Henry Nash Smith and Frederick Anderson also visited Isabel, and in a letter dated October 18, 1954, Isabel informed Smith that the probable source for a number of Twain items that had recently come up for sale was Albert Bigelow Paine. Forty-five years after the scandal, Isabel was still defending her honor.

In November 1955, Isabel turned over all of her personal writings and photographs to the Websters in the hope that they would produce a publishable work, thus reinstating her into the record of Twain's life. The Websters accepted the collection with the understanding that Isabel's memoirs would be included as a permanent part of the Mark Twain Papers. By housing her papers in the same archive as Twain's, Isabel assured scholarly security for herself. Henry Nash Smith acknowledged the gift, reassuring the Websters that Isabel's papers would be kept "in a locked room that houses the Mark Twain Papers (although of course kept separate from the papers belonging to the Estate; and I think they will be quite safe, while they are in our custody)." Doris wrote Smith that Isabel had volunteered to name Samuel Webster as a coauthor, "because of the unfortunate ending of the association, due to the wretched newspaper stories, she has been deeply hurt all her life and wants no publicity. But since she has known Sam it seems to make a great difference to her and if her name and Sam's were combined she would not feel alone and vulnerable." Isabel may have reasoned that using Samuel's name might offer her protection against Clara's fury.

In response to Smith's inquiry, Doris and Sam stoutly defended Isabel's honor:

> We are certain that there was no scandal whatever in the M.T.-IVL relationship. In connection with her diary, Isabel once said wistfully "Do

you think I rave too much about him? I was not in love with him. He was an old man to me." We suggested that perhaps he was in love with her, and she said very simply "No, he was not. There was only one woman in his life, and that was Mrs. Clemens."

Yet, despite all of Isabel's attempts to fly under Clara's radar, they continued to be linked together. In the February 9, 1957, issue of *The New Yorker,* embedded in an essay by Geoffrey T. Hellman entitled "Literary Estate," is an odd reference to both women. In the course of mentioning the sexual content *Letters from the Earth*, Hellman made an unwitting reference about Isabel: "Mark Twain's widow wouldn't allow the book to be published, and his daughter, Mrs. Jacques Samossoud, hasn't as yet allowed it to be published. Bernard DeVoto let me read it when he was literary executor of the Mark Twain estate."

Hal Holbrook first contacted Isabel in 1958, when he was performing Twain in a nearby Greenwich Village nightclub. He had been developing his impression for several years, having given his first performance in 1954. In 1957 he performed *Mark Twain Tonight* as the season opener for the Valley Players, a summer stock company. While Isabel was certainly "a lovely, genuine person," Holbrook had a clear motive in meeting with the elderly woman: by this time, she was one of the last people who had been in close contact with Mark Twain and could describe his intonations and mannerisms. Holbrook became a frequent visitor, and he remembers Isabel as "independent in a rather exciting way. She was somebody special." Their meetings greatly affected him and profoundly influenced his portrayal of Mark Twain. When the two met in her apartment, before Isabel would start talking to Holbrook about Twain, she would pack with tobacco a small meerschaum pipe (the one Twain had given her), pour herself a stiff Scotch (the same kind of liquor she drank with Twain), and prop up the seat cushion on her favorite chair as a backrest so her feet could touch the floor.

Holbrook was placed "in the peculiar position of not being able to record these conversations, despite the fact that nothing but the most charming stories and fine insight into Mark Twain has resulted from them. She is a wonderful recluse, intent on maintaining her privacy, and I was allowed to see her only on the understanding that I would 'never publish' what she told me." Over the years, she had "consistently refused to see or speak to newspaper reporters and writers," and Holbrook acknowledged how fortunate he was to have had several audiences with her: "It is only by the luckiest stroke that she has agreed to speak to me. So I have to honor her wishes." Isabel saw Holbrook perform *Mark Twain Tonight* just once, on a freezing cold evening in the summer of 1958, in Nyack, New York.

After years of declining health, on December 3, 1958, Isabel suffered a heart attack. That afternoon the apartment building janitor entered her tiny apartment using a passkey when she did not respond to his knocking. She was found in a coma and taken by ambulance to St. Vincent's Hospital. The next day, at 4:53 p.m., just eleven days shy of turning ninety-five, Isabel died. She was buried in the Lyon family plot in Farmington, Connecticut, where her plain, granite headstone reads:

Isabel V. Lyon
Dec. 15, 1863
Dec. 4, 1958

After learning of her death, Hal Holbrook sent a condolence note to Isabel's grandnephew, David Moore:

> She was a lovely, genuine person and I have so much respect for her. I admired her very much. I have talked with many people who knew Mr. Clemens, but none of them knew him as she did nor had her deep understanding of him. She impressed me very strongly, and the image of Mark Twain which she gave to me is the strongest one I have and, I believe, the truest one.

In a second letter to Mr. Moore, Holbrook mentioned that he had visited with the Websters and that they had spoken quite a bit about Isabel: "I wish so much that I had seen more of her. She had a better understanding of Mr. Clemens than anyone I know." In 2001, Holbrook recalled Isabel's insistence that Twain be remembered as "a very serious minded man. A man who felt deeply about the world around him and the people in it, an extremely sensitive man, and that his sense of humor came out of this well of seriousness. . . . That was the most important message I carried away from my meeting with Ms. Lyon and I have tried to honor this in my presentation of him on the platform."

Holbrook wrote that Isabel had "left behind some unpublished things, pictures and memorabilia, including a diary of seven years with him which will one day be published, I pray. Her will stipulated that it could not be published until after Clara's death."

In 1959, just a few months after Isabel's death, Holbrook opened *Mark Twain Tonight* at a tiny off-Broadway theater. His performance met with stunning success. That same year he was awarded a special Obie for his Isabel-inspired rendition of Twain. After fifty-six years of performing his one-man show, Holbrook has played the role longer than his subject lived it.

On July 28, 1960, more than a year and a half after Isabel's death, Henry Nash Smith sent the Websters a letter acknowledging receipt of their "typescript of Isabel Lyon's diary." He concurred with them that the 349-page manuscript could not be published while Clara was alive: "I believe it will make a book, and I will be delight[ed] to do anything in connection with the publication that I can." Smith commented that Isabel appeared to be remarkably "free of malice and pettiness, and the diaries, documents that simply could not have been faked, are the evidence."

Smith was correct about Clara, who had continued her surveillance even after Isabel was gone. Immediately upon receiving Smith's letter, the Websters wrote him to say that a close friend of Clara's, Caroline Harnsberger, the author of several books about Twain, had recently paid them a visit, wanting to know the location of Isabel's diaries. Harnsberger told them that she "wanted to 'clear Isabel's name.' We told her that that was the 1st thing Isabel would have wanted." Later the Websters found out that Clara suspected the Websters were in possession of Isabel's diaries and had sent Harnsberger to confirm it. Doris described the mysterious visit: "All very cloak and dagger."

Approximately one month later, the Websters transferred the bulk of Isabel's collection of primary materials to the University of California, where the Mark Twain Papers are housed. Some of Isabel's original materials were given to Vassar College during the late 1960s by a Webster family relative, despite her express wish that all of her materials be transferred to "The Mark Twain section of the University of California." Samuel Webster passed away on March 24, 1962. Doris Webster died five years later, on July 9, 1967. Frederick Anderson, editor of the papers at the time of Doris's death, did not view Isabel's writings with much regard: "It is very difficult to take Miss Lyon's fatuous enthusiasms, expressions of affection, & awe seriously." If the Webster manuscript was ever to be prepared for publication, Anderson opined, it would have to be severely edited.

Doris Webster left a large bequest—several hundred thousand dollars—to the Mark Twain Papers. None of her bequest was used to prepare the Webster manuscript for publication; instead, Frederick Anderson used her gift to support other editorial work. In 1977 there was a brief expression of interest in publishing a coffee-table version of the Webster manuscript with many accompanying photographs; however, the individual proposing the project, John Seelye, was uninterested in Isabel's story:

> Yes I'm sure that much of the . . . diary stuff is not worth printing. But the pictures are, as you realize. . . . Certainly the world is not waiting for the diaries. But if we were to work up a book that balanced selected parts of the diaries with a full range of her photographic work, that might both please the family and the general public.

The proposal came to naught, and the Webster transcription and Isabel's photographs still sit in boxes at the Mark Twain Papers, largely unpublished.

A Twain manuscript that also seemed destined never to see the light of day was suddenly granted a reprieve by Clara. For decades, Clara had refused permission for DeVoto's edited version of *Letters from the Earth* to be published. Suddenly, in November 1960, she changed her mind. *The New York Times* ran an extensive article about the excitement the publication was generating:

> A series of highly inflammatory anti-religious essays written by Mark Twain in his later years will be made public for the first time on Sept. 21 [1962]. Withheld by the humorist's daughter since 1939, when they were edited by the late Bernard DeVoto, the essays will be published by Harper & Row. The pieces, humorous in style but venomous in viewpoint, have been collected in a volume entitled "Letters from the Earth." It was learned yesterday that Mark Twain's 88 year-old daughter, Mrs. Clara Clemens Samossoud, who is an invalid and lives in Mission Beach, Calif., recently agreed to publication on the grounds that "Mark Twain

belonged to the world" and that public opinion had become more toler-ant. It was understood that another factor leading to Mrs. Samossoud's change of mind was her annoyance by Soviet charges that some of her father's ideas were being suppressed in the United States. . . . Mr. DeVoto assumed the editing job after the death in 1937 of Twain's biog-rapher, Albert Bigelow Paine. Harper & Brothers recommended to the estate's trustees that Mr. DeVoto, who was the author of "Mark Twain's America," be asked to prepare for publication material from Twain's unpublished writings. In March 1939, when the edited manuscript was ready for the printer, Mrs. Samossoud objected to parts of it on the ground that they presented a "distorted view" of her father's ideas and attitudes. The project was dropped. Mrs. Samossoud's recent change of heart was partly influenced by Charles Neider, who edited "Autobiogra-phy of Mark Twain" for Harper & Brothers in 1959. . . . "I wrote Mrs. Samossoud on several occasions." . . . "I explained that the public was mature enough to make up its own mind what was in its interest. I felt, too, that Mark Twain should be taken in the round as it were, and that we should not exclude parts of his work because they may not be fash-ionable." It was about that time—Nov. 30, 1960—that the 125th anniversary of Twain's birth was being widely celebrated. Mr. Neider said that Mrs. Samossoud informed him that she had searched her con-science and decided to step aside. "It was a great change and I was rather startled," Mr. Neider recalled. He immediately got in touch with Harper, who decided to go ahead with the manuscript edited by Mr. DeVoto.

Why did Clara finally allow *Letters* to be printed? The answer has far less to do with the Russians than with the demise of Isabel. Isabel, the last person remaining who knew the real reason why Twain had written about adultery and its connection to Clara, had died. With Isabel's passing, Clara believed that the secret the manuscript contained would be safe forever, and the last manuscript her father ever wrote could finally be published.

Clara died two months after the publication of *Letters from the Earth*, at age eighty-eight. At the time of her death she was living with Samossoud at the Bahia Hotel in San Diego. Due to her husband's con-stant gambling, Clara had been forced to sell her Hollywood home in 1951 and auction off most of its contents. The San Diego location was convenient for Samossoud, as it provided easy access to the racetrack at Del Mar.

When Clara was living at the Bahia, Hal Holbrook paid her a visit. He was performing *Mark Twain Tonight* in San Diego and phoned and asked Jacques if she was well enough for a visitor. Jacques was amenable, so Holbrook was ushered into her bedroom for a chat. According to Holbrook, Clara had "a shock of white hair that looks exactly like him. She's got these two eyes staring out from under her eyebrows. All she lacked was a mustache. She looked exactly like Mark Twain." While Holbrook expected that they would talk about her father, Clara appeared to be uninterested. Instead, she volunteered that she had a much better subject for him to play on the stage: "I've had an idea for you, Hal. I think you should do a show where you play Jesus Christ. . . . Yes, I think you could do a very good job of trying to make people understand." Startled, Holbrook replied, "Well, I don't know, I don't know if it would book very well." Clara continued, "I think you could do it. I wish you would. I want you to think seriously about that."

By this time Clara and her daughter were no longer on speaking terms. After Nina spent time at Camarillo State Hospital, her psychiatrist wrote that her "hatred for her mother was well-established." Clara disinherited Nina in her will, leaving everything to her husband. (Nina later successfully sued Samossoud and a settlement was reached.)

As for Nina, Mark Twain's last direct descendent, her final years were excruciatingly lonely ones, as old friends no longer took her drunken late-night calls. When Holbrook was in California, he invited her to a performance of *Mark Twain Tonight,* and Nina accepted. However, she was so inebriated that she was unable to appreciate the show. Nina committed suicide in her apartment on January 16, 1966, at age fifty-five. It is said that her ghost still haunts the hallways of the Highland Towers, going from door to door begging to come inside. Nina was buried in Woodlawn Cemetery in Elmira, a short distance away from Clara. Even in death she would remain separated from her mother; Jacques Samossoud, who died five months after Nina, was buried next to Clara. His grave remains unmarked today, supposedly due to the hatred of the Langdon family.

Eight years after Clara's death, a mysterious and forgotten Twain manuscript came to light. The *New York Times* headline announced,

"Newly Found Mark Twain Letter Accuses Aide of Theft." Forty-nine years after its composition, the "Ashcroft-Lyon Manuscript" was found in a shoebox. Clara had given the manuscript to Julia Langdon Loomis, her mother's niece, to safeguard for her, and sometime over the years, Julia had passed it along to her husband's business associate, Harold R. German. German's daughter discovered Twain's manuscript when she was going through her father's papers. She contacted a dealer, who sold it to the Berg Collection of English and American Literature at the New York Public Library for $25,000, with the restriction that no portions of the manuscript could be quoted. The *Times* did, however, cite Twain's exhortation to "the person who might one day find the manuscript to preserve it for the value of its contents." By this time, all of the people originally concerned were dead, and no one remained who knew the real reason that Twain had written the account or who could question the manuscript's veracity. Twain would have been pleased.

In view of his lifelong reliance upon women, it is unsurprising that Twain spent his final year passionately writing about them. For each of the three women featured in his writings there was a different, tragic ending: Clara was alienated from her father, unable to marry the man she loved, and estranged from her only child; Jean was dead, after years spent suffering with a terrible affliction and unrequited affection; and Isabel was condemned to be the subject of a blackmail document whose author was determined to destroy her name.

When Isabel began her collaboration with Doris and Samuel Webster she was in her late eighties. Money was not the motivating factor that drew her to the past. Twenty-eight years after leaving Twain's side she wrote, "No penalty attaches itself to perfect living—No penalties ever attach themselves to joy." After all those years, what Isabel could not bear was the awareness that her existence had been successfully and systematically erased: first by Twain, then by Clara, and finally by Paine. She desperately wanted people to know that she mattered—that she had been needed and valued by Twain.

While still married to Ashcroft and living in Montreal in the 1920s, Isabel jotted down an insightful and particularly bleak observation:

> Sitting alone in a little room in an old house in Montreal, I am thrown
> back through the years—by a single packet of written matter, which

proves to be the "forms" dictated by Mr. Clemens to me as his private secy. For answer to letters, invitations, the gifts of books—His private secretary—so private that the very mention of me is with held from the world by the turn of fate—Private—

*Insert card issued by the Mogul Egyptian Cigarettes Company, summer 1909–fall 1910. It reads, "A woman is only a woman, but a good cigar's a smoke!"*

# Acknowledgments

This book took too long to complete, sixteen years, and I am deeply grateful to the librarians, scholarly colleagues, archivists, students, collectors, friends, and family who supported me throughout the undertaking. I began the initial research in 1993 while an associate professor of English at the State University of New York at Potsdam, and since then my family moved first to Cedar Rapids, Iowa, where I was dean of the faculty at Coe College for five years, and then to Claremont, California, where I have served as president of Pitzer College for the past eight years. All the while, through many life changes, including the birth of my son in 1996, I kept returning to this project.

I would like to thank the National Endowment for the Humanities for its 1994 summer stipend, which allowed me to do invaluable archival research at the Mark Twain Papers & Project at the University of California at Berkeley; Vassar College; the Mark Twain House in Hartford, Connecticut; and Trinity College. And to SUNY Potsdam for awarding me its 1993–94 Research and Creative Endeavors Grant, which allowed me to work with two wonderful research fellows: Russell Swanker III and Donna Williamson. Special appreciation goes to the reference librarians who assisted me in locating materials in those pre-digitization days: Keith Compeau at SUNY Potsdam, Betty Rogers and Susan Wagner-Hecht at Coe College, and Mark Woodhouse at Elmira College. Quite simply, my work could not have been done without Bob Hirst, the director of the Mark Twain Papers at the University of California, Berkeley, and the support of his scholar-editors Kenneth Sanderson and Victor Fisher. I am indebted to my office staff, Doris Gitzy, Jennifer Berkley, and Natalie Wilson, for their help in preparing materials and providing a listening ear. Special appreciation goes to Andrea Olson at Pitzer College for her superb research skills, Stuart McConnell for his wealth of information about the Gilded Age, and Lee Monroe for his meticulous manuscript editing. Thank you Tom Curley, Alan Finder, and Liliana Trevizan for your assistance in locating primary source materials.

It has been my good fortune to count among my colleagues the Mark Twain scholars Michael Kiskis, Gary Scharnhorst, Ann Ryan, David Smith, Victor Doyno, and the late Hamlin Hill. Their feedback over the years has made this journey infinitely more interesting. I also want to thank the collectors Bob Slotta and Kevin Mac Donnell for their generosity in sharing unpublished Mark Twain materials. To Geoff Ward: I am most grateful for your warm regard and encouragement. To my academic mentor Jay Martin: Your unwavering faith in my abilities for the past twenty-five years has meant more to me than you will ever know. And to Bill Flanagan, my dearest friend: How fortunate I am that you are part of my life.

I am indebted to Bob Bookman for his assistance in bringing this project to its completion; to Melanie Jackson, my agent, whose enthusiasm and support meant the world to me; to Vicky Wilson, my editor at Knopf, for her keen and insightful critical eye; and to Carmen Johnson, who has been so helpful in preparing the manuscript for publication.

One of the rewards of writing biography is the opportunity to meet the descendents and friends of the subjects. Therefore, I would like to express my deepest gratitude to Isabel Van Kleek Lyon's family, David and June Moore, Laura Moore, and Tracy Worthington, for sharing their memories and precious collection of letters and photographs, and to Alice Henderson, one of Nina Gabrilowitsch's closest friends, for her stories and photographs. Thank you to Hal Holbrook, who has "done" Mark Twain longer than Samuel Clemens did, for his memories of his time spent talking with Isabel Van Kleek Lyon.

To my parents, John and Mary Skandera, thank you for encouraging my love of reading as a child and for raising me to appreciate the importance of humor. Finally, to my beloved son, Sparkey, who was born to a mother who writes and who shares my love of reading, this is your book.

Laura E. Skandera Trombley
November 1, 2009

# Notes

## ABBREVIATIONS

For frequently cited names, the following abbreviations are used:

CC      Clara Clemens
JC      Jean Clemens
SLC     Samuel Langhorne Clemens
FD      Frederick Duneka
WDH     William Dean Howells
IL      Isabel Van Kleek Lyon
KM      Kevin Mac Donnell
DW      Doris Webster
SW      Samuel Webster
HW      Harriet Whitmore

For frequently cited libraries and manuscript depositories, the following abbreviations are used:

HL      Huntington Library, San Marino, California
MC      Moore Collection, David Moore, IL's grandnephew
MTM     Mark Twain Memorial, Hartford, Connecticut
MTP     Mark Twain Papers & Project, University of California, Berkeley
NYPL    New York Public Library
SC      Robert Slotta Collection

TC        Trinity College
VC        Vassar College
YU        Yale University

The Isabel Lyon Collection at the Mark Twain Papers & Project includes:

"Ashcroft-Lyon Manuscript," Box 48
Annotated copy of *Mark Twain's Autobiography* (1924) File
Annotated copy of *Mark Twain: A Biography* (1912) File
1903 Daily Reminder: January 3–4, 1903
1905 Daily Reminder #1 (This is a xeroxed copy; the original is in the Antenne-Dorrance Collection, University of Wisconsin.)
1905 Daily Reminder #2
1906 Daily Reminder #1
1906 Daily Reminder #2 (This is a xeroxed copy; the original is in the Harry Ransom Humanities Research Center at the University of Texas at Austin. This daily reminder is an edited copy of 1906 Daily Reminder #1.)
1907 Daily Reminder
1908 Daily Reminder
1903–06 Journal
IL Miscellaneous Mark Twain Notes
Notebook #1: January 31, 1906, to September 8, 1906
Notebook #2: October 23, 1906, to May 31, 1907
Notebook #3: December 17, 1906, to January 17, 1908
Notebook #4: October 5, 1907, to February 17, 1908
Notebook #5: February 2, 1906, to April 1, 1908
Annotated copy of Albert Bigelow Paine, *Mark Twain's Autobiography*, vol. 1 (New York: Harper and Brothers, 1944), (1924) File Subject File, Lyon, IL
Webster [Doris and Samuel] Manuscript

# PREFACE

xiii "Sitting alone in a little room": Personal correspondence to the author from Tracy S. Worthington, April 6, 2002. Undated quotation.
xiii "I am not *an* American": Twain wrote this line in his 1897 notebook in a passage with references to Frank Fuller. There is a debate as to whether Twain is referring to himself or is quoting Fuller. MTP.
xv "a slovenly writer": IL Journals Research; Frederick Anderson note card, and editorial comments, MTP.

xvi Also, her daily reminders: I spent many years laboriously transcribing IL's writings. Happily, her handwriting is quite legible. The primary difficulty I had was in recovering entries that she had tried to cross out. In most cases, I was able to retrieve the information. I tried to be as accurate as possible, despite her idiosyncratic punctuation, and even if it meant occasionally sacrificing proper grammar and correct spelling.

xvi In addition, Isabel made: The unabridged 1906 daily reminder is archived at the Mark Twain Papers & Project, and the abridged (xeroxed) copy is archived at the Harry Ransom Humanities Research Center, at the University of Texas at Austin.

xvi "a liar, a forger": SLC to CC, March 6, 1910, MTP.

## ONE: "TOO PERFECT FOR LIFE"

1 "Today has been very full": January 15, 1905; 1905 Daily Reminder #2, MTP.

3 "contained a hundred people": Albert Bigelow Paine, ed., *Mark Twain's Autobiography* (New York: Harper and Brothers, 1924).

4 "I came in with Halley's Comet": Albert Bigelow Paine, *Mark Twain: A Biography* (New York: Harper and Brothers, 1912).

4 "The Almighty has said": Ibid.

4 "He always seemed to me": Ibid. In vol. 1, chap. 3, Paine prefaces this remark with the words "long afterward, one of those who knew him best said."

4 "COCA, a vegetable product": Mark Twain, "The Turning Point of My Life," *Harper's Bazaar,* February 1910.

6 "I made the great discovery": Milton Meltzer, *Mark Twain Himself* (Philadelphia: University of Pennsylvania, 2002), p. 150.

7 "High and fine literature": SLC to WDH, February 15, 1887, MTP.

7 "one living writer": Professor Richard Burton declared in 1904 that SLC was the "one living writer of indisputable genius" in the United States.

8 "has taken a leading place": Louis Budd, *Our Mark Twain* (Philadelphia: University of Pennsylvania Press, 1983), p. 83.

8 "I am frightened": Ibid., p. 95.

8 "himself high": Ibid., p. 87.

8 One afternoon in the late 1880s: DW interview with IL, undated, handwritten document, IL Miscellaneous Mark Twain Notes, MTP.

8 the Whitmores' six children: Franklin, Jr., Harriet (nicknamed "Hattie"), Ruth, Frederick, William, and Harold. Franklin Whitmore File, MTM.

8 Isabel was let into: IL to DW, September 18, 1956, MTM.

11 "if I can play": DW interview with IL, undated, handwritten document, IL Miscellaneous Mark Twain Notes, MTP.

11 Born on December 15, 1863: IL's siblings were Louise and Charles.

12 Charles was a published writer: "Considerations in favour of Classical Studies" (New York: W. G. Boggs, 1839); "The Power of Intellectual Culture; A Lecture Delivered Before the Tarrytown Lyceum" (New York: Dean and Trevett, 1841); "Oration Delivered in a Grove, Near the Ground on Which Major André Was Taken, at Tarrytown, on the Fourth of July, 1839" (New York: Bryant and Boggs, 1839).

12 Individual lots: Description of Irving Park, Tarrytown, the property of Charles H. Lyon (New York: Wynkoop, Hallenbeck and Thomas, 1859).

12 Making matters worse: William T. Lyon was a longtime headmaster at the prestigious Irving Institute, a preparatory school for boys, located in Tarrytown.

12 The house was located: Miss Porter's mission was to produce women who would lead useful lives, fully grounded in the tenets of professionalism, marriage, motherhood, and household management. To all appearances, IL was in full agreement with the school's goals.

12 Her first known job: Unknown author, "143 Main Street" (unpublished manuscript, July 7, 1972), MC.

12 "Surrounded by French speech": IL to HW, December 3, 1890, MTM.

13 "I cannot tell you": IL to HW, December 3, 1890, MTM.

13 A possible explanation: July 10, 1906, JC Diary April 30–July 21, 1906, HL.

13 "had so much trouble": IL to HW, December 3, 1890, MTM.

13 "$500 a year": IL to HW, December 3, 1890, MTM.

15 "Up go the trolley cars": Quoted in Laura E. Skandera Trombley, *Mark Twain in the Company of Women* (Philadelphia: University of Pennsylvania Press, 1994), p. 14.

16 "could manage to have an opinion": Budd, *Our Mark Twain,* p. 148.

17 "was almost a living statue": Ibid., p. 216.

17 In a manuscript: "143 Main Street" (author's personal collection).

17 Years later, Isabel confided: July 10, 1906, JC Diary April 30–July 21, 1906, HL.

18 This was an era: Nils Retterstøl, "Suicide in a Cultural History Perspective, Part 2," *Suicidologi* 3 (2000).

19 "My dear Friend": Olivia Clemens to HW, June 30, 1902, MTM.

20 "But I said": DW interview with IL, undated, handwritten document, IL Miscellaneous Mark Twain Notes, MTP.

20 "I want to tell you": CC to HW, December 10, 1902, MTM.

20 "so personal": DW interview with IL, undated, handwritten document, IL Miscellaneous Mark Twain Notes, MTP.

21 "Alone I watched": January 1, 1903, 1903 Daily Reminder, VC.

21 "His private humor": Undated, loose page, 1903–05 Box VC.

22 "enchanting": January 6, 1903, 1903 Daily Reminder, VC.

22 "This morning as I sat": January 3, 1903, 1903 Daily Reminder, MTP.

23 Ill at ease: IL, interview by DW, January 5, 1950; Typed transcript, VC.

23 "she looked badly": January 2, 1903, 1903 Daily Reminder, VC.

23 "have been having a sad time": January 6, 1903, 1903 Daily Reminder, VC.

23 "Jean's head got a bad knock": Lewis Leary, ed., *Mark Twain's Correspondence with Henry Huttleston Rogers* (Berkeley: University of California Press, 1969), p. 430.

24 "fright, anxiety": Albert H. Hayes, M.D., *Diseases of the Nervous System: Or Pathology of the Nerves and Nervous Maladies* (Boston: Peabody Medical Institute, 1875), pp. 74–75.

24 Based on descriptions: According to Dr. Peter C. Whybrow, director of the UCLA Neuropsychiatric Institute, "in late adolescence a 'pruning' of the neurons in the brain takes place, as the nervous system matures . . . one of the developmental genes responsible for that pruning may be abnormal (at variance from the usual gene structure) in people who suffer idiopathic epilepsy." Personal correspondence with the author, August 10, 2004.

24 At times she took thrice-daily doses: Jean's primary physician for her epilepsy, Dr. Frederick Peterson, recommended bromides of "sodium salt." See his *Nervous and Mental Diseases* (Philadelphia: W. B. Saunders Company, 1911), p. 644.

24 "constant hebetude": Ibid.

24 "vegetable than animal food": Hayes, *Diseases of the Nervous System,* p. 76.

24 Yet, despite the family's heroic efforts: "Petit mal seizures begin with electrical discharges in a small area of the brain, and the discharges remain confined to that area. Symptoms include abnormal sensations, movements, or psychic aberrations, depending on the part of the brain affected. Convulsive seizures (or grand mal seizures) usually begin with an abnormal electrical discharge in a small area of the brain. The discharge quickly spreads to adjoining parts of the brain, causing the entire area to malfunction. In primary generalized epilepsy, abnormal discharges over a large area of the brain cause widespread malfunction from the beginning. In either case, a convulsion is the body's reaction to the abnormal discharges. In these convulsive seizures, a person experiences a temporary loss of consciousness, severe muscle spasms and jerking throughout the body, intense turning of the head to one side, clenching of teeth, and loss of bladder control. Afterward, the person may have a headache, be temporarily confused, and feel extremely tired. Usually, the person doesn't remember what happened during the seizure." The Merck Manual, Home Edition, chapter 73: "Seizure Disorders."

24 "ever achieve control": John R. Gates, M.D., "Sudden Death in Epilepsy," *The Medical Journal of Allina* 6 (2002): 1.

25 opera glasses: June 21, and June 15, 1903, 1903 Daily Reminder, VC.

25 "if the little cherubs": IL to Frank Whitmore, April 20, 1903, MTM.

25 "I saw Mrs. Clemens twice": IL, undated, handwritten document, IL Miscellaneous Mark Twain Notes, MTP.

25 Isabel was "summoned": June 29, 1903, 1903 Daily Reminder, VC.

26 "Oh she is sweet": June 30, 1903, 1903 Daily Reminder, VC.

26 Bangs and Twain knew: Twain's publishing company printed Bangs's novel *Toppleton's Client: Or, A Spirit in Exile* (1893), and Twain contributed articles to Bangs's magazine, the *Metropolitan* magazine.

27 "How I kept on a strange sympathy": April 23, 1905, 1905 Daily Reminder #2, MTP; fragment in the 1905 Daily Reminder #2, MTP.

28 Twain, thinking that Italy was impossible: June 26, 1903, 1903 Daily Reminder, VC.

28 "This begins my third trip to Europe": November 7, 1903, 1903–06 Journal, MTP.

29 "where Mr. & Mrs. Clemens are established": January 17, 1904, 1903–06 Journal, MTP.

30 "for someday I shall want": January 17, 1904, 1903–06 Journal, MTP.

30 "It was built for Cosimo I.": January 17, 1904, 1903–06 Journal, MTP.

30 "made it quite plain to her": January 17, 1904, 1903–06 Journal, MTP.

31 "At first the high stone walls on either side": January 17, 1904, 1903–06 Journal, MTP.

31 He had always been irresistibly drawn: Laura Skandera Trombley, "Mark Twain's Cross-Dressing Oeuvre," *College Literature* 24 (1997): 82–95.

32 "Perhaps you may be interested": IL to HW, January 8, 1904, MTM.

33 "About January 14": February 28, 1904, 1903–06 Journal, MTP.

33 "I've struck it!": Henry Nash Smith and William M. Gibson, eds., *Mark Twain–Howells Letters* (Cambridge, Mass.: Belknap Press, 1960), p. 778.

33 "Last week we began": January 12, 1904, loose page, 1903–05 Box, VC.

34 "Somewhere in the Bible": March 18, 1904, 1903–06 Journal, MTP.

34 "I dropped out of sight": February 28, 1904, 1903–06 Journal, MTP.

34 "Miss Lyon was pursued by that donkey": CC to Dorothea Gilder, February 1904, SC.

35 "sudden standstill": SLC to FD, February 8, 1904, MTP.

35 "I have reached the very lowest stage": CC to Dorothea Gilder, postmarked February 1904, SC.

36 Olivia wrote back: The meeting never took place. IL to Olivia Clemens, after March 1, 1904, MTM.

37 "to have a word with her": February 14, 1904, loose page, 1903–05 Box, VC.

37 "Mrs. Clemens has not had the good winter": IL to HW, March 8, 1904, MTM.

38 "The past week": Hamlin Hill, *Mark Twain: God's Fool* (New York: Harper and Row, 1972), p. 83.

39 "We sat out of doors": Webster Manuscript, MTP.

39 "And we came over here": April 14, 1904, 1903–06 Journal, MTP.

39 "Mr. Clemens ran right up": Mary Lawton, *A Lifetime with Mark Twain* (1925; reprinted Amsterdam: Fredonia Books, 2004), pp. 228–29.

40 "June 5—Mrs. Clemens": June 5, 1904, 1903–06 Journal, MTP.

40 "Today is the anniversary": June 5, 1905, 1905 Daily Reminder #2, MTP.

40 "The trunks are pulled out": June 16, 1904, 1903–06 Journal, MTP.

41 "to get the 16 Trunks booked": July 15, 1904, 1903–06 Journal, MTP.

41 "strain": SLC to C. J. Langdon, June 13, 1904, MTM.

41 At the cemetery: Lawton, *A Lifetime with Mark Twain,* p. 231.

41 "pale weak exhausted": July 16, 1904, 1903–06 Journal, MTP.

41 "Dear Susy—": July 25, 1904, MTP

43 "[Gorky] could not offend": August 26, 1906, fragment in the 1906 Daily Reminder #1, MTP.

43 "No, I want her here": Doris Webster wrote, "When they moved from Redding to Fifth Ave. Clara thought Isabel should have a room outside, but M.T. said 'no, I want her here. She's like an old pair of slippers to me.'" Doris probably meant Lee instead of Redding, because when Twain moved from Fifth Avenue to Redding, Isabel was provided with a cottage of her own separate from the main house. Webster Interview, 1953, VC.

43 "I wonder if I am glad": July 18, 1904, 1903–06 Journal, MTP.

43 "Oh stretching straining heart": July 28, 1904, 1903–06 Journal, MTP.

43 "Today I have an uplift": August 17, 1904, 1903–06 Journal, MTP.

43 "lost money": February 12, 1905, 1905 Daily Reminder #2, MTP.

43 "Santa Clara went away": July 22, 1904, 1903–06 Journal, MTP.

44 "a broken tendon": July 28, 1904, 1903–06 Journal, MTP.

44 "hysterical": August 3, 1904, 1903–06 Journal, MTP.

44 Rudyard Kipling's *Five Seas:* Isabel mentions a Kipling book with this title. She is likely confusing two titles by Kipling: *The Seven Seas* (1896) and *The Five Nations* (1903).

44 "[Alice] Hegan Rice": July 26, 1904, 1903–06 Journal, MTP.

45 "This house is": November 30, 1904, 1903–06 Journal, MTP.

45 "the real picture": August 12, 1905, loose page, 1903–05 Box, VC.

46 "Tonight at dinner": December 3, 1904, 1903–06 Journal, MTP.

46 "The attitude that one has to assume": December 4, 1904, 1903–06 Journal, MTP.

46 "This evening after dinner we played": November 30, 1904, 1903–06 Journal, MTP.

46 "When Jean is in Mr. Clemens's room": January 2, 1905, 1903–06 Journal, MTP.

47 "a truly wonderful instrument": December 2, 1904, 1903–06 Journal, MTP.

47 The Aeolian was delivered: SLC to CC, September 3, 1905, MTP. The Aeolian resides today at the Mark Twain Museum in Hannibal, Missouri.

47 Over the next few years: IL's Orchestrelle repertoire was composed primarily of classical pieces: Schubert's "Impromptu" (possibly op. 90, no. 3; the "Impromptu" was Jean's favorite), "Unfinished Symphony," first movement, and "Erlkönig" (Twain nicknamed the piece "König Stutil"); Wagner's "Wedding March" from *Lohengrin* and "O du mein holder Abendstern"; the Finale from Tchaikovsky's Symphony no. 6; Beethoven's Adagio from the Piano Sonata op. 13, no. 8, and Andante from Symphony no. 5; *Stabat Mater* (probably Rossini's version); Wagner's *Tannhäuser*'s Overture; Chopin's Sonata no. 2 ("Funeral March") and "Nocturne," op. 37; and the popular "The Last Rose of Summer."

47 "Aeolian satisfies": January 30, 1905, 1905 Daily Reminder #2, MTP.

47 "I have been playing": March 2, 1906, 1906 Daily Reminder #1, MTP.

47 "He is weak": December 23, 1904, 1903–06 Journal, MTP.

48 "He seems quite helpless": January 3, 1905, 1905 Daily Reminder #2, MTP.

48 When he felt a cold coming on: May 26, 1905, 1905 Daily Reminder #2, MTP.

48 His daily intake was approximately forty: "I have been all my life in the habit of taking at least 40"; Twain quoted in "Down to Four a Day," *Boston Daily Globe*, August 3, 1909, p. 9.

48 "Sometimes I think": October 4, 1905, 1905 Daily Reminder #2, MTP.

48 "I doubt if any smoker": August 12, 1905, loose page, 1903–05 Box, VC.

49 "Fuel": December 31, and January 1, 1905, 1905 Daily Reminder #2, MTP.

49 "Today Mr. Clemens": July 24, 1905, 1905 Daily Reminder #2, MTP.

50 "Like a dream edifice": January 2, 1905, 1908 Daily Reminder, MTP.

> This morning when I went into Mr. Clemens's room he asked me something about Moses & the 10 Commandments, and that led up to making Mr. Clemens say "If those ten Commandments had never been written, man would be making some for himself. He has to have a code—he'd be saying—Thou shalt not sit up all night. Thou shalt not drink Coffee at midnight—Thou shalt not eat Cabbage &

beans—" "They would all be Commandments that he is in need of and he couldn't be happy if he wasn't making them to break—"

March 26, 1905, 1903–06 Journal, MTP.

50 Twain entertained the group: Kent R. Rasmussen, *Mark Twain A–Z* (New York: Oxford University Press, 1995), p. 105.

50 "Prosper appeared just then": June 23, 1905, 1905 Daily Reminder #2, MTP.

51 "[Samuel] had been left": December 4, 1904, 1903–06 Journal, MTP.

53 " 'This is the day' ": March 24, 1906, 1906 Daily Reminder #1, MTP.

53 "He went with his father": March 22, 1907, loose page, 1906–07 Box, VC.

53 "I was a little bit of a girl": July 28, 1904, 1903–06 Journal, MTP.

54 With her father, uncle, and brother gone: January 8, 1905, 1905 Daily Reminder #2, MTP.

55 Isabel constantly worried: December 3, 1904, 1903–06 Journal, MTP.

55 "very lonely": March 27, 1905, 1905 Daily Reminder #2, MTP.

55 "strange, nervous": July 10, 1904, 1903–06 Journal, MTP; February 10, 1905, 1905 Daily Reminder #2, MTP.

55 "shut me away": July 9, 1905, 1903–06 Journal, MTP.

55 "Never never on Sea": March 14, 1905, 1905 Daily Reminder #2, MTP.

56 "tampering with the sentinel": Fragment, 1906 Daily Reminder #1, MTP.

56 "She showered very sweet speech": February 15, 1905, 1905 Daily Reminder #2, MTP.

56 "His love for another woman": April 1, 1905, 1905 Daily Reminder #2, MTP.

56 Isabel declined: January 10, 1905, 1905 Daily Reminder #2, MTP.

57 "For 3 days": December 28, 1904, 1903–06 Journal, MTP.

57 "trying to find places": January 2, 1905, 1905 Daily Reminder #2, MTP; December 28, 1904, 1903–06 Journal, MTP.

57 "Quite an interesting man": January 7, 1905, 1905 Daily Reminder #2, MTP.

57 "among Mr. C's papers": February 28, 1905, 1905 Daily Reminder #2, MTP.

57 "he Said that a few days ago": April 22, 1905, 1903–06 Journal, MTP.

57 After the individual had departed: December 13, 1904, loose page, 1903–05 Box, VC.

57 Twain later explained to Isabel: IL, annotated copy of *Mark Twain: A Biography* (1924).

58 "Today Mr Clemens": Scrap piece of paper dated January 14, 1935, 1905 Daily Reminder #2, MTP.

58 "with the Sure enough touch": June 2, 1905, loose page, 1903–05 Box, VC.

59 "writing an appreciation": FD to SLC, April 7, 1905, MTP.
59 "That they lay Their homage": April 22, 1905, 1905 Daily Reminder #2, MTP.
59 In early June, after discussing the matter: June 6, 1905, 1905 Daily Reminder #1, MTP.
59 "you and Jean to arrange": SLC to CC, "Mid-June" 1905, MTP.
59 "Tonight as Mr. Clemens lay": September 5, 1905, loose page, 1903–05 Box, VC.
59 In April 1906: "Mark Twain Letter Sold; Written to Thomas Nast, It Proposed a Joint Tour," New York Times, April 3, 1906.
59 Twain's fetched a higher price: Budd, Our Mark Twain, p. 204.
60 "All the days": September 21, 1905, 1905 Daily Reminder #2, MTP.
60 "piled up 172 little pincushions": October 18, 1905, 1905 Daily Reminder #2, MTP.
60 "Away back when General Grant": September 5, 1905, loose page, 1903–05 Box, VC.
60 "that really if publishers had any sense": August 19, 1905, loose page, 1903–05 Box, VC.
61 "Mr Clemens closed the matter": Fragment, 1906 Daily Reminder #1, MTP.
61 "solemn joy of living": January 19, 1905, 1905 Daily Reminder #2, MTP.
61 "his great—very great beauty": December 13, 1904, loose page, 1903–05 Box, VC.
61 "He is at his best": January 30, 1905, 1905 Daily Reminder #2, MTP.
62 "another Soliloquy King Leopold's": February 10, 1905, 1905 Daily Reminder #2, MTP.
62 "Breathless we sat": February 22, 1905, 1905 Daily Reminder #2, MTP.
63 Doubleday arranged for publication: May 9, 1906, 1906 Daily Reminder #1, MTP.
63 "The disinterested reception": IL, "IVL notes on What Is Man?," Berg Collection, NYPL.
63 "He is so wonderful": March 5, 1905, 1905 Daily Reminder #2, MTP.
63 "This morning I played": August 31, 1905, 1905 Daily Reminder #2, MTP.
64 Jean loved the heavily wooded area: March 3, 1905, 1905 Daily Reminder #2, MTP; March 8, 1905, 1905 Daily Reminder #1, MTP.
64 "eternal Slap": March 10, 1905, 1905 Daily Reminder #2, MTP.
64 "didn't think it would do": March 22, 1905, 1905 Daily Reminder #1, MTP.
64 "Tonight Mr. Clemens read": March 21, 1905, 1905 Daily Reminder #2, MTP.
65 "Life in this way": March 18, 1905, 1905 Daily Reminder #2, MTP.

65  Clara spent the fall: Hill, *Mark Twain: God's Fool,* p. 98.

65  "gained 5 1/2 pounds": February 2, 1905, 1905 Daily Reminder #1, MTP; February 3, 1905, 1905 Daily Reminder #2, MTP.

65  "A Little change": March 30, 1905, 1905 Daily Reminder #2, MTP.

66  "The view is wonderful": May 5, 1905, 1905 Daily Reminder #2, MTP.

66  "found her plump": May 10, 1905, 1905 Daily Reminder #1, MTP.

66  "Oh the anxious hours": May 11, 1905, 1905 Daily Reminder #2, MTP.

66  "Today Mr. Clemens arrived": May 18, 1905, 1905 Daily Reminder #2, MTP.

66  Twain delighted in his summer accommodations: May 23, 1905, 1905 Daily Reminder #2, MTP.

67  "Mr. Clemens spends too much Time": May 21, 1905, 1905 Daily Reminder #2, MTP.

67  "This evening": May 22, 1905, 1905 Daily Reminder #2, MTP.

67  "A great faith has come": June 7, 1905, 1905 Daily Reminder #2, MTP.

68  She was disappointed: June 24, 1905, 1905 Daily Reminder #1, MTP.

68  "when I had leisure": June 30, 1905, 1905 Daily Reminder #2, MTP.

68  "For himself there are": July 4, 1905, 1905 Daily Reminder #2, MTP.

68  "This summer is so exquisite": July 13, 1905, 1905 Daily Reminder #2, MTP.

69  "I study to be useful to him": Shelley Fisher Fishkin, ed., *The Diaries of Adam and Eve* (New York: Oxford University Press, 1996), p. 29.

69  "This afternoon I read": July 25, 1905, loose page, 1903–05 Box, VC.

70  "vividly enlarged and clarified": Amy L. Blair, "Misreading *The House of Mirth,*" *American Literature* 76, no. 1 (March 2004): 150, 153.

70  "We began here": Rudyard Kipling, *Selected Stories from Kipling,* William Lyon Phelps, ed. (New York: Doubleday, 1919), p. 324.

70  "We're two little orphans": Ibid., p. 337.

70  "Here was nothing but silence": Ibid., p. 339.

71  Sophie soon becomes pregnant: Ibid., p. 349.

71  "The mug was worn and dented": Ibid., p. 352.

71  "Santissima has given me a creed": July 27, 1905, 1905 Daily Reminder #2, MTP.

71  "Kipling has given me another": July 25, 1905, 1905 Daily Reminder #2, MTP.

72  " 'Never take anything for granted—' ": October 17, 1905, 1905 Daily Reminder #2, MTP.

72  "Jean has told me": July 16, 1905, 1905 Daily Reminder #2, MTP.

72  "It's terribly Thin ice": May 9, 1905 [printed date], June 10, 1905 [handwritten date], 1905 Daily Reminder #2, MTP.

72  From May to July 1905: Memoranda, 1905 Daily Reminder #2, MTP.

73  "my Sacred charge": August 17, 1904, 1903–06 Journal, MTP.

73  "Now it is a book": May 16, 1905, 1905 Daily Reminder #2, MTP.

73 "feel the uselessness": October 7, 1905, 1905 Daily Reminder #2, MTP.

73 "a prodigious piece of work": September 30, 1905, 1905 Daily Reminder #2, MTP.

74 "A calm dreamlike concentration": IL, 1933 File, VC.

74 "This morning Mr. Clemens": October 1, 1905, 1905 Daily Reminder #2, MTP.

75 She and Clara had not seen each other: November 1, 1905, Daily Reminder #2, MTP.

## TWO: THE GATHERING STORM

77 "I am the only person": February 16, 1908, Notebook #4, MTP.

80 "weak & tired & discouraged": September 26, 1905, 1905 Daily Reminder #2, MTP.

80 Clara "was not a good singer": Russell McLauchlin was the music and drama critic for *The Detroit News* until his retirement in 1955. About the quality of Clara's singing, McLauchlin recounted, "In the long years of Ossip Gabrilowitsch's incumbency with the Detroit Symphony, the wife of his bosom was occasionally presented as soloist, not at the weekend 'pop' but to the stately audience of subscribers. What domestic pressures fruited into those events, I cannot say. All I can say is that they were exceedingly tough on the working press. Mrs. Gabrilowitsch, who was always billed as 'Mme. CC,' was not a good singer." McLauchlin, *O.G. the Incomparable: Memoires of Ossip Gabrilowitsch* (A Keepsake Edition, Beverly, Mass. June 2002); the full text is available on www.twainweb.net.

80 "strongly individual": December 24, 1906, 1906 Daily Reminder #1, MTP.

80 In any case, potential patrons: IL to HW, March 8, 1904, MTM.

80 "My brain is so brittle": December 1, 1905, 1905 Daily Reminder #2, MTP.

80 When Teresa Cherubini: February 6, 1906, and February 11, 1906, Daily Reminder #1, MTP.

81 "against the doctor's advice": Hill, *Mark Twain: God's Fool,* 123.

81 Isabel carefully charted:

| | |
|---|---|
| May 3, 1905 | |
| May 1, 1905 | |
| May 7, 1905 | |
| June 15, 1905 | |
| July 4, 1905 | |
| August 12, 1905 | 3 attacks |
| September 12, 1905 | Jean—Bathroom—10 A.M. |

| | |
|---|---|
| October 14, 1905 | Jean—Study—9:30— |
| October 20, 1905 | Jean—10.30—Bed.     5—PM—Bed—unusually long and severe—Jean is in bad shape. Her malady seems to be increasing in violence— |
| November 14, 1905 | Jean 9.30 |
| November 20, 1905 | Jean—9:30—3 Times |
| November 26, 1905 | Jean. 3 p.m. 8 p.m: Katy |
| December 14, 1905 | Jean—9.30 |
| December 25, 1905 | Jean ill all day—no climax |
| January 1, 1906 | Jean—11—1.20—7 p.m. very severe |
| January 5, 1906 | Jean is not well—Not only has her malady increased—but her whole physical condition is at a low ebb. |
| January 22, 1906 | Jean ill—9—or 8.50—burned on the hot radiator. |

These are various entry dates from the 1906 Daily Reminder #1, MTP.

81  "not any too clear-headed": May 5, 1906, JC Diary April 30–July 21, 1906, 53348 HL.

81  About half of the children: "Petit Mal Seizure," www.mayoclinic.com.

81  "one at 11.30": August 12, 1905, 1905 Daily Reminder #2, MTP.

82  Recent research, however: S. J. Logsdail and B. K. Toone. "Post-ictal Psychoses: A Clinical and Phenomenological Description," *British Journal of Psychiatry* 152 (1988): 246–52.

82  Psychosis usually develops: Ibid., p. 251.

82  "the most common of the episodic epilepsy-related psychoses": C. Christodoulou, M. Koutroumanidis, M. J. Hennessy, R. D. C. Elwes, C. E. Polkey, B. K. Toone, "Postictal Psychosis After Temporal Lobectomy," *Neurology* 59 (2002): 1432–35.

82  According to Dr. John Milton: John Milton, William Rand Kenan, Jr., Professor in Computational Neuroscience at the Claremont Colleges, Personal correspondence, September 8, 2004.

82  "confusion, visual and auditory": O. Devinsky, H. Abramson, K. Alper, L. S. FitzGerald, K. Perrine, J. Calderon, D. Luciano, "Postictal Psychosis: A Case Control Series of 20 Patients and 150 Controls," *Epilepsy Research* 20 (1995): 247–53.

82  Jean's medical history: I shared the record that IL kept of Jean's attacks with John Milton and with Peter C. Whybrow, M.D., director of the Semel Institute of the Department of Psychiatry & Behavioral Science at UCLA. Both concur that Jean's aggressive behavior was the result of a psychotic state (i.e. postictal psychosis) directly linked to her epilepsy.

82 In Isabel's papers, there are two mentions: There is also a handwritten note by SW included in the unpublished Webster manuscript referring to the attack: "This . . . refers to an attack on the maid, Katy . . . Leary, that Miss Lyon told me about. S.C.W." January 5, 1906, 1906 Daily Reminder #1, MTP.

82 "Jean. 3—pm 8 pm <u>Katy</u>": November 26, 1905, 1905 Daily Reminder #2, MTP.

82 In her cryptic fashion:

> *The Fly (William Blake 1794)*
> *Little Fly*
> *Thy summer's play,*
> *My thoughtless hand*
> *Has brush'd away.*
> *Am not I*
> *A fly like thee?*
> *Or art not thou*
> *A man like me?*
> *For I dance*
> *And drink & sing;*
> *Till some blind hand*
> *Shall brush my wing.*
> *If thought is life*
> *And strength & breath;*
> *And the want of thought is death;*
> *Then am I*
> *A happy fly,*
> *If I live,*
> *Or if I die.*

83 "Not only has her malady increased": January 5, 1906, 1906 Daily Reminder #1, MTP.

83 "never to let Jean get between": November 26, 1905, SW, Webster Manuscript, MTP.

84 In a victory for Clara: November 2, 1905, 1905 Daily Reminder #2, MTP.

84 "full and sole authority": *Mark Twain: God's Fool,* Hill, pp. 116–17.

84 "Mary the good little cook": November 8, 1906, 1906 Daily Reminder #1, MTP

84 "After this I'll do my own dirty work": Webster Interview, 1953, VC.

84 "sat in pew 16": September 2, 1905, 1905 Daily Reminder #2, MTP.

85 "would be glad if I would go": December 4, 1905, 1905 Daily Reminder #2, MTP.

85 "That was the reason why": December 5, 1905, 1905 Daily Reminder #2, MTP.

85 "the most notable festive occasion": Budd, *Our Mark Twain,* p. 192.

85 The banquet lasted: Ibid.

86 "I wish it were in my power": "Celebrate Mark Twain's Seventieth Birthday," *New York Times,* December 6, 1905.

86 Twain's speech was so well received: Budd, *Our Mark Twain,* p. 193.

87 "They were not present": "Celebrate Mark Twain's Seventieth Birthday," December 6, 1905.

88 "Col. Harvey is being much criticised": January 18, 1906, 1906 Daily Reminder #1, MTP.

88 "mooned about": January 3–4, 1908, 1908 Daily Reminder, MTP.

89 "Not that I don't like the ones": Webster Interview, 1953, VC.

89 "living as I am": March 22, 1908, 1908 Daily Reminder, MTP.

89 "It is almost as stupid": Alan Gribben, *Mark Twain's Library: A Reconstruction* (Boston: G. K. Hall, 1980), p. 758.

89 "tears mingled": December 15, 1905, 1905 Daily Reminder #2, MTP.

89 "from Mr. Clemens": December 25, 1905, 1905 Daily Reminder #2, MTP.

90 "too much responsibility": Hill, *Mark Twain: God's Fool,* p. 116.

90 "Mr. Clemens found": November 28, 1905, 1905 Daily Reminder #2, MTP.

90 "Mr. Clemens's 70th birthday": November 30, 1905, 1905 Daily Reminder #2, MTP.

90 "Such an impulsive man he is": January 5, 1906, 1906 Daily Reminder #1, MTP.

90 "that there isn't much chance": December 17, 1905, 1905 Daily Reminder #2, MTP.

91 "It was a delight": December 18, 1905, 1905 Daily Reminder #2, MTP.

91 "I was so excited": January 22, 1906, 1906 Daily Reminder #1, MTP.

92 When they visited the bedridden Jean: January 24, 1906, 1906 Daily Reminder #1, MTP.

92 "it had always been his dream": January 9, 1906, 1906 Daily Reminder #1, MTP.

93 In an odd coincidence: February 25, 1906, 1906 Daily Reminder #1, MTP.

93 Paine visited Twain: January 6, 1906, 1906 Daily Reminder #1, MTP.

93 "collecting of the many notes": IL, Annotated copy of Mark Twain's *Autobiography* (1924), p. xxii; File, MTP.

93 "Columbia graphophonic": January 6, 1906, 1906 Daily Reminder #1, MTP.

93 "his wonderful rising color": January 9, 1906, 1906 Daily Reminder #1, MTP.

93 "enchanting & an inspiration": January 12, 1906, 1906 Daily Reminder #1, MTP.

93 "he drifted into the Biography chat": January 14, 1906, 1906 Daily Reminder #1, MTP.

94 "A man can't tell the truth": September 10, 1906, 1906 Daily Reminder #1, MTP.

95 "Who speaks of Care": January 16, 1906, 1906 Daily Reminder #1, MTP.

95 At his daughters' expense: Hill, *Mark Twain: God's Fool,* pp. 121–22.

95 "Jean—11—1.20": 1906 Daily Reminder #1, MTP.

95 "Jean is not well": January 5, 1906, 1906 Daily Reminder #1, MTP.

95 "marked and varied mood changes": C. Christodoulou et al., "Postictal Psychosis After Temporal Lobectomy," pp. 1432–35.

96 "But oh a disturbing element": January 13, 1906, 1906 Daily Reminder #1, MTP.

96 "full of pretty women": January 30, 1906, 1906 Daily Reminder #1, MTP.

96 "This was a tragic day": January 27, 1906, 1906 Daily Reminder #1, MTP.

97 "how at times she was really dangerous": Webster Interview 1948; IL Miscellaneous Mark Twain Notes, MTP.

97 The next day, January 28: January 28, 1906, 1906 Daily Reminder #1, MTP.

97 Susan Crane, Olivia Clemens's older sister: IL actually gave two dates for Susan Crane's arrival. In her entry for January 31, she wrote: "Mrs. Crane arrived this afternoon." The next sentence is crossed out: "Two or three days ago." Susan Crane could have arrived as early as January 28. 1906 Daily Reminder #1, MTP.

97 "I had a very plain talk": February 1, 1906 [printed date], February 2, 1906 [entry date], 1906 Daily Reminder #1, MTP.

97 "pair of ratty old daylight pants": February 2, 1906, Notebook #5, MTP.

98 "keeps away from anything": April 9, 1906, Notebook #1, MTP.

98 "who is going to have charge": February 5, 1906, 1906 Daily Reminder #1, MTP.

98 Peterson was forty-seven years old: E. J. Fine, D. L. Fine, L. Sentz, and E. D. Soria, "Contributions of the Founders of Craig Colony to Epileptology and Public Care of Epileptics: 1890–1915," *Journal of the History of Neuroscience* 4 (1995): 77–100.

98 He served as chairman: Derek Denny-Brown, "Presidents of the Second Fifty Years," *Centennial Anniversary Volume of the American Neurological Association, 1875–1975* (New York: Springer Publishing Company, 1975), pp. 164–67.

98 Peterson was appointed president: "Contributions of the Founders of Craig Colony," p. 78.

98 In his chapter "Epilepsy": Peterson, *Nervous and Mental Disorders,* p. 639.

99 "All these days": February 9, 1906, 1906 Daily Reminder #1, MTP.

99 "As I grow older": February 10, 1906, 1906 Daily Reminder #1, MTP.

99 "Mr. Clemens he suggested": February 24, 1906, 1906 Daily Reminder #1, MTP.

99 "Lakewood, very bad day": March 25, 1906, 1906 Daily Reminder #1, MTP.

100 "quite pale": March 27, 1906, 1906 Daily Reminder #1, MTP.

100 "This is the wretched day": March 24, 1906, 1906 Daily Reminder #1, MTP.

100 An astounding thirty thousand copies: Cynthia Griffin Wolff, introduction to Edith Wharton, *The House of Mirth* (New York: Penguin, 1985), p. vii.

101 "Perhaps I'm discouraged": March 18, 1906, 1906 Daily Reminder #1, MTP.

103 Isabel, like others in Wharton's reading audience: March 18, 1906, 1906 Daily Reminder #1, MTP.

103 thirty-year-old Charlotte Teller Johnson: Charlotte was once married to Frank Minitree Johnson, a Washington, D.C., civil engineer.

104 "her revolutionary tribe": Also present were Tschaykoffshi, Robert Collier, Nikolas Burenin, Arthur Brisbane, David Graham Phillips, Robert Hunter, Ernest Poole, Dr. Walter Weyl, Leroy M. Scott, and Howard Brubaker.

104 "13—such a hellish superstition it is": April 11, 1906, 1906 Daily Reminder #1, MTP.

104 "paid me damn compliments": April 17, 1906, 1906 Daily Reminder #1, MTP.

104 "calamity for me": May 5, 1906, 1906 Daily Reminder #1, MTP.

104 "[Crossed out: I am sitting here": May 6, 1906, 1906 Daily Reminder #1, MTP.

104 The two discussed their various writing projects: April 13, 1906, Berg Collection, NYPL.

105 "twenty-five or twenty-seven years ago": Mark Twain, *What Is Man?,* ed. Shelley Fisher Fishkin, Oxford Mark Twain (New York: Oxford University Press, 1996).

105 "not a 'perfect setting' ": Paine, *Autobiography,* p. xiii; File IL's annotated copy, MTP.

106 When one reads the tally: K. Patrick Ober, *Mark Twain and Medicine* (Columbia: University of Missouri Press, 2003), p. 157.

106 "petit-mals . . . fearfully long": May 4, 1906, JC Diary April 30–July 21, 1906, 53348 HL.

106 "My memory about where the various friends": May 3, 1906, JC Diary April 30–July 21, 1906, 53348 HL.

106 "little short touches of absentmindedness": May 1, 3, 4, 5, 14, 15, 1906, JC Diary April 30–July 21, 1906, 53348 HL.

106 "As soon as I wakened": May 4, 1906, JC Diary April 30–July 21, 1906, 53348 HL.

107 "mental and nervous improvement": June 23, 1906, MTP.

107 "Why must I live on aimlessly": JC Diary April 30–July 21, 1906, 53348 HL.

107 "Two years!": JC Diary April 30–July 21, 1906, 53348 HL.

107 "What can I do?": October 6, 1906, JC Diary September 12–November 30, 1906, 53350 HL.

108 "I think it was a glory of a thing": March 3, 1906, 1906 Daily Reminder #1, MTP.

108 "Jean's insolences": June 10, 1906, 1906 Daily Reminder #1, MTP.

108 While Jean and Isabel enjoyed: September 28, 1906, 1906 Daily Reminder #1, MTP.

108 "In Jean's present condition": September 29, 1906, 1906 Daily Reminder #1, MTP.

108 "I cast my thoughts toward the ones": July 5, 1906, 1906 Daily Reminder #1, MTP.

109 "take hold of the condition mentally": October 3, 1906, 1906 Daily Reminder #1, MTP.

109 "I have seen it only three times": Leary, *Mark Twain's Correspondence with Henry Huttleston Rogers,* pp. 489–90.

109 Jean had a distinctive cry: CC to Julia Langdon, January 23, 1910, MTP.

109 Usually people who experience grand mal seizures: The Merck Manual, Home Edition, chapter 73: "Seizure Disorders."

109 the House of Mirth: Paine, *Autobiography;* annotated copy, p. xiii, MTP.

109 "went to pieces": September 24, 1906, 1906 Daily Reminder #1, MTP.

110 "waiting for the electric lights to go out": June 9, 1906, 1906 Daily Reminder #1, MTP.

110 The Clemens family, with their host of illnesses: The mixing of alcohol and chloral hydrate was contemporaneously known as a Mickey Finn.

110 "[Crossed out: I have to sleep on Bromidia": June 12, 1906, 1906 Daily Reminder #1, MTP.

111 "he is overflowing": May 31, 1906, 1906 Daily Reminder #1, MTP.

111 "Now I'm not sure": October 5, 1906, 1906 Daily Reminder #1, MTP.

111 "his disgust at those who worship": June 3, 1906, 1906 Daily Reminder #1, MTP.

111 "discussion of the Immaculate Conception": June 20, 1906, 1906 Daily Reminder #1, MTP.

111 "After a talk like the ones he gives me": March, 11, 1906, 1906 Daily Reminder #1, MTP.

112 "48 years ago": May 26, 1906, 1906 Daily Reminder #1, MTP.

112 "My soul is not moored": September 9, 1906, 1906 Daily Reminder #1, MTP.

112 Amused by the scarlet stockings: September 7, 1906, 1906 Daily Reminder #1, MTP.

112 "gaudy things": December 27, 1906, 1906 Daily Reminder #1, MTP.

112 "his Suitable white clothes": October 8, 1906, 1906 Daily Reminder #1, MTP.

112 "Darlingly he cocked his head": February 12, 1908, 1908 Daily Reminder, MTP

112 "on a mossy bank": October, 8, 1906, 1906 Daily Reminder #1, MTP.

112 By the fall of 1906: Budd, *Our Mark Twain,* p. 207.

113 "often went off on R[oger]'s boat": DW, undated, handwritten document, IL Miscellaneous Mark Twain Notes, MTP.

113 "I've just been cutting the King's hair": August 25, 1908, 1908 Daily Reminder, MTP.

114 "& rubbed his damp hair": January 20, 1907, fragment in the 1907 Daily Reminder, MTP.

114 "[Crossed out: I didn't think he would want it": March 19, 1906, 1906 Daily Reminder #1, MTP.

115 "But in the afternoon AB": September 28, 1906, 1906 Daily Reminder #1, MTP.

115 "Old Fraud": June 28, 1906, 1906 Daily Reminder #1, MTP.

115 "That is our ritual": August 6, 1906, 1906 Daily Reminder #1, MTP.

115 "if I am good": August 6, 1906, 1906 Daily Reminder #1, MTP.

115 In August, Isabel traveled: August 13, 1906, 1906 Daily Reminder #1, MTP.

115 "the most polished of young creatures": October 29, 1906, 1906 Daily Reminder #1, MTP.

115 At that moment Isabel believed: August 14, 1906, 1906 Daily Reminder #1, MTP.

116 This meant that Clara and Jean: December 29, 1906, 1906 Daily Reminder #1, MTP.

116 Financing would come from his $30,000 agreement: January 12, 1907, 1907 Daily Reminder, MTP.

116 "He won't allow himself": April 9, 1907, 1907 Daily Reminder, MTP.

117 "is the possessor of a rich contralto voice": "Miss Clemens in Concert. Mark Twain Makes a Speech at His Daughter's Debut," *New York Times,* September 23, 1906.

117 She refused: Hill, *Mark Twain: God's Fool,* p. 147.

118 "Katonah plan": October 18, 1906; JC Diary April 30–July 21, 1906, 53348 HL.

118 While the trip north was brief: October 22, 1906, JC Diary September 12–November 30, 1906, HL.

118 Hillbourne Farms was located: From roughly 1905 to 1944, Hillbourne Farms, later known as Hillbourne Club, was a sanitarium specializing in the treatment of epilepsy. Dr. E. A. Sharp created the institution around 1905 on farmland that he had purchased the previous year. By 1910, Dr. Armstrong had replaced Dr. Sharp as the resident doctor and director of Hillbourne. It was around this time that the name changed to Hillbourne Club. In 1944, Dr. Armstrong died. Two years later, Hillbourne morphed into a "vacation resort" under the management of Mr. Herman Bain. Shell Oil used the facility, which then included a "lodge house and three guest houses," for training seminars ("Shell Oil School in Sylvan Setting," New York Times, February 10, 1947). When it was sold, two years later, as a "resort-hotel property on Rte 22," the former Hillbourne property included "three hotel buildings, [a] swimming pool, tennis court, ski run, bowling alleys, gymnasium and stables" ("Resort Hotel Sold," New York Times, May 10, 1949). In 1951, the main two houses on the property, then known as Idlewood Hotel, burned. Two years later Idlewood Holding Corporation sold the land and remaining buildings to the American Legion, post 1575. The American Legion moved to the site in 1956 and opened the swimming and wading pools for use by area residents. In the late 1980s, a portion of the property was sold to establish the Katonah Museum of Art. The art museum and the American Legion still occupy the site. Christina Rae, assistant to the Bedford Town Historian, personal correspondence with the author, July 17, 2006; Frances R. Duncombe, Katonah: The History of a New York Village and Its People (Katonah, N.Y.: Katonah Village Improvement Society, 1961), p. 477; "Hillbourne Club a Private Health Resort," Undated pamphlet, 1910 (Town of Bedford, Office of Town Historian).

118 All this luxury and privacy: "Hillbourne Club."

118 All together Twain would be supporting: Information about Jean's expenses; SLC Holder No. 1 Accountants' Statements and Schedules Accounts Ashcroft-Lyon Affair March 1907 to February 28, 1909, MTP.

119 By comparison, the mean daily pay: Brad Hansen, "The Golden Age of Flexible Wages in the Old Dominion: Labor Market Adjustment in Virginia During the Panic of 1907," www.eh.net/Clio/Conferences/ASSA/ Jan_97/Hansen.shtml.

119 Dr. Edward A. Sharp: Christina Rae, personal correspondence.

119 After their tour: October 22, 1906, JC Diary September 12–November 30, 1906, 53350 HL.

119 Jean was delayed by a day: "Of course my breakfast, all of it came up— even before I had finished eating it. That was proof positive of what was to follow. The attack didn't come on as promptly as the last one, but it came during the forenoon, while the second one was quite late in the

afternoon. For some time I thought that I should be well enough to go out to Katonah on the three o'clock train, but that was a mistaken idea, as I was ill all day long & even after the second attack." October 24, 1906; JC Diary September 12–November 30, 1906, HL.

119 "It was desperately hard": October 25, 1906, JC Diary September 12–November 30, 1906, HL.

120 "heart stretching to have her so": October 25, 1906, 1906 Daily Reminder #1, MTP.

120 Encouraged by Clara's visit: "[Clara] brought me a lovely bunch of pink carnations." October 27, 1906, JC Diary September 12–November 30, 1906, HL.

120 "I began this morning": October 28, 1906, JC Diary September 12–November 30, 1906, HL.

120 "Today nothing of importance has occurred": December 1, 1906, JC Diary December 1, 1906–February 28, 1907, HL.

120 Lard was feared: December 1, 1906 and January 19, 1907, JC Diary December 1, 1906–February 28, 1907, HL.

121 "my own stubbornness and unwillingness": December 8–9, 1906, JC Diary December 1, 1906–February 28, 1907, HL.

121 He did, however, want to hear back: December 9, 1906, JC Diary December 1, 1906–February 28, 1907, 53351 HL.

121 "I dreamed last night of Dr. Sharp": December 16, 1906, JC Diary December 1, 1906–February 28, 1907, HL.

121 "a pretty violent injection": December 17, 1906, JC Diary December 1, 1906–February 28, 1907, HL.

121 "I had often felt": January 14, 1907, JC Diary December 1, 1906–February 28, 1907, HL.

122 Rebelling against all the restrictions: January 9, 16, 26, 1907, JC Diary December 1, 1906–February 28, 1907, HL.

122 patients were only allowed to eat: December 25–27, 1906, JC Diary December 1, 1906–February 28, 1907, HL.

123 Patients could go boating: Boating on the reservoir was very popular; by 1907 there were six hundred boats "used on 'the Lake.' " Duncombe, *Katonah,* p. 235.

123 "Of course, the minute I had done it": December 20, 1906, JC Diary December 1, 1906–February 28, 1907, 53351 HL.

123 To her joy, Scott soon appeared: Hill, *Mark Twain: God's Fool,* p. 167.

123 Jean had her driver: Karen Lystra, *Dangerous Intimacy* (Berkeley: University of California Press, 2004), p. 97.

123 To that end, Hillbourne: "Hillbourne Club."

123 "a professional member": JC Diary December 1, 1906–February 28, 1907, HL.

123 In June he wrote Clara: June 9, 1906, 1906 Daily Reminder #1, MTP.

123 "prodigious piece of work": June 15, 1906, 1906 Daily Reminder #1, MTP.

124 "He is often animated": June 25, 1906, 1906 Daily Reminder #1, MTP.

124 "It is only by means of fertilization": July 8, 1906, 1906 Daily Reminder #1, MTP.

124 After Miss Doty's huffy departure: October 22, 1906, 1906 Daily Reminder #1, MTP.

124 "repeated the gossip": October 22, 1907; undated entry, Notebook #2, MTP.

125 "gave what I dared": October 24, 1907, fragment in the 1906 Daily Reminder #1, MTP.

125 "an adventurer & planning to marry": May 22, 1907, 1907 Daily Reminder, MTP.

125 "I'll get even with you": May 22, 1907, 1907 Daily Reminder, MTP; SW, a sheet of paper attached to July 25, 1907, entry, Webster Manuscript, MTP.

126 "at this base of action": October 27, 1906, 1906 Daily Reminder #1, MTP.

126 "so glad—So selfishly glad": October 31, 1906, 1906 Daily Reminder #1, MTP.

126 He explained to Jean: Hill, *Mark Twain: God's Fool,* p. 157.

126 "not go away from him again": December 12, 1906, 1906 Daily Reminder #1, MTP.

126 "Editor and Executor": Loose page, 1906–07 Box, VC.

127 Now, in addition to acting: December 13, 1906, 1906 Daily Reminder #1, MTP.

127 Of course, Paine's decision to move out: February 3, 1907, 1907 Daily Reminder, MTP.

127 "that isn't the place for AB.": December 25, 1906, 1906 Daily Reminder #1, MTP.

127 "full authority over all literary remains": January 14, 1907, 1907 Daily Reminder, MTP.

127 "Oh King—you are so wonderful": Undated entry, Notebook #2, MTP.

128 "completed the only work": Hill, *Mark Twain: God's Fool,* p. 164.

128 She apparently found Twain's monetary interest: January 3, 1907, 1907 Daily Reminder, MTP.

128 "baked beans & bacon": January 4, 1906, 1907 Daily Reminder, MTP.

129 "Of course there couldn't ever be anybody": January 4, 1907, Notebook #5, MTP.

130 Isabel played the enthusiastic audience: "He makes such a pretty bridge of his hand, which is so beautiful & in his white silk coats which we had made at Vantine's." January 13, 1907, 1907 Daily Reminder, MTP.

130  "The secretary can do anything": January 13, 1907, 1907 Daily Reminder, MTP.

130  "missed so much": January 16, 1907, Notebook #2, MTP.

131  For his enjoyment: January 14, 1908, 1908 Daily Reminder, MTP.

131  "When I go to his room to tell him": February 26, 1907, 1907 Daily Reminder, MTP.

131  "earthquake dream": Undated entry, Notebook #2, MTP.

131  "It was that remark": January 21, 1907, 1907 Daily Reminder, MTP.

132  "98 years ten months": January 23, 1907, 1907 Daily Reminder, MTP.

132  Twain received Fletcher's savvy instruction: January 26, 1907, 1907 Daily Reminder, MTP.

132  "She is a made over creature with happiness": March 26, 1907, 1907 Daily Reminder, MTP.

132  "learning her trade": March 28, 1907, 1907 Daily Reminder, MTP.

132  After a second lightning-quick visit with Isabel: March 5, 1907, 1907 Daily Reminder, MTP.

133  "Here am I missing": April 12, 1907, 1907 Daily Reminder, MTP.

133  "I had reached the grandpapa state of life": April 17, 1908; Mark Twain's Autobiographical Dictations, MTP.

133  "Y.M.C.A. men": March 4, 1906, 1906 Daily Reminder #1, MTP.

134  She was equally pleased: August 5, August 7, and August 9, 1907, 1907 Daily Reminder, MTP.

135  "too splendid": May 3, 1907, 1907 Daily Reminder, MTP.

135  "He is in love with Tuxedo": May 30, 1907, 1907 Daily Reminder, MTP.

135  "Mr. Clemens is carried away": May 29, 1907, 1907 Daily Reminder, MTP.

136  "silk underclothes": June 3, 1907, 1907 Daily Reminder, MTP.

136  "POWER OF ATTORNEY": SLC, May 7, 1907, Box 48, "Ashcroft-Lyon Manuscript," MTP.

137  Isabel's lot improved: Hill, Mark Twain: God's Fool, p. 172.

137  "It is going to be a Strange Summer": June 19, 1907, 1907 Daily Reminder, MTP.

137  "the King would be": July 1, 1907, 1907 Daily Reminder, MTP.

137  "I have not known": Hill, Mark Twain: God's Fool, p. 173.

138  "decided to go home": July 6, 1907, 1907 Daily Reminder, MTP.

138  "I'll get even with you": May 22, 1907, 1907 Daily Reminder, MTP; SW, a sheet of paper attached to July 25, 1907, entry, Webster Manuscript, MTP.

138  Years later, Isabel told Samuel and Doris Webster: DW and SW to Henry Nash Smith, July 1, 1960, MTP.

138  Ironically, a little over a week before: May 3, 1907, 1907 Daily Reminder, MTP.

138 "Colonel Harvey is the mensch to go": May 3, 1907, 1907 Daily Reminder, MTP.

138 "It was a blow to Paine": DW to Betty [Hall] Mack [Mrs. Clifford G.], July 29, 1959, MTM.

138 "lying weak and sick": June 8, 1907, 1907 Daily Reminder, MTP.

139 "thoughtless things": June 21, 1907, fragment in the 1907 Daily Reminder, MTP.

139 "REMEMBER THE PROPRIETIES": June 22, 1907, fragment in the 1907 Daily Reminder, MTP.

139 "TRY NOT TO BE JEALOUS": June 26, 1907, 1907 Daily Reminder, MTP.

139 Standing at the end of the pier: July 22, 1907; fragment in the 1907 Daily Reminder, MTP.

140 "more yet from that devil": July 25, 1907, 1907 Daily Reminder, MTP.

140 "the 'protection' of it": July 26, 1907, 1907 Daily Reminder, MTP.

140 "very tiny drive": July 30, 1907, 1907 Daily Reminder, MTP.

141 "It was Sweet to drive": August 25, 1907, 1907 Daily Reminder, MTP.

141 "he was very Sweet": January 3, 1908, 1908 Daily Reminder, MTP.

141 "until the one hundred thousand words": January 20, 1907, fragment in the 1907 Daily Reminder, MTP.

142 "they poured in": May 23, 1907, 1907 Daily Reminder, MTP.

142 "the loss would be": August 5, 1907, 1907 Daily Reminder, MTP.

142 Twain, on the other hand: October 14, 1907, 1907 Daily Reminder, MTP.

142 "The King's interest in children": February 8, 1908, 1908 Daily Reminder, MTP.

142 "savagely ill": August 30, 1907, 1907 Daily Reminder, MTP.

142 "neuritis in my left neck": June 24, 1907, 1907 Daily Reminder, MTP.

143 Phenacetin: In 1983, phenacetin was removed from usage due to its link to kidney failure. Http://encyclopedia.thefreedictionary.com/Phenacetine.

143 "entire dissatisfaction in my condition": August 30, 1907, 1907 Daily Reminder, MTP.

143 "hopped out of bed": January 4, 1908, 1908 Daily Reminder, MTP.

143 "feel that he wants": January 7, 1908, 1908 Daily Reminder, MTP.

143 She returned to Redding: June 21, 1907, 1907 Daily Reminder, MTP.

143 An alarmed John Howells: Hill, *Mark Twain: God's Fool,* p. 182.

143 Clara's demands: Ibid., p. 202; Rasmussen, *Mark Twain A–Z,* p. 445.

144 She had initially opposed: Lystra, *Dangerous Intimacy,* p. 78.

144 "full of plans for the future home": March 25, 1907, 1907 Daily Reminder, MTP.

144 She commented bitterly: Hill, *Mark Twain: God's Fool,* p. 168.

144 "TO THE EDITOR": March 14, 1907, 1907 Daily Reminder, MTP.

145 "the task of providing enough innocence": Mary Louise Howden, "Mark

Twain as His Secretary at Stormfield Remembers Him; Anecdotes of the Author Untold Until Now," *New York Herald,* December 13, 1925, section 7, pp. 1–4.

145 She christened the residence Stormfield: Hill, *Mark Twain: God's Fool,* p. 205.

145 The revenue from "Extract": Ibid., p. 190.

145 Twain acquiesced: Rasmussen, *Mark Twain A–Z,* pp. 445–46.

145 "She could do what she like[d]": Webster Interview, 1953, VC.

145 "Poor prisoner": June 13, 1907, 1907 Daily Reminder, MTP.

145 "filled with happiness over it": April 24, 1907, 1907 Daily Reminder, MTP.

145 "triple windows": September 12, 1907, 1907 Daily Reminder, MTP.

146 A wing was added for a new kitchen: Webster Interview, 1953, VC.

146 The farmhouse also boasted: April 24, 1908, 1908 Daily Reminder, MTP.

146 Lyonesse: Lyonesse was also referred to as the Lobster Pot and Summerfield by the Clemenses, Isabel, and friends.

146 " 'the magic land' ": June 21, 1907, 1907 Daily Reminder, MTP.

146 In the end, the King slays his enemy:

> Then rose the King and moved his host by night
> And ever pushed Sir Mordred, league by league,
> Back to the sunset bound of Lyonesse—
> A land of old upheaven from the abyss
> By fire, to sink into the abyss again;
> Where fragments of forgotten peoples dwelt,
> And the long mountains ended in a coast
> Of ever-shifting sand, and far away
> The phantom circle of a moaning sea.

146 "Santa misunderstood all my efforts": May 2, 1908, 1908 Daily Reminder, MTP.

147 Her new purchasing power: June 23, 1903, 1903 Daily Reminder, VC.

147 "leisured, urban women": Elaine S. Abelson, *When Ladies Go A-Thieving: Middle-Class Shoplifters in the Victorian Department Store* (New York: Oxford University Press, 1989), p. 6; "shopping" in the nineteenth century had become "linked in the public mind with pleasure and personal freedom."

147 "wonderful place on 15th Street": April 27, 1908, 1908 Daily Reminder, MTP.

147 "to look at rugs": June 10 and September 12, 1907, 1907 Daily Reminder, MTP.

148 "Miss Lyon is working very hard": Hill, *Mark Twain: God's Fool,* p. 203.

148 The first-floor billiard room: November 24, 1908, 1908 Daily Reminder, MTP.

148 Indeed, Stormfield was a grand space: Much more information about Stormfield, along with photographs, can be found in Kevin Mac Donnell's article "Stormfield: A Virtual Tour," *Mark Twain Journal* 44, no. 1/2 (Spring/Fall 2006).

148 In 1908, 90 percent: Jim Rasenberger, *America, 1908: The Dawn of Flight, the Race to the Pole, the Invention of the Model T, and the Making of a Modern Nation* (New York: Scribner, 2007), p. 76.

149 When Twain took up residence: John Cooley, *Mark Twain's Aquarium: The Samuel Clemens Angelfish Correspondence 1905–1910* (Athens: University of Georgia Press, 1991), p. 175.

150 "I shan't ever be able": June 25, 1908, 1908 Daily Reminder, MTP.

151 "the thought of ever going back": Hill, *Mark Twain: God's Fool*, p. 205.

151 Twain had ended his lease: "New York Loses Mark Twain," *New York Times,* September 8, 1908.

151 "packing & clearing out": September 29, 1908, 1908 Daily Reminder, MTP.

152 "The burden of this house": September 3, 1908, 1908 Daily Reminder, MTP.

152 "I wish he wouldn't talk quite so often": Undated entry, 1908, loose page, 1908–09 Box, VC.

152 "every time I try to arrange": Hill, *Mark Twain: God's Fool,* 145.

152 "The King talks so much about his death": January 14,1907, 1907 Daily Reminder, MTP.

152 "track of the hours of the day": September 28, 1907, 1907 Daily Reminder; January 4, 1907, Notebook #5; August 6, 1908, 1908 Daily Reminder, MTP.

152 On multiple occasions: November 2, 1906, 1906 Daily Reminder #1; January 4, 1907, Notebook #5; March 20, 1907, fragment in the 1907 Daily Reminder, MTP.

153 During a long celebratory evening: Twain joined the Lotos Club in 1873, just three years after it was founded. It was the first New York club he joined and is one of the oldest literary clubs in the United States.

153 "pale as death": March 6, 1908, 1908 Daily Reminder, MTP.

153 funeral procession: Hill, *Mark Twain: God's Fool,* p. 175.

153 "architect of his own reputation": Budd, *Our Mark Twain,* p. 19.

154 "An autobiography is the truest": March 14, 1904, MTP.

154 "He was cross": January 26, 1908, 1908 Daily Reminder, MTP.

154 "I have no desire": January 28, 1909, MTP.

155 The horrific episode: "Editor Moffett Dies, Struggling in Surf," *New York Times,* August 2, 1908.

155 "some days I feel": August 17, 1908, MTM.

THREE: "ANOTHER STRIPPED & FORLORN KING LEAR"

159 "atmosphere of adulation": Budd, *Our Mark Twain,* p. 158.

159 "broken my bow": Hill, *Mark Twain: God's Fool,* p. 115.

159 "he didn't get much good": August 2, 1907 [dated September 1, 1907], 1907 Daily Reminder, MTP.

160 "I have just come to the conclusion": "Twain's Daughter Talks About Him," *New York Times,* June 14, 1908.

160 Myron W. Whitney, Jr.: At the height of his career, Whitney was internationally renowned for his beautiful bass voice. At the time of this concert, he was seventy-two years old. "Concerts of the Week," *New York Times,* November 10, 1907. For more on Whitney see http://www .whitneygen.org/archives/extracts/sketch.html.

160 "Mr. Wark and his honest blue eyes": Hill, *Mark Twain: God's Fool,* p. 171.

160 Will was Canadian: 1881 Canadian Census Household Record; Family Search, International Genealogical Index, Church of Jesus Christ of Latter Day Saints.

160 Enormous homes were constructed: Marsha Ann Tate, "Presentation Given at the Cobourg & District Historical Society's 25th Annual Dinner," College of Communications, The Pennsylvania State University, May 24, 2005.

160 The contrast between: Will's father was Irish and worked as the caretaker of Victoria Hall (Cobourg's Town Hall). Canadian Census Household Records.

161 Two years after: Census Dansville Township, Livingston County, New York, Supervisor District 8, ENU 141, enumerator: Frederick B. Maloney. The Jackson Sanatorium offered hydropathic treatments (including cold-water baths, wraps, and sprays), and endorsed a vegetarian diet while forbidding sugar, coffee, tea, alcohol, and tobacco.

161 In March 1907, Isabel expressed: March 29, 1907, 1907 Daily Reminder, MTP.

161 "a long thin black gown": June 1, 1907, 1907 Daily Reminder, MTP.

161 "every night": June 28, 1907, 1907 Daily Reminder, MTP.

161 "I have been dreaming": June 22, 1907, fragment in the 1907 Daily Reminder, MTP.

161 "is beautifuller": August 29, 1907, 1907 Daily Reminder, MTP.

162 "could hear Clara's voice": Charles Wark to SLC, August 13, 1907, HL.

162 During the early months: March 6, 1908.

163 "the fourth letter of credit": Hill, *Mark Twain: God's Fool,* p. 200.

163 "very soon": Ibid., p. 205.

163 "on shares so that Clara": Charles Wark to IL, June 24, 1908; IVL Material Drawer #8, MTP.

163 "He understands perfectly": Oneonta *Star,* August 3, 1918.

164 "dear old W. is more wonderful": Hill, *Mark Twain: God's Fool,* p. 205.

164 Edith had married Wark: Family Search International Genealogical Index, Church of Jesus Christ of Latter Day Saints. The wedding took place at 3:00 p.m. and was announced in *The New York Times,* October 11, 1903, p. 7. Edith Wark was born on September 12, 1875.

164 Will's best man was Francis Rogers: Information about Wark's groomsmen from Jim Leonard, grandnephew of Charles Wark, personal e-mail to the author, January 2, 2008.

164 The couple was blessed: January 11, 1909, torn-out page from date book, 1908–09 Box, VC. Information about Wark's twins from Jim Leonard, personal e-mail to the author.

165 "Miss Clemens will give a reception": "Mark Twain No More a Gay New Yorker," *The World,* September 7, 1908.

165 "contradicted that & many things": September 7, 1908, 1908 Daily Reminder, MTP.

165 "Miss Clemens . . . has been traveling": "New York Loses Mark Twain," *New York Times,* September 8, 1908.

166 "Mr. Littleton is submerged in the Thaw trial": January 9, 1908, 1908 Daily Reminder, MTP.

166 In his brief after-dinner remarks: "Mark Twain Now After Compliments Says at Lotos Club Dinner He's Collecting Them as Some Others Do Stamps," *New York Times,* January 12, 1908.

166 On proud display at the Lotos Club: Paula Uruburu, *American Eve: Evelyn Nesbit, Stanford White; The Birth of the "It" Girl and the Crime of the Century* (New York: Riverhead Books, 2008), p. 59.

167 "are readier to wink at the horrors": August 26, 1906, fragment in the 1906 Daily Reminder #1, MTP.

168 Printing excerpts from the letters: Hill, *Mark Twain: God's Fool,* p. 202.

168 Twain's reaction was to write: January 24, 1908, pages bundled together, 1908–09 Box, VC.

168 Also at Isabel's urging: January 22, 1908, 1908 Daily Reminder, MTP.

168 "Paine could have killed me": January 17, 1908, pages bundled together, 1908–09 Box, VC.

169 "lock the Ms. Trunk": 1936 notes to Mr. Howe regarding 1908, 1908–09 Box, VC

169 "the red Ms. Trunk": September 8, 1908, 1908 Daily Reminder, MTP.

169 "very beautiful": September 7, 1908, 1908 Daily Reminder, MTP.

169 After spending a long weekend: September 17, 1907, 1908 Daily Reminder, MTP.

170 Rents for the suites: The Stuyvesant consisted of twin red-brick buildings side by side; five stories tall, boasting mansard roofs done in the

French style. The ceilings in the apartments were high, and there were brass doorknobs, tin bathtubs in wooden holders, and wood-burning fireplaces. Steven S. Gaines, *The Sky's the Limit: Passion and Property in Manhattan* (New York: Little, Brown, 2005); James Trager, *The New York Chronology: A Compendium of Events, People, and Anecdotes from the Dutch to the Present* (New York: HarperCollins, 2003).

170 Clara rented one: 1909 Financial Documents File, MTP.

170 Tenants' needs were attended to: Lewis Randolph Hamersly, John William Leonard, William Frederick Mohr, Herman Warren Knox, and Frank R. Holmes, *Who's Who in New York City and State* (New York: L. R. Hamersly Company, 1904), p. 337. *The Whole Family* was a novel consisting of twelve chapters, each by a different author. Jordan had invited Twain to contribute, and while he initially expressed interest in the project, he ultimately declined.

170 Clara moved into her new abode: October 6, 1908, 1908 Daily Reminder, MTP; Hill, *Mark Twain: God's Fool,* p. 210.

170 "wonderful sleep in Santa's little apartment": October 7, 1908, 1908 Daily Reminder, MTP.

170 The day after the two men: "Burglars Invade Mark Twain Villa," *New York Times,* September 19, 1908.

171 "she had supposed that her father": October 30, 1908, loose page, 1908–09 Box, VC.

171 Although she called Isabel: October 26, 1906, 1906 Daily Reminder #1, MTP.

171 "Very soon we got out": December 8, 1906; JC Diary December 1, 1906–February 28, 1907, 53351 HL.

172 "I don't in the least hope": December 19, 1906, JC Diary December 1, 1906–February 28, 1907, 53351 HL.

172 "that what I do": January 5, 1907, JC Diary December 1, 1906–February 28, 1907, 53351 HL.

173 "action was low": January 18, 1907, JC Diary December 1, 1906–February 28, 1907, 53351 HL.

173 "cold & that her own idea": January 5, 1907, JC Diary December 1, 1906–February 28, 1907, 53351 HL.

173 "in a Torrent of impossible moods": January 10, 1907, Diary December 1, 1906–February 28, 1907, 53351 HL.

173 He did not return: May 21, 1907, 1907 Daily Reminder, MTP.

173 "Jean's making out a bad case": Entry about Jean in Twain's handwriting May 31, 1907, IL Notebook #2, MTP.

173 "squelched the idea": JC Diary 1907, Katonah, 53352 HL.

174 "Jean may or may not": June 11, 1907, 1907 Daily Reminder, MTP.

174 "the place & the Great pathos": October 27, 1906, 1906 Daily Reminder #1, MTP.

174 On Christmas Day Clara was the only member: December 25, 1906, 1906 Daily Reminder #1, MTP.

174 Nevertheless, despite the awkward circumstances: March 25, 1907, 1907 Daily Reminder, MTP.

175 "distresse[d] beyond words": July 22, 25, 30, and August 2, 5, 1907; JC Diary 1907, Katonah, 53352 HL.

175 "Poor Jean": April 5, 1907, 1907 Daily Reminder, MTP.

175 Isabel then took another: June 12, 1907, 1907 Daily Reminder, MTP.

175 "Oh Terrible—Terrible": October 2, 1907, 1907 Daily Reminder, MTP.

176 "the epileptic temperament rarely improved": October 5, 1907, Notebook #4, MTP.

176 Dr. Peterson felt strongly: Lystra, *Dangerous Intimacy,* p. 112.

176 Her father's Christmas present: Ibid., p. 115.

177 "When the dear Cowles girls": February 16, 1908, Notebook #5, MTP.

177 Isabel telephoned Jean: December 25, 1907, JC Diary December 1, 1906–February 28, 1907, 53351 HL.

177 "Dr. Peterson is glad": December 25, 1907, JC Diary 1907, Katonah, 53352 HL.

177 Considering what people were under treatment for: Jean's leave-taking came just a few short weeks before one of her fellow patients was found dead in a well that was located on the property. Henry Harris Barnard, a New York lumber merchant, had spent two months at Hillbourne Farms under treatment for "nervous prostration" caused by business reverses. Apparently the discovery of Mr. Barnard's body at the bottom of the well, half a mile from the sanitarium, generated a great many rumors. Dr. Sharp was quick to assure the inquiring *New York Times* reporter that Mr. Barnard had not committed suicide: "I am confident it was purely a case of accident. I think the man stumbled into the well." Dr. Sharp's explanation was somewhat at odds with that of the coroner, who stated that Mr. Barnard's death was either accidental or "a case of suicide." Accidental death was certainly the most socially acceptable explanation, and Mr. Barnard's son, having been told by Dr. Sharp that his father had died of "exposure," decided against any further investigation and the family let the matter drop. "Found Dead in Well," *New York Times,* February 12, 1908.

177 She moved to Greenwich: Hill, *Mark Twain: God's Fool,* p. 196.

177 "very very ill": January 9, 1909, 1908 Daily Reminder, MTP.

177 "Enraged" that her father: February 16, 1908, Notebook #4, MTP.

177 The next day Jean suffered: January 10, 1908, 1908 Daily Reminder, MTP.

178 "criticized in Dublin": January 19, 1908, 1908 Daily Reminder, MTP.

178 "We have been sore": February 16, 1908, Notebook #4, MTP.

178 Peterson also thought: Lystra, *Dangerous Intimacy,* p. 126.

178 At the end of March 1908: March 31, 1908, Notebook #5, MTP.

178 "Now Father thinks": JC to Nancy Brush, letter fragment [ca. July 1908], copy, MTP.

179 "Yesterday the news came": August 1, 1908, MTP.

179 "pathetic & wan": September 26, 1908, 1908 Daily Reminder, MTP.

180 In August, Josephine Hobby: Hobby was well compensated, receiving a constant $100 a month. (Hobby was paid twice as much as Isabel.) For her last month she was paid $25. Miss Howden's compensation was much reduced to $35 a month. SLC Holder No. 1 Accountants' Statements and Schedules Accounts, MTP.

180 Isabel spent the remainder of the month: October 1, October 6, and October 8, 1908, 1908 Daily Reminder, MTP.

181 "that she cannot stay": October 9, October 11, and October 19, 1908, 1908 Daily Reminder, MTP.

181 "for there has been no night": October 20, 1908, 1908 Daily Reminder, MTP.

181 "There is such a confusion": October 21, 1908, 1908 Daily Reminder, MTP.

182 "a great pink rose": June 7, 1907, 1907 Daily Reminder, MTP.

182 Plasmon proved to be no exception: For a detailed explanation of Ashcroft and Twain's involvement in Plasmon, see Hill, *Mark Twain: God's Fool*, 101–4.

182 Ashcroft was thirty years old: Box 48, "Ashcroft-Lyon Manuscript," MTP; DW's notes found in IVL Notebook #1. Undated, handwritten document, evidently an interview DW conducted with Lyon; IL Miscellaneous Mark Twain Notes, MTP.

182 "third hand": October 13, 1907, 1907 Daily Reminder, MTP.

182 Ashcroft claimed that Hammond had libeled him: "John Hays Hammond Sued," *New York Times,* October 16, 1907.

183 "trying to reach the door": January 16, 1908, fragment in the 1908 Daily Reminder, MTP.

183 "playing in a drunken haze": January 17, 1908, 1908 Daily Reminder, MTP.

183 "he approved of my method of procedure": January 24, 1908, 1908 Daily Reminder, MTP.

183 By June, Isabel had bestowed: The first mention by Isabel of "Benares" came on June 18, 1908, 1908 Daily Reminder, MTP. According to DW, " 'Bernar' was also a nickname for Ashcroft—They called him 'Bishop of Bernares.' " Handwritten document by IL and DW, IL Miscellaneous Mark Twain Notes, MTP.

183 The name came from one: This was the only Kipling story in which Benares was cited and it was initially published as a newspaper article, between 1887 and 1888. The story was later included in a two-volume

set entitled *From Sea to Sea and Other Sketches,* published in 1900, which Twain owned. Isabel likely first encountered the story in August 1906 after Twain asked her to read Kipling's interview with him (the interview was published in the same volume as the short story). Gribben, *Mark Twain's Library,* p. 378.

184 Benares, now known as Varanasi: Hindus come from all over India to walk down the ghats (steps) leading into the sacred Ganges to bathe and pray at sunrise. Devoted Hindus save all their lives so that when they die their bodies will be burned on a funeral pyre on the riverbank and their ashes dropped into the Ganges.

184 "Day broke over Benares": Rudyard Kipling, "The Bride's Progress," *From Sea to Sea and Other Sketches,* vol. 11 (New York: Doubleday, 1941), p. 393.

184 "The King wandered out from dinner": August 8, 1908, 1908 Daily Reminder, MTP.

185 "ruining [her] mentality": July 26, 1908, 1908 Daily Reminder, MTP.

185 "fenacetine [the drug]": July 26, 1908, 1908 Daily Reminder, MTP.

185 Isabel had probably told Paine: Twain conveniently blamed Phenacentin for Charles Webster's death, rather than admitting his complicity. Hill, *Mark Twain: God's Fool,* p. 202.

185 "nearly Paine had culled": August 8, 1908, 1908 Daily Reminder, MTP.

186 "to courage me up": October 15, 1908, 1908 Daily Reminder, MTP.

186 With this newfound support: October 6, 1908, 1908 Daily Reminder, MTP.

186 "In the late twilight": October 18, 1908, 1908 Daily Reminder, MTP.

186 "gloom that misunderstandings frequently put": October 21, 1908, 1908 Daily Reminder, MTP.

187 With the introduction of the electrified home: The first machine to be electrified was the sewing machine, followed by the fan, then the teakettle and the toaster, with the vibrator coming in fifth. The vacuum and the electric iron would not arrive until a decade later.

187 In the nineteenth century: Rachel P. Maines, *The Technology of Orgasm: "Hysteria," the Vibrator, and Women's Sexual Satisfaction* (Baltimore: Johns Hopkins University Press, 1999).

187 "Relieves all Suffering": Ibid., pp. 101–3.

187 "Snap, ginger, punch": Advertisement copy from *Popular Mechanics,* ca. 1908, author's personal collection.

188 "We had a most lovely evening": October 21, 1908, 1908 Daily Reminder, MTP.

188 "I want Mr. Rogers to buy": Leary, *Mark Twain's Correspondence with Henry Huttleston Rogers*, p. 655.

188 Twain was so enthralled: Receipt for purchase of one set of batteries from the Arnold Electric Company, May 5, 1909, 1909 Financial Documents; "Ashcroft-Lyon Manuscript," p. 1, Box 48, MTP.

189 As a faithful user: Maines, *The Technology of Orgasm,* xv. In the late 1860s Twain asked his good friend Frank Fuller to send him condoms: "Please forward one dozen Odorless Rubber Cundrums—I don't mind them being odorless—I can supply the odor myself." Harriet Elinor Smith and Richard Bucci, eds., *Mark Twain's Letters,* vol. II: *1867–1868* (Berkeley: University of California Press, 1990), p. 240.

189 "misunderstandings fired": October 26, 1908, 1908 Daily Reminder, MTP.

190 "Dear Mrs. Furnas": SLC to Mrs. Furnas (letter copied by IL), October 28, 1908, loose page, 1908–09 Box, VC.

190 " 'That is *good!* ' ": Marginalia on copy of a letter Isabel wrote for Twain, October 28, 1908, loose page, 1908–09 Box, VC.

190 Yet, despite his warning: October 26, 1908, 1908 Daily Reminder, MTP.

190 "trying and terrible": November 11, 1908, 1908 Daily Reminder, MTP.

190 "true and lawful attorneys": Exhibit A, "Ashcroft-Lyon Manuscript," Box 48, MTP; Twain would revoke this power of attorney nearly seven months later (see Hill, *Mark Twain: God's Fool,* p. 213).

191 His actions were also influenced: "Aid for Harte's Daughter. Miss Robson Sends Money and Will Give a Benefit," *New York Times,* January 30, 1907: "Mark Twain wrote: I feel that the American people owe a debt of gratitude to Bret Harte, for not only did he paint such pictures of California as delighted the heart, but there was such an infinite tenderness, such sympathy, such strength, and such merit in his work that he commanded the attention of the world to our country, and his daughter is surely deserving of our sympathy. It was learned yesterday that the publishers of Bret Harte's works have in their possession and in their own right, all the copyrights to the Harte works and that Mr. Harte never at any time had an agreement with them upon a royalty basis. He got $10,000 a year, and never would listen to a royalty arrangement."

192 "very nervous, very worried": October 30, 1908, loose page, 1908–09 Box, VC.

192 "two daughters Clara L. and Jean L. Clemens": "Mark Twain a Corporation," *Washington Post,* December 25, 1908, p. 6.

192 *The Washington Post* reported: The Mark Twain Company would be subsumed under the name of the Mark Twain Foundation in 1978. The Mark Twain Foundation, through its co-trustee Richard A. Watson, is a perpetual charitable trust located in New York City, which possesses the publication rights to all of Mark Twain's writings unpublished at his death. The income from the Mark Twain Foundation is to be used for, among other things, "enabling mankind to appreciate and enjoy the works of Mark Twain." All copyrights on Twain's works are held by Richard A. Watson and JPMorgan Chase Bank as Trustees of the Mark Twain Foundation.

192  "The knowledge that the copyright": "Mark Twain Turns Into a Corporation. The Pen Name Is Incorporated to Save Daughters from Literary Pirates. Family Holds the Stock. With the Expiration of His Copyrights the New Company Will Control All His Works," *New York Times,* December 24, 1908.

192  During his lifetime, the image and pseudonym Mark Twain:

> Twain's influence has not been limited to his career as a writer. His status as a celebrity had a profound cultural impact during his lifetime and his popular image has evolved ever since. Many people don't know Twain through his writings, but instead have a notion of his place in American cultural life based solely on his image and perhaps a few dubious quotations. Twain's name and image were used in the market place from the very beginnings of his literary career in the 1860s until his death in 1910, sometimes with his permission, and much more often without his knowledge. And after his death, his name and image were used to promote products and causes in new and even more distorted ways. . . .
>
> The game of Authors was a popular card game, first manufactured in 1861, and has been produced in more than 200 different versions since. By 1869, Twain was being included in decks. . . .
>
> Twain was widely associated with cigar-smoking, and cigar makers found it profitable to use his image and name. . . .
>
> Twain was known for his wide travels, which made his image especially useful to those in the travel industry. Oldsmobile used [a] picture postcard of Twain to advertise their motor cars in 1906, and Pullman used Twain to advertise its new passenger train car in 1904. Riding the car with Twain were Theodore Roosevelt, Thomas Edison, and others. . . .
>
> Mark Twain Flour was introduced in 1900, just two years after this company began milling flour. . . .
>
> Mark Twain attended many dinners, especially toward the end of his life, and was famous for his after-dinner speeches, so food makers felt entitled to his name. . . .
>
> Visitors to historical sites associated with Twain could send postcards to their friends. . . .
>
> Early visitors to Hannibal could buy Wheelock China plates and sweet dishes (1902–1915) and sterling silver spoons.

Kevin Mac Donnell, "Mark Twain Collectibles": http://etext.virginia .edu/railton/sc_as_mt/merchandiz/macdonnell.html. In 1872 Twain patented his "Mark Twain's Patent Scrapbook," which was the only one of his inventions that turned a profit.

193 "problem native to their constitution": Joshua Wolf Shenk, *Lincoln's Melancholy: How Depression Challenged a President and Fueled His Greatness* (Boston: Houghton Mifflin, 2005), pp. 74–76.

193 "The opportunity to get rich": Scott A. Sandage, *Born Losers: A History of Failure in America* (Cambridge, Mass.: Harvard University Press, 2005), pp. 4–5.

194 His brother Orion: Rasmussen, *Mark Twain A–Z,* pp. 81–82.

194 "I shall never look": Edgar Marquess Branch, Michael B. Frank, and Kenneth M. Sanderson, eds., *Mark Twain's Letters,* vol. I: *1853–1856* (Berkeley: Univerisity of California Press, 1988), p. 195.

195 "striving for success": Sandage, *Born Losers,* p. 5.

195 Twain's method of thwarting: Leary, *Mark Twain's Correspondence with Henry Huttleston Rogers,* pp. 11, 23.

195 "The King last night went gambling": March 3, 1907, Notebook #4, MTP.

196 "His wisdom and steadfastness": Autobiography dictation, MTP.

196 "a big dish of radishes": Coley Taylor, "Our Neighbor Mark Twain," www.twainproject.blogspot.com/; January 2, 1908, 1908 Daily Reminder, MTP.

196 "very very tired": November 21, 1908, 1908 Daily Reminder, MTP.

197 "Will came early": November 25, 1908, 1908 Daily Reminder, MTP.

197 But Thanksgiving Day 1908: Wark is no longer mentioned by Isabel in her daily reminder, with the lone exception of her exchange with Mrs. Twichell on January 11, 1909. The last check Wark received for services rendered totaled $400 and had been written seven months earlier. Nichols, Clara's violinist, would continue to be paid into 1909; the last check to her was for $150 and dated March 1, 1909, for "services prior to February 28th"; SLC Holder No. 1 Accountants' Statements and Schedules.

197 "There is a heavy": torn-out page from date book, 1908–09 Box, VC.

198 Isabel's only reference to: Twain would later claim that Jean had become dissatisfied with her treatment by Dr. von Reuvers and Dr. Peterson, although there is no mention by Jean or Isabel at the time of any issues concerning her care (see Hill, *Mark Twain: God's Fool,* p. 214). In 1909, Jean wrote Bébé that she had contradicted Dr. Peterson in a recent visit when he claimed that he had been the one to make her come back from Berlin: "I laughed, saying but you haven't made me go home" (Ibid., p. 249).

198 She was initially placed: Ibid., p. 225.

198 "Why should there be an age": Ibid., p. 45.

199 "his voice rang out": January 1, 1903, 1903 Daily Reminder, VC.

199 That same evening: January 19, 1907, 1907 Daily Reminder, MTP.

199 Over the next three months: February 13, March 27, and April 7, 1907, 1907 Daily Reminder, MTP.

199 "Such a rich personality,"Isabel effused: December 18, 1908, 1908 Daily Reminder, MTP.

200 "Miss Clara Clemens": *New York Times,* December 21, 1909.

200 Clara recovered with lightning speed: December 21, 1908, 1908 Daily Reminder, MTP.

200 "Gabrilowitsch played to us for an hour": December 21, 1908, 1908 Daily Reminder, MTP.

200 Two days later: December 23, 1908, 1908 Daily Reminder, MTP.

201 "Gabrilowitsch & I walked down": December 29, 1908, 1908 Daily Reminder, MTP.

201 In fact, Clara would not resurface: January 25, 1909, yellow printed date book, 1908–09 Box, VC.

201 "the engagement was broken": Samuel Clemens to Helen K. Blackmer, October 13, 1909, YU. There are several conflicting accounts regarding the nature of Clara and Ossip's relationship in 1901. Clemens claimed in the letter he wrote to Helen Blackmer that he had "wanted this wedding 8 years ago, when the engagement was broken twice in 6 months." In a letter Clemens sent to Elizabeth Wallace on November 10, 1909, he claimed that Clara and Ossip "were engaged years ago—twice. Broken both times, to Mrs. Clemens's great regret" (HL). Hill states that in 1901 Clara was "visiting altogether too much with the young pianist Ossip Gabrilowitsch, in the United States on a tour, to please her parents. . . . Her father opposed marriage" (Hill, *Mark Twain: God's Fool,* p. 44).

201 In a written statement: "Mark Twain Philosophizes at His Daughter's Wedding," *New York Herald,* October 7, 1909, p. 12.

201 Twain's claim regarding Clara's supposed engagement: Hill, *Mark Twain: God's Fool,* p. 44.

201 "all the Hartford world": January 11, 1909, torn-out page from date book, 1908–09 Box, VC.

201 The framework can be found: Mark Twain, *Wapping Alice,* introduction and afterword by Hamlin Hill (San Francisco: Arion Press, 1981).

202 "to stay right in this room": January 9, 1909, torn-out page from date book, 1908–09 Box, VC.

202 "He knows that we love him": February 12, 1909, torn-out page from date book, 1908–09 Box, VC.

202 "His reading of Shakespeare": February 13, 1909, torn-out page from date book, 1908–09 Box, VC.

203 This entry, from February 13, 1909: Twain scholars have looked for Isabel's journal or daily reminder for 1909 without success. There are a few torn pages from a date book in the special collections archive at VC, and that is all that remains of her written record for that year. Clara spent years trying to find Isabel's personal writings.

203 "the psychic moment hasn't come yet": IL to Harriet Whitmore Enders (Mrs. John Ostrom Enders), February 16, 1909, MTM.

203 "any engagement announcement": IL to Harriet Whitmore Enders (Mrs. John Ostrom Enders), February 16, 1909, MTM.

204 "Plenty of time there is now": January 21, 1909; yellow printed date book, 1908–09 Box, VC.

204 "Dear Mr. Clemens": Undated typescript; "Ashcroft-Lyon Manuscript," Box 48, MTP.

204 "wants me to but I wouldn't": Webster Interview, January 5, 1950, typed transcript, VC.

205 "wouldn't hear of it": Ibid.

205 "shamefaced, embarrassed, hesitating": "Ashcroft-Lyon Manuscript," Box 48, MTP.

206 With Isabel absent: Mary Lawton considered CC "the best beloved of all my friends." Although she acted in stage productions in New York City in the early 1900s, she apparently was unsuccessful as an actress, and promoted herself as a psychic. Lawton wrote a book providing a portrayal of Twain that likely pleased Clara. Twain identifies Lawton as a psychic in the "Ashcroft-Lyon Manuscript," p. 399, Box 48, MTP.

206 "being driven almost crazy": Hill, *Mark Twain: God's Fool,* pp. 218–19.

206 "taking various things": Webster Interview, January 5, 1950, typed transcript, VC.

206 "before the break came": Ibid.

206 "Carnellian beads": JC to Joseph Twichell, June 14, 1909, MTP.

207 A few months later, Ashcroft: Hill, *Mark Twain: God's Fool,* p. 226; Ralph Ashcroft to John Stanchfield, July 30, 1909, MTP.

207 "I have no suspicions": Hill, *Mark Twain: God's Fool,* pp. 220–21.

207 Twain may have thought: Twain used the term "General Clean-Up Day" in the "Ashcroft-Lyon Manuscript" to describe the events of March 13, 1909. Box 48, MTP.

207 "and not to those of any member or members": "Ashcroft-Lyon Manuscript," Box 48, MTP.

208 Twain read and signed: For her Christmas gift, Twain had relieved Isabel of $500 of her debt. On "General Clean-Up Day," Ashcroft offered Twain notes for $1,000, and to Twain's surprise informed him that Isabel would be returning his $500 Christmas gift. Hill, *Mark Twain: God's Fool,* p. 221; "Ashcroft-Lyon Manuscript," Box 48, MTP.

208 "Cupid has been active": 1908–09 Box, VC.

209 Present were friends: "Part of Mark Twain Married While the Humorist Looks On," newspaper unknown, March 18, 1909, MTM. Names of the wedding guests from the "Ashcroft-Lyon Manuscript," Box 48, MTP.

209 "The first one of you": Doris and SW to Henry Nash Smith, July 1, 1960, MTP.

209 *The Hartford Courant* erroneously reported on March 19, 1909, that Clara attended with her father. In the Ashcroft-Lyon manuscript Twain wrote the names of the wedding guests and did not include Clara.

209 "a pity that a singer": "Miss CC Sings," *New York Times,* April 14, 1909.

211 "give Miss Lyon her notice": Hill, *Mark Twain: God's Fool,* p. 223.

211 "she found it was a very kind letter": Webster Interview, January 5, 1950; typed transcript, VC. On the contract Twain wrote the following entry:

> Canceled Apl 15 by written notice to take affact May 15/09
> Two months' salary Paid by check. SLC

"Ashcroft-Lyon Manuscript," Box 48, MTP.

211 "Remember, whatever I do": Webster Interview, January 5, 1950; typed transcript, VC.

211 Ashcroft had purchased: Hill, *Mark Twain: God's Fool,* p. 226; in the "Ashcroft-Lyon Manuscript," Twain noted that Ashcroft had purchased the farmhouse and acreage for $7,200 "& saved us $600 thereby": Box 48, MTP, p. 255. "Mark Twain Adds 150 Acres to Farm," *New York Times,* April 9, 1909.

212 "Wisdom, judgment, penetration": July 18, 1909, MTP.

212 "They would not want me": JC to Nancy Brush, July 29, 1909, MTP.

213 "I had a call this morning": "Ashcroft-Lyon Manuscript," p. 165, Box 48, MTP.

213 He closed by recognizing: Ralph Ashcroft to SLC, April 29, 1909, "Ashcroft-Lyon Manuscript," pp. 171–72, Box 48, MTP.

214 "a man who had been in his employ": "Ashcroft-Lyon Manuscript," p. 166, Box 48, MTP.

214 His fears about Miss Watson: SLC Holder No. 1 Accountants' Statements and Schedules.

214 The first lines Twain composed: While the draft to Howells was the first piece he composed, Twain later added two forewords to the manuscript: a letter to Adolph S. Ochs, publisher and owner of *The New York Times,* and a note to the "Unborn Reader."

215 "rotten eggs": "Ashcroft-Lyon Manuscript," p. 2, Box 48, MTP.

215 "Man, let me tell you": "Ashcroft-Lyon Manuscript," pp. 6–7, Box 48, MTP.

215 After a year of infrequent and unfocused autobiography dictations: Isabel recalled that while *Harper's* did not want to publish "Is Shakespeare Dead?," they were contractually obligated to do so. Colonel Harvey asked Isabel to try to restrain Twain, saying that his public wanted to see "only the humorous side of him. And the comment is that he is slipping intellectually." February 17, 1909, as transcribed in her notes, NYPL, as quoted in Hill, *Mark Twain: God's Fool,* p. 218.

215 "one great crime": "Ashcroft-Lyon Manuscript," p. 45, Box 48, MTP.

216 "She would . . . stretch herself": "Ashcroft-Lyon Manuscript," p. 34, Box 48, MTP.

216 Here Twain borrowed the language: The love triangle of Florence Evelyn Nesbit, Stanford White, and Harry K. Thaw culminated in Thaw's murder of White on November 28, 1905. Constant newspaper coverage contained lurid details about the sex lives of all three individuals.

216 "Doesn't it sound like print?": SLC to WDH, "Ashcroft-Lyon Manuscript," Box 48, MTP.

217 "This is terrible, terrible": "H. H. Rogers Dead, Leaving $50,000,000," *New York Times,* May 20, 1909.

217 To his dismay: For his work Weiss was paid $372.05 by check signed by JC on October 4, 1909; cancelled checks dated 1886–1910, MTP.

217 "Clara finally said": "Ashcroft-Lyon Manuscript," pp. 421–22, Box 48, MTP.

218 "I had a burning desire": Michael Kiskis, ed., *Mark Twain's Own Autobiography* (Madison: University of Wisconsin Press, 1990), pp. 81–82.

218 "most amazing document": SLC to William R. Coe, June 16, 1909, MTM.

218 "took large quantities": JC to Joseph Twichell, June 14, 1909, TC.

218 "before me personally": "Ashcroft-Lyon Manuscript," Box 48, MTP.

218 In a personal recollection entitled "Our Friend Mark Twain" by Helen Nickerson Upson (*The Redding Times,* June 2, 1960), Twain offered a second explanation as to why he signed the power of attorney document. With his angry daughters in attendance, instead of claiming that he had been hypnotized, he informed John N. Nickerson that he had been tricked: "A trusted friend of mine who has recently married a 'man of experience' brought me a document to sign without in any way explaining it—and I was foolish enough to require no explanation. At the moment I was concentration on the writing of a script and, as was my custom, took the paper and quickly signed as she directed without reading it and I supposed the matter was dismissed, but this morning, to my horror, I discovered that I have signed over to a trusted friend ABSOLUTE Power of Attorney over everything that I possess and I cannot spend so much as a nickel! without her O.K. Could any man have been a bigger damned fool?? Eventually she consented to withdraw if a certain [piece] of Mr. Clemens treasured real estate (and he owned property in several states) could be turned over to her. As Mr. Clemens was convinced this was the only way out he acceded. Dad took care of the transaction and the case was closed" (http://twainproject.blogspot.com/ 2009/11/new-stormfield-articles.html). Twain latter inscribed a copy of *Innocents Abroad* to Nickerson: "The sane man readeth first but the ass signeth without looking" (http://www.twainquotes.com/Autographs .html). This second rationale, that Twain unwittingly changed his power

of attorney is as implausible as his claim that he was hypnotized for years.

218 After Ashcroft's April meeting: Hill, *Mark Twain: God's Fool*, p. 221.

219 In the audit report: SLC Holder No. 1 Accountants' Statements and Schedules, MTP.

219 Naturally Clara excluded mention: June 14, 21, 28, 1909; clippings, newspapers unknown, VC.

219 "I believe the whole trouble": "Wants Mark Twain to Explain to Her," *New York Times,* July 15, 1909.

220 This time Clara accompanied Lark: Hill, *Mark Twain: God's Fool,* pp. 234–35.

220 "inveigled into transferring": Ralph Ashcroft to John B. Stanchfield, July 30, 1909, MTM.

220 Ashcroft asserted that a total: Ralph Ashcroft to John B. Stanchfield, July 30, 1909, MTM.

220 His not so very subtle intimation: Ralph Ashcroft to John B. Stanch- field, July 30, 1909, MTM.

221 "One's vocal ambitions": "Ashcroft Accuses Miss Clara Clemens," *New York Times,* August 4, 1909.

221 "It involves an attack": *Connecticut Courant,* August 9, 1909.

221 Noteworthy were two checks: Folder 2, statements of Miss Watson, of Mr. Ashcroft, and letters, etc., of J. B. Stanchfield's office; Statements and Accounts Ashcroft-Lyon 1907–1909; and "Ashcroft-Lyon Manu- script," Box 48, MTP.

222 "The differences between Mark Twain and his daughter": "Mark Twain Suits All Off. All Litigation Between Him and the Ashcrofts Is Finally Dropped," *New York Times,* September 13, 1909.

222 "The facts in my case": "Ashcroft-Lyon Manuscript," Box 48, MTP.

223 The officers for the Mark Twain Corporation: Rasmussen, *Mark Twain A–Z,* p. 304.

223 As for Isabel, her hopes: Notes by Samuel C. & DW on talk with Mrs. Lyon, March 5, 1948; Webster Interview, IL Miscellaneous Mark Twain Notes, MTP.

223 In keeping with earlier contracts: "Ashcroft-Lyon Manuscript," Box 48, MTP.

224 Along with fighting with Ashcroft: Katy's account is succinct: "When he first come out to Redding he was pretty near dying" (Lawton, *A Life- time with Mark Twain,* p. 309). In her memoir *My Husband Gabrilowitsch* (New York: Harper and Brothers, 1938), Clara offers a hyperbolic tale of how a visiting neighbor happened to mention that Gabrilowitsch was ill in a New York City hospital and that she and Katy had immediately rushed to his side. She also claimed that "after a night of prayer," upon

seeing Gabrilowitsch in his hospital bed she knew that "God would work a miracle" and save his life (pp. 47–49).

224 "a terrible operation": Lawton, *A Lifetime with Mark Twain,* p. 306; Hill, *Mark Twain: God's Fool,* p. 243; Paine, *Biography* (vol. 3), described Gabrilowitsch as having been "invalided through severe surgical operations, and for a long time rarely appeared, even at meal-times" (p. 1505).

224 He was diagnosed: SLC to Mrs. John Paul Jones, October 21, 1909: "G. is pretty well run down. He was here in the house all summer recovering from three operations for the mastoid process" (MTP).

224 Symptoms include difficulty: According to the online Merck edition, "symptoms appear two or more weeks after acute otitis media develops, as the spreading infection destroys the inner part of the mastoid process. A collection of pus (abscess) may form in the bone. The skin covering the mastoid process may become red, swollen, and tender, and the external ear is pushed sideways and down. Other symptoms are fever, pain around and within the ear, and a creamy, profuse discharge from the ear. The pain tends to be persistent and throbbing. Hearing loss is progressive." www.merck.com/mmhe/sec19/ch220/ch220h.html.

224 The operating physician: B. Heine, *Operations on the Ear: The Operations for Suppurative Otitis Media and its Intracrania Complications* (New York: William Wood and Company, 1908), p. 44.

224 A large, unsightly scar: McLauchlin, in *O.G. the Incomparable,* recalled that Gabrilowitsch, "had what is sometimes called 'wild hair' and he wore the highest starched collars ever seen. We all wondered where he bought them. There was one theory that his wife made them in her sewing-room." Gabrilowitsch's peculiar sartorial excess may have been an attempt to hide the scar from his operations.

225 "I've always heard": Ibid.

225 "just as I used to rub": Lawton, *A Lifetime with Mark Twain,* p. 309.

225 The program lasted nearly two hours: Paine, *Biography,* p. 1522.

225 A profusion of guests: *New York Herald,* October 7, 1909, p. 1.

225 "We shall now hear": McLauchlin, *O.G. the Incomparable,* p. 6. Mary Lawton offered a kinder version of Twain's statement: "Of course, my daughter Clara is going to sing too. My daughter is not so famous as these gentlemen, but she's ever so much better looking" (*A Lifetime with Mark Twain,* p. 308).

225 " 'Katy, the date is set' ": Clara Clemens, *My Husband Gabrilowitsch,* pp. 50–51.

226 "will wed Gabrilowitsch": Hill, *Mark Twain: God's Fool,* p. 243.

226 "News of the wedding": "Russian Pianist to Wed Mark Twain's Daughter," *New York Herald,* October 6, 1909, p. 1.

226 Twain attempted to defend: "Miss Clemens Weds Mr. Gabrilowitsch," *New York Times,* October 7, 1909.

226 "had signed for a concert tour": Paine, *Biography,* p. 1523.

226 On the surface a reasonable explanation: Hill, *Mark Twain: God's Fool,* p. 244.

226 "Gabrilowitsch was leaving for Europe": *Musical America,* October 12, 1909, MTP.

227 "had been nursing her husband": Mark Twain, "The Death of Jean," http://www.online-literature.com/twain/1316/.

227 "argued with him in vain": Marie Nichols, "Marie Nichols Tells Intimate Stories of Humorist's Life," *The Campus,* Sarah Lawrence College, May 4, 1931.

227 Before the wedding: Clemens, *My Husband Gabrilowitsch,* p. 51.

227 The Associated Press was duly notified: Paine, *Biography,* p. 1524.

227 "he wished to": "Twain Philosophizes at His Daughter's Wedding," *New York Herald,* October 7, 1909, p. 12.

227 the guest list for his daughter's nuptials: The Reverend Joseph Twichell presided, Jean was the bridesmaid, and Jervis Langdon served as the groomsman. Also in attendance were Julia Loomis, Susan Crane, Mrs. John B. Stanchfield, Dr. Quintard, Miss Ethel Newcomb, the Richard Watson Gilders, the Charles Hapgoods, Clara Gordon, Dr. Angenette Parry, Marie Nichols, William Dean Howells, Miss Foot, Miss Comstock, Miss Mary Lawton, the Albert Bigelow Paines, Theodore Gaillards, the Frank Spragues, the E. F. Bauers of New York, and the A. M. Wrights of Boston. Paine, *Biography,* pp. 1523–24; Lawton, *A Lifetime with Mark Twain,* pp. 311–14; Hill, *Mark Twain: God's Fool,* pp. 243–44.

228 "two or three tragically solemn things": *Post-Standard,* October 7, 1909.

228 "service for which I am most thoroughly grateful": SLC to Augusta M. D. Ogden, October 13, 1909, United States Library of Congress.

228 The Associated Press issued a release: "Sensation Promised," *Los Angeles Times,* October 14, 1909.

230 'No suit that I know of": "Clara Clemens in a Mysterious Suit," New York *American,* October 14, 1909, p. 2.

230 "willful and malicious interference": Personal correspondence to the author from Arlene Prater, June 1, 2006. The *Chicago Sun-Times* ran a front-page news story on July 1, 2007, about a husband who successfully sued his wife's lover for alienation of affection. The husband was granted monetary damages. As of 2007, eleven states remain where alienation of affection is legally actionable.

230 "He is an excellent man": "Mystery in Quest of Pianist's Wife," *New York Herald,* October 14, 1909, p. 7. Campbell was a criminal lawyer and fifty

percent of a two-man firm, Pentecost and Campbell. That same month Campbell was mentioned in a brief paragraph in *The New York Times* as the lawyer representing a yogi and seer from Brooklyn who had been arrested for sending his female clients who had come to him for "spiritual treatment to the offices of Henry T. Rodman & Co., where they were led to invest in some highly unprofitable mining securities" ("$12,000 Bail for Garnett," *New York Times,* October 20, 1909).

231 "who does not feel kindly": "Pianist's Bridal Trip Deferred," *New York Herald,* October 17, 1909, p. 6.

231 "Mr. Gabrilowitsch's statement": "Denies Daughter of Mark Twain Is Sued," New York *American,* October 17, 1903, section II, p. 1.

232 "troubled for fear": JC to Joseph Twichell, October 17, 1909, TC.

232 The next day a check for $1,000: Cancelled Checks 1886–1910, MTP.

232 "At this very day Ashcroft": SLC, Notebook 49, 1910, MTP.

233 "phrasing. [Twain] had exhausted": Paine, *Biography,* p. 1533.

233 "During twenty-three days": Mark Twain, *Letters from the Earth,* ed. Bernard DeVoto (New York: Harper and Row, 1962), pp. 40–41.

234 On November 20, 1909: SLC to Helen Allen, October 30, 1909, Beinecke Rare Book and Manuscript Library, YU.

234 The newlyweds spent their first weeks: Clemens, *My Husband Gabrilowitsch,* p. 52.

234 Twain and Paine had sailed: Paine, *Biography* p. 1541. Hill gives November 18 as the sailing date (*Mark Twain: God's Fool,* p. 249); Twain, in a letter to Dorothy Quick on November 18, wrote that the sailing date would be November 20 (MTP).

234 "past 5 months": SLC to Dorothy Quick, November 18, 1909, MTP.

234 "was not at all ill": Paine, *Biography,* p. 1544.

234 At Twain's specific request, no news: JC to Mr. Dunne, November 30, 1909, MTP.

234 "Don't begin right off": JC to Nancy Brush, July 29, 1909, MTP.

234 "real jealousy": JC to Marguerite Schmitt, October 19, 1909 (collection of Hamlin Hill, copy at, MTP).

235 "The principle reason": JC to Marguerite Schmitt, November 7, 1909 (collection of Hamlin Hill, copy at, MTP).

235 "I began to be absent-minded": July 17, 1906; JC Diary April 30–July 21, 1906, 53348 HL.

235 On the morning of Christmas Eve: Taylor, "Our Neighbor Mark Twain."

235 To her utter horror: Lawton, *A Lifetime with Mark Twain,* 321.

235 "She's happy now": Ibid., p. 322.

235 This initial diagnosis: The following day the Associated Press sent a release that was picked up by papers across the country. *The Fresno Morning Republican* carried the story, entitled "Mark Twain's Daughter Dies."

An excerpt from the article provided the cause of death: JC "died not directly from drowning, as was first supposed, but more probably of strangulation due to an attack of epilepsy, or from heart failure. The body was found in the bath tub with the head only partly submerged and medical examination tonight showed that the lungs contained little water." December 5, 1909.

235 Jean died seven months shy: In a 1989 American Neurological Association article, researchers reported that "sudden unexpected death without obvious cause accounts for a substantial portion of reported deaths among epileptics; however, this phenomenon is still not widely recognized nor appreciated." A more recent article, entitled, "Sudden Death in Epilepsy," published in the winter 1997 issue of *The Medical Journal of Allina,* states that epileptic patients who had never been able to achieve complete seizure control, who had suffered from epilepsy for years possibly from the result of a head injury, and who were between twenty and forty years of age and in excellent health except for epilepsy were viewed as at a high risk for sudden death. Jean fit those parameters.

235 "I am already rejoicing": SLC to Mai H. Rogers Coe, December 27, 1909, MTM.

236 "She is out of it all": SLC to HW, December 28, 1909, MTM.

236 "constitute my family henceforth": SLC to Mary B. Rogers, December 29, 1909 (Columbia University, New York).

236 "If a word would do it": For the online text of "The Death of Jean," see http://www.online-literature.com/twain/1316/.

236 Her epilepsy had never been cured: Clara Clemens, *My Father Mark Twain* (New York: Harper and Brothers, 1931), p. 283.

237 "Who loves to steal a while away": SLC to Albert Bigelow Paine, January 14, 1910, SC.

237 "Who feeds on bromide and on Scotch": Hill, *Mark Twain: God's Fool,* p. 268.

237 "A year later—No more association": January 21, 1909; yellow printed date book, 1908–09 Box, VC.

238 "In your guess of a year ago": SLC to CC, March 6, 1910, MTP.

238 Clara later professed: Clemens, *My Father Mark Twain,* pp. 288–89; Hill, *Mark Twain: God's Fool,* p. 257.

## EPILOGUE

241 "Clemens was sole": William Dean Howells, *My Mark Twain* (New York: Harper & Brothers: 1910).

243 "We have called him the greatest": Obituary, *New York Times,* April 22, 1910.

244 Afterward, for two hours: Associated Press story, April 24, 1910; Hill, *Mark Twain: God's Fool,* pp. 266–67.

244 "1909—The humorist and his daughter": "Events in Mark Twain's Life," *Sheboygan Daily Press,* Sheboygan, Wisconsin, April 29, 1910.

245 "going about everywhere": CC to HW, June 25, 1910, MTM.

246 "About 'Miss Lyon' I can so well understand": CC to HW, August 5, 1910, MTM.

246 Actually, the lawyer had been sent: Hill, *Mark Twain: God's Fool,* p. 267.

247 "I had hoped it would be a boy": Lawton, *A Lifetime with Mark Twain,* pp. 334–35.

247 "sad that [Nina] inherited": McLauchlin, *O.G. the Incomparable.*

247 "very fine": CC to HW, April 7, 1913, MTM.

248 "After 21 years": IL, 1936 File, VC.

248 "The building of the new home": Paine, *Biography,* p. 1446.

248 "As soon as this is begun": Hill, *Mark Twain: God's Fool,* p. 268.

249 "with total neglect of all duties": Divorce decree of Isabel V. Lyon and Ralph Ashcroft (copy, author's personal collection).

249 "very unsatisfactory": Webster Interview, January 5, 1950, typed transcript, VC.

249 Isabel went back to New York City: DW to Betty (Hall) Mack (Mrs. Clifford G. Mack), July 29, 1959, MTM.

249 Ashcroft married a second time: Hill, *Mark Twain: God's Fool,* p. 268.

249 At the time of his death: *New York Times,* January 9, 1947, p. 24; "Ashcroft-Lyon Manuscript," Box 48, MTP.

250 Clara insisted upon: McLauchlin, *O.G. the Incomparable.*

250 Wife and daughter did not attend: Caroline Thomas Harnsberger, *Mark Twain's Clara, or What Became of the Clemens Family* (Evanston, Ill.: The Press of Ward Schori, 1982).

250 A model of the memorial: I discovered the model of Twain and Olivia in the storage room of the Elmira Historical Society when I was doing research for my biography *Mark Twain in the Company of Women* (Philadelphia: University of Pennsylvania Press, 1994).

251 DeVoto had to seek her permission: Rasmussen, *Mark Twain A–Z,* p. 111.

252 This bickering led to the resignation: Ibid., p. 304.

252 Wecter and Clara enjoyed: Personal correspondence to the author from Robert Hirst, October 9, 2000.

252 Anderson passed away suddenly: Rasmussen, *Mark Twain A–Z,* p. 433.

253 In August 1940, Clara asked her lawyer: Charles Tressler Lark was the assistant of John B. Stanchfield, Twain's Elmira-based attorney. He continued to work for Clara into the 1940s (Hill, *Mark Twain: God's Fool,* p. 238).

253 "were jealous of [Isabel's] entirely friendly relation": Letter from Charles

Tressler Lark, counselor at law, to Bernard DeVoto, Subject File, MTP. It is curious that DeVoto, who published his biography *Mark Twain at Work* (Cambridge, Mass.: Harvard University Press, 1942) two years after receiving this letter, never mentioned it. DeVoto instead argued that the pronounced pessimism of Twain's later years did not require any explanation—that his bitterness was in agreement with the literature of reality. DeVoto went on to claim that Twain's fictive powers did not wane toward the end, and that he was also unaffected by the travails and deaths of the women in his life. In retrospect, it seems incredible that DeVoto could have made this claim with this letter in his possession unless he felt a particular allegiance to Clara (or felt pressured to leave such unpleasant matters unmentioned in his work).

254 "pawned her off on nannies": Author's interview with Alice Henderson, July 29, 2006.

255 His losses were so great: Harnsberger, *Mark Twain's Clara,* p. 176.

255 DeVoto specifically suspected: Personal correspondence to the author from Robert Hirst, August 27, 2000.

255 Treasured memorabilia: Webster Interview, March 5, 1948, IL Miscellaneous Mark Twain Notes, MTP; Webster Interview, 1953, VC.

255 Among her friends and family: Charles Tressler Lark, counselor at law, to Bernard DeVoto, Subject File, MTP.

255 "You are certainly a tough human being": William Howe to IL, October 26, 1933, MC.

256 A lover of hats and colorful dresses: Charles Tressler Lark to Bernard DeVoto, Subject File, MTP.

256 Stubbornly independent: "Dear Mrs Bunce: Your interesting letter asking about the disposition of the furnishings in the New York house, came at an unfortunate time for me, & I owe you an explanation for my apparent discourtesy in not answering. I was slowly recovering from a recurrent heart attack which stops all activities, mental or physical until energy returns." IL to Eleanor Bunce (Mrs. John Lee), March 14, 1956, MTM; DW to Henry Nash Smith, December 5, 1958, Subject File, MTP.

258 "inside a voluminous dress": DW, undated handwritten document, IL Miscellaneous Mark Twain Notes, MTP.

258 "Oh, but he is lovable": Webster Manuscript, MTP.

259 Isabel informed Smith: October 18, 1954, MTP.

259 The Websters accepted the collection:

> Dear Mr. Smith:
>
> When you were East about two years ago, and came in to see me, you expressed the hope that any notes I might have, would Some day find their way into the right hands; Therefore you will be glad to know

that in November, 1955, I turned over To Mr Samuel C. Webster & wife, all notes, diaries, & photographs covering my 6½ years with Mr. Clemens. And with them my written wish that Some day they would be Transferred by Mr. Webster & wife, To The Mark Twain section of the University of California.

Sincerely Yours
Isabel V. Lyon

IL to Henry Nash Smith, March 5, 1958, MTP.

259 "in a locked room": August 8, 1960, MTP.

259 "because of the unfortunate ending of the association": November 1, 1954, Subject File, MTP.

259 Isabel may have reasoned: Isabel also offered to have her name "effaced from the record, at first insisting that her name be omitted from the title page, but of course that is impossible for a book of this sort." Such was the power of the "Ashcroft-Lyon Manuscript." DW and SW to Henry Nash Smith, July 30, 1960, MTP.

259 "We are certain that there was no scandal": DW and SW to Henry Nash Smith, July 1, 1960, MTP.

261 "It is only by the luckiest stroke": Hal Holbrook to Robert D. Wallace, June 10, 1958, Subject File, MTP.

261 That afternoon the apartment building janitor: MC, December 26, 1958.

261 She was found in a coma: A second version exists of Isabel's death. "She had fallen in her apartment, and was not able to get up and it was quite a while before anyone knew it. Some of her friends feel that the great mistake was to take her to the hospital—something she always dreaded. She had a heart attack as they were lifting her into the ambulance. It was her new neighbor in the front apartment who started things by sending for the police, although Mrs. Lyon had called her doctor, she had said all she needed was to sit quietly in her chair." DW to Henry Nash Smith, December 5, 1958, MTP.

261 The next day, at 4:53 p.m.: Certificate of Death, City of New York, #156–58–125638.

261 "She was a lovely, genuine person": January 11, 1959, MC.

261 "I wish so much": January 21, 1959, MC.

261 "a very serious minded man": Personal correspondence to the author from Hal Holbrook, July 5, 2001.

262 "left behind some unpublished things": Hal Holbrook to Robert D. Wallace, February 10, 1959, Subject File, MTP.

262 "I believe it will make a book": Henry Nash Smith to DW and SW, July 28, 1960, MTP.

262 "wanted to 'clear Isabel's name'": DW and SW to Henry Nash Smith, July 30, 1960, MTP.

262 Some of Isabel's original materials: "Isabel gave [the Websters] the diaries etc., as a block, which only got split in two when the husband of Sam's older sister Alice Jane Webster showed up one day during Doris's dotage or near dotage and took possession of all the letters and stuff she had. That's the cache of stuff that ended up at Vassar College, even though Doris fully intended to give it to the Mark Twain Papers." Personal correspondence to the author from Robert Hirst, August 27, 2000.

263 "It is very difficult to take": Isabel Van Kleek Lyon Journals Research; Frederick Anderson note card and editorial comments, MTP.

263 Doris Webster left a large bequest: Personal correspondence to the author from Robert Hirst, August 27, 2000.

263 "Yes I'm sure that much": John Seelye to Frederick Anderson, March 18, 1977, MTP.

263 "A series of highly inflammatory anti-religious essays": "Anti-Religious Work by Twain, Long Withheld, to Be Published: Author's Daughter, Who Barred Release of Venomous 'Letters from the Earth' in Thirties, Now Agrees to Printing," *New York Times,* August 24, 1962.

265 When Clara was living at the Bahia: Hal Holbrook, informal talk at the Center for Mark Twain Studies, Elmira, New York, August 8, 2009.

265 After Nina spent time: Harnsberger, *Mark Twain's Clara,* p. 222.

265 When Holbrook was in California: Hal Holbrook, informal talk at the Center for Mark Twain Studies, Elmira, New York, August 8, 2009.

266 "Newly Found Mark Twain Letter": *New York Times,* June 25, 1970.

266 "No penalty attaches itself": January 15, 1905, 1905 Daily Reminder #2, MTP.

266 "Sitting alone in a little room": Personal correspondence to the author from Tracy S. Worthington, April 6, 2002. Undated quotation.

# Permissions Acknowledgments

The previously unpublished writings of Mark Twain, Olivia Louise Langdon Clemens, Clara Clemens, and Jean Clemens are copyright © 2009 by Richard A. Watson and JPMorgan Chase Bank as Trustees of the Mark Twain Foundation, which reserves all reproduction or dramatization rights in every medium.

Quotation and photograph reproduction is made with the permission of the University of California Press and Robert H. Hirst, general editor, Mark Twain Papers & Project at Berkeley.

Quotation is made with the permission of the Mark Twain House & Museum, Hartford, Connecticut.

Quotation is made with the permission of Vassar College Libraries.

Reproduction of photographs is made with the permission of Robert Slotta.

Reproduction of photographs is made with the permission of Kevin Mac Donnell.

Jean Clemens's diaries are reproduced by permission of the Huntington Library, San Marino, California.

Isabel Van Kleek Lyon's daily reminders, notebooks, and journal are reproduced by permission of the Isabel Lyon Heirs.

The source for the letter from Samuel L. Clemens to Helen Allen, October 30, 1909, is the Yale Collection of American Literature, Beinecke Rare Book and Manuscript Library.

The source for the letter from Samuel L. Clemens to Charlotte Teller Johnson, April 13,1906, is the Henry W. and Albert A. Berg Collection of English and American Literature at the New York Public Library; Astor, Lenox and Tilden Foundations.

# Index

Page numbers in *italics* refer to illustrations.